MW00678936

Entrepreneurship, Sustainable Growth and Performance

Entrepreneurship, Sustainable Growth and Performance

Frontiers in European Entrepreneurship Research

Edited by

Hans Landström

Professor in Business Administration, Institute of Economic Research, School of Economics and Management, Lund University, Sweden

Hans Crijns

Professor, Centre for Entrepreneurship, Vlerick Leuven Gent Management School, Belgium

Eddy Laveren

Professor of Finance and Entrepreneurship, Department of Accounting and Finance, University of Antwerp, Belgium

David Smallbone

Professor of Small Business and Entrepreneurship, Small Business Research Centre, Kingston University, UK

IN ASSOCIATION WITH THE ECSB

Edward Elgar

Cheltenham, UK • Northampton, MA, USA

Published by
Edward Elgar Publishing Limited
The Lypiatts
15 Lansdown Road
Cheltenham
Glos GL50 2JA
UK

Edward Elgar Publishing, Inc.
William Pratt House
9 Dewey Court
Northampton
Massachusetts 01060
USA

A catalogue record for this book
is available from the British Library

Library of Congress Cataloguing in Publication Data

Research in Entrepreneurship and Small Business Conference (20th: 2007: Brussels)
Entrepreneurship, sustainable growth and performance: frontiers in European entrepreneurship research/edited by Hans Landström . . . [et al.].
p. cm.
Papers presented at the 20th annual Research in Entrepreneurship and Small Business Conference held in Brussels in Nov. 2006.
Includes bibliographical references and index.
1. Entrepreneurship—Europe. 2. Entrepreneurship—Research—Europe. 3. Sustainable development—Europe. I. Landström, Hans. II. Title.
HB615.R48 2007
338'.04094—dc22

2008023881

ISBN 978 1 84720 853 8

Printed and bound in Great Britain by MPG Books Ltd, Bodmin, Cornwall

Contents

List of contributors vii
Foreword by Friederike Welter ix

PART I INTRODUCTION

1 Introduction 3
Hans Crijns, Eddy Laveren, Hans Landström and David Smallbone

2 Looking back at 20 years of entrepreneurship research: what did we learn? 13
Per Davidsson

PART II ENTREPRENEURS AND THEIR ROLE

3 The hunt for the Heffalump continues: who is the Flemish entrepreneur? 29
Eva Cools

4 How do you react to entrepreneurship education? An examination of the role of predispositions in an enactive mastery experience of entrepreneurship 54
Frédéric Delmar and Régis Goujet

5 Why do they use financial bootstrapping? A quantitative study of new business managers 77
Joakim Winborg

PART III ENTREPRENEURSHIP IN FAMILY FIRMS

6 Transgenerational entrepreneurship: exploring entrepreneural orientation in family firms 93
Mattias Nordqvist, Timothy G. Habbershon and Leif Melin

7 Financing and growth behavior of family firms: differences between first- and next-generation-managed firms 117
Vincent Molly, Eddy Laveren and Ann Jorissen

8 The link between family orientation, strategy and innovation in Dutch SMEs: lagged effects 141
Lorraine M. Uhlaner, Sita Tan, Joris Meijaard and Ron Kemp

PART IV PERFORMANCE OF NEW VENTURES

9 New venture teams: the relationship between initial team characteristics, team processes and performance 163
Daniela A. Almer-Jarz, Erich J. Schwarz and Robert J. Breitenecker

10 Entrepreneurs' human capital and early business performance 194
Espen John Isaksen

11 Direct and indirect effects of entrepreneurial and market orientations on the international performance of Spanish and Belgian international new ventures 215
María Ripollés, Andreu Blesa, Diego Monferrer and Ysabel Nauwelaerts

PART V PROCESSES AND ENTREPRENEURSHIP

12 Emergency entrepreneurship: creative organizing in the eye of the storm 243
Bengt Johannisson and Lena Olaison

13 On the role of academic staff as entrepreneurs in university spin-offs: case studies of biotechnology firms in Norway 267
Olav R. Spilling

14 Innovation at the intersection of market strategy and technology: a study of digital marketing adoption among SMEs 299
Vladimir Vanyushyn

15 Employment growth of new firms 324
Erik Stam, Petra Gibcus, Jennifer Telussa and Elizabeth Garnsey

Index 353

Contributors

Daniela A. Almer-Jarz, Klagenfurt University, Austria

Andreu Blesa, Universitat Jaume I, Spain

Robert J. Breitenecker, Klagenfurt University, Austria

Eva Cools, Vlerick Leuven Gent Management School, Belgium

Hans Crijns, Vlerick Leuven Gent Management School, Belgium

Per Davidsson, Queensland University of Technology, Australia and Jönköping International Business School, Sweden

Frédéric Delmar, EM Lyon, France

Elizabeth Garnsey, University of Cambridge, UK

Petra Gibcus, EIM Business and Policy Research, the Netherlands

Régis Goujet, EM Lyon, France

Timothy G. Habbershon, Babson College, USA

Espen John Isaksen, Bodø Graduate School of Business, Norway

Bengt Johannisson, Växjö University, Sweden

Ann Jorissen, University of Antwerp, Belgium

Ron Kemp, Wageningen Universiteit, the Netherlands

Hans Landström, Lund University, Sweden

Eddy Laveren, University of Antwerp, Belgium

Joris Meijaard, Erasmus Universiteit Rotterdam, the Netherlands

Leif Melin, Jönköping International Business School, Sweden

Vincent Molly, University of Antwerp, Belgium

Diego Monferrer, Universitat Jaume I, Spain

Ysabel Nauwelaerts, Lessius University College and Catholic University Leuven, Belgium

Mattias Nordqvist, Jönköping International Business School, Sweden and Babson College, USA

Lena Olaison, Copenhagen Business School, Denmark and University of Essex, UK

María Ripollés, Universitat Jaume I, Spain

Erich J. Schwarz, Klagenfurt University, Austria

David Smallbone, Kingston University, UK

Olav R. Spilling, NIFU STEP, Norway

Erik Stam, University of Cambridge, UK

Sita Tan, EIM Business and Policy Research, the Netherlands

Jennifer Telussa, EIM Business and Policy Research, the Netherlands

Lorraine M. Uhlaner, Nyenrode Business Universiteit, the Netherlands and Max Planck Institute of Economics, Germany

Vladimir Vanyushyn, Umeå University, Sweden

Joakim Winborg, Halmstad University, Sweden

Foreword

With this book, the European Council for Small Business and Entrepreneurship (ECSB) presents the third volume in a series of papers from the annual Research in Entrepreneurship and Small Business Conference (RENT). RENT XX, held in Brussels in November 2006, celebrated the anniversary of an event that started as a small workshop in Brussels 20 years ago. Today RENT has grown to become one of Europe's best known and globally recognized conferences in the entrepreneurship field. RENT is organized jointly by the European Institute for Advanced Studies in Management (EIASM) and the ECSB.

This book assembles selected best papers, discussing facets of the overall topic of RENT XX, namely 'Entrepreneurship: a driver for sustainable growth in a global and knowledge-based environment'. I thank the editors and reviewers who assisted in selecting papers for their great effort. With this book and series, ECSB continues to offer a look into current European entrepreneurship research, thus facilitating knowledge transfer and international discussions.

Friederike Welter
President, ECSB

PART I

Introduction

1. Introduction

Hans Crijns, Eddy Laveren, Hans Landström and David Smallbone

The field of entrepreneurship and small business studies has prospered and grown considerably in recent years in all European countries, with remarkable developments taking place in the research frameworks and methodologies used. Progress in the field of entrepreneurship is not only triggered by the exchange of ideas and new analyses inside the research community. It is also triggered by the growing emphasis on entrepreneurship in policy agendas and business communities all over Europe, which has stimulated dialogue between the research community and communities of practice.

New and small firms, rather than large ones, are the main providers of new jobs in most economies. Countries exhibiting the highest rates of entrepreneurship tend to exhibit greater subsequent decreases in unemployment rates. Research suggests that entrepreneurship provides a positive contribution to economic growth, although GDP growth is influenced by many other factors. Nevertheless, it is often argued that the key to economic growth and productivity improvements is entrepreneurial capacity. By 2010 the European Union aims to become the most competitive and dynamic knowledge-based economy in the world, capable of sustainable economic growth with more and better jobs and greater social cohesion. In 2001 the European Council agreed on a strategy for sustainable development, adding an environmental dimension to the Lisbon strategy. The Council recognized the need for radical transformation of the economy in order to create some 15 million new jobs by 2010. A friendly environment for starting and developing businesses is central to reaching these goals.

Even though we can say that there are positive signs regarding entrepreneurship and small firms around Europe in general, and that the field of entrepreneurship research has grown significantly in all European countries, we have to remind ourselves that Europe is a very heterogeneous continent which not only provides different conditions for entrepreneurship and small businesses, but also shows very different research traditions between countries.

We shall argue that entrepreneurship and small business research in Europe has several characteristics (see Landström, 2005 for a more detailed discussion). First, as already stated, Europe is a heterogeneous continent, and entrepreneurship and small business research is characterized by its diversity. There are major differences between countries and regions – there are various contextual settings that influence entrepreneurship and small businesses, and these are reflected in different topics chosen among researchers in different countries. This book covers a number of different topics – from the individual entrepreneur and entrepreneurial teams to strategic considerations, finance in SMEs and corporate entrepreneurship.

Second, in order to stimulate development in society, entrepreneurship and small business policies in Europe are both more controversial and more subject to intensive public attention than in the USA. This makes the research of contextual differences interesting. Contextual differences not only influence the research topics chosen but are also reflected in the level of analysis in research. For example, European researchers focus more strongly than their US counterparts on an aggregate level of analysis. The interest in a more aggregated level of analysis is partly shown in the selection of chapters for the book. The focus on the individual and firm levels of analysis is strong in the book, but we can also find chapters focusing on entrepreneurship as a societal phenomenon, comparisons between countries, regional aspects of entrepreneurship and the development of new ventures in different industries.

Third, there is an acceptance of a broader range of methodological approaches among European researchers, which means greater methodological openness compared to US scholars. European researchers and doctoral students have consequently been trained in a greater range of methodologies than their US counterparts. Over time, we have seen a trend in entrepreneurship and small business research, not least in the USA, becoming more and more a 'one-methodological field', relying to a great extent on survey and archival methods, and an increased use of sophisticated statistical methods for data analysis (Landström, 2005). The methodological openness in European entrepreneurship and small business research is reflected in the methods used in the studies presented in this book. For example, several chapters in the book are based on more qualitative methodologies, such as case studies.

Finally, the diversity of entrepreneurship and small business research in Europe influences not only the topics chosen, the level of analysis and the methodological approaches in the studies, but is also reflected in the research communities of the various countries. There is a very great variation in research traditions between countries – not only in terms of the size of the research community but also in the researchers' disciplinary backgrounds and epistemological concerns. As can been seen in the book, many different disciplines are represented – from psychology, sociology, social psychology, management, innovation and regional studies. Even if many studies in the book are based on some 'normal science approach' (Aldrich and Baker, 1997), we can find a diversity of epistemological concerns among the researchers in the book, such as interpretive approaches and social constructivistic research.

Having emphasized the heterogeneity in European entrepreneurship and small business research, we must admit that the majority of chapters selected for this volume are based on some form of international research agenda. Scientific activities are becoming increasingly international. Aldrich (2000) talks about 'isomorphism' as a mechanism through which scholars learn about each other's work. There are many forces that have the potential to bring scholars from different countries closer together. Research is becoming more and more international (conferences, joint projects, international journals, visiting scholars and so on) and international activities are increasing in importance, which promotes the dissemination of approaches. There is also the growing importance of international English-language journals, which promote a common standard of evaluation and professional prestige and which institutionalize norms of professionalism within the field; and there are similar reward systems evolving in Europe as in the USA. Thus many forces are working towards international convergence and uniformity in entrepreneurship and small business research – in common with most scientific fields. At the same time, it is important for European scholars to maintain the diversity that we find among researchers in Europe, and that we systematically develop the specific research areas and paradigms that characterize entrepreneurship and small business research in Europe.

INTRODUCTION TO THE THEMES OF THE BOOK

The chapters in this book cover four themes, each of which illustrates a key dimension in the overall theme of entrepreneurship, sustainable growth and performance.

First, there are the *entrepreneurs*, who are the people involved in entrepreneurship. We are all familiar with successful entrepreneurs, who act as demonstrator cases of the entrepreneurship phenomenon, although the phenomenon itself may appear more abstract. Entrepreneurs matter to both new and old organizations. For new companies, their strengths and weaknesses are typically those of the founding entrepreneur. The firm's success then depends strongly on the entrepreneur's capabilities and competences to develop the organization. However, the organization and the team are also important as key elements in the entrepreneurial process. It is impossible to reduce entrepreneurship to the entrepreneur alone or to the team or to the organization, since the relationships between the three are also important, together with the strategies followed.

A particular place in the entrepreneurship community is taken by the concept of *family business*, defined as firms where ownership is controlled by a family unit, with family members typically involved in management. In such situations relations between family members and with other stakeholders, as well as with resources, raise specific issues. In many European countries family businesses play an important role in creating employment and value, as well as in incubating and financing new businesses. Family firms have gained increasing attention in the economics and finance literature due to research showing that the majority of firms around the world are controlled by their founders or their founders' descendants.

The third theme brings in business *performance*, over time. An understanding of what drives an organization's growth and performance is critical for both managers and founders trying to achieve competitive advantage, as well as for policy makers seeking to attain a healthy economy. Performance also influences the future development potential and managerial activities of a company.

The emphasis in the fourth theme is on the *processes* in which entrepreneurs and their firms operate. It considers how entrepreneurs cope with environmental factors in which both they and the venture are embedded. It focuses on evolutionary perspectives and processes, with various factors influencing performance changing over time. Entrepreneurship as a phenomenon operates in a continually changing environment, which itself is shaped by the entrepreneurial processes themselves. It also includes their role as agents of change in a wider meaning of the concept.

PART I: INTRODUCTION

The first contribution is written by Per Davidsson, who makes some personal and critical reflections on the development of the field of entrepreneurship research, paying particular attention to European contributions. Davidsson assesses what participants of European research conferences have learnt over the past 20 years. He also discusses future challenges of entrepreneurship research and reflects on the past and future roles of European research in this field.

PART II: ENTREPRENEURS AND THEIR ROLE

In Chapter 3 Eva Cools offers insight into what typifies Flemish entrepreneurs. Her analysis is based on trait variables (tolerance for ambiguity, self-efficacy, proactive personality, locus of control, need for achievement) but also cognitive styles (individual and organizational behaviour characteristics), which are used to compare entrepreneurs with non-entrepreneurs. These trait and cognitive characteristics are also used to predict variances in entrepreneurial orientation (EO). This study shows that entrepreneurs score significantly higher on all trait characteristics than non-entrepreneurs. For cognitive styles (as measured with the Cognitive Style Indicator), the study shows that non-entrepreneurs score higher on the knowing and planning style. No differences are found for the creating style. With regard to the link between the entrepreneur's profile and EO, the author finds a significant contribution of tolerance for ambiguity and proactive personality to EO.

The purpose of the study by Frédéric Delmar and Régis Goujet, which is reported in Chapter 4, is to examine how experience on an entrepreneurship course, constructed as a mastery experience, is influenced by personal predispositions, such as intentions, self-efficacy and previous vicarious experience. The purpose is also to examine how this mastery experience affects changes in intention and self-efficacy. Using data from 958 French business school students, enrolled in a compulsory entrepreneurship course, Delmar and Goujet find that intention is an important factor defining the level of learning measured as self-efficacy, but that it has a weaker effect than previous self-efficacy. This is in line with previous research that has examined the relationship between task characteristics and motivation. The authors discuss the role of entrepreneurial education in the acquisition of entrepreneurial self-efficacy and intentions, and the mediating effect of previous entrepreneurial exposure.

In Chapter 5 Joakim Winborg examines the relative importance of the entrepreneur's motives for using financial bootstrapping in new businesses. Financial bootstrapping is defined as methods of securing the use of resources without relying on long-term external finance. Another goal of the study is to identify the managerial and business factors that influence the motives for using this type of financing method. Based on a questionnaire sent to 120 new business managers, the findings show that 'lower costs' is the most commonly reported motive, followed by 'lack of capital' and surprisingly 'fun in helping others and getting help'. In the analysis managers were classified in one of two groups, namely 'economic motives' and 'economic and existential motives'. The analysis shows significant differences between the two groups when it comes to the owner's situation, the need for long-term finance, the type of company, the line of industry, and the manager's driving force and relative experience.

PART III: ENTREPRENEURSHIP IN FAMILY FIRMS

In Chapter 6 Mattias Nordqvist, Timothy Habbershon and Leif Melin investigate transgenerational entrepreneurship in family firms, which they define as a family's mindset and capabilities to continue their entrepreneurial legacy of social and economic wealth creation across generations. Combining and integrating literature on corporate entrepreneurship and family firms, the authors investigate what characterizes entrepreneurship in owner-families and family firms and how entrepreneurship can be maintained and reproduced across generations. The authors conclude that a family firm does not have to be entrepreneurial across all dimensions of entrepreneurial orientation (EO) to reach desired entrepreneurial performance outcomes. Based on in-depth case research, Nordqvist, Habbershon and Melin suggest that the risk-taking and competitive aggressiveness dimensions of the EO are less important in family firms. Conversely, they propose that specific characteristics of family firms, such as autonomy, innovativeness and proactiveness, are more common dimensions of EO, with greater implications for transgenerational entrepreneurship. Contrary to some earlier studies, they observe that over time and across generations characteristics that support a sustained entrepreneurial orientation can emerge alongside increased family orientation. This lends support to the argument that family firms can stay entrepreneurial, even with increasing family involvement.

In Chapter 7 Vincent Molly, Eddy Laveren and Ann Jorissen examine the financing and growth behaviour of 613 small and medium-sized family firms, by using concepts of internal and sustainable growth. The aim of the study is to highlight intergenerational differences in family firms by using first-generation family firms as a reference category for describing the behaviour in later generations of family firms. Empirical evidence shows that the type of generation actively involved in the management of a family firm is not neutral to the financing and growth decisions of the company, as first-generation family firms seem to realize higher debt levels, lower cash holdings and faster growth rates in comparison with third-generation family firms. Based on a comparison of actual and internal/sustainable growth rates, regression analysis further shows that next-generation managed family firms have a stronger preference for internal financing instead of an excessive level of indebtedness in funding their growth. The results give support for the idea that second- and especially third-generation family firms seem to be more constrained in their growth behaviour due to more conservative financial policies.

In Chapter 8 Lorraine Uhlaner, Sita Tan, Joris Meijaard and Ron Kemp investigate the links between family orientation, strategy and innovation. The authors conclude that family orientation has a negligible negative impact on the innovation performance of SMEs. They found that more family-oriented firms are likely to report fewer innovations than less family-oriented firms, even when controlling for size, age, sector and differences in strategy. Although this conclusion implies that the family orientation may indeed be an obstacle for innovation, most of this effect can be explained by differences in strategy. In particular, companies following certain approaches to strategy (greater risk orientation, greater growth orientation, more formal strategic process, more focus, innovation differentiation, less emphasis on price discounting) are likely to report a greater level of innovation performance than those who do not. However, family orientation has a small, but statistically significant effect on innovation performance, both direct and indirect.

PART IV: PERFORMANCE OF NEW VENTURES

The key research question considered in Chapter 9 focuses on whether team foundations achieve better performance in new ventures than solo entrepreneurs. However, new venture teams are also exposed to risks, for example, if team members do not have complementary competences and/or if they have communication problems. Daniela Almer-Jarz, Erich Schwartz and Robert Breitenecker investigate the relationship between the initial characteristics of the team, such as size, heterogeneity and the experience of the team, as well as characteristics of team processes, such as work norms, communication, fluctuation and new venture performance. The empirical results indicate that team size and communication have a significant influence on new venture performance, whereas fluctuation, in terms of team member entry and exit, does not.

In Chapter 10 Espen John Isaksen investigates performance differences in newly started businesses. A human capital model focusing on the business founder's key human capital attributes is developed. A distinction is made between the entrepreneur's general and specific human capital. Derived hypotheses are tested using a representative sample of 264 new independent businesses surveyed at two points in time. The first round of data collection took place shortly after the businesses had entered a Norwegian business register. Follow-up data relating to the dependent variable, early business performance, were separated from the presumed explanatory factors by approximately 19 months. The reported findings suggest that two out of three selected specific human capital variables (that is, business ownership experience and business similarity) were significantly associated with superior early business performance. General human capital variables (that is, the level of education, years of work experience and management experience) were not found to be related to early business performance.

In Chapter 11 María Ripollés, Andreu Blesa, Diego Monferrer and Ysabel Nauwelaerts analyse how entrepreneurial and market orientations influence the performance of international ventures, based on data gathered from Spanish and Belgian new ventures. The Spanish sample shows a positive and significant relationship between entrepreneurial orientation, market orientation and international performance. Market orientation also has a positive and significant relationship with international positional advantages. Finally, international positional advantages have a positive and significant relationship with international performance. In the Belgian case the analysis shows a positive and significant relationship between entrepreneurial orientation and market orientation, and between international positional advantages and international performance. In the case of Spain, entrepreneurs who promote an entrepreneurial orientation can enhance international performance if their companies adopt market orientation. However this does not hold in the case of Belgian international new ventures.

PART V: PROCESSES AND ENTREPRENEURSHIP

In Chapter 12 Bengt Johannisson and Lena Olaison argue for recognition of different perspectives on entrepreneurship, suggesting that it is not possible to conclusively generate models and/or conceptualize entrepreneurship once and for all. The authors associate entrepreneurship with imaginative ways of dealing with ruptures in the everyday life context of individuals. They propose that such ruptures may initiate processes that uncover and (re)produce entrepreneurship, which remain invisible when 'business as usual' rules in society. Johannisson and Olaison investigate creative organizing in the face of (natural) catastrophes and conceptualize 'emergence entrepreneurship' accordingly.

In Chapter 13 Olav Spilling focuses on the complex processes that may follow attempts to develop a new business based on research results and, in particular, on the role of academic staff in such processes, particularly with respect to how they might contribute as entrepreneurs in the formation of new spin-off businesses. Spilling develops qualitative insights into processes of commercialization and the role of academic staff in such processes using a longitudinal case study approach, based on four spin-off, biotechnology firms. The four cases illustrate that processes of commercialization may be characterized by complexity, turbulence and a high level of uncertainty. Spilling recognizes the different roles that academic staff may take in the processes of commercialization: the entrepreneurial professor with a high commitment to entrepreneurial tasks as well as research; the industrial entrepreneur with a high commitment to entrepreneurial tasks and less commitment in research; the research oriented entrepreneur with a high commitment to research activities and less in entrepreneurial tasks; and the production manager with a low commitment to research as well as the entrepreneurial tasks of the firm, but who still has an important role in managing the production of the new company. In academic milieus there are often perceived conflicts between academic and commercial activities, and there may be significant barriers to developing a more entrepreneurial culture.

In Chapter 14 Vladimir Vanyushyn argues that the opportunities inherent in the digitization of marketing and selling activities are substantial and that going on-line can lead to a number of benefits for a business, including more efficient business processes, round the clock operations, flexible pricing, rapid internationalization, increased market reach, cost reduction and better targeting of products. Vanyushyn's study aims to identify and examine antecedents of digitization of marketing and sales by smaller manufacturing firms. To do so, three partially overlapping, but nonetheless conceptually and empirically distinct groups of studies, are reviewed and integrated. The first group of studies, which are commonly found in mainstream management and marketing journals, approach digitization from the innovation perspective. The second group, represented mostly by information and management science publications, is grounded in technology acceptance models that evaluate the perceived usefulness and ease of use of an IT application. The third approach examines digitization from a product-market strategy perspective. It is suggested that these three approaches are rather compartmentalized and have been weakly integrated in the literature. Vanyushyn seeks to test alternative models incorporating various combinations of predictors of digitization and to suggest and test an integrative model.

Finally, in Chapter 15 Erik Stam, Petra Gibcus, Jennifer Telussa and Elizabeth Garnsey suggest that new firms must demonstrate dynamic capabilities to reconfigure their resource base as needed. Dynamic capabilities are the organizational and strategic routines by which firms achieve new resource combinations. The authors analyse the association between dynamic capabilities and new firm growth, controlling for measures of firm resources, characteristics of the entrepreneur and aspects of the environment. The central research question discussed in the chapter is: 'How strong is the relationship between dynamic capabilities and the growth of new firms?' The empirical results show that many variables (that is, an entrepreneurial team, educational level, business-ownership experience, technical experience, industry experience, gender and new product development) do not have the presumed relationship. The level of start-up capital only partly has the expected positive association. Employment growth ambitions have a strong positive association with firm growth in general. Growth path dynamics should be viewed in terms of the inherent problems of firm growth and the changing ability of firms to solve these problems by accumulating firm-specific competences and dynamic capabilities.

REFERENCES

Aldrich, H.E. (2000), 'Learning together: national differences in entrepreneurship research', in D.L. Sexton and H. Landström (eds), *The Blackwell Handbook of Entrepreneurship*, Oxford: Blackwell, pp. 5–25.

Aldrich, H.E. and T. Baker (1997), 'Blinded by the cites. Has there been progress in entrepreneurship research?', in D.L. Sexton and R.W. Smilor (eds), *Entrepreneurship 2000*, Chicago, IL: Upstart, pp. 377–400.

Landström, H. (2005), *Pioneers in Entrepreneurship and Small Business Research*, New York: Springer.

2. Looking back at 20 years of entrepreneurship research: what did we learn?

Per Davidsson

INTRODUCTION

As one of the participants of the first RENT conference in 1987, and one of those who have stayed in this field of research, I was invited to deliver a keynote address at the 20th anniversary of RENT in November 2006. This short chapter is largely based on that keynote address. What follows are some personal and hopefully provocative, yet constructive, reflections on the development of the field of entrepreneurship research with a particular eye to European contributions. Before proceeding I should emphasize that I have not undertaken a systematic review of the past 20 years of research, and despite the title I shall confine my discussion about what we have learnt to a few fundamental ways in which research results have made us rethink the entrepreneurship phenomenon and how it can be researched. I shall then turn to the (remaining) challenges of entrepreneurship research and reflect on the past and future roles of European research in this field.

It should be pointed out that I am fully aware that my sometimes critical remarks are made by possibly the greatest of sinners or traitors in relation to the issues I raise. I have explored empirically more than I have developed or tested theory, and I have researched a broad range of entrepreneurship phenomena rather than building a tighter research stream. At the same time that I propagate designs that reduce heterogeneity problems, I lead a research project that has among the worst such problems one could imagine. Despite my call for supporting European research institutions or infrastructure, I have not been a regular attendee at RENT in recent years, and I have not systematically sent my best RENT papers to the leading European journal, *Entrepreneurship and Regional Development*. I even left the European continent (for Australia; not North America), although I retain a part-time position at the Jönköping International Business School (JIBS) in Sweden. Then again, this half insider, half outsider position can be useful for assessing and reflecting upon where European entrepreneurship research stands today. As regards being a target of the criticism I deliver, I definitely count myself as an insider.

THE EARLY CONFERENCES

In order to assess what we have learnt over the past 20 years I found it useful to check the proceedings from the first RENT conferences – in Brussels, 1987, Vienna, 1988 and Durham, 1989. What is most striking about such a reading exercise is that the research of the time was largely directed at mapping out the field, that is, to broadly explore entrepreneurial phenomena. This includes still quite readable, conceptual organizing efforts by thought leaders of the time, such as Alan Gibb, Bengt Johannisson and Josef Mugler, as well as many broad-based or in-depth – but largely atheoretical – empirical explorations that have not stood the test of time to the same extent. However, these early empirical explorations were absolutely essential to the further development of the field. Through them grew a close-up familiarity with the phenomenon that was indispensable for our subsequent ability to ask the relevant questions, improve research design and correctly interpret or assign meaning to empirical findings.

Striking in the proceedings from the first few conferences is also the broad variety of research approaches before some convergence or conformism set in (the same goes for the North American development of the field; see, for example, the *Frontiers of Entrepreneurship Research* from 1981 and 1982). This variety includes some very interesting 'false starts'. One example is viewing entrepreneurship as a career issue (rather than a myopic focus on one individual-venture combination at one point in time, thus blurring levels of analysis and disregarding the non-entrepreneurship options). Early take-up of this idea could have led to a faster move towards longitudinal designs and attention to level-of-analysis issues. Another example is the use of computer simulation as an approach to learn about entrepreneurial phenomena. Failing to build on these early attempts may be regarded opportunities foregone for European entrepreneurship research. However, it is encouraging that at long last they seem to have been re-invented. At the recent Academy of Management meeting in Philadelphia (August 2007) some of the most interesting sessions (see Academy of Management Meeting 2007 programme, sessions 293, 333 and 1420) addressed precisely these issues – careers-oriented theory development, simulation of serial entrepreneurship, and the building of longitudinal data bases that allow studies on how individuals enter, team up and exit independent business ownership over time. Even more encouraging is that Europe-based researchers had leading roles in all of these sessions.

TWENTY YEARS – WHAT DID WE LEARN?

When you are in the middle of something that develops gradually it is easy to become unimpressed and conclude that we have not come far enough, fast enough (Low, 2001). However, at least in part this perception is false and due to internalization and taking earlier achievements for granted. The fact is that our knowledge about entrepreneurial phenomena has grown dramatically over the past couple of decades. A look back at what the research output looked like 20 years ago clearly suggests that such is the case. Apart from thousands of more specific and detailed insights, I think that the following are among the more important strides forward that have been made:

- We have come to understand that the population of independent businesses is numerically dominated by largely non-growing and non-innovative entities that do not exercise much 'entrepreneurship' most of the time (for example, Samuelsson, 2004; Storey, 1994).
- Yet it has been firmly established that small, independent businesses are an important force in the economy – for innovation (for example, Acs and Audretsch, 1990), job creation (for example, Davidsson et al., 1998) and regional development (for example, Fritsch and Mueller, 2004). There is still some debate as regards to what extent this is attributable to a small minority of high-growth/high-potential businesses versus the incremental improvements introduced by large numbers of more mundane ventures. In all likelihood these proportions vary across time and space.
- Importantly, we have come to realize that entrepreneurship is about newness rather than about organizational smallness. Hence the entire field has drifted from an entrepreneurship/small business position to a focus on the creation of new economic activity regardless of organizational context (Davidsson, 2004; Shane and Venkataraman, 2000).
- We have learnt that entrepreneurship is not as much about innate qualities of special individuals as the early research assumed. Personality differences do exist on average between 'entrepreneurs' and others (for example, Collins et al., 2004) but such variables explain but a few per cent of the variance. Moreover, over the course of their lives a rather large and internally heterogeneous chunk of the human population are at some stage actively involved in business

start-ups or other entrepreneurial activities (for example, Delmar and Davidsson, 2000).

- Hence individual level research has taken off in several directions that lead to more teachable and learnable insights, such as cognition (for example, Gustafsson, 2004; Mitchell et al., 2002) and behaviour (for example, Gartner, 1988; Samuelsson, 2004), including examination of habitual (serial and portfolio) entrepreneurs. The latter is an example of a sub-field where European researchers have played a leading role (for example, Alsos and Kolvereid, 1998; Westhead and Wright, 1998)
- A very central insight is that entrepreneurship is much more a *social* game than an individual one. The most striking characteristic of successful entrepreneurs is perhaps their ability to identify, cultivate and use other people's competencies. This insight has led to an increased focus on issues, such as networking, teams and social capital (for example, Davidsson and Honig, 2003; Hoang and Antoncic, 2003; Ruef et al., 2003; note also early European contributions, such as Birley, 1985; Johannisson, 1986).
- The limited early success with research on the individual level led to fruitful redirection towards examination of what features of regional environments are conducive of entrepreneurship (for example, Reynolds et al., 1994) as well as the characteristics and dynamics of 'clusters' (for example, Braunerhjelm et al., 2000); 'industrial districts' (for example, Becattini, 1991) and 'innovative milieux' (Maillat, 1998). These more aggregate level analyses exemplify another domain where European researchers have made major contributions to comparatively strong empirical generalizations.
- Similarly, we have increasingly understood that for policy-making purposes we need to look at institutional arrangements rather than at qualities of individuals. Arguably, under the right institutional arrangements enough entrepreneurs will come forward for the benefit of the economy at large (Baumol, 1990; Davidsson and Henrekson, 2002).
- The drift away from myopic preoccupation with individual characteristics has also led to progress on the entrepreneurial process (for example, Bhave, 1994; Sarasvathy, 2001; Van de Ven et al., 1999) and on the fit between the individual(s) and the venture idea (for example, Shane, 2000). However, these are arguably areas where we have as yet only scratched the surface.

Obviously, the above bullet points represent but a rudimentary sketch of some of the more important insights that have been attained. Each bullet point above could easily be expanded to a full length review chapter in its own right. Similarly, regarding other aspects of entrepreneurship, there are thousands of pieces of the jigsaw puzzle that have been put in place by the research efforts of the past decades.

THE CHALLENGE AHEAD

However, perhaps more than anything else we have come to realize that entrepreneurship is a complex, heterogeneous and multi-level phenomenon. Very different types of individuals enact an array of business ideas with very different inherent qualities, and for different reasons. Survival does not necessarily mean success, and neither does growth; in the same vein, discontinuance is not necessarily synonymous with failure (Davidsson, 2008). Further, a successful venture does not necessarily mean a happy entrepreneur; highly successful entrepreneurs occasionally create a failing venture, and what looks like a positive or negative outcome on the venture level may have an influence in the opposite direction on the economy as a whole. Moreover, what contributes to a successful outcome may vary across industries, spatial contexts, time periods and stages of a venture's development. To complicate even more things, the theoretically contributing factors may not be possible to operationalize in the same, comparable way across ventures in these different contexts.

Phenomenon-driven research conducted by researchers with a passionate interest in the object of their research has made it possible for us to gradually understand just how complex and heterogeneous the world of entrepreneurship really is. When research starts from a genuine interest in the phenomenon it is natural to strive for 'complete' understanding of the 'entire' phenomenon as it presents itself 'in the real world'. This calls for a study of the 'entire population' or a representative sample thereof. For a researcher with a more qualitative bent the corresponding lure would be case studies of the grounded, 'thick description' type. In either case, the researcher would want to include 'all relevant variables' in the study. This is what much of the early research in this field has looked like.

The problem is that when there is a large number of factors involved, which have variable measurability and effects, our analysis techniques and cognitive capacities may not suffice to disentangle the true nature of the relationships. Hence the many confusing, apparently conflicting results and lack of cumulative growth of knowledge in many areas of entrepreneurship research. To make matters worse, even if we were able to arrive at 'true' results there is no guarantee that the descriptively valid results thus gained translate into valid, normative advice.

For these reasons we should welcome the current transition to more theory-driven research in more narrow empirical settings. As one of the biggest sinners in that regard I am certainly not suggesting that phenomenon-driven research is wrong. What I am suggesting is that it is very, very demanding. I am also suggesting that in order to make further progress we need more theory-driven research.

Unlike phenomenon-driven research, theory-driven research does not start from an interest in what is going on 'out there' at a particular time in a particular place. This means that the entire, theoretically relevant population is not accessible because if the theory is valid it should hold in other places and at other times as well. The task then becomes to test the theory on one theoretically relevant population – and then hopefully to repeat that test on other, equally relevant populations. Neither does theory-driven research aspire to 'complete understanding'; the research confines itself to examination of a limited set of pre-specified relationships as predicted by some theory. Other influences on the dependent variable are relevant only to the extent that they threaten to blur the focal relationships. Hence they are preferably 'designed away', for example, through randomization in an experimental setting. And indeed, experimental research on entrepreneurial phenomena has increased in recent years, sometimes extending to research questions one would initially doubt would lend themselves to experimentation (for example, Brundin et al., 2008).

However, for practical and/or ethical reasons it can be argued that most research questions in entrepreneurship cannot be examined through experimentation. Barring experimental control the primary route to reduced complexity and heterogeneity is to focus the study on a more narrowly defined sample, that is, one where the entities share many characteristics rather than varying widely on every dimension. Let me mention a few studies that have impressed me in that regard.

Using a sample from the North American architectural woodwork industry, careful operationalizations, a longitudinal design, structural equations modelling and inclusion of a few key control variables, Baum and Locke (2004) were able to show that psychological characteristics of the founders, such as passion and tenacity, significantly influence the growth of the firms. That is, by reducing measurement error as well as unmeasured heterogeneity and other sources of model misspecification they were able to demonstrate the effects of a type of variable for which previous research has found it hard to arrive at firm conclusions.

Similarly, using a sample of law firms founded in the Greater Vancouver area between 1990 and 1998, Cliff et al. (2006) addressed the age-old question of whether it is industry insiders or outsiders who are more innovative. By focusing on one industry and one type of innovation they were able to assess innovativeness in a reliable and comparable way. Their results suggest that neither complete outsiders nor those at the core of the industry but rather those with experience from the periphery of the industry were the primary contributors of organizational innovation. Addressing this question across different industries would likely have been an impossible task as it would force the researchers to rely on 'one-size-fits-all' assessments of core variables, such as 'innovation', 'industry core' and 'industry periphery'.

Another Canadian example is Usher and Evans (1996), who examined how organizational adaptation versus selection/replacement combined to change the population of petrol stations in Edmonton, Alberta, from 1959 to 1988. This is an example of researchers being able to identify an empirical context that is distinct enough and has undergone enough change in order to serve as a fruitful testing ground for the theories they were interested in.

Finally, to include an example of case-based research, we have Shane's (2000) study of all the individuals associated with all the ventures – successful and unsuccessful – that were based on one and the same basic technological breakthrough. This allowed him to focus on the specific role of prior knowledge and to make a compelling argument that in every case it would have been impossible to swap teams or venture ideas. Each team was uniquely equipped to discover and/or exploit their particular idea; there is no way they would have come up with the ideas the other teams were pursuing. The obvious implication is that it may not be meaningful to discuss entrepreneurial 'opportunities' separately from the individuals who pursue them (Dimov, 2004).

The point here is that although we may have zero interest in architectural woodwork firms, the city of Edmonton and so on, the specific and very narrow empirical contexts in which these studies were undertaken allowed them to arrive at comparatively clear findings that we feel really teach us something. This is also thanks to the theoretical input and interpretations that give the findings meaning. For sure, 'final proof' would require replication in other, equally theoretically relevant contexts. However, to my mind, analytical generalization from well-designed studies like these is much more convincing than statistical inference based on empirical fact-finding where theoretical interpretation is lacking.

Again, I am not saying that phenomenon-driven research is wrong or that we did not learn anything from it over the past decades. On the contrary, I believe phenomenon-driven exploration was a necessary step before turning to more theory-driven research and I think it is still warranted in some areas, such as real time study of venture creation processes. Having said that, I also believe the theoretical and methodological sophistication of discipline-based research should be the main road forward for entrepreneurship research. However, it would be naïve to think that such a transition comes without costs or risks. We may have been lacking in terms of theoretical and methodological sophistication at the time of the early RENT conferences but there sure was close-up familiarity with and genuine interest in the phenomena. If future entrepreneurship research is to be carried out in separate disciplinary silos by researchers whose primary considerations are to impress academic colleagues and adding lines to their CVs, nothing has been gained. As pointed out by Low (2001), 'entrepreneurship as specific domain' and 'entrepreneurship belongs in the disciplines' are mutually dependent perspectives. Our research needs disciplinary input (and recognition) but we also need the community that prevents us from drifting away from relevance and reality checks.

EUROPE VS NORTH AMERICA

I distinctly remember a discussion with the late, great Mike Scott at one of the first RENT conferences. The topic of our discussion was European versus North American entrepreneurship research and we were in full agreement that European research compared favourably. I do not think Europe has kept that lead. For example, it was no accident that all my examples of impressive pieces of work using narrow samples were North American.[1] However, to this day I believe European research is more curiosity-driven and characterized by greater paradigmatic diversity, which can be great strengths. For example, from ten years at Jönköping International Business School I can fondly recall doctoral dissertations representing an amazing diversity of theoretical and methodological approaches. A longitudinal survey study adhering to the ideal of scientific realism (Wiklund, 1998) would be followed by a Foucaultian discourse analysis (Ahl, 2002); an ethnography (Wigren, 2003); a multi-method, real time case study approach (Brundin, 2002); a theory-driven, experimental study (Gustafsson, 2004) and yet another longitudinal survey approach (Samuelsson, 2004). Accepting such variety can be high risk but also extremely enriching.

By contrast, North American research tends to be paradigmatically narrow. In my darker moments I would also hold that it tends to be overly geared towards quantity and minimum publishable units; towards enhancing careers and adding lines to CVs rather than being curiosity-driven or concerned about having an impact on practice; by overly emphasizing 'packaging' and 'selling' of stories and results rather than reflecting sound academic honesty and professional scepticism, and by sometimes displaying make-believe theory-drivenness when the true research process was highly explorative.

And yet, the tip of that iceberg produces the 'best', most influential and most cited research, and the past couple of decades of entrepreneurship research have been characterized by increased North American influence. There is no research infrastructure in Europe that can really compare with its North American counterparts. RENT and the ad hoc books that come from it have never achieved the same status as the Babson (BCERC) conference and its proceedings, the *Frontiers of Entrepreneurship Research* (which was a very important outlet in the early days). EURAM does not have the central role that the Academy of Management (and its 2200 member strong Entrepreneurship Division) enjoys. European researchers often make the *Journal of Business Venturing* and *Entrepreneurship Theory and Practice* their preferred targets. By contrast, while the respective editors should be lauded for improving the quality and status of *Entrepreneurship and Regional Development* and the *International Small Business Journal* they are far from reaching the same 'impact factors' and it is rare that North American scholars submit their work to them before it has been rejected in a couple of better preferred outlets.

Is this a problem at all? Should and could not European researchers contribute through the dominant North American system – and help change it where change is called for? Yes, they could – and they do. Many contributions in the leading conferences and journals, and many well cited papers, are authored or co-authored by Europeans. As shown in Table 2.1, a superficial analysis indicates that European (based) researchers do exceedingly well as they account for the vast majority of top cited articles in major entrepreneurship journals regardless of the home of the journal.

However, there is trouble in paradise. Firstly, the large, continental European countries are not represented in the table other than by an Asian scholar trained in the USA who works for a truly international institution that happens to be located on French soil (INSEAD). Second, the European dominance in the table may be happenstance due to a few outliers during the first years of the new millennium. Third, it is uncertain whether the entries in the table stand for anything distinctly European other than by birthplace or university affiliation. Despite the results in the table it is my sense that European research – and certainly a distinctly European discourse – is under-represented in the top end that truly gives the field direction. This would likely show in a similar analysis of influential works published in leading disciplinary and mainstream management journals. As a case in point, there are few Europeans among the recipients of The International Award for Entrepreneurship and Small Business Research.

Table 2.1 Most cited works published 2000–07 in ISI/WoS (SSCI) listed entrepreneurship journals (each journal's top two according to Google Scholar)

Journal	Journal home	Work	GS citations	Author based in
JBV	USA	Davidsson and Honig (2003)	183	Sweden/Israel
JBV	USA	Hoang and Antoncic (2003)	117	France/Slovenia
ETP	USA	Ucbasaran et al., (2001)	87	UK
ETP	USA	Davidsson and Wiklund (2001)	80	Sweden
JSBM	USA	Dhanaraj and Beamish (2003)	39	USA/Canada
JSBM	USA	Sadler-Smith et al. (2003)	33	UK
ERD	UK	Delmar and Davidsson (2000)	128	Sweden
ERD	UK	Chell and Baines (2000)	69	UK
SBEJ	NL/US	Carree et al. (2002)	101	The Netherlands
SBEJ	NL/US	DuRietz and Henrekson (2000)	82	Sweden
ISBJ	UK	Daniel et al. (2002)	61	UK
ISBJ	UK	Freel (2000)	52	UK

Note: JBV = *Journal of Business Venturing*; ETP = *Entrepreneurship Theory and Practice*; JSBM = *Journal of Small Business Management*; ERD = *Entrepreneurship and Regional Development*; SBEJ = *Small Business Economics Journal*; ISBJ = *International Small Business Journal*; GS= Google Scholar.

Language barriers may be one restricting factor. To the extent that intellectually leading discourses exist in the other major European languages, they do not seem to reach the international community, which restricts their communication to English. However, I doubt that language is the major factor. I admit to speculation here, but I feel that one reason for European research to be less influential than it should be is that to a lesser degree than the North Americans have we accepted that in order to make strong contributions in a maturing field it may be necessary to develop and stick to a narrow research stream rather than jumping from topic to topic according to one's own current curiosity (in this regard I am obviously one of the greatest sinners on the planet). It is also increasingly necessary to team up as it becomes more and more inconceivable that one individual would possess all the theoretical, methodological and other skills necessary to contribute at the frontier. I believe North American researchers more than Europeans have embraced these realities.

I have noted above that the European 'infrastructure' of entrepreneurship research is not as strong as (the top end) of its North American counterpart. Is there anything we can do about that? Well, hopefully not by trying to weaken a perceived 'enemy'. Most of my moments are bright rather than dark, and in these moments I think the North American academic system – despite admitted flaws – has something going for it. Hence I use much of my time trying to contribute to it (and change it in what marginal ways I can), and I would encourage others to follow suit. However, a dose of sound competition is good for all. Therefore some spicing up of European outlets for entrepreneurship research would be good for European and North American scholars alike – as well as for those representing other parts of the globe. 'Everybody' knows that regular paper presentation sessions at conferences do not always lead to the most stimulating exchange. Some innovation that yields more intellectually rewarding conference experiences should not be too far fetched (or too hard to implement) an idea. Similarly, when reflecting upon it 'everybody' realizes that if academic publishing started today we would not let the limitations of Gutenberg's innovation restrict the format for how we share our research findings. Why don't we get a chance to comment upon and rate published articles (other than beforehand as anonymous reviewers)? Why don't authors get a chance to respond to our objections, update their work or share what new insights they have gained post publication? By applying some creativity and readily available new technology European research outlets would have a great opportunity to improve their positions. This would presumably lead to sound competition and some counter balancing of the excesses of the North American system. Ultimately, the winner would be the accumulation and diffusion of knowledge about one of the most important phenomena in our societies: entrepreneurship.

NOTE

1. There are European examples of the same kind, for example, Karl Gratzer's fantastic reconstruction of the automated restaurant industry in Sweden or Mario Raffa's comprehensive, longitudinal study of the development of software firms – but they are typically not as well 'marketed' and hence not as influential. See Gratzer (1999) and Raffa et al. (1996) for some of the fragments that are available in English.

REFERENCES

Acs, Z.J. and D.B. Audretsch (1990), *Innovation and Small Firms*, Cambridge, MA: MIT Press.

Ahl, H.J. (2002), *The Making of the Female Entrepreneur*, Doctoral dissertation, Jönköping: Jönköping International Business School.

Alsos, G.A. and L. Kolvereid (1998), 'The business gestation process of novice, serial and parallel business founders', *Entrepreneurship Theory and Practice*, **22**(4), 101–14.

Baum, J.R. and E.A. Locke (2004), 'The relationship of entrepreneurial traits, skill, and motivation to subsequent venture growth', *Journal of Applied Psychology*, **89**(4), 587–98.

Baumol, W.J. (1990), 'Entrepreneurship: productive, unproductive and destructive', *Journal of Political Economy*, **98**(5), 893–921.

Becattini, G. (1991), 'The industrial district as a creative milieu', in G. Benko and M. Dunford (eds), *Industrial Change and Regional Development: The Transformation of New Industrial Spaces*, London: Belhaven, pp. 102–14.

Bhave, M.P. (1994), 'A process model of entrepreneurial venture creation', *Journal of Business Venturing*, **9**, 223–42.

Birley, S. (1985), 'The role of networks in the entrepreneurial process', *Journal of Business Venturing*, **3**(1), 107–17.

Braunerhjelm, P., B. Carlsson, D. Cetindamar and D. Johansson (2000), 'The old and the new: the evolution of polymer and biomedical clusters in Ohio and Sweden', *Journal of Evolutionary Economics*, **10**(5), 471–88.

Brundin, E. (2002), *Emotions in Motion: Leadership during Radical Change*, Doctoral dissertation, Jönköping: Jönköping International Business School.

Brundin, E., H. Patzelt and D. Shepherd (2008), 'Managers' emotional displays and employees' willingness to act entrepreneurially', *Journal of Business Venturing*, **23**(2) 221–43.

Carree, M., A. van Stel, R. Thurik, R. and S. Wennekers (2002), 'Economic development and business ownership: an analysis using data of 23 OECD countries in the period 1976–1996', *Entrepreneurship and Regional Development*, **19**(3), 271–90.

Chell, E. and S. Baines (2000), 'Networking, entrepreneurship and microbusiness behaviour', *Entrepreneurship and Regional Development*, **12**(3), 195–215.

Cliff, J.E., P.D. Jennings and R. Greenwood (2006), 'New to the game and questioning the rules: the experiences and beliefs of founders who start imitative versus innovative firms', *Journal of Business Venturing*, **21**, 633–63.

Collins, C.J., P.J. Hanges and E.A. Locke (2004), 'The relationship of achievement motivation to entrepreneurial behavior: a meta-analysis', *Human Performance*, **17**(1), 95–117.

Daniel, E., H. Wilson and H. Myers (2002), 'Adoption of e-commerce by SMEs in the UK', *International Small Business Journal*, **20**(3), 253–70.

Davidsson, P. (2004), *Researching Entrepreneurship*, New York: Springer.

Davidsson, P. (2008), 'Interpreting performance in entrepreneurship research', in P. Davidsson (ed.), *The Entrepreneurship Research Challenge*, Cheltenham, UK and Northampton, MA, USA: Edward Elgar.

Davidsson, P. and M. Henrekson (2002), 'Institutional determinants of the prevalence of start-ups and high-growth firms: evidence from Sweden', *Small Business Economics*, **19**(2), 81–104.

Davidsson, P. and B. Honig (2003), 'The role of social and human capital among nascent entrepreneurs', *Journal of Business Venturing*, **18**(3), 301–31.

Davidsson, P. and J. Wiklund (2001), 'Levels of analysis in entrepreneurship research: current practice and suggestions for the future', *Entrepreneurship Theory and Practice*, **25**(4), 81–99.

Davidsson, P., L. Lindmark and C. Olofsson (1998), 'The extent of overestimation of small firm job creation: an empirical examination of the "regression bias"', *Small Business Economics*, **10**, 87–100.

Delmar, F. and P. Davidsson (2000), 'Where do they come from? prevalence and characteristics of nascent entrepreneurs', *Entrepreneurship and Regional Development*, **12**, 1–23.
Dhanaraj, C. and W. Beamish (2003), 'A resource-based approach to the study of export performance', *Journal of Small Business Management*, **41**(3), 242–61.
Dimov, D.P. (2004), 'The individuality of opportunity recognition: a critical review and extension', in J.E. Butler (ed.), *Opportunity Identification and Entrepreneurial Behavior*, Greenwich, CT: IAP, pp. 135–62.
DuRietz, A. and M. Henrekson, M. (2000), 'Testing the female underperformance hypothesis', *Small Business Economics*, **14**(1), 1–10.
Freel, M.S. (2000), 'Barriers to product innovation in small manufacturing firms', *International Small Business Journal*, **18**(2), 60–80.
Fritsch, M. and P. Mueller (2004), 'Effects of new firm formation on regional development over time', *Regional Studies*, **38**(8), 961–75.
Gartner, W.B. (1988), ' "Who is an entrepreneur?" is the wrong question', *American Small Business Journal*, **12**(4), 11–31.
Gratzer, K. (1999), 'The making of a new industry – the introduction of fast food in Sweden', in B. Johannisson and H. Landström (eds), *Images of Entrepreneurship Research – Emergent Swedish Contributions to Academic Research*, Lund, Sweden: Studentlitteratur, pp. 82–114.
Gustafsson, V. (2004), *Entrepreneurial Decision-Making*, Doctoral dissertation, Jönköping: Jönköping International Business School.
Hoang, H. and B. Antoncic (2003), 'Network-based research in entrepreneurship: a critical review', *Journal of Business Venturing*, **18**(2), 165–87.
Johannisson, B. (1986), 'Network strategies: management technology for entrepreneurship and change', *International Small Business Journal*, **1**(1), 19–30.
Low, M. (2001), 'The adolescence of entrepreneurship research: specification of purpose', *Entrepreneurship Theory and Practice*, **25**(4), 17–25.
Maillat, D. (1998), 'Innovative milieux and new generations of regional policies', *Entrepreneurship and Regional Development*, **10**(1), 1–16.
Mitchell, R.K., L. Busenitz, T. Lant, P. McDougall, E.A. Morse and J.B. Smith (2002), 'Towards a theory of entrepreneurial cognition: rethinking the people side of entrepreneurship', *Entrepreneurship Theory and Practice*, **27**(2), 93–104.
Raffa, M., G. Zollo and R. Caponi (1996), 'The development process of small firms', *Entrepreneurship and Regional Development*, **8**(4), 359–72.
Reynolds, P.D., D.J. Storey and P. Westhead (1994), 'Cross-national comparisons of the variation in new firm formation rates', *Regional Studies*, **28**(4), 443–56.
Ruef, M., H.E. Aldrich and N.M. Carter (2003), 'The structure of organizational founding teams: homophily, strong ties, and isolation among U.S. entrepreneurs', *American Sociological Review*, **68**(2), 195–222.
Sadler-Smith, E., Y. Hampson, I. Chaston and B. Badger (2003), 'Managerial behavior, entrepreneurial style, and small firm performance', *Journal of Small Business Management*, **41**(1), 47–67.
Samuelsson, M. (2004), *Creating New Ventures: A Longitudinal Investigation of the Nascent Venturing Process*, Doctoral dissertation, Jönköping: Jönköping International Business School.
Sarasvathy, S. (2001), 'Causation and effectuation: towards a theoretical shift from economic inevitability to entrepreneurial contingency', *Academy of Management Review*, **26**(2), 243–88.

Shane, S. (2000), 'Prior knowledge and the discovery of entrepreneurial opportunities', *Organization Science*, **11**(4), 448–69.

Shane, S. and S. Venkataraman (2000), 'The promise of entrepreneurship as a field of research', *Academy of Management Review*, **25**(1), 217–26.

Storey, D.J. (1994), *Understanding the Small Business Sector*, London: Routledge.

Ucbasaran, D., P. Westhead and M. Wright (2001), 'The focus of entrepreneurship research: contextual and process issues', *Entrepreneurship Theory and Practice*, **25**(4), 57–80.

Usher, J.M. and M.G. Evans (1996), 'Life and death along gasoline alley: Darwinian and Lamarckian processes in a differentiating population', *Academy of Management Journal*, **39**(5), 1428–66.

Van de Ven, A.H., D. Polley, R. Garud and S. Venkataraman (1999), *The Innovation Journey*, Oxford: Oxford University Press.

Westhead, P. and M. Wright (1998), 'Novice, portfolio, and serial founders: are they different?', *Journal of Business Venturing*, **13**, 173–204.

Wigren, C. (2003), *The Spirit of Gnosjö: The Grand Narrative and Beyond*, Doctoral dissertation, Jönköping: Jönköping International Business School.

Wiklund, J. (1998), *Small Firm Growth and Performance: Entrepreneurship and Beyond*, Doctoral dissertation, Jönköping: Jönköping International Business School.

PART II

Entrepreneurs and their Role

3. The hunt for the Heffalump continues: who is the Flemish entrepreneur?

Eva Cools

INTRODUCTION

Given the importance of entrepreneurial activities for economic growth, wealth creation, business expansion and technological progress, numerous studies on entrepreneurship exist (Wickham, 2004). These studies seek to understand how opportunities are discovered, created and exploited, by whom and with what consequences (Shane and Venkataraman, 2000). To answer the question 'who is an entrepreneur', researchers tried to identify the unique characteristics of an entrepreneur by borrowing concepts from the trait psychology domain (Landström, 1999; Shook et al., 2003). Although this has been one of the earliest and most frequently visited domains in the history of entrepreneurship research, it failed to answer this key question (Sadler-Smith, 2004). Research that has tried to identify attitudes, traits, behaviors or characteristics of entrepreneurs did not yield unequivocal findings (Cromie, 2000). However, as some scholars contend, it remains worthwhile to study the entrepreneurial profile as there is no entrepreneurship without the entrepreneur (Hisrich, 2000; Steyaert, 2004). Consequently, the aim of the research project in this chapter is to get more insight into what typifies Flemish entrepreneurs and what distinguishes them from non-entrepreneurs. Given the criticism on the trait approach, this study differs from previous studies on the profile of the entrepreneur in two respects.

Firstly, we add a cognitive perspective, beside the trait approach. The fairly recent adoption of the cognitive perspective in entrepreneurship research seems a promising evolution to continue answering the 'who is the entrepreneur' question (Baron, 2004). The cognitive view of entrepreneurship provides alternative lenses to explore entrepreneurship related phenomena, as it focuses on detecting knowledge structures and mental models that entrepreneurs use to make assessments, judgments or decisions involving opportunity evaluation, venture creation and growth (Mitchell et al., 2002). An interesting concept in this regard are cognitive styles, defined as the way in which people perceive stimuli and how they use this information for guiding their behavior (Hayes and Allinson, 1998). Cognitive styles influence people's preferences for different types of knowledge gathering, information processing and decision making, which are all key tasks an entrepreneur is daily confronted with (Leonard et al., 1999). Although cognitive styles provide an alternative means to conceptualize the characteristics of entrepreneurs, they have not yet received much attention in entrepreneurship literature (Sadler-Smith, 2004).

Secondly, we use the different traits and cognitive characteristics to examine entrepreneurial orientation (EO). EO refers to a firm's strategic orientation, capturing specific entrepreneurial aspects of decision-making styles, methods and practices (Lumpkin and Dess, 1996). The failure to identify a set of dispositional characteristics of entrepreneurs has led some scholars to shift their attention to entrepreneurial behavior, conceptualized as the firm's EO (Krauss et al., 2005; Poon et al., 2006). Most studies on EO focus on its relationship with organizational performance (Wiklund, 1999; Zahra and Covin, 1995). Recently, some scholars have defended the usefulness of studying the link between the entrepreneur's trait characteristics and EO (Lumpkin and Erdogan, 2004; Poon et al., 2006). They emphasize that the founders and executives of organizations can exert important influences on the firm's actions. At this moment, few studies have examined EO as a dependent variable, investigating the link between several trait characteristics and EO. The link between entrepreneurs' cognitive styles and entrepreneurial orientation has (as far as we know) not been studied yet.

With the study in this chapter, we continue the hunt for the Heffalump to answer the 'who is the entrepreneur' question (Bouckenooghe et al., 2005). The Heffalump is a character from Winnie-the-Pooh that has been hunted by many individuals using various ingenious trapping devices, but no one has succeeded in capturing it so far. All who claim to have caught sight of it report that it is enormous, but they disagree on its particularities (Steyaert, 2004; Wickham, 2004). Several aspects give the research project in this chapter a unique dimension:

1. the integration of the trait and the cognitive approach to examine the entrepreneurial profile
2. the comparison of entrepreneurs and non-entrepreneurs on these cognitive and trait characteristics and
3. the examination of the impact of the entrepreneur's cognitive and trait characteristics on entrepreneurial orientation.

CONCEPTUAL FRAMEWORK AND HYPOTHESES

To introduce the conceptual framework of the study, we focus on the different concepts that are included in the research design: traits, cognitive styles and entrepreneurial orientation.

The Trait Approach

As already stated, many studies have aimed to identify the particular qualities of entrepreneurs. There is substantial literature on those traits that purport to predispose individuals to act in an entrepreneurial way (Bridge et al., 2003). Different characteristics are attributed to entrepreneurs, such as a strong need for achievement, an internal locus of control or risk-taking propensity. However, some recent reviews in the entrepreneurship field refer to the inconsistent research results with regard to several of these characteristics. Cromie (2000) and Vecchio (2003), for instance, refer to studies that did not find a difference between entrepreneurs and non-entrepreneurs for locus of control and need for achievement. Delmar (2000) argues that the inconsistency in trait research is due to the large number of traits that are linked to entrepreneurship, the different ways in which similar traits are operationalized and the supposed static nature of entrepreneurial traits in many of these studies. This led to increased criticism on this approach, even to the extent that it is questioned whether entrepreneurs do indeed score higher on particular characteristics than non-entrepreneurs (Bridge et al., 2003; Vecchio, 2003). Given the criticism on the trait approach, several authors suggest that identifying a cluster of relevant traits might be more useful to assess the entrepreneurial personality than focusing on a single characteristic (Cromie, 2000; Johnson, 1990). On the basis of an extensive literature review, we choose to simultaneously include five prominent entrepreneurial traits in our research, hereby focusing on a mixture of extensively studied concepts (such as locus of control, need for achievement) and newer perspectives (such as proactive personality) (Hansemark, 2003; Shane et al., 2003). In this way the study in this chapter is a unique opportunity to check whether the criticism on the trait approach is warranted.

Tolerance for ambiguity

When there is insufficient information to structure a situation, an ambiguous situation is said to exist. The way in which people deal with this ambiguous situation reflects their tolerance for ambiguity (Furnham and Ribchester, 1995). People with high tolerance for ambiguity find ambiguous situations challenging and strive to overcome unstable and unpredictable situations to perform well. People with low tolerance for ambiguity see ambiguous situations as threats. Dealing with uncertainty, risks and continuous changes are part of the entrepreneurial job (Markman and Baron, 2003; McMullen and Shepherd, 2006). Research found that entrepreneurs eagerly undertake the unknown and willingly deal with and manage uncertainty (Koh, 1996). Whetten et al. (2000) found that managers with high tolerance for ambiguity were more entrepreneurial in their actions.

Self-efficacy

Self-efficacy is a person's belief about their chances of successfully accomplishing a specific task (Bandura, 1997). Self-efficacy is a motivational construct that influences people's choices of activities, goal levels, persistence and performance in a variety of contexts (Zhao et al., 2005). There is increased attention for the role of self-efficacy in the study of entrepreneurship, implying research on entrepreneurial career preferences, intentionality, new venture formation and performance (Chen et al., 1998; Markman et al., 2002). Research on self-efficacy concludes that it is an important factor to clarify entrepreneurial intentions and behavior (Boyd and Vozikis, 1994; Neck et al., 1999). People need to believe in their capacity to succeed in starting and running a new business before they will do so.

Proactive personality

Bateman and Crant (1993) define a proactive personality as a dispositional construct that refers to individual differences in the extent to which people take action to influence and change their environment. Research on the entrepreneurial profile concluded that proactive behavior is a characteristic of entrepreneurs (Becherer and Maurer, 1999; Kickul and Gundry, 2002). According to Drucker (1985), entrepreneurs see change as the norm. They always search for change, respond to it and exploit it as an opportunity. Crant (1996) found that having a proactive personality to a large extent clarified the entrepreneurial intentions of MBA students.

Locus of control

Locus of control refers to the extent to which people attribute the source of control over events to themselves (internal locus of control) or to external circumstances (external locus of control) (Rotter, 1966). Boone et al. (1996) conclude that many entrepreneurs eventually succeed due to an internal locus of control, as this helps them to overcome setbacks and disappointments and leads to higher firm performance. Blau (1993) found that an internal locus of control was positively related to the initiative dimension of performance. This means that people with an internal locus of control engaged more frequently in innovative and spontaneous performance that go beyond basic job requirements. However, some studies failed to distinguish entrepreneurs and non-entrepreneurs concerning their locus of control (Chen et al., 1998; Cromie, 2000).

Need for achievement

Need for achievement refers to a desire to accomplish something difficult, to excel and do better than others to achieve a sense of personal accomplishment (McClelland, 1961). Several studies found a positive effect of high need for achievement on entrepreneurial behavior and on firm performance (Collins et al., 2004; Johnson, 1990). Entrepreneurs must persistently aim at working on their goals, need to continuously enhance their performance and have to cope with challenging tasks (Utsch and Rauch, 2000), which are characteristics of high achievers. However, Cromie (2000) refers to different studies that could not identify differences in the need for achievement of entrepreneurs and other groups, such as managers or university professors. On the basis of previous research with these five traits and following the majority of studies that found a higher score for these characteristics among entrepreneurs, we propose:

Hypothesis 1: Entrepreneurs will score higher on each of these traits than non-entrepreneurs.

The Cognitive Approach

Recently, a more cognitive oriented approach has been introduced in the entrepreneurship domain (Baron, 2004; Mitchell et al., 2004). Rather than focusing on dispositional traits that distinguish entrepreneurs from non-entrepreneurs, it includes all aspects of entrepreneurial cognition that can potentially play a role in the entrepreneurial process. The cognitive perspective starts from the idea that some people are better in recognizing opportunities for two major reasons (Mitchell et al., 2002). On the one hand, they possess information that is necessary to identify an opportunity and, on the other hand, they have the cognitive properties necessary to exploit them.

In line with this cognitive approach, we examine the entrepreneur's cognitive style. A cognitive style influences how people look at their environment for information, how they organize and interpret this information and how they use these interpretations for guiding their actions (Hayes and Allinson, 1998). Cognitive styles are considered to be fundamental determinants of individual and organizational behavior that manifest themselves in individual workplace actions and in organizational systems, processes and routines (Sadler-Smith and Badger, 1998). A large variety of cognitive style dimensions has been identified by researchers over the years

(Hodgkinson and Sadler-Smith, 2003; Rayner and Riding, 1997). However, much cognitive style research has been done in educational settings, leading to a lack of instruments for use in organizations (Allinson and Hayes, 1996). Recently, Cools and Van den Broeck (2007) reported on the development of a reliable, valid and convenient cognitive style instrument – the Cognitive Style Indicator (CoSI) – for use with managerial and professional groups. Reliability, item and factor analyses confirm the internal consistency and homogeneity of three cognitive styles: a knowing, a planning and a creating style.

People with a knowing style search for facts and data. They want to know exactly the way things are and tend to retain many facts and details. They like to search for rational solutions. People with a planning style are characterized by a need for structure. Planners like to organize and control, and prefer a well structured work environment. They attach importance to preparation and planning to reach their objectives. People with a creating style tend to proliferate ideas and like experimentation. They can deal with uncertainty and prefer freedom. We use this model in our research project, as previous research already demonstrated the value of the CoSI model to distinguish entrepreneurs from non-entrepreneurs (Bouckenooghe et al., 2005).

Kickul and Krueger (2004) conclude from their study with entrepreneurs that cognitive styles play an important role in entrepreneurial thinking. According to their view, entrepreneurs with different cognitive styles do not necessarily perceive different opportunities (although they may), but it seems from their study that they got there by different cognitive paths. Allinson et al. (2000) propose that cognitive styles are an alternative way of differentiating entrepreneurs from non-entrepreneurs. Goldsmith and Kerr (1991) reported a higher score on an innovative cognitive style for students following an entrepreneurship class. Similarly, Buttner and Gryskiewicz (1993) found a more innovative cognitive style for entrepreneurs than for managers in large established organizations. Stewart et al. (1998) concluded from their research that entrepreneurs had a more innovative cognitive style than managers of large organizations, who tended to prefer a more adaptive, analytical cognitive style. Allinson et al. (2000) found that entrepreneurs were more intuitive in their cognitive style than the general population of managers. However, no style differences were found between the entrepreneurs and the senior managers and executives in their samples. Based on previous cognitive style studies with entrepreneurs and using the terminology of the CoSI model, we propose that:

Hypothesis 2: Entrepreneurs will score higher on the creating style than non-entrepreneurs. We expect that entrepreneurs will score lower on the knowing and the planning style.

Entrepreneurial Orientation

Entrepreneurial orientation (EO) refers to the top management's strategy in relation to innovativeness, proactiveness and risk taking (Kreiser et al., 2002; Poon et al., 2006). Innovativeness refers to a firm's willingness to engage in and support new ideas, novelty, creative processes and experimentation that may result in new products, services or technological processes. Proactiveness refers to the propensity of a firm to take an opportunity-seeking, forward-looking perspective characterized by the introduction of new products and services ahead of the competition and by acting in anticipation of future demand. Risk taking refers to the extent a firm is willing to make large and risky resource commitments, and to make decisions and take action without certain knowledge of probable outcomes. Firms with an entrepreneurial orientation are willing to innovate, to be proactive relative to marketplace opportunities and to take risks (Covin and Slevin, 1991). Although EO has been conceptualized as a firm-level behavioral process of entrepreneurship, the behavior of the firm and that of the entrepreneur are likely to be the same in entrepreneur-led firms (Poon et al., 2006).

Most EO studies focus on the relationship between the degree of entrepreneurial orientation and firm performance. However, these studies have yielded ambiguous results. Several studies found a positive relationship between entrepreneurial orientation and firm performance (Wiklund, 1999; Zahra and Covin, 1995). Other studies showed that there is no significant relationship between EO and firm performance (Auger et al., 2003). Lumpkin and Dess (1996) summarized different possible models on the relationship between EO and performance, suggesting moderator as well as mediator variables. Only a few studies have examined EO as a dependent variable (Lumpkin and Erdogan, 2004; Poon et al., 2006).

Traits as antecedents of EO

A review of the entrepreneurship literature reveals some theoretical models (Aloulou and Fayolle, 2005; Lumpkin and Dess, 1996) and empirical works (Krauss et al., 2005; Lumpkin and Erdogan, 2004; Poon et al., 2006) that suggest that traits might influence entrepreneurial orientation. However, there is little evidence for selecting particular traits (and not others) as antecedents of EO. We select tolerance for ambiguity, self-efficacy, proactive personality and need for achievement from our trait variables. These traits all have theoretical links with EO and also received considerable attention in entrepreneurship studies. Previous research found that being innovative, risk taking and proactive requires tolerance for ambiguity (Lumpkin and Erdogan, 2004). Self-efficacy is assumed to have an impact on people's willingness to introduce new products, to be proactive towards the environment and to take risks (Poon et al., 2006). Having a proactive personality results in proactive behavior, meaning a willingness to change the status quo, and a tendency to identify opportunities and improve things (Crant, 2000). Previous studies found that achievement motivation is positively correlated with a preoccupation with future goals (proactiveness) and with personal innovativeness (Lumpkin and Erdogan, 2004). Locus of control is not included in the model. Although some scholars formulate theoretical relationships between locus of control and EO (Boone et al., 1996; Lumpkin and Erdogan, 2004), a recent study found no predictive effect of an internal locus of control on EO (Poon et al., 2006).

Cognitive style differences as antecedents of EO

Researchers used cognitive styles as a basis for studying decision-making behavior, conflict handling, strategy development and group processes (Leonard et al., 1999). As cognitive styles are individual preferences with regard to information processing, it can be assumed that these differences lead to variation in the way entrepreneurs see strategy (Hough and Ogilvie, 2005; Manimala, 1992; Sadler-Smith, 2004). According to Gallén (1997), research on managerial characteristics and strategy suggested that creative managers can be found in innovative firms, while more bureaucratically oriented managers can be found in stable firms. Gallén (2006) found that analytical types more often described the defender strategy as the most viable option (that is, offering a stable set of products and competing mainly based on price, quality, service and delivery), while more intuitive types preferred a prospector firm strategy (that is, having a broad product definition, striving to be first in the market and focusing on change and innovation). In an early study on the link between cognitive styles and strategic decision making Nutt (1990) found that cognitive style differences are a key factor in explaining the likelihood of taking strategic action and the perceived risk seen in this action. We do not know of prior studies that linked cognitive styles with EO. Given the limited prior research on the antecedents of EO, we formulate a rather general hypothesis:

Hypothesis 3: Both trait variables (tolerance for ambiguity, self-efficacy, proactive personality and need for achievement) and cognitive styles will explain a significant amount of variance in entrepreneurial orientation after controlling for the effects of age, firm size and firm age.

METHOD

The study in this chapter is part of a research project under the authority of the Flanders District of Creativity, which is a Belgian government institution that aims to stimulate entrepreneurship, innovation and creativity in Flanders.

Samples and Procedure

We collected the data of this study in March 2006 with a survey instrument sent out by email to 1797 Flemish entrepreneurs and 422 healthcare managers. We drew the samples from the database maintained by a leading Western European business school. There is little consensus among scholars regarding the definition of entrepreneurship (Curran and Blackburn, 2001). For the sample of entrepreneurs, we selected people who indicated in the function categories owner or general manager of the firm from the database. We used two additional sampling criteria: a firm size limit of 500 employees and the exclusion of schools (or institutes) and firms within social profit. The maximum limit of 500 employees is consistent with the definition of 'small businesses' according to the US Small Business Administration. We used the exclusion of schools and social profit firms to avoid having public sector organizations in this sample. We selected the sample of healthcare managers (from hospitals as well as nursing homes) from the same database. We used a relatively broad approach and include managers of all ranks and departments.

We gave people a website link, where they could complete the questionnaire. We pre-tested the survey with academics and entrepreneurs to check whether the questions were clear and understandable. We revised potentially confusing items. In the end 177 entrepreneurs (10 per cent response rate) and 60 healthcare managers (14 per cent response rate) participated in our research. Using the internet or email is a new and promising data collection tool, as it is cheap and efficient. However, the experience is that the response rates are quite low compared to alternatives because people easily ignore requests for cooperation in such research studies (Spector, 2001).

Mean age of the entrepreneurs in this study is 47.46 ($SD = 9.19$) and about 88 per cent are men. They represent a wide variety of sectors, including industry and production (30 per cent), services (36 per cent), distribution and trade (11 per cent), ICT and new technology (14 per cent) and other (9 per cent, such as the building sector). The mean age of the firms in this sample is 37.49 years. However, this mean represents a wide variance, ranging from firms younger than 5 years and ones older than 100 years ($SD = 39.01$). Most firms in our study employ 10 to 50 people (32 per cent), while the other 68 per cent is almost equally spread between firms of less than 10 employees, 51 to 99 employees, 100 to 199 employees and 200 to 499 employees.

Of the healthcare managers in the study, 71 per cent are men and the mean age is 45.82 ($SD = 7.84$), which is comparable to the sample of entrepreneurs. This sample includes 52 per cent general directors, 31 per cent directors or senior managers and 17 per cent middle managers. The majority work in the general management department (68 per cent), 22 per cent work within the nursing and care department and 10 per cent in the financial and administrative department. The firm size of this sample is also diverse. Seven per cent employ 10 to 50 people, 28 per cent 51 to 99 people (the majority), 27 per cent 100 to 199 people, 13 per cent 200 to 499 people and 25 per cent more than 500 people.

Measures

To select the measures of the study in this chapter, we consider the relevance of the instruments for entrepreneurs as well as non-entrepreneurs. For instance, we find a general locus of control scale and a general self-efficacy scale most appropriate for our research design rather than a firm-level scale or one focused on specific entrepreneurial activities. To limit the length of the survey, we search for short scales (such as the five-item Need for Achievement scale of Steers and Braunstein, 1976). If a short measure is not available, we select a number of items from a larger scale, choosing those items that showed the highest factor loadings as indicated in the original scale development and validation articles. All scales in the survey (unless otherwise indicated) use a five-point Likert scale format from 1 (typifies me not at all) to 5 (typifies me completely). We create a composite score for each scale by averaging the responses across the items used for the measure. Higher scores on a measure reflect higher levels of the construct.

Tolerance for ambiguity

We assess tolerance for ambiguity with ten items, taken from the willingness-to-change sub-scale of the Innovativeness scale (Hurt et al., 1977) and the Need for Cognitive Closure scale (Webster and Kruglanski, 1994). Given the criticism on several tolerance for ambiguity scales (Furnham and Ribchester, 1995; Grenier et al., 2005), we choose to measure the construct with these subscales. The alpha reliability of this scale is 0.73.

Self-efficacy

We measure self-efficacy with six items from the 17-item General Self-Efficacy scale developed by Sherer et al. (1982). This is the most widely used instrument to measure general self-efficacy (Chen et al., 2001). The alpha reliability of this scale is 0.61.

Proactive personality

We assess proactive personality with six items from Bateman and Crant's (1993) 17-item Proactive Personality scale. The alpha reliability of this scale is 0.73.

Locus of control

We excerpt a seven-item scale from Rotter's (1966) Internal-External (I-E) scale to measure locus of control (Kreitner et al., 2002). We use a Likert-scale version of this measure (Poon et al., 2006), with higher scores reflecting higher internality. The alpha reliability of this scale is 0.72.

Need for achievement

We assess achievement motivation with the achievement need subscale of the Manifest Needs Questionnaire (Steers and Braunstein, 1976). The scale consists of five items, with an alpha reliability of 0.56 in this sample.

Cognitive styles

We assess cognitive styles with the 18-item Cognitive Style Indicator (CoSI) (Cools and Van den Broeck, 2007). The CoSI distinguishes a knowing style (four items, $\alpha = 0.76$), a planning style (seven items, $\alpha = 0.82$) and a creating style (seven items, $\alpha = 0.78$).

Entrepreneurial orientation

We use the scales of Covin and Slevin (1989) and Miller and Toulouse (1986) to measure entrepreneurial orientation. Only the entrepreneurs complete this measure. The response format of this scale uses a five-point Likert scale on which the entrepreneurs have to indicate the extent to which the items represent their firm's strategy. The EO scale distinguishes between three sub-dimensions: innovativeness (three items, $\alpha = 0.78$), proactiveness (four items, $\alpha = 0.88$) and risk taking (three-items, $\alpha = 0.77$). The overall reliability of the EO scale is 0.90.

Analyses

As the variables used in the analyses come from the answers provided by a single respondent, we check the possibility that the relationships among the variables are the result of common method variance by conducting Harman's (1967) one-factor test (as suggested by Podsakoff and Organ, 1986). A substantial amount of common method variance will be shown if one factor accounts for the majority of covariance in the variables. However, exploratory factor analysis of the dependent and independent variables results in 17 factors with Eigenvalues greater than one (accounting for 70 per cent of the variance), with the first factor accounting for only 17 per cent of the total variance and the second and third factor each accounting for 10 per cent and 6 per cent, respectively, of the total variance.

To compare entrepreneurs and non-entrepreneurs on the different cognitive and trait characteristics (Hypotheses 1 and 2), we perform independent sample *t* tests, investigating the means of the two groups for each of the variables.

We perform hierarchical regression to analyze the extent to which we can use different trait and cognitive variables to predict variance in entrepreneurial orientation (Hypothesis 3), entering the variables in three steps. Model 1 contains only control variables: age, firm size and firm age. Model 2 consists of the control variables and the four trait characteristics: tolerance for ambiguity, self-efficacy, proactive personality and need for achievement. Model 3, in its turn, adds the cognitive styles to the previous model.

RESULTS

Descriptive Statistics

We summarize the correlations of the variables in Table 3.1, together with the corresponding means, standard deviations and alpha reliabilities. All trait variables (except locus of control) are significantly correlated among one another. This is consistent with previous research on these traits (Judge et al., 1999; Poon et al., 2006). Looking at the correlations among the cognitive styles, we find a strong positive correlation between the knowing and planning style ($r = 0.58$, $p < 0.001$). However, item and factor analyses justify the distinction between the two styles.

Looking further at the correlations in Table 3.1, it is remarkable that the creating style shows a strong correlation with different trait variables and with entrepreneurial orientation ($r = 0.39$, $p < 0.001$). Previous research on cognitive styles found that people with an intuitive cognitive style prefer to leave options open, can tolerate ambiguity, like to restructure situations, have a proactive personality and are self-confident (Kickul and Krueger, 2004; Kirton, 1994; Myers et al., 2003). Furthermore, we find a significant negative correlation between a planning style and tolerance for ambiguity ($r = -0.30$, $p < 0.001$). Stewart et al. (1998) have already shown that there is considerable variation between entrepreneurs, with different types of entrepreneurs demonstrating different risk preferences. Finally, looking at

Table 3.1 Descriptive statistics, scale reliabilities and correlations of study variables

Variable	1	2	3	4	5	6	7	8	9
1. Locus of control	(0.72)								
2. Self-efficacy	0.27***	(0.61)							
3. Tolerance for ambiguity	0.07	0.38***	(0.73)						
4. Proactive personality	0.38***	0.61***	0.50***	(0.73)					
5. Need for achievement	0.32***	0.57***	0.53***	0.62***	(0.56)				
6. Knowing style	0.17*	0.28***	−0.08	0.22**	0.27***	(0.76)			
7. Planning style	0.14*	0.15*	−0.30***	0.05	0.11	0.58***	(0.82)		
8. Creating style	0.17*	0.36***	0.58***	0.53***	0.50***	0.19**	0.05	(0.78)	
9. Entrepreneurial orientation	0.01	0.18*	0.47***	0.35***	0.37***	−0.06	−0.12	0.39***	(0.90)
Mean	3.18	3.70	3.29	3.71	4.10	3.69	3.70	4.02	3.44
Standard deviation	0.58	0.63	0.51	0.52	0.50	0.65	0.60	0.50	0.74

Notes: Alpha reliabilities are shown in parentheses on the diagonal; * $p<0.05$, ** $p<0.01$, *** $p<0.001$.

entrepreneurial orientation, the highly significant correlation of EO with tolerance for ambiguity is notable ($r=0.47$, $p<0.001$). We also find a significant correlation between EO and need for achievement ($r=0.37$, $p<0.001$) and EO and proactive personality ($r=0.35$, $p<0.001$).

Comparing Entrepreneurs and Non-entrepreneurs

Table 3.2 represents the results of the comparison of the entrepreneurs and non-entrepreneurs on the trait and cognitive styles. As can be seen in Table 3.2, the entrepreneurs score higher on all traits than the healthcare managers. Hence, Hypothesis 1 is confirmed. Hypothesis 2 is only partly confirmed. Comparison of the cognitive style profiles of the two samples in our study reveals that healthcare managers score significantly higher on the knowing and the planning style than entrepreneurs. We find no significant difference for the creating style. Interestingly, when comparing healthcare managers with entrepreneurs from the service sector ($n=64$), all differences between the two samples remain significant, except for the knowing style ($t(121)=-1.69$, $p=0.09$) and tolerance for ambiguity ($t(120)=1.72$, $p=0.09$). These additional analyses suggest that the findings in Table 3.2 are probably due more to being an entrepreneur or not than to the sector of employment. In contrast to other studies (Begley, 1995), additional analyses within the sample of entrepreneurs reveals that no significant differences can be found for any of the traits when looking at a number of demographics (such as age, gender, education level, tenure, sector, firm size and firm age).

Table 3.2 Comparison entrepreneurs and non-entrepreneurs

Variable	Entrepreneurs		Managers		Comparison	
	M	*SD*	*M*	*SD*	*t*	*df*
Tolerance for ambiguity	3.34	0.51	3.16	0.50	2.39*	(227)
Self-efficacy	3.79	0.61	3.42	0.61	3.99***	(229)
Proactive personality	3.80	0.51	3.44	0.47	4.79***	(228)
Locus of control	3.27	0.53	2.95	0.65	3.79***	(228)
Need for achievement	4.18	0.45	3.87	0.57	3.76***	(227)
Knowing style	3.64	0.66	3.86	0.60	−2.21*	(232)
Planning style	3.64	0.58	3.86	0.63	−2.48*	(231)
Creating style	4.05	0.49	3.94	0.51	1.52	(233)

Note: * $p<0.05$, ** $p<0.01$, *** $p<0.001$.

Trait and Cognitive Variables as Predictors of Entrepreneurial Orientation

To study the effect of the cognitive and trait variables on entrepreneurial orientation, we perform hierarchical regression analysis (Table 3.3). Exploration of Table 3.3 reveals that Model 2 (control and trait variables) is a better predictor of EO than Model 1 (control variables) ($\Delta R^2 = 0.27$; $F(4,141) = 12.82$, $p < 0.001$). Model 3 (adding cognitive styles) in its turn is a better predictor than the default zero model ($R^2 = 0.28$; $F(10,138) = 5.45$, $p < 0.001$), but it is no significant improvement compared to Model 2 ($\Delta R^2 = 0.01$; $F(3,138) = 0.67$, $p = 0.57$). These findings suggest that Model 2 is the best fitting model. Consequently, Hypothesis 3 is only partially confirmed. Two of the traits seem to be significant contributors of entrepreneurial orientation. Specifically, people with higher tolerance for ambiguity show higher entrepreneurial orientation ($\beta = 0.35$, $p < 0.001$), as well as being more proactive people ($\beta = 0.21$, $p < 0.05$). Need for achievement shows a positive relationship with EO, but only at the $p < 0.10$ level of significance ($\beta = 0.18$, $p = 0.08$). Although previous research identified self-efficacy as an important antecedent of EO (Poon et al., 2006), we find a significant negative effect ($\beta = -0.20$, $p < 0.05$).

Table 3.3 Hierarchical regression of trait and cognitive characteristics on entrepreneurial orientation

Variables	Model 1		Model 2		Model 3	
	β	*t*	β	*t*	β	*t*
Constant		10.23***		0.28		0.27
Age	0.04	0.50	0.07	0.92	0.07	0.84
Firm size	0.02	0.20	−0.06	−0.73	−0.07	−0.92
Firm age	−0.09	−1.04	0.01	0.06	0.003	0.04
Tolerance for ambiguity			0.35	4.05***	0.33	2.89**
Self-efficacy			−0.20	−2.05*	−0.18	−1.80†
Proactive personality			0.21	2.00*	0.21	1.95†
Need for achievement			0.18	1.80†	0.19	1.81†
Knowing style					−0.13	−1.38
Planning style					0.07	0.68
Creating style					0.03	0.27
R^2		0.01		0.27***		0.28***
ΔR^2				0.26***		0.01

Note: $p<0.10$, *$p<0.05$, ** $p<0.01$, *** $p<0.001$.

DISCUSSION AND CONCLUSION

The aim of the study in this chapter is to contribute to further insights into who the entrepreneur is. Two aspects give our research a unique character in comparison with other studies on the entrepreneurial profile. Firstly, we integrate the trait and the cognitive approach. Studying a cluster of traits rather than one single characteristic is suggested to be a useful approach to assess the entrepreneurial personality (Cromie, 2000). Given the promise of the new cognitive perspective within entrepreneurship research (Baron, 2004), several authors recognize the relevance of studying cognitive style differences of entrepreneurs (Allinson et al., 2000; Sadler-Smith, 2004). Moreover, we compare entrepreneurs and non-entrepreneurs on these traits and cognitive styles, which contributes to further clarification of differences between entrepreneurs and non-entrepreneurs. Secondly, we use these trait and cognitive variables as antecedents to clarify entrepreneurial orientation. Most studies on EO look at the link with organizational performance. Research on EO as a dependent variable is currently scarce (Lumpkin and Erdogan, 2004; Poon et al., 2006).

Discussion of Findings

Our findings demonstrate that Flemish entrepreneurs score higher on tolerance for ambiguity, self-efficacy, proactive personality, an internal locus of control and need for achievement than the non-entrepreneurs in the study. These results are consistent with previous trait studies that found that entrepreneurs had higher tolerance for ambiguity than non-entrepreneurs (Koh, 1996), higher levels of self-efficacy (Chen et al., 1998), a more proactive personality (Becherer and Maurer, 1999), an internal locus of control (Vecchio, 2003) and a stronger need for achievement (Collins et al., 2004). These findings suggest that entrepreneurs are currently better equipped to deal with the numerous uncertainties and changes that characterize the current work surroundings than healthcare managers. Fortunately, many of these traits can be learned and developed, implying that effective training programs can play an important role to strengthen people's profiles. In this respect this research project shows that entrepreneurship and management education may not only focus on technical and managerial skills. It is equally, or even more, important to give attention to fostering entrepreneurial drive in business education. This means stimulating particular characteristics (such as self-efficacy, need for achievement and proactive personality) (Florin et al., 2007; Peterman and Kennedy, 2003). Whetten et al. (2000) also emphasize the importance of intrapersonal skills for effective management. This means, in their perspective, developing self-awareness based on a thorough analysis of one's strengths and weaknesses.

With regard to cognitive style differences, we find a higher score for the knowing and the planning style for non-entrepreneurs than for entrepreneurs. This indicates a larger focus on rationality and procedures from managers of the healthcare sector than from entrepreneurs. We find no differences for the creating style. Although previous research found a higher score on an innovative cognitive style for entrepreneurs than for non-entrepreneurs (Buttner and Gryskiewicz, 1993: Goldsmith and Kerr, 1991) this is not confirmed in our study. However, this finding is consistent with the previous research of Allinson et al. (2000). They found no differences for an intuitive cognitive style between entrepreneurs and senior managers. Managers at higher levels, like entrepreneurs, also face uncertainty, time pressure, ambiguity and incomplete information, which needs an intuitive problem solving approach. These findings suggest that it is not necessarily a creating style that typifies entrepreneurs. In contrast, it seems that higher levels of knowing and planning styles hamper entrepreneurship. The knowing style is characterized by a focus on facts and figures, a high level of rationality and avoidance of risks. The planning style is characterized by an urge for control, a focus on structures, procedures and planning and a need for certainty. These characteristics might imply that people with these styles see more risk in entrepreneurship and experience higher levels of uncertainty, which curbs their enthusiasm to become an entrepreneur.

Understanding the interplay between people's preferences and their day-to-day workplace behavior is crucial for designing and implementing effective individual development efforts (Berr et al., 2000). As cognitive styles are considered to be fairly stable characteristics of people (Clapp, 1993), this does not imply changing one's style, but rather learning about the consequences of having a particular style. Importantly, no style is inherently better than another. Sadler-Smith and Badger (1998) emphasize the importance of style versatility (that is, having a mixture of cognitive style profiles) at the organizational level for effective innovation. Individuals with a more intuitive cognitive style are expected to be more effective in the initiation phase of the innovation process (that is, the stage in which new ideas are generated), whereas individuals with a more analytical style may be better in the implementation phase (that is, the stage in which ideas are put into practice). Consequently, effectively managing individual cognitive styles and strategies to facilitate versatility is an important issue for organizations to stimulate organizational learning and innovation (Leonard and Straus, 1997; Sadler-Smith and Badger, 1998).

With regard to the link between the entrepreneur's profile and EO, we find a significant contribution of tolerance for ambiguity and proactive personality to EO. Previous research identified tolerance for ambiguity as one of the most important variables in explaining managerial coping with organizational change (Judge et al., 1999). Research found that entrepreneurs with a higher tolerance for ambiguity own the most innovative and entrepreneurial firms (Entrialgo et al., 2000; Rigotti et al., 2003). Similarly, proactive behavior is considered to be an important variable in the context of organizational success (Crant, 2000). According to Kickul and Gundry (2002), entrepreneurs with a proactive personality choose a strategic orientation for their firms that permits flexibility and change in response to surrounding business conditions. In contrast to other studies, we find no significant contribution of a need for achievement to EO and a negative contribution of self-efficacy (Entrialgo et al., 2000; Poon et al., 2006). However, the findings with regard to the need for achievement and self-efficacy should be treated with caution, given the low internal consistencies observed for the scales in our research (Cronbach alpha lower than 0.70).

Research Limitations

Some limitations of this study should be taken into account for further research. Due to the initial sampling procedure and the data collection method, we cannot be totally sure whether the samples are representative for their populations. This coverage problem is inherent to online surveying. A replication of this study with another sample of Flemish entrepreneurs might strengthen our findings. Additionally, it is necessary to continue and cross-validate this study with data from multiple sources, as we now depend on self-reporting data. We used self-reporting questionnaires, using a single data source, which implies that respondents can unduly influence the result. Certainly with regard to the measurement of entrepreneurial orientation, it might be useful to include responses from more than one data source in further research. According to Curran and Blackburn (2001), a high proportion of small firms have two or more owner-managers, partners or directors, which suggests that it might be better to aggregate responses of several entrepreneurs from one company to measure EO.

Furthermore, due to availability and access problems, we compared entrepreneurs only with healthcare managers. To examine the consistency of the findings in this chapter, further research should also look at the comparison with other types of managers for two major reasons. Firstly, as trait studies within entrepreneurship did not succeed in identifying those factors that are unique to entrepreneurs, a major criticism on studies that compare entrepreneurs with non-entrepreneurs is that these traits are common to successful people, including managers (Boyd and Vozikis, 1994). Our study could not fully address this criticism as we only included healthcare managers. Secondly, although previous studies on entrepreneurs' cognitive styles did not find differences between entrepreneurs and senior managers in their samples with regard to the intuitive cognitive style (Allinson et al., 2000), they did find differences for lower-level managers. Due to the sample size of the non-entrepreneurs in our study and the limited number of lower-level managers within this sample ($n = 10$), we could not examine this further.

As there is little prior research on EO as a dependent variable, there was little theoretical and empirical basis on which to identify relevant models for hierarchical regression analyses. Further research is needed to stimulate our understanding of variances in entrepreneurial orientation. In this regard it is also important to carefully select the right measures to assess the variables, as the low internal consistencies of the self-efficacy and need for achievement scales in our study imply that our results should be treated with caution. As we selected for several trait concepts items from larger scales and also applied these scales in different settings from those for which they were originally developed, questions about their validity can be raised (Begley, 1995).

Finally, it can be of interest to take a longitudinal perspective rather than a cross-sectional one, linking trait variables to entrepreneurial intentions, and later on to entrepreneurial orientation to learn more about the entrepreneurial profile. For instance, locus of control and self-efficacy are considered to be learned characteristics that can change over time (Hansemark, 2003). A longitudinal study, in which dependent and independent variables are kept apart, can contribute to further examining the predictive power of various traits. Moreover, comparing potential entrepreneurs with actual entrepreneurs and various types of corporate managers, preferably in a longitudinal setting, can stimulate the advancement of the knowledge about what distinguishes entrepreneurs from other types of managers.

Conclusion

This research project fits well within the call of Landström (1999) to integrate a variety of perspectives in one study to further advance research on entrepreneurship. Through the exploration of a cluster of traits and the cognitive style profiles of entrepreneurs and the comparison with non-entrepreneurs, on the one hand, and the link with entrepreneurial orientation, on the other hand, we are convinced that we contributed to the advancement of entrepreneurship research. To further stimulate research on the proclivity to entrepreneurship, the field of entrepreneurship research can benefit from a novel approach. Building further on the call of

Landström (1999), it can be an interesting endeavor in future research to integrate a variety of research methods in one study to advance entrepreneurship research. Taking into account the limitations of this research project, we are convinced that multi-source, multi-method and longitudinal studies on the entrepreneurial profile will contribute to the advancement of the entrepreneurship field.

ACKNOWLEDGEMENTS

We are grateful to the Flanders District of Creativity (www.flandersdc.be) for their financial support to execute this research project. A revised version of this paper has been published in the winter 2008 issue of the *Journal of Small Business Strategy*.

REFERENCES

Allinson, C.W. and J. Hayes (1996), 'The Cognitive Style Index: a measure of intuition-analysis for organizational research', *Journal of Management Studies*, **33**(1), 119–35.

Allinson, C.W., E. Chell and J. Hayes (2000), 'Intuition and entrepreneurial behaviour', *European Journal of Work and Organizational Psychology*, **9**(1), 31–43.

Aloulou, W. and A. Fayolle (2005), 'A conceptual approach of entrepreneurial orientation within small business context', *Journal of Enterprising Culture*, **13**(1), 21–45.

Auger, P., A. Barnir and J.M. Gallaugher (2003), 'Strategic orientation, competition, and internet-based economic commerce', *Information Technology and Management*, **4**(2), 139–64.

Bandura, A. (1997), *Self-efficacy: The Exercise of Control*, New York: Freeman.

Baron, R.A. (2004), 'The cognitive perspective: a valuable tool answering entrepreneurship's basic "why" questions', *Journal of Business Venturing*, **19**(2), 221–39.

Bateman, T.S. and J.M. Crant (1993), 'The proactive component of organizational behavior: a measure and correlates', *Journal of Organizational Behavior*, **14**(2), 103–18.

Becherer, R.C. and J.G. Maurer (1999), 'The proactive personality disposition and entrepreneurial behavior among small company presidents', *Journal of Small Business Management*, **37**(1), 28–36.

Begley, T.M. (1995), 'Using founder status, age of firm, and company growth rate as the basis for distinguishing entrepreneurs from managers of smaller businesses', *Journal of Business Venturing*, **10**(3), 249–63.

Berr, S.A., A.H. Church and J. Waclawski (2000), 'The right personality is everything: linking personality preferences to managerial behaviors', *Human Resource Development Quarterly*, **11**(2), 133–57.

Blau, G.J. (1993), 'Testing the relationship of locus of control to different performance dimensions', *Journal of Occupational and Organizational Psychology*, **66**(2), 125–38.

Boone, C., B. De Brabander and A. Van Witteloostuijn (1996), 'CEO locus of control and small firm performance: an integrative framework and empirical test', *Journal of Management Studies*, **33**(5), 667–99.

Bouckenooghe, D., E. Cools, K. Vanderheyden and H. Van den Broeck (2005), 'In search for the Heffalump: an exploration of cognitive style profiles among Flemish entrepreneurs', *Journal of Applied Management and Entrepreneurship*, **10**(4), 58–75.

Boyd, N.G. and G.S. Vozikis (1994), 'The influence of self-efficacy on the development of entrepreneurial intentions and actions', *Entrepreneurship Theory and Practice*, **18**(4), 63–90.

Bridge, S., K. O'Neill and S. Cromie (2003), *Understanding Enterprise: Entrepreneurship and Small Business* (2nd edn), New York: Palgrave Macmillan.

Buttner, E.H. and N. Gryskiewicz (1993), 'Entrepreneurs' problem-solving styles: an empirical study using the Kirton Adaption/Innovation theory', *Journal of Small Business Management*, **31**(1), 22–31.

Chen, C.C., P.G. Greene and A. Crick (1998), 'Does entrepreneurial self-efficacy distinguish entrepreneurs from managers?', *Journal of Business Venturing*, **13**(4), 295–316.

Chen, G., S.M. Gully and D. Eden (2001), 'Validation of a new general self-efficacy scale', *Organizational Research Methods*, **4**(1), 62–83.

Clapp, R.G. (1993), 'Stability of cognitive style in adults and some implications: a longitudinal study of the Kirton Adaption-Innovation Inventory', *Psychological Reports*, **73**(3), 1235–45.

Collins, C.J., P. Hanges and E.A. Locke (2004), 'The relationship of need for achievement to entrepreneurship: a meta-analysis', *Human Performance*, **17**(1), 95–117.

Cools, E. and H. Van den Broeck (2007), 'Development and validation of the Cognitive Style Indicator', *Journal of Psychology*, **141**(4), 359–87.

Covin, J.G. and D.P. Slevin (1989), 'Strategic management of small firms in hostile and benign environments', *Strategic Management Journal*, **10**(1), 75–87.

Covin, J.G. and D.P. Slevin (1991), 'A conceptual model of entrepreneurship as firm behaviour', *Entrepreneurship Theory and Practice*, **16**(1), 7–25.

Crant, J.M. (1996), 'The proactive personality scale as a predictor of entrepreneurial intentions', *Journal of Small Business Management*, **34**(3), 42–9.

Crant, J.M. (2000), 'Proactive behaviour in organizations', *Journal of Management*, **26**(3), 435–62.

Cromie, S. (2000), 'Assessing entrepreneurial inclinations: some approaches and empirical evidence', *European Journal of Work and Organizational Psychology*, **9**(1), 7–30.

Curran, J. and R.A. Blackburn (2001), *Researching the Small Enterprise*, London: Sage.

Delmar, F. (2000), 'The psychology of the entrepreneur', in S. Carter and D. Jones-Evans (eds), *Enterprise and Small Business*, London: Pearson Education, pp. 142–3.

Drucker, P.F. (1985), *Innovation and Entrepreneurship: Practice and Principles*, New York: Harper & Row.

Entrialgo, M., E. Fernández and C.J. Vázquez (2000), 'Characteristics of managers as determinants of entrepreneurial orientation: some Spanish evidence', *Enterprise and Innovation Management Studies*, **1**(2), 187–205.

Florin, J., R. Karri and N. Rossiter (2007), 'Fostering entrepreneurial drive in business education: an attitudinal approach', *Journal of Management Education*, **31**(1), 17–42.

Furnham, A. and T. Ribchester (1995), 'Tolerance of ambiguity: a review of the concept, its measurement and applications', *Current Psychology*, **14**(3), 179–200.

Gallén, T. (1997), 'The cognitive style and strategic decisions of managers', *Management Decision*, **35**(7/8), 541–51.

Gallén, T. (2006), 'Managers and strategic decisions: does the cognitive style matter?', *Journal of Management Development*, **25**(2), 118–33.

Goldsmith, R.E. and J.R. Kerr (1991), 'Entrepreneurship and Adaption-Innovation theory', *Technovation*, **11**(6), 373–82.

Grenier, S., A.-M. Barrette and R. Ladouceur (2005), 'Intolerance of uncertainty and intolerance of ambiguity: similarities and differences', *Personality and Individual Differences*, **39**(3), 593–600.

Hansemark, O.C. (2003), 'Need for achievement, locus of control and the prediction of business start-ups: a longitudinal study', *Journal of Economic Psychology*, **24**(3), 301–19.

Harman, H.H. (1967), *Modern Factor Analysis* (2nd edn), Chicago, IL: University of Chicago Press.

Hayes, J. and C.W. Allinson (1998), 'Cognitive style and the theory and practice of individual and collective learning in organizations', *Human Relations*, **51**(7), 847–71.

Hisrich, R.D. (2000), 'Can psychological approaches be used effectively: an overview', *European Journal of Work and Organizational Psychology*, **9**(1), 93–6.

Hodgkinson, G.P. and E. Sadler-Smith (2003), 'Complex or unitary? A critique and empirical re-assessment of the Allinson-Hayes Cognitive Style Index', *Journal of Occupational and Organizational Psychology*, **76**(2), 243–68.

Hough, J.R. and D.T. Ogilvie (2005), 'An empirical test of cognitive style and strategic decision outcomes', *Journal of Management Studies*, **42**(2), 417–48.

Hurt, H.T., K. Joseph and C.D. Cook (1977), 'Scales for the measurement of innovativeness', *Human Communication Research*, **4**(1), 58–65.

Johnson, B.R. (1990), 'Towards a multidimensional model of entrepreneurship: the case of achievement motivation and the entrepreneur', *Entrepreneurship Theory and Practice*, **14**(3), 39–54.

Judge, T.A., C.J. Thoresen, V. Pucik and T.M. Welbourne (1999), 'Managerial coping with organizational change: a dispositional perspective', *Journal of Applied Psychology*, **84**(1), 107–22.

Kickul, J. and L.K. Gundry (2002), 'Prospecting for strategic advantage: the proactive entrepreneurial personality and small firm innovation', *Journal of Small Business Management*, **40**(2), 85–97.

Kickul, J. and N. Krueger (2004), 'A cognitive processing model of entrepreneurial self-efficacy and intentionality', in S.A. Zahra et al. (eds), *Frontiers of Entrepreneurship Research*, Wellesley, MA: Babson College, Center for Entrepreneurial Studies, pp. 607–19.

Kirton, M.J. (ed.) (1994), *Adaptors and Innovators: Styles of Creativity and Problem Solving*, New York: Routledge.

Koh, H.C. (1996), 'Testing hypotheses of entrepreneurial characteristics: a study of Hong Kong MBA students', *Journal of Managerial Psychology*, **11**(3), 12–25.

Krauss, S.I., M. Frese, C. Friedrich and J.M. Unger (2005), 'Entrepreneurial orientation: a psychological model of success among Southern African small business owners', *European Journal of Work and Organizational Psychology*, **14**(3), 315–44.

Kreiser, P.M., L.D. Marino and K.M. Weaver (2002), 'Assessing the psychometric properties of the entrepreneurial orientation scale: a multi-country analysis', *Entrepreneurship Theory and Practice*, **26**(4), 71–94.

Kreitner, R., A. Kinicki and M. Buelens (2002), *Organizational Behaviour* (2nd European edn), London: McGraw-Hill.

Landström, H. (1999), 'The roots of entrepreneurship research', *New England Journal of Entrepreneurship*, **2**(2), 9–20.

Leonard, D. and S. Straus (1997), 'Putting your company's whole brain to work', *Harvard Business Review*, **75**(4), 111–21.

Leonard, N.H., R.W. Scholl and K.B. Kowalski (1999), 'Information processing style and decision making', *Journal of Organizational Behavior*, **20**(3), 407–20.

Lumpkin, G.T. and G.G. Dess (1996), 'Clarifying the entrepreneurial orientation construct and linking it to performance', *Academy of Management Review*, **21**(1), 135–72.

Lumpkin, G.T. and B. Erdogan (2004), 'If not entrepreneurship, can psychological characteristics predict entrepreneurial orientation? – a pilot study', *ICFAI Journal of Entrepreneurship Development*, **1**(1), 21–33.

Manimala, M.J. (1992), 'Entrepreneurial heuristics: a comparison between high PI (pioneering-innovative) and low PI ventures', *Journal of Business Venturing*, **7**(6), 477–504.

Markman, G.D., D.B. Balkin and R.A. Baron (2002), 'Inventors and new venture formation: the effects of general self-efficacy and regretful thinking', *Entrepreneurship Theory and Practice*, **27**(2), 149–65.

Markman, G.D. and R.A. Baron (2003), 'Person-entrepreneurship fit: why some people are more successful as entrepreneurs than others', *Human Resource Management Review*, **13**(2), 281–301.

McClelland, D.C. (1961), *The Achieving Society*, New York: Van Nostrand.

McMullen, J.S. and D.A. Shepherd (2006), 'Entrepreneurial action and the role of uncertainty in the theory of the entrepreneur', *Academy of Management Review*, **31**(1), 132–52.

Miller, D. and J.M. Toulouse (1986), 'Strategy, structure, CEO personality and performance in small firms', *American Journal of Small Business*, **10**(3), 47–62.

Mitchell, R.K., L. Busenitz, T. Lant, P.P. McDougall, E.A. Morse and H.B. Smith (2002), 'Toward a theory of entrepreneurial cognition: rethinking the people side of entrepreneurship research', *Entrepreneurship Theory and Practice*, **27**(2), 93–104.

Mitchell, R.K., L. Busenitz, T. Lant, P.P. McDougall, E.A. Morse and H.B. Smith (2004), 'The distinctive and inclusive domain of entrepreneurial cognition research', *Entrepreneurship Theory and Practice*, **28**(6), 505–18.

Myers, I.B., M.H. McCaulley, N.L. Quenk and A.L. Hammer (2003), *MBTI Manual: A Guide to the Development and Use of the Myers-Briggs Type Indicator*, Palo Alto, CA: Consulting Psychologists Press.

Neck, C.P., H.M. Neck, C.C. Manz and J. Godwin (1999), '"I think I can; I think I can": a self-leadership perspective toward enhancing entrepreneur thought patterns, self-efficacy, and performance', *Journal of Managerial Psychology*, **14**(6), 477–501.

Nutt, P.C. (1990), 'Strategic decisions made by top executives and middle managers with data and process dominant styles', *Journal of Management Studies*, **27**(2), 173–94.

Peterman, N.E. and J. Kennedy (2003), 'Enterprise education: influencing students' perceptions of entrepreneurship', *Entrepreneurship Theory and Practice*, **28**(2), 129–44.

Podsakoff, P.M. and D.W. Organ (1986), 'Self reports in organisational reports: problems and prospects', *Journal of Management*, **12**(4), 531–44.

Poon, J.M.L., R.A. Ainuddin and S.H. Junit (2006), 'Effects of self-concept traits and entrepreneurial orientation on firm performance', *International Small Business Journal*, **24**(1), 61–82.

Rayner, S. and R.J. Riding (1997), 'Towards a categorization of cognitive styles and learning styles', *Educational Psychology*, **17**(1/2), 5–27.

Rigotti, L., M. Ryan and R. Vaithianathan (2003), 'Tolerance of ambiguity and entrepreneurial innovation', *Working Papers, Duke Fuqua School of Business*, 1 January.

Rotter, J.B. (1966), 'Generalized expectancies for internal and external control of reinforcement', *Psychological Monographs: General and Applied*, **80**(1), 1–28.

Sadler-Smith, E. (2004), 'Cognitive style and the management of small and medium-sized enterprises', *Organization Studies*, **25**(2), 155–81.

Sadler-Smith, E. and B. Badger (1998), 'Cognitive style, learning and innovation', *Technology Analysis and Strategic Management*, **10**(2), 247–65.

Shane, S. and S. Venkataraman (2000), 'The promise of entrepreneurship as a field of research', *Academy of Management Review*, **25**(1), 217–26.

Shane, S., E.A. Locke and C.J. Collins (2003), 'Entrepreneurial motivation', *Human Resource Management Review*, **13**(2), 257–79.

Sherer, M., J.E. Maddux, B. Mercandante, S. Prentice-Dunn, B. Jacobs and R.W. Rogers (1982), 'The self-efficacy scale: construction and validation', *Psychological Reports*, **51**(2), 663–71.

Shook, C.L., R.L. Priem and J.E. McGee (2003), 'Venture creation and the enterprising individual: a review and synthesis', *Journal of Management*, **29**(3), 379–99.

Spector, P.E. (2001), 'Research methods in industrial and organizational psychology: data collection and data analysis with special consideration to international issues', in N. Anderson, D.S. Ones, H.G. Sinangil and C. Viswervaran (eds), *Handbook of Industrial, Work, and Organizational Psychology. Volume 1: Personnel Psychology*, London: Sage, pp. 10–26.

Steers, R.M. and D.N. Braunstein (1976), 'A behaviorally-based measure of manifest needs in work settings', *Journal of Vocational Behavior*, **9**(2), 251–66.

Stewart, W.H., W.E. Watson, J.C. Carland and J.W. Carland (1998), 'A proclivity for entrepreneurship: a comparison of entrepreneurs, small business owners, and corporate managers', *Journal of Business Venturing*, **14**(2), 189–214.

Steyaert, C. (2004), 'Entrepreneurship without entrepreneurs? Reclaiming a(n other) psychology of entrepreneurship studies', RENT XVIII conference paper, Copenhagen, November.

Utsch, A. and A. Rauch (2000), 'Innovativeness and initiative as mediators between achievement orientation and venture performance', *European Journal of Work and Organizational Psychology*, **9**(1), 45–62.

Vecchio, R.P. (2003), 'Entrepreneurship and leadership: common trends and common threads', *Human Resource Management Review*, **13**(2), 303–27.

Webster, D.M. and A.W. Kruglanski (1994), 'Individual differences in need for cognitive closure', *Journal of Personality and Social Psychology*, **67**(6), 1049–62.

Whetten, D., K. Cameron and M. Woods (2000), *Developing Management Skills for Europe* (2nd edn), Harlow: Pearson Education.

Wickham, P.A. (2004), *Strategic Entrepreneurship* (3rd edn), Harlow: Pearson Education.

Wiklund, J. (1999), 'The sustainability of the entrepreneurial orientation-performance relationship', *Entrepreneurship Theory and Practice*, **24**(1), 37–48.

Zahra, S. and J. Covin (1995), 'Contextual influence on the corporate entrepreneurship-performance relationship: a longitudinal analysis', *Journal of Business Venturing*, **10**(1), 43–58.

Zhao, H., S.E. Seibert and G.E. Hills (2005), 'The mediating role of self-efficacy in the development of entrepreneurial intentions', *Journal of Applied Psychology*, **90**(6), 1265–72.

4. How do you react to entrepreneurship education? An examination of the role of predispositions in an enactive mastery experience of entrepreneurship

Frédéric Delmar and Régis Goujet

INTRODUCTION

In this chapter we examine the role of entrepreneurial education in the acquisition of entrepreneurial self-efficacy and intentions, and the mediating effect of previous entrepreneurial exposure. Both sociological theories and social psychology theories, such as the theory of self-efficacy (Bandura, 1997), underline the important interaction between individual predispositions and supporting environments to shape motives and abilities. These theories state that individuals develop their skills and expectations depending on how supporting different contexts have been in relation to the individual predispositions. That is, a person with predispositions towards entrepreneurship, such as creativity and risk taking, will develop skills and motives that are going to drive that person in such a direction if they are exposed to supporting environments. However, that same person might choose another career if exposed to different situations that either allow those dispositions to progress in another direction (for example, mountaineering) or result in them being suppressed. Moreover, a person that does not have such predispositions will not react favourably to situations that demand risk taking and creativity. The process is not deterministic because people construct a meaning from their experience when shaping their own personal development. From the perspective of entrepreneurship, this is interesting as people will react and learn differently to the same entrepreneurial experience according to their disposition and their constructed meaning. This learning experience is important later on when they assess the possibility of engaging in entrepreneurship. However, we do not know what shapes the construction of meaning and how skill and motives are developed in an entrepreneurial setting.

Our purpose is to empirically examine the role of self-efficacy and of intentions in the context of entrepreneurial training to see who reacts, and how, to a practical experience in entrepreneurship by measuring their change in entrepreneurial self-efficacy and intentions. Both self-efficacy and intentions can be seen as important outcomes of entrepreneurship courses. A course might have an objective to encourage the willingness to create an independent business or to develop new skills and competencies, or both. The question is, how do students react and learn, and what the mediating factors are affecting those reactions and learning?

We argue that the effect of an enactive mastery experience on entrepreneurial self-efficacy and intentions is moderated by individual predispositions. We test a model of how initial self-efficacy, intentions and predispositions to entrepreneurship interact with an enactive mastery experience to possibly change entrepreneurial self-efficacy and intentions. We test for causality directions among the concepts.

Empirically, we test our basic argument on a sample of 958 undergraduate students from three yearly cohorts that have followed a course in new venture creation over a period of five months. We measure their self-efficacy and intention both prior to the course and after the course has been completed. The chosen design allows us to mitigate some of the most well-known methodological drawbacks that exist in entrepreneurship research.

We believe such research is important for three reasons. First, it sheds light on the importance of entrepreneurial experience and how it affects both the willingness to engage in self-employment, and the ability to perform. Entrepreneurial experience is one of the most well-known predictors of self-employment and performance, but we know surprisingly little of what skills are developed and how (Cooper et al., 1994; Shane and Stuart, 2002). Second, it directs the attention to policy related questions, such as 'does more training in entrepreneurship among young people result in more adults becoming entrepreneurs?' Thus governments wishing to increase the level of entrepreneurship in their economies should care about the content of training (for example, training focusing primarily on experience and acting on reflection and abstraction) and how people react to this content based on individual predispositions. Third, from a pedagogical perspective, teachers in entrepreneurship have to understand what kind of skills can be developed and how situations have to be contextualized for different students.

The chapter is organized as follows. In the first section we discuss recent research on how the two concepts of self-efficacy and intention are linked together, and what the results are of previous studies examining the two constructs in the research domains of entrepreneurship and social psychology. Based on our review we then develop a set of hypotheses. In the method section, we discuss the participants, the design, the measures and the analyses used. We also discuss the advantages and disadvantages with our chosen approach. Thereafter, we present the results of the analyses. The implications for research and practice, limitations of the study and possible future research are discussed in our final section.

THEORY DEVELOPMENT

Self-efficacy and intentions have attained a central position in entrepreneurship literature, but to a certain degree they represent somewhat separate sets of literature. Intentions have been used largely in studies trying to establish the validity of the theory of planned behaviour to predict entry into self-employment (Kolvereid, 1996; Kolvereid and Isaksen, 2006; Krueger and Carsrud, 1993). Intention is the formulation of a choice of behaving in a certain direction (Ajzen, 1991). Both constructs are thus related directly to behaviour, but are also supposed to affect each other (Armitage and Conner, 1999). Self-efficacy is about a person's beliefs in their ability to mobilize the motivation, cognitive resources and courses of actions needed to control events in their life. Perceived self-efficacy is also positively related to the behaviour of starting one's own business and exploring new opportunities (Chen et al., 1998; Krueger and Dickson, 1994). Recent research in motivation suggests an important interaction between the two concepts where self-efficacy is a strong complement or replacement to the perceived behavioural control component in the theory of planned behaviour (Kolvereid and Isaksen, 2006).

However, self-efficacy is not just a sub-component or a development of Ajzen's theory of planned behaviour. On the contrary, self-efficacy has been shown to have a strong motivational impact in itself. For example, Baum et al. (2001) have demonstrated that the relationship between the personality of the entrepreneur and performance of the firm is mediated by situation specific goals and self-efficacy. Moreover, Baum and Locke (2004) conducted a six-year follow-up study to examine how the entrepreneur's passion and tenacity interact to affect the success of the venture as a whole. These two traits were found to have indirect rather than direct effects on firm performance through goal setting and self-efficacy.

We also find a relationship between self-efficacy and task or job characteristics, especially in situations such as the creation of a new venture that demands a high degree of autonomy for learning and development. Such situations or environments provide an individual with an opportunity to grow, because one has to have (1) discretion over the way work is performed, (2) timing control in terms of one's influence over scheduling of work and (3) discretion in setting performance goals. Such a context provides individuals with a mastery experience.

However, these opportunities for individual growth will only be taken by individuals high in self-efficacy. When people believe themselves to be inefficacious, they are likely to exert little or no effort even in environments that provide opportunities for growth. Conversely, when people view their environments as controllable (which for them is an important characteristic), they are motivated to exert fully their perceived self-efficacy, which in turn enhances their likelihood of success (Bandura, 2001). If they are successful, feedback about their success is likely to reinforce their perception of self-efficacy.

While self-efficacy is by definition related to the characteristics of the specific situation, the formation of intention is less so. However, change in both intention and self-efficacy is mediated by previous experiences. Individuals that have been exposed to entrepreneurship through family ties, for example, will have less change in their perceived entrepreneurial self-efficacy and intentions than participants with less exposure. The latter group will have a higher variance in perceived self-efficacy both before and after the practical experience. An investigation of this moderating effect allows us to see under which circumstance participants develop skills and motives and how they perceive this experience.

Thus, a mastery experience will reinforce and stabilize people's perception of self-efficacy and intentions if they have had prior exposure, but will force others with less experience to reassess their perceptions. Hence some will discover first hand what entrepreneurship can mean and others will be reassured in their perceptions. The consequences are that the latter group will have more stable perceptions, and therefore a higher probability to act in accordance with them, and the former group will have formed less discordant perceptions about their skills and motives in this specific domain, and will be less likely to engage in a behaviour that they do not control (Sheeran and Abraham, 2003).

Consequently, both the concept of intention and the concept of self-efficacy are closely related to entrepreneurship and especially entry into self-employment, even if self-efficacy has a wider or deeper effect on behaviour as it is not only limited to choice but also to a feeling of control in a specific situation. We have seen that they are related to each other, but that the causal direction is not determined. Bandura (1997; 2001) argues in his social regulation theory that self-efficacy is affected by feedback loops. Similarly, Ajzen (1995) also argues for the importance of feedback in his model. Therefore we are inclined to believe that self-efficacy is influenced by intentions, and vice versa. Both are mediated by previous experiences, but self-efficacy seems to a higher degree to be dependent on the characteristics of the task to be developed. Furthermore, entrepreneurship education seeks to influence one or both concepts. In the following section we develop hypotheses to examine the relationship between the two, and how mediating effects are likely to moderate the results.

Hypotheses

Motivation theories rest on the building block that our motivations affect our behaviour. Motivation affects the choice of behaviour, the longevity of the behaviour and the level of effort (Kanfer, 1991). An individual's intention to create an independent venture reflecting attitudes and subjective norms in Ajzen's theory of planned behaviour (Ajzen, 1991) affects their choice to do so, the willingness to sustain this choice over time and at what level of effort.

Unless motivation is relatively constant over time, and until the behaviour is performed, prediction will be weak (Ajzen, 1995). Empirically, research has found that stable motivations are good predictors of behaviour while unstable motivations have no association with behaviour (Sheeran et al., 1999). Stability of intentions over time is also associated with a higher probability that over time the individual will encounter the specific situation that will commit the individual to engage in the behaviour. That is to say, people often develop intentions, but related to those intentions they develop implementation intentions that specify when, where and how behaviour is likely to lead to the successful achievement of their choice.

The important thing here is that intention implementation allows people to switch from a conscious effort to control their behaviour to being unconsciously led by situational cues (Gollwitzer, 1999). In our case our subjects are young and are following a general programme of management. The fact that they have an enactive experience now should not affect their intentions, as this situation probably differs extensively from the situation they imagine would lead them to become entrepreneurs. Such a situation could arise after they have finished their education, accumulated a number of years of work experience and identified a valuable opportunity. Thus this experience does not lead them to reconsider their intentions, because it does not correspond to the specific situation that will commit them to engage in entrepreneurship.

Consequently, we believe, based on our review of the literature on motivation, that intention should remain relatively stable over time to be effective, and relatively little affected by feedback if the feedback is not related to specific cues related to intention implementation. Therefore we state:

Hypothesis 1: Intentions at time 1 have a positive effect on intentions at time 2.

The search for knowledge and the perception of knowledge is closely related to the choice that we make. Therefore we argue that individuals that have formed a strong intention to act as entrepreneurs will also develop a strong perception of knowledge, which will be based on the actual accumulation of relevant experiences and skills (that is, the basis for self-efficacy which is based on the perception of abilities and skills). Intentions can therefore be said to cause an increase in self-efficacy if the individual is placed in a situation that allows them to behave in such a way that successful achievement is possible. Basically, if intentions are aligned with the characteristics of the task, then learning is made easier and subsequent achievement is made easier (Harackiewicz and Elliot, 1993; Rigby et al., 1992). Consequently, we believe that:

Hypothesis 2: Intentions at time 1 have a positive effect on self-efficacy at time 2.

Self-efficacy as a construct resembles the perceived behavioural control component of the theory of planned behaviour. Actually, Ajzen in his seminal article from 1991 makes a direct connection to Bandura's work on self-efficacy, stating that: 'perceived behavioural control . . . is most compatible with Bandura's concept of self-efficacy . . . The theory of planned behaviour places the construct of self-efficacy belief or behavioural perceived control within the more general framework of the relations among beliefs, attitudes, intentions, and behaviour' (Ajzen, 1991, p. 185).

Perceived behavioural control as a concept has been replaced more and more by the concept of self-efficacy as the theory of planned behaviour has evolved (Conner and Armitage, 1998). It is evident that if an individual controls the necessary resources and opportunities, then the probability of behavioural achievement increases. Of greater interest from a psychological perspective than actual control is the perception of behavioural control and its impact on intention and actions. The perception of control is a good indicator of actual control, and thus should have an impact on intentions and behaviour (Ajzen, 1991).

Hypothesis 3: Self-efficacy at time 1 has a positive effect on intentions at time 2.

As described above, the relationship between self-efficacy and intentions is far from clear. Several claims have been made in the literature, and there is a need for a closer examination of the interplay of these two constructs as they are potentially important in our understanding of how motivation is developed when students or other individuals are subjected to an entrepreneurial mastery experience. Both concepts are related directly to behavioural achievement and performance. People high in intention are more likely to act than people low in intention. People higher in self-efficacy are more likely to act than people lower in self-efficacy. Moreover, intentions are influenced by self-efficacy and self-efficacy is influenced by intentions.

However, we do not know exactly which of the two is most easily changeable, and why. It might be that intentions are relatively stable over time, and that a mastery experience does not change the willingness to act, but that it changes the perception of control and knowledge (self-efficacy). That is, the effect of a mastery experience is not a change in choice to do something, but is a change in energy deployed in the behaviour should the right situation arise in the future. Moreover, self-efficacy is about a person's belief in their ability to mobilize the motivation, cognitive resources and courses of actions needed to control events. This has an effect on how the mastery experience is perceived. We predict that the level of self-efficacy at the beginning of the experience will have a direct positive impact on the self-efficacy at the end of the experience because it allows the individual to test the validity of their perceptions. If intentions are stable over time while self-efficacy is not, but is influenced by the mastery experience, we will have a strong indication that such experience influences foremost a person's belief in their ability to mobilize the motivation, cognitive resources and courses of actions needed to control events rather then the intention to act. This leads us to our next hypothesis:

Hypothesis 4: Self-efficacy at time 1 has a stronger impact on self-efficacy at time 2 than intentions had at time 1.

We argue that change in both intention and self-efficacy is mediated by previous experiences. Individuals that have been exposed to entrepreneurship through family ties, for example, will have less change in their perceived entrepreneurial self-efficacy and intentions than participants with less exposure. The latter group will have a higher variance in perceived self-efficacy both before and after the practical experience. A mastery experience, such as the one proposed in our research design where students are asked to create a business plan for a new venture that could be launched, will reinforce and stabilize people's perception of self-efficacy and intentions if they have had prior exposure, but will force others with less experience to reassess their perceptions. Hence some will discover first hand what entrepreneurship can mean and others will be reassured in their perceptions.

The consequences are that the latter group will have more stable perceptions, and therefore a higher probability to act in accordance with them, and the former group will have formed less discordant perceptions about their skills and motives in this specific domain, and will be less likely to engage in a behaviour that they do not control (Sheeran and Abraham, 2003). Feedback on achievement is central to the theory of self-efficacy, and to the theory of planned behaviour as information of past experience is the root of intentions and behaviour (Doll and Ajzen, 1992).

We focus specifically on vicarious experience, which is the second strongest source of efficacy information, as none of the course participants has any previous practical experience of entrepreneurship. It is based on social comparative inference, where the attainments of others who are similar to oneself are judged to be diagnostics of one's own capabilities. Here parents and other close family members play a crucial role. As a consequence, in our final set of hypotheses we state:

Hypothesis 5: Individuals with previous vicarious experience will have a higher increase in self-efficacy than individuals with less experience.

Hypothesis 6: Individuals with previous experience will have a higher increase in intentions than individuals with less experience.

METHOD

Participants

The participants all come from an elite business school in France. We are working with three cohorts of students (year 2002, 2003 and 2004). They have all participated in a compulsory five-month course taken during their first year, named 'Project Venture Creation'. In total, 958 students have taken the course, with 313 students in 2002 and 325 students in 2004. Women comprise 55.18 per cent the group. The age of the students ranges from 20 to 22. All students have been through the French education system and have come from the 'Classes Préparatoires'. These 'classes' cover a very selective two-year preparatory programme that starts after the students' high school graduation and allows them, if they succeed, to integrate the best French business schools. Hence we are dealing with a group of high ability and high achievement.

Design

We use a repeated measure design where participants of the programme are given an initial questionnaire before they start and a second questionnaire at the end of the programme before they receive their final grades.

The purpose behind 'Project Venture Creation' is for the students to discover entrepreneurship and the different functions of a firm. The course covers a period of five months where the students in groups of six (men and women) are asked to develop a business plan around a new venture. During this period they have to assemble a maximum of information to enable them to construct a business plan and to defend it in a final business plan competition. They have the opportunity of presenting their project and interacting with the professor at least once every two weeks, but apart from these fixed meetings they are very autonomous. The goal is to create a situation where they have to work independently and decide themselves about their level of commitment and achievement, while at the same time having to gather information outside of the school. They are asked to seek out potential customers, suppliers and other stakeholders that can help them to validate and develop their project. The programme is perceived as the most important course during this year as many students are recruited to their first job based on their course performance. Hence the programme is a mastery experience characterized by a high degree of autonomy for learning and development. As such, participants (1) have to have discretion over the way work is performed, (2) control timing in terms of its influence over work scheduling and (3) exercise discretion in setting performance goals.

The design has some important advantages. First, there is no self-selection in the process as the course is mandatory. Second, we can assume equal general ability among the students as they have a similar social background and have been selected by the school on the same criteria. Third, they are in the same age range and are aware of the importance of succeeding in this course for their future careers. Fourth, they have the same access to resources. Fifth, because none of the students have any previous practical experience in entrepreneurship, we do not have a problem with heterogeneity in experiences. Finally, it allows us to examine the change in our two independent variables.

Hence this design allows us to mitigate for well-known method problems due to high heterogeneity in entrepreneurship groups that are trying to measure entrepreneurial behaviour or performance. Thus our study has high internal validity.

An important drawback is that we do not have access to a control group. Our choice of analysis techniques does mitigate this drawback to a certain degree. A further disadvantage is the sacrifice of external validity for internal validity as we measure behaviour among students in a controlled setting rather than among real-life entrepreneurs. However, based on research in psychology testing the external validity of experimental data, we are confident that our results will also have some validity for real-life entrepreneurship (Neale and Liebert, 1986).

Measures

We are interested in what causes change in intention and self-efficacy over time. The two concepts were extracted using a principal component analysis followed by a varimax rotation factor analysis. The specific wording of the items included in the concepts as well as the related reliability measures are presented in Table 4.1. The Cronbach's alpha varies between 0.67 for the intention measures at time 1 to 0.71 for the self-efficacy measure. According to Peterson (1994) these values can be considered satisfactory, but not exceptionally high.

We measure previous entrepreneurial exposure or vicarious experience with a single question, asking the participants if they have people close to them that are owner-managers of a small business or are entrepreneurs. Four responses are possible starting with the lowest value of 1 if they have no one close to them in the previously mentioned categories. A value of 2 is

Table 4.1 Measurement summary for the constructs of study

Construct/ dimension	Conceptual definition/Approach	No. of items	Coeff. Alpha at T1	Coeff. Alpha at T2
Self-efficacy		3	.71	.69
	I believe that I have the necessary competencies in terms of personality to create my own business	1–4		
	I think that I have the necessary skills to create a business	1–4		
	I think I have a high probability to succeed should I choose to start my own business	1–4		
Intention		2	.67	.69
	I want to create my own business in the future	1–4		
	I intend to create my own business as soon as possible	1–4		

attributed if they have friends who are entrepreneurs. A value of 3 is attributed if they have family who are entrepreneurs. Finally, a value of 4 is given if they have both friends and family who are entrepreneurs. The higher the value, the higher the vicarious experience of entrepreneurship.

We use a number of control variables. We control for the impact of attitudes by using three separate attitude measures that do not load on the same factor. The three questions ask the respondents if they admire entrepreneurs, believe that entrepreneurs contribute to economic wealth and if entrepreneurs have to work harder than others. We also control for the grade that the participants receive. The grade is given to the group, and is a good control for group level effects and for performance. The grade is given by two professors who have evaluated both the written business plan and the presentation. We also control for the educational background of participants with a dummy variable coded 1 if they have a high school degree in the hard sciences or 0 if they have a high school degree in social or human sciences. Finally, we had controls for sex, the professions of their fathers and mothers and for the cohort. The base cohort is 2002.

Analysis

Our hypotheses suggest relatively complex causal relationships between intention and self-efficacy. Specifically, they state dual causality between intention and self-efficacy, and that there are important feedback loops, but they also suggest we have both fixed effect and random effects to consider. Normally, the best way to analyze our data would be to create a fixed effect model as it allows us to mitigate the problem directly without having a control group. However, such an approach is not possible as our hypotheses state that time invariant factors, such as previous experience, affect the change in our dependent variable. To fully test our model, we use a combination of a fixed and random effect approach to mitigate the latter problem and a cross-lagged regression to handle the former problem related to dual causality.

We rely on cross-lagged regression analysis to handle dual causality. Cross-lagged regression is used to determine the causal relationship between constructs that are measured at least twice (Cohen and Cohen, 1983). It has been used in several studies to clearly identify the causal relationship between constructs where correlations have been noted in past research. For example, studies have examined the causal relationship between employee satisfaction and organizational effectiveness (Koys, 2001), between communication effectiveness and innovativeness (Lind and Zmud, 1991) or if political talk shows influence the audience or whether the audience is merely selecting sources consistent with previous political attitudes (Yanovitzky and Capella, 2001).

The cross-lagged model requires two separate analyses to be performed. First, intention at time 2 was regressed on intention at time 1 and self-efficacy at time 1. Second, self-efficacy at time 2 was regressed on intention at time 1 and self-efficacy at time 1. In addition, a comparison of the size of the regression coefficients tells us which causal relationships were stronger. Since we measured intention and self-efficacy in both employment and sales, this gave us a total of four different regression analyses.

The mixed random effect and fixed effect approach is suggested by Halaby (2004). The approach is done in two steps. First, two random effect models are estimated. The first model estimates the variance in the dependent variable at time 1. The second model estimates the variance in the dependent variable at time 2. All this allows us to test the effect of time invariant predictors. If the coefficient changes significantly between the models, then the exogenous treatment is affected by the time invariant variables and not only by its entry value. The second step consists of a fixed effect regression where the time variant variables are regressed on the changes in the dependent variable. This enables us to estimate the change effect better.

RESULTS

Tables 4.2 and 4.3 present the means, standard deviations and correlations for the two time periods. None of the correlation tables display any alarmingly high correlations that could distort the estimation of the standard error of the coefficients in a significant way. Furthermore, we do not observe any standard deviations that are abnormally high.

Our first step in our analyses to test our hypotheses is to examine if we can observe a significant change between time 1 and time 2. A significant change is an indication that the exogenous treatment has had an effect on our dependent variables. The average difference in perceived self-efficacy between time 1 and time 2 is significantly different from zero (mean $=0.41$, standard deviation $=0.05$, $p<0.000$). The average difference in intention between time 1 and time 2 is not significantly different from zero (mean $=-0.04$, standard deviation $=0.04$, $p<0.80$). The result that intention has not changed significantly is a first indication that our first hypothesis might be supported. That is, intentions are in general stable motivators that should not normally be affected by the kind of mastery experience to which the course participants were subjected.

Table 4.2 Correlation matrix at time 1

Variable	Mean	St. dev.	1	2	3	4	5	6	7	8	9	10	11	12	13	14
1. Ent exposure	2.26	1.16	1.00													
2. Intention	4.86	1.41	0.18	1.00												
3. Admiration	3.43	0.69	0.16	0.23	1.00											
4. Economic wealth	3.58	0.58	0.11	0.18	0.26	1.00										
5. Working more	3.27	0.74	0.10	0.09	0.17	0.19	1.00									
6. Education	0.55	0.50	−0.06	0.04	0.00	−0.05	0.04	1.00								
7. Sex	1.55	0.50	0.00	−0.25	−0.02	−0.12	−0.07	0.04	1.00							
8. Social background	1.18	0.38	−0.08	−0.01	0.02	−0.01	−0.03	−0.06	0.00	1.00						
9. Father white collar	0.47	0.50	−0.03	0.00	−0.03	−0.03	−0.02	0.11	0.01	−0.32	1.00					
10. Father business leader	0.13	0.34	0.22	0.09	0.07	0.07	0.06	−0.06	−0.04	−0.13	−0.37	1.00				
11. Mother white collar	0.25	0.43	0.05	0.02	−0.07	−0.04	0.03	0.03	0.04	−0.16	0.23	0.02	1.00			
12. Mother business leader	0.02	0.14	0.10	−0.02	0.04	0.01	0.05	−0.01	0.01	−0.04	−0.11	0.17	−0.08	1.00		
13. Cohort 2003	0.36	0.48	0.01	−0.04	−0.10	−0.10	0.00	0.12	0.01	−0.02	0.16	0.00	0.08	0.05	1.00	
14. Cohort 2004	0.33	0.47	0.01	0.01	0.05	0.06	−0.03	−0.06	0.04	−0.03	0.10	0.00	0.11	−0.02	−0.52	1.00

Notes: $N = 760$; correlations greater than 0.07 are significant at $p < 0.05$; and those greater than 0.10 are significant at $p < 0.01$.

Table 4.4 shows the results from our two step analyses. Models 1 through 3 show the results when we use intention as a dependent variable. Models 4 through 6 show the results when we use self-efficacy as a dependent variable. Models 1 and 4 present the results of the regressions at time 1. Models 2 and 5 present the results of the regression at time 2 where we test the causal direction of self-efficacy and intentions. Finally, Models 3 and 6 present the results of the fixed effect regressions. Concerning the control variables, we see that attitudes towards entrepreneurs are somewhat important, and that we have an expected sex effect, where women in general score lower on both intention and self-efficacy. Grades have, as anticipated, a strong effect. Teams and individuals that have worked and feel that they have achieved something important have also strengthened both their intentions and self-efficacy.

Hypotheses 1 and 3 are related to the prediction of intentions. Hypothesis 1 states that intentions at time 1 affect intentions at time 2. Hypothesis 3 states that self-efficacy at time 1 should also have an effect. We have already seen that the change between the two measurement points is not statistically significant. Model 2 confirms Hypotheses 1 and 3. Intention at time 1 has a positive effect on intention at time 2 (coeff. 0.49, s.e. 0.04, $p<0.001$). Individuals high in intention at time 1 are also likely to be high in intention at time 2. The same pattern is repeated for self-efficacy. Self-efficacy at time 1 has a positive effect on intention at time 2 (coeff. 0.14, s.e. 0.03, $p<0.001$). The effect of intentions is significantly larger than for self-efficacy when we test for a difference in coefficient strength ($F=33.20$, $p<0.0001$).

Hypothesis 2 is related to the prediction of self-efficacy at time 2 and is tested in Model 2. Hypothesis 2 states that intentions at time 1 should have an effect on self-efficacy. We find support for both hypotheses. People high in intention are more likely to be high on self-efficacy at the end of the course (coeff. 0.41, s.e. 0.04, $p<0.001$). Hypothesis 4 is related to the relative strength between intention and self-efficacy. To test this hypothesis, we investigate to see if the coefficients are significantly different from each other. We find support for Hypothesis 4. Self-efficacy at time 1 has a significantly stronger coefficient than intentions on self-efficacy at time 2 ($F=25.48$, $p<0.0001$).

Hypotheses 5 and 6 suggest that previous experience or specifically vicarious experience has a moderating effect on change in intentions and self-efficacy. We test these hypotheses with two models (Models 4 and 5). The first tests the effect at the entry to the course (time 1) and the second tests the effect at the exit of the course (time 2). By comparing the two models we can see if the coefficients are significant and if there is a change in the coefficient value between the two measurement points. Thereby, we can

Table 4.3 Correlation matrix at time 2

Variable	Mean	St.dev.	1	2	3	4	5	6
1. Intention t2	4.90	1.47	1.00					
2. Intention t1	4.91	1.42	0.61	1.00				
3. Self-efficacy t2	8.34	1.44	0.54	0.34	1.00			
4. Self-efficacy t1	7.93	1.50	0.44	0.54	0.49	1.00		
5. Ent exposure	2.26	1.16	0.14	0.19	0.15	0.16	1.00	
6. Grade	13.83	2.52	0.04	−0.05	0.10	−0.04	0.00	1.00
7. Admiration	3.42	0.70	0.26	0.22	0.20	0.14	0.16	0.01
8. Economic wealth	3.55	0.59	0.15	0.14	0.17	0.18	0.13	−0.03
9. Working more	3.50	0.63	0.18	0.11	0.17	0.12	0.04	−0.02
10. Education	0.56	0.50	0.04	0.03	0.02	0.03	−0.07	0.04
11. Sex	1.53	0.50	−0.26	−0.26	−0.20	−0.26	−0.01	0.06
12. Social background	1.19	0.39	0.01	0.00	−0.03	−0.12	−0.09	0.05
13. Father white collar	0.47	0.50	−0.01	−0.04	−0.08	0.01	0.00	−0.08
14. Father business leader	0.13	0.34	0.06	0.10	0.08	0.10	0.21	0.02
15. Mother white collar	0.24	0.43	−0.01	0.01	−0.03	0.05	0.06	−0.07
16. Mother business leader	0.02	0.15	−0.03	−0.03	0.04	0.01	0.10	0.01
17. Cohort 2003	0.36	0.48	−0.01	−0.05	−0.02	−0.02	0.02	−0.14
18. Cohort 2004	0.33	0.47	0.02	0.00	0.01	0.01	0.02	−0.03

Note: $N = 688$; correlations greater than 0.08 are significant at $p < 0.05$; and those greater than 0.10 are significant at $p < 0.01$.

separate the entry effect from the effect that is caused by the external treatment. Even if we find a significant effect at the bivariate level of analysis of vicarious experience on intention and self-efficacy at time 1, where people high in self-efficacy and intention are also high in vicarious experience, the result does not stand in the regression models. Furthermore, we do not observe that the coefficients change or that they are significant. Consequently, we do not find support for Hypotheses 5 and 6.

The fixed effect models show that if there is a change in self-efficacy, there is likely to be a change in intentions and vice versa. This indicates that for some participants intentions did change significantly, as did self-efficacy. For those where a change did occur, that change had an impact on their level of self-efficacy and intention. At this point we can only speculate if there are systematic sources to these changes. An examination of the different intention models does not offer any guidance. However, when we examine the models predicting self-efficacy, we see that the sex of the participants may be important. The coefficient for sex between Models 4 and

Table 4.3 (continued)

7	8	9	10	11	12	13	14	15	16	17	18
1.00											
0.38	1.00										
0.29	0.23	1.00									
0.01	−0.07	−0.02	1.00								
−0.01	−0.10	−0.11	0.06	1.00							
−0.10	−0.03	−0.03	−0.05	0.02	1.00						
−0.02	−0.02	0.00	0.09	0.02	−0.32	1.00					
0.09	0.07	0.06	−0.08	−0.04	−0.13	−0.36	1.00				
−0.03	−0.04	−0.03	0.03	0.08	−0.17	0.26	0.00	1.00			
0.02	0.03	0.01	−0.01	0.02	−0.05	−0.12	0.18	−0.08	1.00		
−0.02	−0.02	−0.05	0.13	0.01	−0.01	0.16	0.01	0.07	0.05	1.00	
−0.03	−0.03	−0.03	−0.05	0.03	−0.07	0.11	0.01	0.13	−0.02	−0.52	1.00

5 changes dramatically from –0.36 to –0.19. This indicates that male participants and female participants react somewhat differently and that their point of departure is different. The dummy variable measures the intercept and indicates that women are lower in self-efficacy than men at time 1. As we have not stated a formal hypothesis, we choose not to conclude anything in a more definitive manner. In analyses not shown here we also test for a number of interaction effects between previous experience, sex, intentions and self-efficacy. We did not find any significant results.

We conclude from the previous results that intentions are difficult to change (no significant change between the two points of observations), but that self-efficacy is more easily affected (a significant and positive change). Figure 4.1 summarizes the changes in the two dependent variables. We have also seen that self-efficacy has a relatively stronger effect on self-efficacy than intention. We therefore conclude that our treatment has an effect on self-efficacy because it works well as a mastery experience, and allows the participants to test and develop their knowledge rather than to change their choices.

Table 4.4 Regressions at time 1 and time 2

Intention	Model 1 Coeff.	T1 (s.e.)	Model 2 Coeff.	T2 (s.e.)	Model 3 Coeff.	Diff. (s.e.)
Intention			0.49	(0.04)***		
Self-efficacy	0.43	(0.03)**	0.14	(0.03)***	0.26	(0.03)***
Ent. exposure	0.11	(0.04)**	0.01	(0.04)		
Grade			0.05	(0.02)**		
Admiration	0.26	(0.07)**	0.26	(0.07)***	0.09	(0.07)
Economic wealth	0.07	(0.08)	−0.03	(0.08)	0.04	(0.08)
Working more	−0.05	(0.06)	0.18	(0.07)*	0.05	(0.06)
Education	0.14	(0.09)	0.07	(0.09)		
Sex	−0.42	(0.09)***	−0.32	(0.09)***		
Social background	0.25	(0.13)*	0.17	(0.12)		
Father white collar	0.04	(0.11)	0.01	(0.11)		
Father business leader	0.19	(0.15)	−0.07	(0.15)		
Mother white collar	0.09	(0.11)	−0.03	(0.10)		
Mother business leader	−0.34	(0.31)	−0.19	(0.30)		
Cohort 2003	−0.12	(0.11)	0.27	(0.11)*		
Cohort 2004	−0.06	(0.11)	0.26	(0.11)*		
Constant	0.56	(0.48)	−0.67	(0.54)	−0.14	(0.05)**
n		726		721		708
Adj.*R2*		0.32		0.41		0.10

Note: t $p<0.10$, * $p<0.05$, ** $p<0.01$, *** $p<0.001$.

DISCUSSION

The results are potentially important for entrepreneurship researchers, educators and policy makers. The strength of our approach comes from our design that allows us to control for a number of problems that have previously hindered entrepreneurship research to respond in a satisfactory manner to what elements in a person's experience lead to the development of skills and motives driving them towards entrepreneurial activity. Our study might not be able to answer if people will engage in entrepreneurship or not, but it will be able to shed some light on the processes that leads individuals to develop dispositions towards entrepreneurship, that is, the acquisition of perceived self-efficacy in entrepreneurship. Related to our theoretic departure, we developed a set of hypotheses that we tested on a sample of 958 French business school students who have taken a compulsory course in entrepreneurship.

Table 4.4 (continued)

Self–efficacy	Model 4 Coeff.	T1 (s.e.)	Model 5 Coeff.	T2 (s.e.)	Model 6 Coeff.	Diff. (s.e.)
Intention	0.48	(0.04)***	0.07	(0.04)t	0.34	(0.04)***
Self-efficacy			0.41	(0.04)***		
Ent. exposure	0.04	(0.04)	0.06	(0.04)		
Grade			0.07	(0.02)***		
Admiration	0.13	(0.07)t	0.18	(0.08)*	0.12	(0.08)
Economic wealth	0.25	(0.09)**	0.05	(0.09)	0.20	(0.09)*
Working more	0.14	(0.06)*	0.19	(0.08)*	0.09	(0.07)
Education	0.07	(0.09)	0.03	(0.10)		
Sex	−0.36	(0.10)***	−0.19	(0.10)t		
Social background	−0.45	(0.13)**	0.04	(0.13)		
Father white collar	0.01	(0.11)	−0.24	(0.12)*		
Father business leader	0.05	(0.16)	−0.15	(0.16)		
Mother white collar	0.04	(0.11)	−0.06	(0.11)		
Mother business leader	0.06	(0.33)	0.25	(0.33)		
Cohort 2003	0.03	(0.12)	0.16	(0.12)		
Cohort 2004	0.01	(0.12)	0.18	(0.12)		
Constant	4.66	(0.47)***	2.50	(0.59)***	0.41	(0.05)***
n	726		692		708	
Adj.*R2*	0.30		0.29		0.11	

We argued that one role that entrepreneurship courses play is that it allows participants to more correctly assess their self-efficacy. We find empirical support for this statement. We find that the course participants changed in their self-efficacy, but not in their intention. This change in self-efficacy is attributed to a mastery experience where they are able to set their own work conditions under high autonomy. In line with previous work we find that tasks characterized by such high autonomy provide a fertile ground for learning if a person is already high in self-efficacy. That is, people already high in self-efficacy are most likely to develop an even higher perception of control when they are given the freedom to do so. People who are low in initial self-efficacy are less likely to be able to take advantage of such a situation.

We have also argued that intentions should remain stable over time, as a mastery experience does not lead the participants to fundamentally

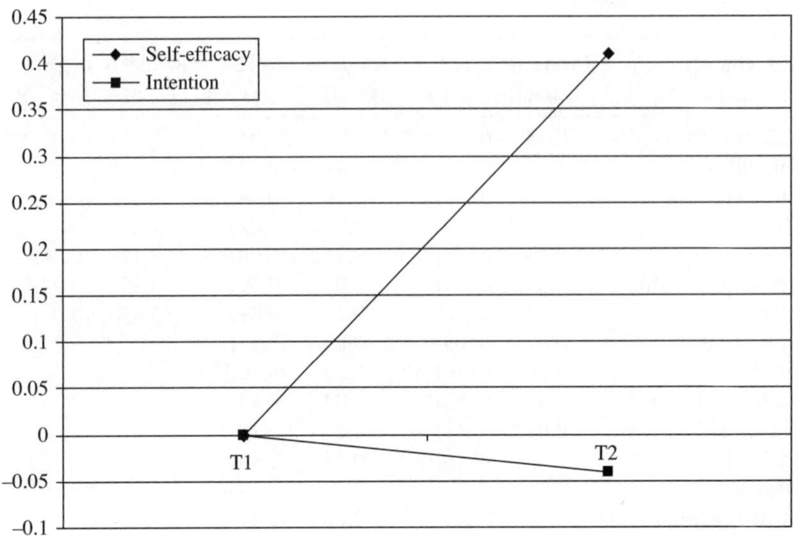

Figure 4.1 Change in sample mean in intention and self-efficacy after the mastery experience

re-examine the foundations of their intended choice if cues related to the implementation of the intention are activated. This claim found empirical support. The proposed mechanism is that intentions are subject to change only if the individuals encounter a specific situation that will commit them to engage in the behaviour. If such a situation is not encountered, then intentions are not acted upon and not easily changed. The situational clues that allow a person to test an intention are based on an unconscious intention of when, where and how behaviour is likely to lead to a successful achievement of the choice. We do not believe that young students entering a general programme with little practical knowledge or experience related the course to their own future choices and intentions, because it does not reflect the situation in which they would expect to engage in such a behaviour. Consequently, we are not likely to observe such a change if we do not construct a situation that engages such clues.

We argued that people with previous vicarious experience have a more correct assessment of their self-efficacy than do people with less vicarious experience. Consequently, we will expect different reactions to an enactive mastery experience where less experienced people to a greater degree will reassess their self-efficacy based on this new experience. We did not find support for this argument.

Implications

To sum up, as we stated in our introduction, people will create different meanings from the same situation, where some will find it supporting and others suppressing relative to their intention and level of self-efficacy. Such knowledge about how situations are experienced and how, as a result, skills and motives are formed is important to entrepreneurship research because it allows us to better understand the role of experience in the entrepreneurial process. Both scholars in management and economics have recognized the importance of entrepreneurial experience (Delmar and Shane, 2006; Jovanovic and Nyarko, 1995; Otani, 1996), but we know little of the inner functioning of such experiences. Moreover, this research points to the importance of understanding the stable motivations in predicting future behaviour.

From a pedagogical point of view, we need more research about how initial individual predispositions affect the way the students acquire new skills in entrepreneurship and how they intend to use them in the future. We believe that our results are important as they show that perception of competence and control are the easiest factors to affect, at least when a similar programme format is used. It also shows that participants learn to believe that there are skills and competencies related to the successful launch of a new venture, and that it is not only a question of pure commitment to the task, and to 'just do it'.

Finally, for policy makers such knowledge is important because it points to the necessity of developing programmes that better accommodate individual needs, meaning that programme content for people with very low perceived self-efficacy in entrepreneurship should probably have different designs from programme content for people with high perceived self-efficacy. The use of teams in our programmes somewhat offsets this effect, but teams can only be used if the participants are interested in pursuing the same opportunity. For participants that already have an idea in their head and are high in self-efficacy, tasks high in autonomy are probably preferable. For participants that already have an idea in their head but are low in self-efficacy, tasks high in autonomy are probably not preferable because they will not lead to a favourable learning environment. Here other types of pedagogies need to be developed.

Limitations

This research suffers from several limitations. First, we do not use measures validated by other researchers. Hence the operationalization of our constructs can to a certain degree be questioned. However we believe that the wording of our items does not differ too much from other efforts in entrepreneurship, and we are therefore confident that they largely reflect the underlying concepts. Another limitation is that we do not have a control group, despite trying to adapt appropriate analysis techniques that mitigate some of the problems with examining causality. A control group would have made the examination of the underlying causality more direct. We can at this point only infer causality by claiming that our conclusions are in line with the principles of Granger causality.

Future Research

The number of limitations present in our study coupled with the important issue of the role of entrepreneurship education opens up a number of possibilities for future research. We need to better understand how different situations affect the learning process of people with different predispositions to entrepreneurship. We have seen that there are different goals to entrepreneurship courses, and that people are differently affected by the characteristics of the course. This difference is to a high degree related to previous predispositions in terms of intentions and self-efficacy, and is moderated by the characteristics of the course. We need to develop a deeper understanding about this mechanism in order to create courses that are appropriate to a larger variety of people coming to entrepreneurship with different motives.

Moreover, we need to better assess the durability of self-efficacy related to entrepreneurship which goes back to our question in the introduction: 'does more training in entrepreneurship among young people result in more adults becoming entrepreneurs?' If self-efficacy was easily affected by the experience described in the study, and if young people are affected, it is logical to wonder what the durability or temporal stability of such motivators is. That is, it is only possible to answer yes if intentions are high and stable, and that the positive changes in self-efficacy can be assumed to be stable over time or until the individual is faced with a situation where the situational clues to entrepreneurship are activated. Nonetheless, for the moment, we only know that we can increase their self-efficacy and that intentions are stable.

REFERENCES

Ajzen, I. (1991), 'The theory of planned behavior', *Organizational Behavior and Human Decision Processes*, **50**, 179–211.

Ajzen, I. (1995), 'Attitudes and behavior', in A.S.R. Manstead and M. Hewstone (eds), *The Blackwell Encyclopedia of Social Psychology*, Oxford, UK: Blackwell Publishing pp. 52–7.

Armitage, C.J. and M. Conner (1999), 'The theory of planned behaviour: assessment of predictive validity and "perceived control" ', *British Journal of Social Psychology*, **38**, 35–54.

Bandura, A. (1997), *Self-Efficacy: The Exercise of Control*, New York: W.H. Freeman and Company.

Bandura, A. (2001), 'Social cognitive theory: an agentic perspective', *Annual Review of Psychology*, **52**, 1–26.

Baum, J.R. and E.A. Locke (2004), 'The relationship of entrepreneurial traits, skill, and motivation to subsequent venture growth', *Journal of Applied Psychology*, **89**(4), 587.

Baum, R.J., E.A. Locke and K.G. Smith (2001), 'A multidimensional model of venture growth', *Academy of Management Journal*, **44**(2), 292–303.

Chen, C.C., P. Gene Greene and A. Crick (1998), 'Does entrepreneurial self-efficacy distinguish entrepreneurs from managers?', *Journal of Business Venturing*, **13**(4), 295–316.

Cohen, J. and P. Cohen (1983), *Applied Multiple Regression/Correlation Analysis for the Behavioral Sciences* (2nd edn), Hillsdale, NJ: Lawrence Erlbaum Associates.

Conner, M. and C.J. Armitage (1998), 'Extending the theory of planned behavior: a review and avenues for further research', *Journal of Applied Social Psychology*, **28**(15), 1429–64.

Cooper, A.C., F.J. Gimeno-Gascon and C.Y. Woo (1994), 'Initial human and financial capital as predictors of new venture performance', *Journal of Business Venturing*, **9**, 371–95.

Delmar, F. and S. Shane (2006), 'Does experience matter? The effect of founding team experience on the survival and sales of newly founded ventures', *Strategic Organization*, **4**(3), 215–47.

Doll, J. and I. Ajzen (1992), 'Accessibility and stability of predictors in the theory of planned behavior', *Journal of Personality and Social Psychology*, **63**(5), 754–6.

Gollwitzer, P.M. (1999), 'Implementation Intentions', *American Psychologist*, **54**(7), 493–503.

Halaby, C.N. (2004), 'Panel models in sociological research: theory into practice', *Annual Review of Sociology*, **30**, 507–44.

Harackiewicz, J.M. and A.J. Elliot (1993), 'Achievement goals and intrinsic motivation', *Journal of Personality and Social Psychology*, **65**(5), 904–15.

Jovanovic, B. and Y. Nyarko (1995), 'The transfer of human capital', *Journal of Economic Dynamics and Control*, **19**(5–7), 1033.

Kanfer, R. (1991), 'Motivation theory and industrial and organizational psychology', in M.D. Dunnette and L.M. Hough (eds), *Handbook of Industrial and Organizational Psychology*, vol. 1 (2nd edn), Palo Alto, CA: Consulting Psychologists Press Inc., pp. 75–170.

Kolvereid, L. (1996), 'Prediction of employment status choice intentions', *Entrepreneurship Theory and Practice*, **21**(1), 47–57.

Kolvereid, L. and E. Isaksen (2006), 'New business start-up and subsequent entry into self-employment', *Journal of Business Venturing*, **21**(6), 866–85.

Koys, D.J. (2001), 'The effects of employees satisfaction, organizational citizenship behavior, and turnover on organizational effectiveness: a unit-level, longitudinal study', *Personnel Psychology*, **54**, 101–14.

Krueger, N.F.J. and A.L. Carsrud (1993), 'Entrepreneurial intentions: applying the theory of planned behavior', *Entrepreneurship and Regional Development*, **5**(4), 315–30.

Krueger, N.F.J. and P.R. Dickson (1994), 'How believing in ourselves increases risk taking: perceived self-efficacy and opportunity recognition', *Decision Sciences*, **25**(3), 385–400.

Lind, M.L. and R.W. Zmud (1991), 'The influence of a convergence in understanding between technology providers and users on information technology innovativeness', *Organization Science*, **2**(2), 195–217.

Neale, J.M. and R.M. Liebert (1986), *Science and Behavior: An Introduction to Methods of Research* (3rd edn), Englewoods Cliffs, NJ: Prentice-Hall.

Otani, K. (1996), 'A human capital approach to entrepreneurial capacity', *Economica*, **63**(250), 273–89.

Peterson, R.A. (1994), 'A meta-analysis of Cronbach's coefficient alpha', *Journal of Consumer Research*, **21**, 381–91.

Rigby, C.S., E.L. Deci, B.C. Patrick and R.M. Ryan (1992), 'Beyond the intrinsic-extrinsic dichotomy: self-determination in motivation and learning', *Motivation and Emotion*, **16**(3), 165–85.

Shane, S. and T. Stuart (2002), 'Organizational endowments and the performance of university start-ups', *Management Science*, **48**(1), 154–70.

Sheeran, P. and C. Abraham (2003), 'Mediator of moderators: temporal stability of intention and the intention-behavior relation', *Personality and Social Psychology Bulletin*, **29**(2), 205–15.

Sheeran, P., S. Orbell and D. Trafimow (1999), 'Does the temporal stability of behavioral intentions moderate intention-behavior and past behavior–future behavior relations?', *Personality and Social Psychology Bulletin*, **25**(6), 721–30.

Yanovitzky, I. and J.N. Capella (2001), 'Effect of call-in political talk radio shows on their audiences: evidence from a multi-wave panel analysis', *Journal of Public Opinion Research*, **13**(4), 377–97.

5. Why do they use financial bootstrapping? A quantitative study of new business managers

Joakim Winborg

INTRODUCTION

In recent years empirical research has shown the importance of financial bootstrapping methods for the financing of new and small businesses (see, for example, Freear et al., 1995; Harrison and Mason, 1997; Winborg and Landström, 1997; 2001; Harrison et al., 2004; Van Auken, 2005). The study by Freear et al. (1995) was the first empirical study to examine the importance of financial bootstrapping for new businesses. Among other things, they found that, on average, the businesses examined managed to develop by means of bootstrapping and had no or only marginal long-term external finance, over a five-year period. A recent study by Neeley (2003) also demonstrates the important role played by financial bootstrapping, as a large percentage of the businesses examined used bootstrapping to some extent. Moreover, the findings presented by Winborg and Landström (2001) indicate a positive influence on profitability from using some kinds of financial bootstrapping methods.

The first references to financial bootstrapping in the literature define it as methods for securing the use of resources without relying on long-term external finance (Freear et al., 1995). Winborg (2000) argues that, on the basis of this definition, bootstrapping methods can be divided into four categories: methods that eliminate the outflow of financial means, methods that minimize the outflow of financial means, methods that delay the outflow of financial means and, finally, methods that speed up the inflow of financial means. Some of the methods in the latter two categories are included in other concepts, such as cash management. On the basis of the first two categories (that is, eliminate or minimize the outflow of financial means) the present study defines financial bootstrapping as methods aimed at securing the use of resources at relatively low or no cost. According to this narrower definition, bootstrapping involves securing equipment and competence as well as handling marketing at below market price. On the other hand, sharing resources and splitting the total cost does not qualify as bootstrapping unless the total cost of the resources is below market price.

Previous research focused on examining the relative use of different bootstrapping methods per se, whereas the underlying motive for using financial bootstrapping received very little attention. Furthermore, bootstrapping has emerged as a label for methods to be applied in the absence of internal and/or external financial means. In other words, financial bootstrapping has been viewed as the last resort in most studies. For example, Bhide (1992) claims that bootstrapping is about launching a business despite modest personal financial means. In line with this, Van Auken and Neeley (1998) consider bootstrapping as methods that are used when personal savings and loans from financial institutions are either exhausted or unavailable.

However, it seems fair to assume that there are other motives besides lack of capital. Based on this assumption, Winborg (2005) undertook an explorative study of four Swedish new businesses to empirically examine the motives for applying financial bootstrapping. The findings revealed that in most cases the use of bootstrapping is actually a deliberate choice, implying the existence of an explicit motive. Furthermore, the study revealed no less than ten fundamentally different motives for using bootstrapping. The most common motives were: lower costs, lack of capital, reduced risk and the wish to manage without external finance. The findings resulted in a tentative model of factors pertaining to characteristics of the manager and the business, which appeared to influence the motives. As the findings in Winborg (2005) were based on a small number of cases, the overall implication was to test the generalization of the findings using a larger sample of new businesses, which was the point of departure of the present study. More specifically, the aim was to carry out a survey in order to: (1) examine the relative importance of different motives for using financial bootstrapping in new businesses and (2) identify factors pertaining to the manager and the business that have an influence on the motives.

EARLIER RESEARCH ON FINANCIAL BOOTSTRAPPING

Bhide (1992) was one of the first researchers to highlight the potential of financial bootstrapping for the financing of new and small businesses. One of the first empirical studies was undertaken by Freear et al. (1995) and examined the use of bootstrapping among new software businesses in the USA. This study was replicated by Harrison and Mason in 1997 in their investigation of new software businesses in Northern Ireland. Furthermore, Winborg and Landström (1997; 2001) examined the use of financial bootstrapping methods among Swedish small businesses in different sectors. More recent empirical studies are Neeley (2003) and Van Auken (2005), both of which dealt with US small businesses. On the basis of the findings of the above-mentioned studies, it can be concluded that the most common methods included the purchase of used instead of new equipment, renting locations on favorable terms and delaying compensation to the owner/manager.

To date, most research on financial bootstrapping has focused on the relative use of different bootstrapping methods, whereas the underlying motive has received little attention. Furthermore, in earlier research, bootstrapping seems to have been a label for methods employed when internal and/or external finance is not available (see, for example, Bhide, 1992; Van Auken and Neeley, 1998). In other words, business managers were assumed to use bootstrapping as a last resort. At the same time, we know from earlier research on small business finance that there are a number of factors (besides lack of capital) that influence the overall financing decisions. For example, the need for independence and the goals of the business influence how finance is handled (see, for example, Barton and Matthews, 1989; Norton, 1991). Using the same reasoning, it seems fair to assume that there are motives other than lack of capital behind the use of bootstrapping.

Based on this assumption, Winborg (2005) undertook an explorative study of four new businesses to empirically examine the motives for applying bootstrapping. The interview data clearly indicate that the use of bootstrapping is a deliberate choice, implying the existence of an explicit motive. A total of ten different motives were identified. As can be seen in Table 5.1, lower costs, lack of capital and risk reduction were the three most frequently mentioned motives.

In the study by Winborg (2005) it is proposed that the different motives identified can be placed in one of two groups: economic and existential. The findings presented in Table 5.1 show that the most important motives are economic in nature. However, it is interesting to note that there are also several different existential motives, such as work satisfaction and the wish to learn. Furthermore, a tentative model of the factors that influence the various motives was developed. These factors refer to the characteristics of the business as well as of the manager. Of the four businesses examined, one was found to differ from the others in many ways. Its manager mentioned only economic motives for using bootstrapping, whereas the managers of the other three businesses referred to both economic and existential motives. This difference can be attributed to factors relating to the business and the manager. The most obvious differences were found in the area of the driving force behind starting the business, start-up experience and the propensity to take risks. When it came to driving force, the manager

Table 5.1 Motives for using financial bootstrapping

Motive	Number of times mentioned
Lower costs	20
Lack of capital	17
Reduce risk	10
Manage without external finance	6
Save time	5
Work satisfaction	5
Freedom of action	5
Wish to learn	4
Trust in relatives/friends	2
Gain legitimacy	1

Source: Winborg (2005).

who only stressed economic motives was found to focus mainly on the success of the business as such and on making the business highly profitable. On the other hand, the managers in the other three businesses stated that being personally acknowledged by their customers was the main driving force. As regards start-up experience, the managers were found to differ a great deal. The manager who stressed solely economic motives had been previously involved in several start-ups, whereas the other managers had no prior start-up experience. Finally, the findings of the exploratory study revealed that the manager who reported strictly economic motives was far more willing to take risks than the managers of the other three businesses. In addition to these three factors, the analysis indicated some differences with regard to growth ambition, perceived possibilities to attract external finance and owner situation in the business.

OVERALL RESEARCH DESIGN

The purpose of this study was fulfilled by undertaking a survey of managers of new businesses. In this section, the design of the survey, the sample and data collection and, finally, the analysis of data will be presented.

Design of the Survey

The questions included in the survey were developed on the basis of the findings presented in Winborg (2005). The relative importance of different motives for using bootstrapping was examined by means of one question,

Table 5.2 Variables examined and operationalization

Variables	Operationalization
Motives for using bootstrapping	1 = Yes, 0 = No for: lower costs, manage without external finance, lack of capital, risk reduction, freedom of action, save time, fun helping others/getting help from others, other motive, no explicit motive
Characteristics of the business	
Size of business	Number of employees
Age of business	Years since registration
Line of industry	1 = Manufacturing, 2 = Service, 3 = Other
Type of company	1 = Limited company, 2 = Other
Owner situation	1 = External owner, 0 = No external owner
Long-term finance secured	1 = Yes, 0 = No
Characteristics of the manager	
Sex	1 = Male, 2 = Female
Age	Number of years
Level of education	1 = Less than 4 years university and 2 = 4 years or more university
Growth ambition sales	5-point scale ranging from unimportant (1) to very important (5)
Growth ambition employees	5-point scale ranging from unimportant (1) to very important (5)
Driving force; profit	5-point scale ranging from unimportant (1) to very important (5)
Driving force; personal development	5-point scale ranging from unimportant (1) to very important (5)
Experience of the line of industry	Number of years in this line of industry
Experience as manager	Number of years in a management position
Start-up experience	Number of businesses started

in which the respondents were asked to indicate whether or not they had at some time dealt with the need for resources in their business at relatively low or no cost (for example, by borrowing and/or sharing resources). The managers who answered in the affirmative were thereafter asked to indicate the most important motives for dealing with the need for resources in this way from a list of motives taken from Winborg (2005).

As can be seen in Table 5.2, the categorization of motives presented in Winborg (2005) was changed to some degree in the present study. At first glance it may appear that the motives 'Work satisfaction' and 'Wish to learn' were not used. However, these two motives are grouped into one new motive labeled 'Fun helping others and getting help'. In Winborg (2005) it can be seen that 'Work satisfaction' includes motives such as 'Fun helping others' and 'Fun to work with others'. Furthermore, the motive 'Wish to learn' was found to be about learning by obtaining help from others. The motives 'Trust in relatives/friends' and 'Gain legitimacy' were shown to be of little importance in the study by Winborg (2005) and were therefore not included as independent categories in the present study. However, as indicated in Table 5.2, the respondent could tick the alternative 'Other motive' and, if marked, the respondent was asked to describe this other motive.

The respondents could indicate as many of the motives as they wanted. Furthermore, the survey also included independent variables referring to the business and the manager that were assumed to influence the motive. The specific independent variables were selected on the basis of the tentative findings in Winborg (2005) complemented by earlier findings on financial choice in small businesses (see Barton and Matthews, 1989; Winborg, 2000). The variables and their operationalization are presented in Table 5.2.

Data Collection

The data for this study were collected as part of a larger project on the establishment of new businesses in business incubators. The sample consists of new businesses established in three different incubators in the southwest of Sweden: 'Innovationsgruppen' incubator related to Halmstad University in Halmstad, 'Framtidens Företag' incubator attached to Göteborg University in Göteborg and 'Chalmers Innovation' incubator associated with Chalmers University of Technology in Göteborg. Only new business managers that are currently in the incubator or that left less than one year ago are included. Furthermore, only managers that have been in the incubator for at least three months are included. I received assistance from the management teams of the three incubators in identifying a total of 120 managers who met these criteria. The questionnaire was distributed by mail at the end of May 2006 and reminders were sent to non-respondents after two weeks. Those managers who failed to respond to the reminder were then contacted by phone. The data collection concluded in early August 2006. In total 91 usable responses were received (response rate 76 per cent). The most common reason for not participating in the survey was lack of time. This was especially true for the managers establishing their business attached to Chalmers Innovation, who explained that they received many surveys and that they simply did not have the necessary time.

Data Analysis

The analysis focused on identifying the relations between independent variables pertaining to the business and the manager and the motives for using financial bootstrapping. The findings presented in Winborg (2005) indicate that the motives can be classified as either economic or existential in nature. As a first step in the analysis it was decided to classify the respondents according to these two groups. The respondents who indicated solely economic motives were placed in one group. As just one respondent indicated the existential motive without making reference to the economic motives, it was decided that the second group should include all respondents who referred to both economic and existential motives.

Out of the 91 respondents, 11 had never used bootstrapping and accordingly did not answer the question related to motives. Furthermore, three of the remaining 80 respondents gave no answer to the question on the motives for using bootstrapping. Thus the classification is based on the information from 77 respondents. Of these, 41 were classified as having strict economic motives (group 1) and 36 as having both economic and existential motives (group 2).

After the categorization the analysis focused on identifying significant differences between these two groups in terms of the variables presented earlier (see Table 5.2 for the variables examined). In the analysis chi-square and t-tests were undertaken. Since this study is the first to statistically examine variables that have an impact on the motives for bootstrapping, all differences with a p-value of less than 0.10 were considered statistically significant.

PRESENTATION OF THE FINDINGS

This section presents the findings from the study. The presentation starts with a description of the sample in terms of variables related to the business as well as the manager. Thereafter, the findings concerning the relative importance of the motives for using financial bootstrapping are discussed. The findings from the analysis of factors that have an impact on the motives are presented in the following section.

Description of the Sample

The businesses included in this study have an average of 2.5 employees and have existed for slightly more than two years since the date of first registration. A majority are active in the service sector (54 per cent), 24 per cent are engaged in manufacturing while the remaining 22 per cent operate in other sectors, such as trade. More than 60 per cent of the businesses are limited companies. In terms of ownership, just over 50 per cent of the businesses have taken in new partners or undergone a change of ownership. Finally, less than 30 per cent of the managers stated that long-term financial needs have been secured. When it comes to characteristics of the managers, they are on average 31 years old and 75 per cent of them are male. The majority (72 per cent) have a university degree representing at least four years of study, although only 4 per cent have a PhD. Concerning their ambitions for growth, almost all managers strive to increase sales (an average of 4.6 on a 5-point scale), whereas the interest in growth in terms of the number of employees is much weaker (2.7 on the 5-point scale). When asked about the driving force behind starting and running the business, the wish to make profits was found to be equally important as the wish to develop personally (both have a mean of 4.4 on a 5-point scale). With regard to experience, the managers have, on average, almost four years of experience in their present line of industry and two years experience of management positions prior to the start of their present business. Concerning start-up experience, the data revealed that the managers had started an average of two businesses (including the one referred to in the survey).

Motives for Using Financial Bootstrapping

As described in the method section, the managers were first asked to state whether they ever used bootstrapping methods, that is, had managed to handle the need for resources at relatively low or no cost. The data revealed that as many as 88 per cent had used bootstrapping methods to some extent. This finding is completely in line with earlier research showing that most new and small businesses had employed financial bootstrapping (see, for example, Neeley, 2003).

The managers who claimed to have used bootstrapping were then asked to indicate the underlying motives behind their decision. It is interesting to note that no manager ticked the alternative ‘I have no explicit motive’, implying that the use of financial bootstrapping was a deliberate choice. This is completely in line with the findings presented in the explorative study by Winborg (2005). Furthermore, the data revealed a total of 260 answers given by the managers concerning the motives behind the use of bootstrapping, which means that, on average, each manager had three motives. This finding is interesting, as it confirms the assumption that the decision to engage in financial bootstrapping is not only due to a lack of capital (see Winborg, 2005).

Table 5.3 Relative importance of the different motives for using bootstrapping

Motive	Per cent of managers who consider motive important
Lower costs	89%
Lack of capital	50%
Fun helping others and getting help	46%
Save time	45%
Manage without external finance	39%
Risk reduction	38%
Freedom of action	18%

When it comes to the relative importance of the different motives, we can see from Table 5.3 that 'Lower costs' was by far the most important (mentioned by 89 per cent of the managers as important). In second place came 'Lack of capital' (mentioned by 50 per cent), and in third place 'Fun helping others and getting help' (mentioned by as many as 46 per cent). Moreover, 'Saving time', 'Managing without external finance' and 'Reducing risk' were mentioned by quite a large number. On the other hand, relatively few stated that 'Freedom of action' was an important motive for using financial bootstrapping. Finally, only one manager ticked the alternative 'Other motive' and explained that it had to do with 'Social aspects'. However, 'Social aspects' is strongly related to the category 'Fun helping others and getting help', which is already included in the study. When the findings of this study are compared with those of Winborg (2005), it is obvious that the two most important motives are the same in both studies ('Lower costs' and 'Lack of capital'). At the same time, 'Fun helping others and getting help' and 'Saving time' were found to be of much greater importance in the present study than in Winborg (2005).

As indicated in the study by Winborg (2005), some of the motives are strictly economic in nature such as 'Lower costs' and 'Lack of capital', whereas others, such as 'Fun helping others and getting help', can be seen as more existential. In line with the findings in Winborg (2005), the present study shows that the most important motives are economic.

ANALYSIS

As previously described, the respondents were classified and divided into one of two groups: 'economic motives' and 'economic and existential motives'. The first group includes all respondents who ticked at least one of the strictly economic motives 'Lower costs', 'Lack of capital' and 'Manage without external finance', but not the existential motive 'Fun helping others and getting help'. This group comprised 41 respondents. The criterion for placing a respondent in the second group was that they had marked one or more economic motives in addition to the existential motive mentioned above.

Chi-square and t-tests were undertaken to identify significant differences between the two groups in terms of variables pertaining to the business and the manager. In Table 5.4 the results of the analysis are summarized. As already mentioned, all differences with a *p*-value of less than 0.10 were considered statistically significant, which is due to the fact that this is the first statistical study on the subject. The table reveals significant differences in six of the variables examined. The analysis clearly shows that the owner situation influenced the motives reported. Relatively few of the managers

Table 5.4 Differences between the two groups of motives

Variables	Group 1 'Economic motives'	Group 2 'Economic/ Existential motives'	Level of significance
Number of employees	2.8	2.4	0.67
Age of business	2.8	2.3	0.31
Line of industry	34% manufacturing	11% manufacturing	0.05*
Type of company	76% limited companies	56% limited companies	0.06*
External owners	63% of businesses	25% of businesses	0.00*
Long-term finance secured	36% of businesses	14% of businesses	0.06*
Sex	78% men	69% men	0.39
Age of manager	31 years	30 years	0.41
Educational level	78% 4 years university	67% 4 years university	0.26
Experience of sector	4.5 years	2.9 years	0.09*
Experience as manager	2.2 years	1.5 years	0.37
Start-up experience in total	2 businesses	1.9 businesses	0.88
Growth ambition sales	4.7 (5-point scale)	4.5 (5-point scale)	0.39
Growth ambition employees	2.9 (5-point scale)	2.5 (5-point scale)	0.17
Increase profit	4.5 (5-point scale)	4.3 (5-point scale)	0.23
Personal development	4.2 (5-point scale)	4.7 (5-point scale)	0.01*

Note: * $p = 0.10$ or less.

(25 per cent) who mentioned both economic and existential motives had taken in new partners or undergone a change of ownership. The opposite is true of the group who mentioned strictly economic motives ($p = 0.00$). This difference can, of course, be explained by the fact that the managers who had not taken in new partners or who had not undertaken any change of ownership had far more freedom to have motives other than strictly economic ones. This freedom is probably restricted in a business with a new owner demanding a return on their investment.

Furthermore, the findings from the analysis show a significant difference between the two groups in terms of representation of different sectors ($p = 0.05$). In the first group, 'economic motives', there were a relatively large number of manufacturing businesses in comparison with the 'economic and existential motives' group, which instead included a relatively large number of businesses active in the service and other sectors (such as trade). The difference in terms of sectors can in turn be explained by the various possibilities to practice bootstrapping. It can be assumed that it is easier to collaborate and share resources in service businesses than in manufacturing businesses. For example, it seems fair to say that it is more difficult to handle the need for machines and production capacity by means of bootstrapping compared to handling the need for complementary competence in the service sector. Assuming that service businesses find it easier to tap into the resources of others, we can also conclude that this behavior will lead to the development of deeper relationships with resource providers than is the case with new manufacturing businesses. Discussing so-called relational contracting, Macneil (1978; 1980) argues that in profound relationships the motive for exchange between parties is complex, including economic as well as non-economic (existential) aspects.

The analysis also revealed a significant difference between the two groups when it comes to representation of types of company. Relatively many businesses in the group with strictly economic motives are limited companies. This probably relates to differences between the two groups in terms of the number of businesses that have taken in new partners or undergone a change of ownership as discussed earlier. If you want to obtain new partners, it is natural to run the business as a limited company. Finally, the two groups also differ when it comes to handling long-term finance. Relatively more of the businesses in the group with strictly economic motives managed to secure long-term finance compared to the other group, which is probably due to the above-mentioned fact that far more of the businesses in this group have taken in new partners or undergone a change of ownership.

When it comes to the characteristics of the manager, the analysis demonstrated significant differences for two of the variables, namely driving force and experience of the sector. Table 5.4 illustrates that the group reporting both economic and existential motives also indicated a significantly greater interest in personal development in comparison with the group that mentioned strictly economic motives. On the other hand, the managers in the latter group reported a relatively stronger wish to increase profits (although this difference was not significant). These findings associated with the influence of driving force are interesting, as they indicate a strong correlation between the fundamental driving force for starting and running a business and the motive for applying bootstrapping. Furthermore, Table 5.4 shows a significant difference as regards relative experience of the sector. The managers reporting strictly economic motives had an average of 4.5 years experience, which is approximately 1.5 years more than the managers who had mixed motives. This result is supported by the explorative findings presented in Winborg (2005), which revealed that managers who lacked experience reported that, in addition to economic reasons, bootstrapping was a means of personal development and learning (that is, existential motives).

Taken together, we can conclude that the owner situation, line of industry, type of company, need for long-term finance, driving force and experience of the sector are the variables that significantly influence the motives for using financial bootstrapping. The influence of the owner situation, the need for long-term finance as well as the driving forces were also identified in the explorative study by Winborg (2005). However, in contrast to that study, neither growth ambition nor start-up experience significantly influenced the motives behind the use of bootstrapping in the present study, as can be seen in Table 5.4. At the same time, although not significant, the findings nevertheless show that (as concluded in Winborg, 2005) managers who had strictly economic motives were more growth-oriented.

CONCLUSIONS AND IMPLICATIONS FOR FUTURE RESEARCH

This section presents the overall conclusions as well as implications for future research. The findings show that almost nine out of ten managers used financial bootstrapping at some point in time. It was somewhat surprising that all of the managers who used bootstrapping claimed that there was an explicit motive behind the decision, implying that bootstrapping was very much a deliberate choice. On average, each manager mentioned three different motives for engaging in bootstrapping, which indicates that the decision is complex and far from merely due to lack of capital.

With regard to the relative importance of the motives, the analysis shows that 'Lower costs' was the most important, followed by 'Lack of capital' and, slightly surprisingly, the existential motive 'Fun helping others and getting help'. On the other hand, 'Freedom of action' was the least important motive of those examined. The two most important motives are identical to the findings of the explorative study by Winborg (2005). However, in that study the two motives were found to be more or less equal in importance, whereas in the present study 'Lower costs' was found to be much more important than 'Lack of capital'. The motives for using bootstrapping can, in turn, be classified as either economic or existential in nature. The findings clearly show that economic motives are the most important, although existential aspects are of some importance.

In addition to the aim of examining the importance of different motives, this study also seeks to identify variables that influence them. For this reason, the respondents were classified into one of two groups: 'economic motives' and 'economic and existential motives'. The analysis shows that the owner situation, type of company, line of industry, need for long-term finance, driving force and experience of the line of industry all have a significant impact on the motives. On the other hand, it was surprising that growth ambition and start-up experience did not appear to have any significant influence, as indicated by the tentative findings of Winborg (2005).

In more general terms, the findings imply that the opportunity for the different motives behind bootstrapping is restricted by the way in which the business is run. If the business is a limited company with new owners having entered, the opportunity for motives other than strictly economic ones is extremely limited. The results also indicate that differences between businesses in various lines of industry in terms of values and norms are obvious with regard to the attitude to finance and, more specifically, the reasons for engaging in financial bootstrapping.

The conclusions presented above are based on data from new businesses established in business incubators. It can be questioned whether the findings are applicable to all new businesses or if they are specific to incubator businesses. Therefore future research should build upon this study by examining the motives behind the use of financial bootstrapping among new businesses in general.

Furthermore, it would be interesting for future research to extend this study to other countries. As conditions differ between countries (for example, legislation and norms/values), it seems reasonable to assume that the motives for using financial bootstrapping also differ. However, we do not know this for a fact. Thus it is up to future researchers to explore this aspect. Finally, the findings presented in this study show that the specific business situation has a major influence on the underlying motives. However, the data in the present survey did not allow us to study the process in which the motives behind the use of bootstrapping are formed and how they change over time. An interesting subject for future research would be to develop our understanding of this process.

REFERENCES

Barton, S.L. and C.M. Matthews (1989), 'Small firm financing: implications from a strategic management perspective', *Journal of Small Business Management*, **27**, 1–7.

Bhide, A. (1992), 'Bootstrap finance: the art of start-ups', *Harvard Business Review*, November–December, 109–17.

Freear, J., J.E. Sohl and W.E. Wetzel Jr (1995), 'Who bankrolls software entrepreneurs?', paper presented at the 15th Annual Babson College Entrepreneurship Research Conference, London, UK.

Harrison, R.T. and C.M. Mason (1997), 'Entrepreneurial growth strategies and venture performance in the software industry', paper presented at the 17th Annual Babson College Entrepreneurship Research Conference, Boston, USA.

Harrison, R.T., C.M. Mason and P. Girling (2004), 'Financial bootstrapping and venture development in the software industry', *Entrepreneurship and Regional Development*, **16**, 307–33.

Macneil, I.R. (1978), 'Contracts: adjustment of long-term economic relations under classical, neoclassical, and relational contract law', *Northwestern University Law Review*, **72**, 854–905.

Macneil, I.R. (1980), *The New Social Contract. An Inquiry into Modern Contractual Relations*, New Haven, CT: Yale University Press.

Neeley, L. (2003), 'Distinctive resource acquisition behaviors among U.S. entrepreneurs: small enterprises, their managers and bootstrap financing within cultural and economic contexts', paper presented at the 23rd Annual Babson College Entrepreneurship Research Conference, Boston, USA.

Norton, E. (1991), 'Capital structure and small growth firms', *Journal of Small Business Finance*, **1**, 161–77.

Van Auken, H.E. (2005), 'Differences in the usage of bootstrap financing among technology-based versus nontechnology-based firms', *Journal of Small Business Management*, **43**, 93–103.

Van Auken, H.E. and L. Neeley (1998), 'Evidence of bootstrap financing among small start-up firms', *Entrepreneurial and Small Business Finance*, **5**, 235–49.

Winborg, J. (2000), '*Financing small businesses. Developing our understanding of financial bootstrapping behavior*', PhD Thesis, School of Economics and Management, Lund University, Sweden.

Winborg, J. (2005), 'Motives for using financial bootstrapping in new businesses', paper presented at RENT XIX Conference, Naples, Italy.

Winborg, J. and H. Landström (1997), 'Financial bootstrapping in small businesses – a Resource-based view on small business finance', in P.D. Reynolds, W.D. Bygrave, N.M. Carter, P. Davidsson, W.B. Gartner, C.M. Mason and P.P. McDougall (eds), *Frontiers of Entrepreneurship Research*, Wellesley, MA: Babson College, pp. 471–85.

Winborg, J. and H. Landström (2001), 'Financial bootstrapping in small businesses: examining small business managers' resource acquisition behaviors', *Journal of Business Venturing*, **16**, 235–54.

PART III

Entrepreneurship in Family Firms

6. Transgenerational entrepreneurship: exploring entrepreneurial orientation in family firms

Mattias Nordqvist, Timothy G. Habbershon and Leif Melin

INTRODUCTION

Scholars seem to agree that corporate entrepreneurship is a useful concept to address how firms engage in change and renewal processes to maintain and improve their competitiveness. Entrepreneurial orientation (EO) represents a growing stream of literature on corporate entrepreneurship that focuses on decision-making styles and practices related to the entrepreneurial activities of firms. Recently, EO scholars have pointed to the need to explore the characteristics of EO and its dimensions in various types of organizations in greater depth (Lumpkin and Dess, 1996; Lyon et al., 2000). The underlying assumption is that EO might differ in important ways between organizational contexts.

Family firms are often considered to be the most common type of business firms, yet many management theories do not take the family dimension and involvement into account (Dyer, 2003). We argue in this chapter that family firms constitute a unique context for entrepreneurship. For instance, enduring interactions between individuals, the family and the firm may create specific family-related bundles of resources and capabilities that constrain or facilitate entrepreneurial activities (Habbershon et al., 2003). In addition, longer investment and ownership horizons (James, 1999) mean that many family firms strive for transgenerational entrepreneurship (Habbershon and Pistrui, 2002).

In the scarce literature on entrepreneurship in family firms it is possible to see two contradictory streams. One depicts family firms as a context where entrepreneurship flourishes and the other views family firms as conservative, introvert and inflexible (Zahra, 2005). However, both streams in the literature agree that more research is needed into entrepreneurial processes in family firms, and especially on EO in this type of organization (Naldi et al., 2007; Habbershon and Pistrui, 2002; Zahra et al., 2004).

The purpose of this chapter is therefore to draw on the EO construct (Miller, 1983; Covin and Slevin, 1989; 1991; Lumpkin and Dess, 1996) to investigate what characterizes transgenerational entrepreneurship in family firms and explore the conditions under which certain dimensions of EO are more present than others for high-performing family firms. In our analysis we also draw on the concept of duality, a theoretical notion which considers that two opposing principles might simultaneously form an entity without becoming a unity (Jackson, 1999; Achtenhagen and Melin, 2003). The duality notion is useful in our conceptual work since it helps us to capture the tensions of the family business context that we observe in both the literature review and the empirical fieldwork.

We make three contributions to the literature. First, we pay in-depth attention to the role of firm characteristics as context in EO studies, illustrated by the family firm context in this chapter. Second, we add to the literature on entrepreneurship in family firms by drawing on the established conceptual framework of entrepreneurial orientation to enhance the understanding of corporate entrepreneurship in the context of family business. Third, by applying the perspective of dualities, we move the fields of family business studies and entrepreneurship beyond the trade-off view of whether family firms have positive or negative characteristics in relation to entrepreneurial behavior. The chapter is structured as follows. We first review previous EO and family firm literature as well as the concept of duality. Second, we discuss the research approach and methods used in the empirical work. Third, we present our cases and the interpretive analysis with our findings about the role of three dualities for the entrepreneurial orientation in the studied firms. Finally, we provide some conclusions and implications, address the main limitations of the study and offer some possible avenues for future research.

ENTREPRENEURIAL ORIENTATION AND FAMILY FIRMS

We lean on Lumpkin and Dess's (1996, p. 136) influential definition of EO as 'the processes, practices, and decision-making activities that lead to new entry' where new entry is 'the act of launching a new venture'. They suggest five dimensions which determine if a firm has an EO. Proactiveness is about 'acting in anticipation of future problems, needs of changes', meaning a forward-looking perspective and search for new opportunities that are 'accompanied by innovative or new venture activity' (Lumpkin and Dess,

1996, p. 147). Risk-taking consists of activities 'such as borrowing heavily, committing a high percentage of resources to projects with uncertain outcomes and entering unknown markets' (Lyon et al., 2000, p. 1056). Innovativeness refers to 'a firm's tendency to engage in and support new ideas, novelty, experimentation, and creative processes that may result in new products, services, or technological processes' (Lumpkin and Dess, 1996, p. 142), while autonomy is about 'the independent action of an individual or a team in bringing forth an idea or a vision and carrying it through to completion' (Lumpkin and Dess, 1996, p. 140). This often means flexible organizational structures and open communication. Finally, competitive aggressiveness refers to 'a firm's propensity to directly and intensively challenge its competitors to achieve entry or improve position, that is, to outperform industry rivals in the market place' (Lumpkin and Dess, 1996, p. 148). Competitive aggressiveness can be reactive – a new entry that is an imitation of an existing product or service would be considered entrepreneurial if the move implies an aggressive, 'head-to-head' confrontation on the market.

The five dimensions of EO are separate but related constructs. It has been established that firms can vary in terms of how proactive, risk-taking, innovative, autonomous and competitively aggressive they are (Lumpkin and Dess, 1996). Firms do not have to be equally entrepreneurial across all five dimensions, even if the five dimensions are positively correlated (Rauch et al., 2004). The strength of EO dimensions and possible outcomes, such as growth and profitability, are often suggested to vary with context (Lumpkin and Dess, 1996; Covin et al., 1990). Firm type, size, ownership and age are possible contextual factors with a potential impact on EO. In this chapter our focus is on contextual features of family firms with a potential impact on EO.

Family firms are often depicted as a distinct type of firm (Gersick et al., 1997; Sharma et al., 1997; Habbershon et al., 2003). In particular, the family business literature addresses the consequences of the overlap between the family and the firm. A common argument is that family interests often impact on firm behavior, including entrepreneurial actions, with negative outcomes for the firm (Whiteside and Brown, 1991; Habbershon and Pistrui, 2002). For instance, the growth goal of a family member active in firm operations can be in conflict with non-active family members' desires for personal wealth accumulation (Hoy and Verser, 1994). A common assumption is that the family impedes on the growth and prosperity of the business especially in later generations.

Studies looking into entrepreneurship and family firms have, for instance, shown that a strong family-related business culture may impact on the ability to create and maintain entrepreneurial capabilities of family firms (Hall et al., 2001; Zahra et al., 2004). Naldi et al. (2007) studied the risk-taking dimension of EO. They found that family firms take risks, but less so than non-family firms and that risk-taking is negatively related to performance in family firms. Martin and Lumpkin (2003) found decreasing levels of EO measures on autonomy, risk-taking and competitive aggressiveness as later generations are involved in the family firm. They conclude that while founding generations are more motivated by entrepreneurial concerns, these become replaced with family concerns and an increasing family orientation through successive generations that appears to be in conflict with entrepreneurial orientation.

These findings suggest that family firms exhibit characteristics which may allow the family firm to be viewed as a unique context for EO. This is in line with Habbershon et al. (2003) who identify the close and long-lasting interactions between individuals, the firm and the family as a key feature of family firms with impact on organizational processes and behaviors, such as entrepreneurship. The unique systemic interactions in the family firm context give rise to unique bundles of resources and capabilities, labeled 'familiness' (Habbershon and Williams, 1999) that may both constrain and facilitate entrepreneurial activities. These insights lend support to our assumption that family firms can exhibit contextual features with impact on the characteristics and dimensions of EO. In order to investigate the specifics of the family firms and their impact on EO, a holistic and systemic approach is needed. Furthermore, the duality concept can help us to move beyond the role of balancing acts noted in previous corporate entrepreneurship literature (for example, Burgelman, 1983).

THE CONCEPT OF DUALITY

Jackson (1999, p. 549) argues that a duality simultaneously considers two opposite principles which might form an entity without becoming a unity. This means that analyzing just one pole of the duality does not capture its underlying logic. The notion of duality can be adapted to discuss tensions, which can only be fruitfully managed in their entirety. The challenge is not to choose between the two different poles but to accept, support and manage their simultaneous existence (Achtenhagen and Melin, 2003).

An important part of the distinctiveness of family firms as an organizational context is the systemic interactions between the individual, the firm and the family. These interactions from various forces give rise to simultaneously present tensions. From a duality approach, these tensions differ amongst family firms. And within a specific family firm they differ over time. This means that they cannot be managed in a 'one size fits all' solution. Traditionally, contradictions and tensions originating from the interactions between the family and the firm have been viewed as predominantly negative (Whiteside and Brown, 1991). Only recently have entrepreneurship scholars provided frameworks that address the positive outcomes of such tensions (for example, Habbershon et al., 2003). This view is in line with duality reasoning where authors argue that successfully managing these forces, tensions and contradictions in organizations might have positive outcomes (Poole and Van de Ven, 1989; Janssens and Steyaert, 1999). An example of a duality in the realm of entrepreneurship is 'risk-taking and calculating behavior', and an example of a duality from the family business arena is the 'family and the business'. Finally, two examples from the more general field of management are 'centralization and decentralization' and 'globalization and localization'. The notion of duality thus helps us to understand that the innovative challenge is not to choose between either one of two different poles or options but to manage their simultaneous existence (Achtenhagen and Melin, 2003).

We argue that the notion of dualities is relevant given the characteristics of the family firm, since it allows us to discuss tensions, dilemmas and perceived paradoxes that can be fruitfully managed in their entirety. In our view managing dualities is essentially about keeping tension-continuums with impact on entrepreneurial orientation taut. It therefore reflects a mindset or a way of thinking (Evans and Doz, 1992) that fruitfully integrates family firm and EO literature. Family firms are complex social entities that need to be studied holistically and systemically. Theorizing that allows and includes the ambiguity inherent in organizational life is therefore motivated to capture dualities as well as their relation to EO in the family firm arena.

METHODOLOGY

Several scholars of EO have called for more in-depth and qualitative research designs in order to better grasp and conceptualize the characteristics and dimensions of entrepreneurial orientation (Lumpkin and Dess, 1996; Lyon et al., 2000), including family firms (Zahra et al., 2004). The research reported here is based on epistemological underpinnings that put the lived experiences and narratives of human actors in the center. Drawing on an interpretive approach (Morgan and Smircich, 1980; Alvesson and Sköldberg, 2000), we were inspired by grounded theory (Glaser and Strauss, 1967; Strauss and Corbin, 1998) when conducting the research. The principles constant comparison (collecting and analyzing data simultaneously) and theoretical sampling (the findings and emerging theory determines the data to collect next) (Glaser and Strauss, 1967) guided the longitudinal research on entrepreneurial processes in two medium-sized family firms.

The two firms were conveniently sampled (Yin, 1994), based on the following criteria: (1) notable entrepreneurial activities during the last 30 years of development in line with their respective prioritized performance outcomes (that is, the sampled firm should have proven entrepreneurial performance in terms of innovation and new venture creation), (2) belonging to different B2B industries (one traditional manufacturing firm and one advanced service firm to include both old and new economy), (3) at least two generations of family involved as owners and managers to capture the transgenerational family involvement, and (4) access to the firm, the family and the processes under investigation. Table 6.1 summarizes the main characteristics of the studied firms, here called BFS and Habo to maintain their anonymity.

The data collection was designed to enable historical reconstructions and descriptions of real-time actions. The first author of this chapter, Mattias Nordqvist, conducted a total of 67 interviews with people at different levels and with different relations to the firms to capture holistic and perspective-rich descriptions. Family members were interviewed first; non-family board member and top managers, second; and other actors from the same and other categories last in a snowball fashion (cf. Glaser and Strauss, 1967). All interviews were audio taped, transcribed verbatim and guided by a questionnaire with rather open thematic questions. The aim was to facilitate the respondent to give an undirected and narrative account at the beginning of the interview, while asking more specific questions later. Site visits were also made, especially company tours, observation of one strategic planning meeting (Habo), and casual interactions with employees and family members in order to immerse and support a richer understanding of the empirical settings (Langley, 1999). Following Pettigrew (1990) we compiled, as a first level of interpretation, the empirical material into detailed and process-oriented case descriptions. Emerging insights guided our further reading of theory, which also led to new data collection. This systematic interplay between theory and data is recommended in grounded theory-inspired research (Eisenhardt, 1989; Suddaby, 2006) and points to the iterative, creative way of conducting research where a clear separation of theory and data is not seen as an ideal (Strauss and Corbin, 1998). In the next interpretive stage we started to code the data more systematically according to the five dimensions of EO, and the conceptual framework suggesting that the uniqueness of family firms for their entrepreneurial behavior originates from the systemic interactions between the family, the individual and the firm. In this process we also started to search for patterns in the empirical material that could be interpreted as key themes/conceptual categories for

*Table 6.1 Key characteristics of the two family firms**

Key characteristics	*Habo 1999/2003*	*BFS 1999/2003*
Multidivisional group structure	No/No	Yes/Yes
No. of employees (group)	210/414	150/118
No. of employees (focus firm)	210/414	129/87
No. of family members working	Five/four	Three/Two
Total operating income (focus firm)	410/801 SEKm	390/151 SEKm
Profitability (net profit)	38/9.9 SEKm	62/1.4 SEKm
Growth last 5 years (turnover)	96%	−56%*
Growth last 5 years (employees)	100%	−33%
Industry	Manufacturing of agricultural machines (B2B)	Financial services (B2B)
Industry growth (time of study)	Low/Low	High/low
Year founded	1962	1906
Current generation (managing)	2nd/2nd	2nd/2nd, 3rd
No. of core families as owners	Three	Two
No. of family board members	Six/Six	Two/Four
External board members	No/Yes	Yes/Yes
External chairman of the board	No/No	No/No
Family CEO (group)	−/−	Yes/Yes
Family CEO (focus firm)	Yes/Yes	No/Yes
Formal education level of group CEO	−/−	MBA/MBA
Formal education level of CEO	Grade school, 7 years/Grade school 7 years	MSc, Business/ MSc, Business
Managerial experience outside firm, group CEO	−/−	No/No
Managerial experience outside firm, CEO	No/No	Yes/Yes

Note: * These firms were divided into several firms in 1998–99, growth estimated 1998–2003 for these firms.

understanding the specifics of EO in the family firm context. The focus was on exploring whether some dimensions in the EO construct were more visible and important than others in order to understand the entrepreneurial activities, as well as the family's involvement in these.

The themes/conceptual categories that we searched for had to directly address the family influence on EO. In this interpretive process, which was supported by evolving reading of the literature, the role of three dualities became apparent, even if at this point we did not use the language of duality to label our observations. However, searching for a way to interpret the meaning of these three themes, we soon turned to the duality concept. The three identified dualities were: (1) the Historical and New Paths duality, (2) the Independence and Dependence duality and (3) the Formality and Informality duality. These dualities not only increased our understanding of the unique systemic family firm context on EO, but also aided our understanding of the relative presence and importance of different dimensions of EO. In brief, we found that, rather than families embracing one aspect of the duality, their entrepreneurial context was established by viewing the dualities as 'tension-continuums' which are kept taut by 'pulling on' both sides of the continuum simultaneously. Naming the three dualities and reinterpreting their meaning for EO in the two case firms, we reiterated the analysis, complementing it with theoretical support in order to conceptualize our findings and generate analytical generalizations to elaborate and adjust current theory (that is, EO in the context of transgenerational family firms). Analytical generalizations mean that we generalize to theory rather than to a population of firms (c.f. Yin, 1994). The result of our research thus needs to be further explored and tested empirically before statistical generalization is possible and/or the extent to which the found dualities can be applied to non-family firms as well.

In the following empirical section we present the three dualities/themes identified, integrated with case descriptions. To visualize the family business context we focus particularly on how the systemic interactions between individuals, the firm and the family relate to EO. It should be pointed out, however, that this type of presentation mode misses some of the richness and direct experience of the interviewees' narratives and actions.

ILLUSTRATIONS OF EO IN TWO FAMILY FIRMS

The Historical/New Path Duality

Family firms are known for their tradition, a characteristic that is often seen as a source of inertia and constraint on entrepreneurial behavior. Our study suggests, however, that the path dependent histories of family firms are not always negative, but are a tension with which families wrestle. When the 'historical paths' are seen in conjunction with their 'new paths', we discovered a duality that helps understand decisions and strategies observed in family firms. This tension-continuum shows how the demands for stability from the owner-family's legacy are balanced with the firm's need for renewal and entrepreneurial activities in order to stay competitive. We interpret the Historical/New Path continuum as providing the two firms with both an 'anchor' and 'adaptive' capabilities for entrepreneurial behavior. Sometimes, but not always, this duality is driven by tensions between the old and the young generations.

In the case of BFS, the Historical/New Path continuum is seen overtly in their motto 'tradition and novel thinking'. This front door demonstration of keeping the tension taut underlines that the firm intentionally strives to combine the historical legacy and strengths with demands for renewal and change in order to remain competitive. The family has been in banking since 1906 and from 1911 the main business has been stock brokerage. In the early 1990s Charles Borgman launched his vision of 'the bank of the twenty-first century'. Describing their firm, the family is careful to note that they are 'strong believers in continuity that has a long-term view on enterprising'. They also communicate that the firm is family-owned and family members are proud of their heritage as described on their website, 'Despite our strong traditions we are constantly looking ahead for new challenges and opportunities.'

Maintaining his father's main focus of the business on securities trading and investment banking, Mr Borgman developed the firm during the 1960s, 1970s and early 1980s with the launch of several innovative products and services. One was the Borgman Stockmarket Guide. This innovation contained a revolutionary new way of conducting financial analyses of publicly traded firms in Sweden. It formed the basis for additional businesses within BFS that would be very successful during the 1970s and 1980s. During the 1980s and early 1990s BFS grew even more rapidly as a result of innovations and diversification made possible by a general deregulation of financial markets. BFS was, for instance, the first stock brokerage in Sweden trading on the fixed income market in 1988 and in 1996 among the first two to start trading securities over the internet.

Mr Borgman was group CEO until 2003 when his son Ted Borgman replaced him. Three years earlier he had returned to the firm to work closely with his father. He wanted to learn from him and his way of thinking and managing. Ted Borgman describes himself as 'very different' from his father and more like his grandfather, who was more interested in the core business – securities trading – whereas his father is more interested in 'building and growing businesses'. As CEO, Ted Borgman moved from a highly diversified firm to a more focused firm that deals with the traditional core business. Much of the previous diversification was led by a non-family CEO through risky IT ventures. During that era the firm moved away from its core competence, that is to say, their 'tradition', overemphasizing renewal through increasingly unrelated diversification. Both loyal employees and customers were having trouble recognizing the 'old, stable Borgman'. Together with his father, Ted Borgman returned the firm to its soul – with improved profitability and a lower degree of risk-taking.

Habo started in 1962 when the founder, a farmer, felt the need for better products and equipment. He invented a new type of clod-crusher that he began selling when neighboring farmers understood that the innovative construction was efficient. Over the years, the owner-family and Habo has always embraced their history as farmers. Some say that farming is still their core business. Remembering that farming is part of their history is what forms the basis of their renewal commitments. Habo's commitment to both the historical and newness through innovation is what allows them to focus on customers and market trends and less on moves among competitors. This posture was observed, for instance, during a strategic planning meeting where the consultant facilitator pushed for conducting better analysis of competitors. The CEO replied, 'I can't see how analyzing our competitors will improve our products and make farming more efficient for our customers.' With a solid base in key-products for farming, Habo has been able to continuously innovate and launch new products such as a seed-drill and a harrow that has revolutionized the market and created new standards for competitors. Following their tradition, they are careful to maintain the close contacts with farming practice and have a wide network of colleagues and customers in their international markets where they test innovations and capture trends.

To institutionalize their history and tradition, Habo turned the barn, where the founder had started production, into an industry museum. The family is also famous for hosting customers in their home, 'at least until we grew so that it was impossible to make sandwiches for all the customers', one family member reported. In keeping with their commitment to new paths, they bought a nearby farm, transforming it into a testing farm for new products and as a customer meeting place. Keeping the tension taut between old and new paths enables them to engage in a dialogue about their different family risk profiles. Mr Smith, the CEO, eldest son and main owner in the second generation, personifies the ambitious growth target of 20 per cent. 'Perhaps it's not such a big deal to achieve it one year, but if you can do it year after year for ten years, then it becomes exciting,' he says. The other five family members would prefer a lower growth target, since they don't see the point in growing into a large firm where the character of the family firm might get lost.

The Independence/Dependence Duality

We found that family and firm level autonomy was a positive trait for EO when held in tension with a sense of dependence upon other 'forces and sources' of feedback. Family ownership and control allows the family firm to be entrepreneurial through autonomous actions, but it is also critical to seek contributions to their entrepreneurial commitments from different actors outside the owner-family, indicating a certain degree of dependence.

Through their history, BFS has demonstrated a positive dependence on people outside the core family members. They have had an active board with highly competent external members since the late 1960s. These board members have often acted to legitimize and control in line with increasing demands from outside monitors in the financial services industry, but they have advised on many new venture ideas and renewal projects. In BFS many ideas for new ventures came from Charles for many years and, in later phases, many ideas and initiatives for organizational renewal came from his son. However the contribution from non-family employees has also been crucial, especially during the 1980s and 1990s. In this period BFS grew considerably as a result of new products and ventures. For instance, the internet-based stock brokerage was clearly in line with Charles's overall vision of the bank of the twenty-first century, but it originated with and was launched by a non-family CEO.

Charles has worked actively to attract the 'best and the brightest' of the graduates from business schools. For many years the firm was seen as a 'nursery' for the future financial elite in Sweden. While the family ownership has made it difficult at times to retain talented people who wanted to become partners and co-owners of the firm, the family has nevertheless always viewed non-family leaders as critical to their success. At the other end of the continuum, the desire to keep ownership within the family is described as an advantage for long-term development, giving BFS autonomy to act in the marketplace. Family leaders point out that their independence (from other firms and/or large power-blocks in the Swedish business community) gives them freedom to act as they prefer. This is seen as an advantage because they do not have to follow the short-term trends in the financial industry. The focus on autonomy to act is manifested in Charles's principle to maintain high equity ratios whatever the cost. This is frustrating for many in the firm. They argue that they could expand much faster and more aggressively if this principle was loosened. Charles and other family members are aware of this critique, but today they prefer slower growth than to become dependent on either outside financiers or on risky investments in new ventures. Their shared view is that even if risk is taken in new ventures, risk should be 'controlled' and 'minimized'.

In Habo the owner-family has realized that it needs to show more dependence on non-family leadership if they want to grow. The family has always been very visible and active in both ownership and management. The firm has never had a non-family CEO, and Mr Smith's long tenure is characterized by his dominance in both product and market development. The head of sales and marketing in Scandinavia and the head of production are also family members. It was not until 2002 that an external member was elected to the board. Since the 1990s, they have tried to institutionalize their dependence by organizing product development into two areas with more than 30 employees: firstly, adjusting and refining existing products and, secondly, innovating and creating new products. The head of product development is a non-family member, though Mr Smith is heavily involved.

In 2003 Habo recruited a head of administration and finance, which was a new position, in order to free more time for the CEO to work with product and market development. Market development through internationalization during the late 1980s and 1990s was a key to growth. A family member was initially responsible for this area, but it was not until a non-family manager was recruited that expansion really took place. With this growth and involvement of non-family leaders, some family members have worried about losing control. In order to counter these fears, the family has attempted to recruit and hire managers and other key people who have similar values as the family. Value perpetuation is thus a necessary condition for the family to assume more dependence on others within the organization. There is awareness that Habo might be too dependent on a small number of individuals for its continued growth, especially on Mr Smith with his ability to transform 'unpronounceable customer needs to desired innovations', as a top manager puts it.

When it comes to finances and risk profile, the family does not want to be dependent on outsiders, but rather to act more autonomously. Growth has always been financed from retained profits; they have a tradition of low dividends, and family members have rather low salaries. They also refuse to use excessive debt to grow. 'We're not dependent on anyone financially, there's no one that can put pressure on us to act in a certain way,' one family member stated. This financial position makes the firm flexible and more long-term oriented. 'They prioritize growth goals and intend to expand differently than other growth firms. Their strategy for growth is different and it is largely rooted in the spirit of entrepreneurship within Habo,' a non-family member says. The independence provided by family ownership is also important in the eyes of their customers who, when given a choice, prefer to do business with 'people like themselves and who can talk their language'. This family autonomy is a competitive advantage, providing family leaders with the opportunity to keep family ownership and control.

The Formality and Informality Duality

The third tension continuum is that of informality and formality. A hallmark of family firms is their reliance on informal and intuitive organizational practices. This has been noted as both an advantage, especially in early stage companies and entrepreneurial actions, but also as a potential disadvantage, since over time family firms need to move to more formal structures and practices in order to continue their growth (for example, Gersick et al., 1997). By placing the two perspectives on the tension-continuum we see that in our cases families may pull on both sides of the continuum. We found that the ability to manage the tension between an increased need for formalization as a result of growth and the informal and flexible way of working needed to provide a creative climate for new entrepreneurial ideas and new ventures is pivotal to maintain long-run EO.

Many describe the climate in BFS as flexible, informal and creative, offering freedom for co-workers to come up with new ventures and ideas for improvements. This working style is attached to the leadership style of Mr Borgman. Mark Borgman, his father, was stricter and more interested in keeping close control on both employees and the firm's development. During Mr Borgman's time the flexible working style that characterizes the company is an open atmosphere, informal interaction and strategic discussions with employees. Mr Borgman dislikes formalization and has tried to avoid it as much as possible during the growth process. However during the 1980s and late 1990s increased demands from industry-related regulators and monitoring authorities meant that more formal procedures and routines were forced to be implemented. Returning to the family firm, Ted Borgman also gave priority to 'structure and create some kind of order, with a clearer division of responsibilities between different parts of the firm'. He reported that some co-workers enjoyed the open and informal working style and closeness to the owners, but adds that many also felt that expectations and rules were unclear, which led to frustration. He also implemented a more structured strategic planning process, unlike his father, who never worked with formal planning. He referred to his informal interactions and mutual testing of new ideas with key employees and the spontaneous and unstructured vision talks that he gives to the board as the strategic planning process of the firm. He stated that 'an entrepreneurial firm is one with visible, active and decisive ownership with visions'.

Interviewees reported that informality and flexibility are important to maintaining 'the creative and entrepreneurial spirit' that has characterized the firm since Mr Borgman took over in the late 1960s. This gives rise to a quick decision-making process, where new ideas, rapidly and without prestige or too many demands, can be tested among quickly assembled groups. One non-family manager pointed to the advantage of having the main owner 'only half a wedge' away and his son as the boss. 'If I get the go ahead from them, I know it's just to act.' It would be bad to 'formalize this away' even if some admit that 'some order' is needed. One example of this type of order that still has informality is the 'sauna club' started by Ted, where key actors meet 'with some regularity but under informal circumstances' to discuss new ventures and organizational changes.

There were also attempts to formalize the owner-family's relation with the firm, but the family council did not find its role in relation to the rest of the governance structure. The owner-family's influence in the firm's development is now channeled through the board where three family members serve. Nevertheless, voices remain within the owner-family that would like to formalize their influence to a greater extent, especially since not all family members completely share the view on how to achieve the overall goal of profitability.

For many years Habo has kept the 'small, family firm character' with close relations between the owners and the employees. Many people working in the firm are easy-going and rooted in both the village of Habo and the local farming community. Most members of the owner-family are social, which has supported the informal and open atmosphere in the firm. The founder is still a common sight at the firm and likes to talk about how both the organization and its products can be improved. For many years a formal strategic planning process did not exist. Instead the CEO and the non-family marketing manager traveled to customers to gather impressions and ideas for new products. Once back at the firm, they talked informally with other people to start the actual product development process. Lately, however, there has been increased formalization, largely because of the growth achieved. The recruitment of a head of administration and finance is a result of this movement. Moreover, an external consultant has helped to implement a vision planning process where a group of six to seven top managers (including two family members) meet regularly to analyze and finalize the five, three and one year vision of the firm's development. The vision planning process meant that both the family and the employees could share a clearer view on the direction of the firm for the future. There is some fear that too much trust is put in the formal strategic work and that 'people stop thinking continuously about the future and about new products', according to the consultant. Another aspect of the formalization is that the expressed vision is then approved or dismissed by the board. The latter also have more regular meetings since the external board member was included. Both within the family and within the vision group there is a concern that the flexibility, informality and friendly climate that characterizes the firm will disappear as more structure and procedures are implemented to secure the organization. There is especially a risk that foreign subsidiaries of the company are not embraced by the same values and attitudes of the mother company, as the CEO explained. For this reason, the firm recruited its first Human Resources Management (HRM) manager in 2002, who, together with the CEO, works to 'define and write down the culture, so that we can spread our entrepreneurial spirit'. Several non-family members reported that a main reason why they work at Habo is the nice and open character of the firm. New ideas and initiatives are encouraged, they say, and it is easy to get hold of family members to explore the ideas. 'Everybody works hard here. We support and trust each other. It is possible to realize yourself here and it's more fun to work for a visible owner that you're also good friends with. But there is also a risk that this disappears when we grow and we get new people here that are not embraced by and used to this,' says a top manager.

INTERPRETIVE ANALYSIS

Having established the family context of our case firms around the dualities presented as three tension-continuums, we can move to an interpretive analysis of how these relate to the firm's EO. Our empirical observations suggest that in the two family firms the five dimensions of EO may be decoupled when explaining their importance and impact for transgenerational entrepreneurial performance. Interpreting EO with the two case firms as a basis, it is revealed that a firm does not have to be entrepreneurial across all dimensions of EO to reach desired performance outcomes over time. Drawing on the notion of dualities we can see how family firm characteristics, conceptualized as the three tension-continuums, give rise to a specific impact on EO.

In order to systematically elaborate on the relationship of these tension-continuums and the EO of the two case firms, we provide Table 6.2 as our outline. The table shows the three tension-continuums/dualities by the five dimensions of EO with interpretive evaluations of their respective strength. The interpretations are only meant to provide relative comparisons of the

Table 6.2 The three dualities and EO in the two family firms

	Risk-taking	Aggressiveness	Proactiveness	Innovativeness	Autonomy
Historical paths/New paths	−−	−−−	+	+++	+
Independence/ Dependence	−−−	−−	++	+++	+++
Informality/ Formality	−−	−−	+++	+++	++

relationships rather than measurements of outcomes. One – or +, for example, indicates a mild positive or negative relationship, while two or three suggest stronger positive or negative relationships.

The Relative Seclusion of the Risk-taking and Competitive Aggressiveness Dimensions

Our interpretation is that when actors in the two family firms keep the three tension-continuums taut, there are less signs of risk-taking and competitive aggressiveness in comparison to proactiveness, innovativeness and autonomy. When risk-taking is defined as 'borrowing heavily, committing a high percentage of resources to projects with uncertain outcomes and entering unknown markets' (Lyon et al., 2000, p. 1056), interviewees gave little voice to this behavior, leading us to characterize it as a negative (−) relationship overall. This is in line with previous literature in which family firms have been shown to be longer-term oriented with low tolerance for bold risk (Zahra et al., 2004); when they have taken a considerable risk it has been found that it has negative implications for performance (Naldi et al., 2007). Less aggressive risk-taking may relate to a fear of losing the family legacy wealth (James, 1999; Schulze et al., 2003) and/or family reputation (Bartholomeusz and Tanewski, 2006), which are not reasons voiced in our study.

However, we also interpret that less aggressive risk posture does not necessarily mean less innovativeness and proactiveness in entrepreneurial activities. The duality of Independence/Dependence gave the family firms more freedom to act independently in relation to competitors and the external environment, that is, with less boldness and risk. Correspondingly, the more that family members engaged in activities that demonstrated their dependence on others (such as boards and trusted employees), the more they were comfortable advancing, but along more traditional paths. In Habo, for instance, with the family's strong value of independence and a growing dependence, they moved into international markets, but did so in a low risk fashion, which was consistent with their relationship-based and local knowledge-building approach. In comparison to Dependence/Independence, we saw that risk-taking had less of a relationship with Historical/New Paths and even less so with Informality/Formality. In the two family firms Historical/New Paths led actors to pursue the firms' normal entrepreneurial growth, rather than seeking more risky options. Their Informality/Formality did not encourage risk-taking, but neither did it seem to discourage it.

Similarly, we suggest that Independence/Dependence and Historical/New Paths have a negative connection to competitive aggressiveness as shown in Table 6.2. Very few interviewees gave voice to a need to 'take a competitor head on' (Lumpkin and Dess, 1996). This characteristic of family firms was also widely experienced as important by non-family members. Ironically, as the family became more dependent on non-family people in the firm, it gave them more confidence in their ability to build competencies to compete without overly considering actions by competitors. As noted above, in both firms Historical/New Paths were so interactive that the families viewed their new paths as extensions of their historical paths. They knew that entrepreneurial performance was historically tied to 'newness' in relation to customers and this drove their entrepreneurial actions, rather than a focus on the behavior of their competitors. As with the risk-taking dimension, Informality/Formality seemed to be less of a factor in relation to competitive aggressiveness. This interpretation seems to be in keeping with Martin and Lumpkin (2003), in that there are decreasing levels of competitive aggressiveness and risk-taking as firms pass through the generations. It also finds support in studies showing that family firms often focus more on their internal capability building and competitive resource base than on external strategizing (Miller and LeBreton-Miller, 2005; Nordqvist, 2005).

The Primacy of the Proactiveness and Innovativeness Dimensions

Both BFS and Habo could be described as proactive in their entrepreneurial behavior. There were many descriptions of how strategic initiatives were 'anticipating and pursuing opportunities' and 'acting in anticipation of future problems, needs or changes' (Lumpkin and Dess, 1996; Lyon et al., 2000). We suggest that the Informality/Formality duality is the most meaningful with respect to the ability to act proactively. Habo, for example, was characterized by an entrepreneurial spirit and creativity that promoted proactive innovation. Actors felt that this proactive innovation capability was sustained by the informal climate that was rooted in their farming culture, which was shared by the whole family and several key non-family employees. There were also descriptions of close customer connections in the farming community as a key driver of entrepreneurship and innovation. Similarly, actors in BFS described their firm as much more proactive when compared to others in the financial services sector, which they attributed to the informal practices associated with leading family members, especially Mr Borgman. At the same time, more formal practices increased in importance in both firms, for example in the way strategizing took form.

Independence/Dependence was also related to the firms' proactiveness, though with somewhat less intensity as indicated in Table 6.2. One reason why actors described themselves as proactive in their innovations was because they believed they could be. They saw a family-based independence of the firm to act 'as they saw fit'. Similarly, as they built new capabilities through dependence (adding non-family board members and managers to the family core), this reinforced their need to be proactive. Lastly, as illustrated in Table 6.2, Historical/New Paths had slightly less connection to proactiveness. This is explained by the fact that while both families were clearly committed to New Paths, their Historical Paths led them to being somewhat less proactive than they could have been.

We interpret that innovativeness most fully describes the overall entrepreneurial behavior of the two firms. Non-family and family members in both firms described significant investments in R&D in the core business, as well as notable support for new ideas, experimentation and creative processes, which resulted in new products services and technological advancements. This is in line with the notion of innovativeness in Lumpkin and Dess (1996). Correspondingly, we describe the relationship of innovativeness to all three tension-continuums as equally strong in Table 6.2. Habo and BFS made renewal through innovation part of their Historical Path. The New and Historical were fully integrated, especially in Habo. Similarly, actors in both firms believed that their family-related independence gave them freedom to act. This separated their innovation capabilities from their competitors, at least within their growth/risk profile parameters. As the families and their firms built more dependence capabilities, they did so in a way that also enhanced and/or ensured their innovative capabilities. Pulling on the ends of the Independence/Dependence tension-continuum thus fostered their innovativeness.

In some respects, the informality of the firms described by interviewees can be interpreted as a critical part of their innovativeness. Because so much of their innovation was rooted in intuitive actions and they associated these actions with informality, it was hard for them to imagine that they could be equally innovative in a more formal atmosphere. But family members in both firms were intentionally pulling on the Formality side of the continuum. They realized that they were outgrowing their 'pure' informality-based intuition and needed to add new and more formal approaches. Strategic planning was one method used to add formality, as was building new human resource capabilities that were tied to their family-based values. As a consequence, keeping the Informality/Formality tension-continuum taut seems to be critical to enduring innovativeness and EO in family firms.

Extending the Autonomy Dimension

While autonomy, in the sense of granting freedom inside the organization to be creative, to push for ideas and to change current ways of doing things (Lumpkin and Dess, 1996) and open communication and flexible organizational structures (Miller, 1983), had a strong meaning on all three tension-continuums, History/New Paths seemed less so than the other tension-continuums and could also be interpreted as having a mildly negative impact on the autonomy dimension of EO (see Table 6.2). In both firms the tradition was rooted in the family, their culture and history. The family's commitments to 'the new' were seen as dependent upon family leadership involvement and capability building. This family dominance can be interpreted as putting some constraints on allowing people to act autonomously. The families didn't stop creative actions, but they often viewed their involvement as critical, thereby slowing down some entrepreneurial activities championed by non-family members. In other words, the family presence and involvement, to some extent, hampered the part of the autonomy dimension, which Martin and Lumpkin (2003, p. 2) refer to as the ability for organizational members to 'carry ventures through to completion without relying on the support or approval of others'. In this family context the 'others' were not just managers, but also different family members seen as representing ownership. Informal leadership and the involvement of family members, originating not just from their formal position in the firm but also from their family membership, bred the belief that the family leaders were irreplaceable and unreplicable, representing unique resources in their firms, which can be interpreted in the following way.

The autonomy dimension of EO in the family firm context is also about family (often older) members letting go and leaving entrepreneurial space for new actors. Experiencing a lack of this space, it is difficult and often frustrating for other family or non-family actors to feel the autonomy they need to act entrepreneurially. In the cases we studied, we observed that when moving towards a more taut tension with Formality, the firms also moved, despite greater formalization, towards greater autonomy for a wider group of individuals. This movement towards Formality in both cases is why we describe it as having a stronger impact on autonomy than Historical/New Paths. However, we describe the EO dimension of autonomy as being most strongly related to Independence/Dependence. Because family members so clearly felt and highly valued their independence, the priority given to independence was seen as an important legacy to pass on over generations. Over time and across generations, however, the families and the firms also developed more dependence on non-family members, which can be seen to increase the internal organizational autonomy, while possibly decreasing the external family autonomy.

This touches on an interesting expansion of the EO autonomy dimension, emerging from our research. We interpret the impact of the Independence/Dependence duality on EO as having a meaning that extends beyond the traditional notion of autonomy. Until today, the EO literature sees autonomy as internal autonomy related to empowering individuals and teams within an organization, providing them with sufficient freedom to be creative (Miller, 1983; Lumpkin and Dess, 1996). In our cases we see that EO in the family firm context is at least as much about external autonomy. The family firms we studied contain actors with a desire to be autonomous in relation to external constituents, such as banks, financial markets, suppliers and customers. They also had a desire to be autonomous in relation to what they perceived as 'too much non-family influence' in their entrepreneurial activities. In both firms the external autonomy can be interpreted as a central value in their family's way of being entrepreneurial over time. Still, even if a strong sense of autonomy towards external stakeholders and monitors characterizes these two family firms, there is also a need to seek support and feedback from actors outside both the family and the firm in order to avoid being too closed and introvert (Zahra et al., 2004). This means that family firms who keep the Independence/Dependence tension taut generate both an internal and external autonomy, which support maintaining an EO. This is an interesting expansion of the EO construct that should be further explored in future research.

CONCLUSIONS AND IMPLICATIONS

Supported by previous literature (for example, Lumpkin and Dess, 1996; Lyon et al., 2000), we conclude that a family firm does not have to be entrepreneurial across all dimensions of EO to reach desired entrepreneurial performance outcomes. We propose that family firm characteristics give rise to at least three dualities with evident impact on EO: Historical/New Paths, Independence/Dependence and Informality/Formality. Based on our in-depth case research we suggest that the risk-taking and competitive aggressiveness dimensions of the EO are less important in family firms, where the three identified dualities are present and kept taut. Conversely, we propose that specific characteristics of family firms as seen in these dualities mean that autonomy, innovativeness and proactiveness are more present dimensions of EO and with greater meaning for transgenerational entrepreneurship. This conclusion supports the assertion that dimensions of EO may occur in different combinations depending on the context (Lumpkin and Dess, 1996), and that the effectiveness of EO is related to the contexts in which organizational activity takes place (Lumpkin et al., 2006).

Contrary to some earlier studies, we see that both over time and across generations characteristics that support a sustained entrepreneurial orientation can emerge alongside increased family orientation. Martin and Lumpkin (2003) concluded that while founding generations are more motivated by entrepreneurial actions, these were replaced with family concerns and a greater family orientation in later generations. Our cases suggest that family firms can be more entrepreneurial, especially on the proactiveness, innovativeness and autonomy dimensions and, thereby, sustain an EO for transgenerational entrepreneurship. This lends support to the argument that family firms can stay entrepreneurial, even with increasing family concerns and involvement. However, in tune with the notion of managing dualities, it requires a certain way of thinking and acting (Evans and Doz, 1992). This observation is in line with previous arguments by Habbershon and Pistrui (2002) on the distinctive mindset of 'enterprising families'. It is also supported by Zahra et al. (2004) who, drawing on RBV, found that family-influenced cultures perpetuated within family firms potentially promote and sustain entrepreneurial activities.

With the application of the duality perspective we have shown that family orientation and entrepreneurial orientation are not necessarily contradictory. To maintain an EO and support transgenerational entrepreneurship we suggest owner-families manage the three dualities as tension-continuums and keep them taut. This view is different from the dichotomous view of competing demands between the family and the firm that require trade-off decisions towards one side or the other, which hampers entrepreneurship. This polarized view has, for a long time, dominated the family firm literature. Indeed, the concept of dualities addresses tensions and seeming contradictions that arise from opposite forces, which are simultaneously present in activities in most organizations. However, in line with Poole and Van de Ven (1989), we have found that the three dualities seen as tension-continuums have, if kept taut, constructive meaning for EO over time. To keep these tensions taut means that some dimensions of EO are more present and critical than others.

Implications, Limitations and Future Research

From a practice perspective we conclude that for a family firm to stay entrepreneurial over time and maintain an EO across generations there must be an awareness of the three family-related dualities and intentional strategies designed to accept and manage them. Managing the three dualities means simultaneously 'pulling on both ends' of the tension-continuums, rather than leaning too much towards one side of the duality. For instance, family and non-family managers must both intentionally cultivate the Historical Paths that led to their success while simultaneously developing New Paths. Practitioners must therefore seek to capitalize on their Informality while bringing more Formality to their organization. They must act out of their sense of Independence while creating more Dependence on the views and involvement of non-family members. This approach is very different from the current thinking and practice in the fields of family business and entrepreneurship.

The research reported in this study is not without limitations. Given the early stage of knowledge in this particular area, our approach has been deliberately broad and exploratory. A more focused study on, for instance, the innovativeness or the risk-taking dimension of EO in the family firm context would have revealed more detailed insights about parts of the EO constructs, rather than the broader contribution of our research. In our empirical study we investigated two firms that had a clear record of entrepreneurial processes and outcomes. Although our purpose was to explore entrepreneurial family firms, comparing entrepreneurial with non-entrepreneurial family firms would probably have made other processes and activities visible than those we have interpreted. Moreover, family firms are not a homogenous population. Using the label family firms, as we have done, may lead to the impression that we treat all family firms as the same. That is not the case. Indeed, the heterogeneous nature of the family firm population is, we believe, a main argument to compare family firms rather than the more traditional approach to compare family and non-family firms.

We believe there is a large potential in future research that further elaborates on the EO construct in the family firm context, perhaps by using other supporting theories and methodologies. For instance, investigating EO in family firms through a systematic use of the resource-based view and theories of dynamic capabilities would be interesting. To complement our research approach we believe it would be interesting to detect larger patterns and relationships of EO in a large sample of family firms using survey data and other quantitative research methods, thus making statistical generalizations possible. Finally, we need to study both other categories of family firms and non-family firms using the duality perspective in order to find out if the three dualities presented here – the Historical/New Paths duality, the Independence/Dependence duality and the Formality/Informality duality – can be applied to other firms as well.

REFERENCES

Achtenhagen, L. and L. Melin (2003), 'Managing the homogeneity-heterogeneity duality', in A.R. Pettigrew, A. Whittington, L. Melin, C. Sánchez-Runde, F.A.J. Van den Bosch, W. Ruigrok and T. Numagami (eds), *Innovative Forms of Organizing: International Perspectives*, London: Sage, pp. 301–27.

Alvesson, M. and K. Sköldberg (2000), *Reflexive Methodology*, London: Sage.

Bartholomeusz, S. and G.A. Tanewski (2006), 'The relationship between family firms and corporate governance', *Journal of Small Business Management*, **44**(2), 245–67.

Burgelman, R.A. (1983), 'Corporate entrepreneurship and strategic management: insights from a process study', *Management Science*, **29**(12), 1349–64.

Covin, J.G. and D.P. Slevin (1989), 'Strategic management of small firms in hostile and benign environments', *Strategic Management Journal*, **10**(1), 75–87.

Covin, J.G. and D.P. Slevin (1991), 'A conceptual model of entrepreneurship as firm behavior', *Entrepreneurship Theory and Practice*, **16**(1), 7–25.

Covin, J.G., D.P. Slevin and T.J. Covin (1990), 'Content and performance of growth-seeking strategies: a comparison of small firms in high-and low-technology industries', *Journal of Business Venturing*, **5**, 391–412.

Dyer, G.W. Jr (2003), 'The family: the missing variable in organizational research', *Entrepreneurship Theory and Practice*, **27**(4), 401.

Eisenhardt, K.M. (1989), 'Building theories from case study research', *Academy of Management Review*, **15**(4), 532–50.

Evans, P. and Y. Doz (1992), 'Dualities: a paradigm for human resource and organizational development in complex multinationals', in V. Pucik, N.M. Tichy and K.K Barnett (eds), *Globalizing Management: Creating and Leading the Competitive Organization*, New York: Wiley, pp. 85–106.

Gersick, K.E., J.A. Davis, M. McCollom Hampton and I. Lansberg (1997), *Generation to Generation: Life cycles of the Family Business*, Boston, MA: Harvard Business School Press.

Glaser, B.G. and A.L. Strauss (1967), *The Discovery of Grounded Theory: Strategies for Qualitative Research*, New York: Aldine.

Habbershon, T.G. and J. Pistrui (2002), 'Enterprising families domain: family-influenced ownership groups in pursuit of transgenerational wealth', *Family Business Review*, **15**(3), 223–37.

Habbershon, T. and M.L. Williams (1999), 'A resource-based framework for assessing the strategic advantages of family firms', *Family Business Review*, **12**(1), 1–26.

Habbershon, T.G., M.L. Williams and I.C. MacMillan (2003), 'A unified systems perspective of family firm performance', *Journal of Business Venturing*, **18**, 451–65.

Hall, A., L. Melin and M. Nordqvist (2001), 'Entrepreneurship as radical change in family business: exploring the role of cultural patterns', *Family Business Review*, **14**(3), 193–208.

Hoy, F. and T.G. Verser (1994), 'Emerging business, emerging field: entrepreneurship and the family firm', *Entrepreneurship Theory and Practice*, **19**(1), 9–23.

Jackson, W.A. (1999), 'Dualism, duality and the complexity of economic institutions', *International Journal of Social Economics*, **26**(4), 545–58.

James, H.S. (1999), 'Owners as manager, extended horizons and the family firm', *International Journal of the Economics of Business*, **6**(1), 41–55.

Janssens, M. and C. Steyaert (1999), 'The world in two and a third way out? The concept of duality in organization theory and practice', *Scandinavian Journal of Management*, **15**(2), 121–39.

Langley, A. (1999), 'Strategies for theorizing from process data', *Academy of Management Review*, **24**(4), 691–710.

Lumpkin, G.T. and G.G. Dess (1996), 'Clarifying the entrepreneurial orientation construct and linking it to performance', *Academy of Management Review*, **21**(1), 135–72.

Lumpkin, G.T., W.J Wales and M.D. Ensley (2006), 'Assessing the context for corporate entrepreneurship: the role of entrepreneurial orientation', in M. Rice and T. Habbershon (eds), *Praeger Perspectives on Entrepreneurship*, Vol. III, Westport, CA: Praeger Publishers, pp. 49–77.

Lyon, D.W., G.T. Lumpkin and G.G. Dess (2000), 'Enhancing entrepreneurial orientation research: operationalizing and measuring a key strategic decision making process', *Journal of Management*, **26**(5), 1055–85.
Martin, W.L. and G.T. Lumpkin (2003), 'From entrepreneurial orientation to family orientation: generational differences in the management of family businesses', paper presented at the 22nd Babson College Entrepreneurship Research Conference, Babson College, Wellesley, MA, USA.
Miller, D. (1983), 'The correlates of entrepreneurship in three types of firms', *Management Science*, **29**(7), 770–91.
Miller, D. and I. LeBreton-Miller (2005), *Managing for the Long Run: Lessons in Competitive Advantage from Great Family Businesses*, Boston, MA: Harvard Business School Press.
Morgan, G. and L. Smircich (1980), 'The case for qualitative research', *Academy of Management Review*, **5**(4), 491–500.
Naldi, L., M. Nordqvist, K. Sjöberg and J. Wiklund (2007), 'Entrepreneurial orientation, risk taking and performance in family firms', *Family Business Review*, **10**(1), 33–47.
Nordqvist, M. (2005), 'Understanding the role of ownership in strategizing: a study of family firms', JIBS Dissertation Series, no. 029, Jönköping International Business School, Sweden.
Pettigrew, A. (1990), 'Longitudinal field research on change: theory and practice', *Organization Science*, **1**(3), 267–92.
Poole, M.S. and A.H. Van de Ven (1989), 'Using paradox to build management and organizational theories', *Academy of Management Review*, **14**(4), 562–78.
Rauch, A., J. Wiklund, M. Freese and G.T. Lumpkin (2004), 'Entrepreneurial orientation and business performance: cumulative empirical evidence', paper presented at the 23rd Babson College Entrepreneurship Research Conference, Glasgow, UK.
Schulze, W.S., M.H. Lubatkin and R.N. Dino (2003), 'Toward a theory of agency and altruism in family firms', *Journal of Business Venturing*, **18**, 473–90.
Sharma, P., J.J. Chrisman and J.H. Chua (1997), 'Strategic management of the family business: past research and future challenges', *Family Business Review*, **10**(1), 1–36.
Strauss, A. and J. Corbin (1998), *Basics of Qualitative Research: Techniques and Procedures for Developing Grounded Theory* (2nd edn), Thousand Oaks, CA: Sage.
Suddaby, R. (2006), 'From the editors: what grounded theory is not', *Academy of Management Journal*, **49**(4), 633–42.
Whiteside, M.F. and F.H. Brown (1991), 'Drawback of a dual systems approach to family firms: can we expand our thinking?', *Family Business Review*, **4**(4), 383–95.
Yin, R.K. (1994), *Case Study Research: Design and Methods* (3rd edn), Newbury Park: Sage.
Zahra, S.A. (2005), 'Entrepreneurial risk taking in family firms', *Family Business Review*, **18**(1), 23–40.
Zahra, S.A., J.C. Hayton and C. Salvato (2004), 'Entrepreneurship in family vs. non family firms: a resource based analysis of the effect of organizational culture', *Entrepreneurship Theory and Practice*, **28**(4), 363–81.

7. Financing and growth behavior of family firms: differences between first- and next-generation-managed firms

Vincent Molly, Eddy Laveren and Ann Jorissen

INTRODUCTION

The interest in family business studies has increased rapidly over the years, leading to a distinctive legitimate field of study in organizational research. Up until now, there has been considerable interest in exploring family businesses' financial structure and performance, mainly based on a comparison of family firms considered as a 'homogeneous group' with their non-familial counterparts. Recently, however, researchers in family business studies are encouraged to reconsider the definition of a family firm, which will no longer start from the idea of an either or scenario but instead from the varying extent and nature of family involvement in a firm (Astrachan et al., 2002; Sharma, 2002; Tsang, 2002). We try to capture this central idea of a 'heterogeneity approach' in family business studies by distinguishing between different generations of family firms, which can make future comparisons with non-family businesses more meaningful. The aim in this chapter is to use first-generation family firms as a reference category for describing the behavior in later generations of family firms.

Several authors agree on the fact that the success of family firms depends on the effective management of the overlap between the family and the business, as they aim to achieve a combination of both financial and non-financial goals (Sharma, 2004). In this respect, one of the biggest challenges of family firms lies in the accommodation of the path of growth to the availability of financial resources in order to maintain control within family boundaries. We try to further refine previous insights into the financing and growth behavior of family firms by using the concepts of 'sustainable growth' and 'internal growth' (Higgins, 1977; Kyd, 1981; Demirgüç-Kunt and Maksimovic, 1998). This will reveal useful information on the influence that a firm's capital structure and financing decisions have on the growth realized by the company. More specifically, we shall look in this chapter at the financing sources that small and medium-sized private family firms prefer and whether this choice is consistent over different generations of family firms.

The chapter is structured as follows: the next section starts with a literature review resulting in the formulation of testable hypotheses. The third section provides information on the sample and discusses the statistical methodology. In the fourth section the empirical results are presented. A discussion and conclusions are included in the final section.

LITERATURE REVIEW AND FORMULATION OF HYPOTHESES

Financing Behavior in Family Firms

When studying different generations of family firms, the most referenced work in this respect is the book of Gersick et al. (1997), who describe three broad phases of family firm ownership dispersion, besides the development over time in the family and the business sub-system. According to them, a family firm can undergo three general stages of ownership starting with the founding owner or couple holding the shares, after whom second-generation sibling partners may jointly own the firm, and finally ownership passes to a third-generation cousin consortium in which ownership is widely dispersed throughout the family. According to the authors, family firms going through this evolution could experience better conditions in seeking debt finance from financing institutions. Especially if the transition of the firm from one generation to the next is managed successfully, these companies could build on long-term and solid relationships with their bank, giving them the status of more reliable debtors. They also point to the importance of financial planning in light of current and anticipated retirements of family members. If family businesses move from founder- to descendant-controlled family firms, the probability increases that more family members want to be bought out. Given that internal funds are limited, an increased need for external financial means (for example, debt) can be expected from the moment next-generation family members take over the business. Based on these literature findings, one could expect higher debt levels in second- and third-generation family firms.

Contrary to the above formulated ideas, other authors like Anderson et al. (2003) found evidence that bondholders can consider the transfer of a family business from the founder to the next generation as harmful to their wealth, leading them to provide less capital to descendant-controlled family firms, unless higher interest yields can be incurred. This is in line with Jensen and Meckling's theory (1976), which states that agency costs can arise due to asymmetric information between shareholders and bondholders. The idea behind this reasoning is that succession in family firms can involve less qualified founder-descendants to lead the company if the selection of a candidate is solely based on the existence of family ties, resulting in a detrimental effect on company performance. In addition, an increase in the number of active and passive shareholders can be expected after succession, leading to higher dividend payout ratios and less attention for reinvesting retained earnings (Schwass, 2005). As more persons like brothers and sisters, aunts and uncles, cousins and in-laws get involved in the business, intra-family conflicts and rivalry could also arise, as shown by Davis and Harveston (1999) and Harvey and Evans (1995). They identified a pattern of rising conflict with each succession in a family business. In this way, second- and third-generation managed family firms are expected to be more financially constrained in comparison with their founder-controlled counterparts, leading to lower levels of debt in their capital structure.

Besides the agency theory, researchers often start from the frameworks of the 'pecking order theory'. According to Myers (1984) firms have a preferred hierarchy for financing decisions. The highest preference is to use internal financing before resorting to any form of external funds. This idea also holds true with respect to family firms, where several authors found that most owners of family firms are eager to pay off debt (for example, Ward, 1987; Coleman and Carsky, 1999; Romano et al., 2001; Miller and Le Breton-Miller, 2005). Over time, when the company starts to prosper, they avoid an excessive level of indebtedness. If cash is generated, it will mainly be used to reduce the amount of debt in the capital structure of the company. This line of reasoning totally complies with the family's strong desire to successfully transfer a healthy company over different generations as a way of safeguarding the wealth, the security and the tradition of the family. Failure of the company would be seen as a violation of the family's name and a huge loss of the life work created by the founder. Miller and Le Breton-Miller (2006) found that this stress on firm survival may result in a conservative financial policy, namely lower levels of debt and larger cash holdings.

Finally, with respect to the owner's descendants, Kaye and Hamilton (2004) identified that they are usually less willing to take risk compared to their parents. As they have a higher preference for wealth preservation instead of further wealth creation, this can result, amongst other things, in a lower debt-oriented capital structure and higher cash levels. In other words, we expect lower levels of debt and larger cash holdings from the moment next-generation family members get involved in the company. This brings us to the following hypotheses:

Hypothesis 1a: First-generation family firms will realize higher debt levels compared to second- and third-generation family firms.

Hypothesis 1b: First-generation family firms will realize lower cash levels compared to second- and third-generation family firms.

Growth Behavior in Family Firms

In empirical literature on family businesses there exists some discrepancy with respect to the influence that different generations exert on the firm's growth behavior. Zahra (2005) found that from the moment new generations of family members become actively involved in the company, a higher focus on wealth increase and strategic renewal will arise. The author explains this behavior based on the idea that with each succession in a firm, new family members bring fresh knowledge and insights into the company, positively affecting the incentive to innovate. Similar evidence was found by the study of Fernández and Nieto (2005), although here the internationalization strategy of different generations of family firms is emphasized. A positive influence could be identified between the evolution in family firms over generations and the decision to internationalize. Again new ideas, new strategies and better prepared family members were mentioned as the main motive behind this evolution. So, based on these findings we could expect that next-generation family firms will realize higher growth figures compared to their first-generation counterparts.

However, contrary to these findings, several researchers revealed opposite results with respect to the effect of family business succession on growth behavior. They typically state that the growth of family businesses is strongly connected to the study of lifecycle issues. Ward's model (1987) for example, starts from the complex interactions between the family and the business, to find evidence that family firms can differ according to their sought goals and priorities, which shift over time. In this way, firms exist where the business serves the family (family orientation) or where the family serves the business (business orientation). In accordance with this model, evidence was found that first-generation family firms are less family oriented in comparison with subsequent generations, and that firms with a business orientation have a higher capacity to grow (Dunn, 1995; Cromie et al., 1995). Reid et al. (1999) used these same ideas to suggest that first-generation family firms grow at a faster rate compared with subsequent generations of family firms, and that for the latter type of firms family goals (family orientation) become more desirable than 'rational economic issues' like growth. Referring to the entrepreneurial orientation concept, first introduced by Miller (1983) and further developed by Covin and Slevin (1986; 1989), Martin and Lumpkin (2003) found that in successive generations entrepreneurial orientation tends to diminish and give way to family orientation, as stability and inheritance concerns become the businesses' principal drivers.

McConaughy and Phillips (1999) compared growth between founder- and descendant-controlled family firms. They found that second- and later generation family firms invest less in capital equipment and R&D, and exploit less new technologies and markets, leading to slower growth compared to founder-controlled family firms. Miller and Le Breton-Miller (2006) came to the same conclusion of slower growth as generations in family firms progress. According to their research, an explanation for this evolution can be found in the increasing demand for dividends as family businesses enter second or later generations, thus strongly reducing the availability of financial means needed to support the firm's development and growth.

In several studies agency theory forms the basis for explaining performance differences. By investigating alignment of interests between managers and owners, several authors have indicated that family firms suffer less from 'misalignment costs' due to the almost perfect overlap among owners and managers. However, recently, attention has been drawn towards the existence of altruism or specific features of family firms, such as free riding, ineffective managers, and the non-alignment of interests among the non-employed family shareholders and the top management team, which can all increase agency costs and thus lead to lower growth (Bruce and Waldman, 1990; Kellermanns and Eddleston, 2004). As it is expected that the existence of these problems increases as family firms develop, lower growth figures can be assumed in later generation family firms. Based on these literature findings, we therefore hypothesize that:

Hypothesis 2: First-generation family firms will grow faster compared to second-and third-generation family firms.

Linkage Between Financing and Growth Behavior

In any company there usually exists a complex relationship between investment, financing and profit distribution decisions and the financial performance and rate of growth which are achieved. Far from being seen as merely an ex post outcome of the many operating and financial decisions an owner-manager has taken, the rate of growth of a business enterprise should be considered as a strategic decision variable in the same sense that planned capital expenditures, target capital structure and desired profit distributions are ex ante decisions made in light of the strategic and financial goals of a company. The rate of growth, for instance, can be so high that the enterprise concerned is unable to fund the additional current and fixed assets which become necessary. If the expansion continues, it is inevitable that a point will be reached where funding of further growth requires either that profit retentions be increased or that the enterprise seeks external financing. With regard to SMEs it is very realistic to assume that they have less financial funds available and also a more limited access to external funds (for example, Chittenden et al., 1996; Sogorb-Mira, 2005). Here bankruptcy can become the consequence of outstanding success.

There have been a number of attempts in the literature to formalize the understanding of the important relationship between investment, financing and profit distribution decisions and the rate of enterprise growth in small to medium-sized enterprises (for example, McMahon et al., 1993; Berger and Udell, 1998; Berggren et al., 2000; Becchetti and Trovato, 2002; Gregory et al., 2005). Probably the most well known and widely accepted concept referring to the linkage between financing and growth behavior is that of 'sustainable growth'. This concept, also known as 'supportable', 'affordable' or 'attainable' growth, is well described in both the academic literature and practitioner journals. The most referenced version goes back to Higgins (1977) and Kyd (1981) who defined this term as the annual growth rate that is consistent with the firm's established financial policies, given that the company wants to maintain a target dividend payout ratio and a target capital structure without issuing new equity. It can be derived from the following equation:

$$\mathrm{D}_t = g_t * \mathrm{Assets}_{t-1} - \mathrm{Earnings}_t * b_t \qquad (7.1)$$

where D_t represents the amount of borrowing needed at time t if the firm is to grow at a rate of g_t, and b_t is the proportion of the firm's earnings after interest and taxes that are retained for reinvestment. The expression clearly shows that the external financing need can be derived from the difference between the required investment for a company growing at g_t per cent and the internally available capital for investment, given a constant dividend payout ratio.

Based on Equation (7.1) two different estimates of a firm's maximum attainable growth rate can be calculated: the internally financed growth rate and the sustainable growth rate. With regard to the first measure, it is expected that no external financial means will be used, so that growth is funded by exclusively relying on internal financial means. In this way, by equating D_t to zero and solving the equation for g_t, the following model can be derived:

$$IG = b_t * ROA_0 \tag{7.2}$$

where ROA_0 can be defined as the ratio of earnings after taxes and interest in period t to total assets based on opening figures (period $t-1$).

In accordance with Demirgüç-Kunt and Maksimovic (1998) we could also derive the sustainable growth rate (SG) which expresses the maximum growth rate that can be financed without resorting to external equity finance or altering the present financial structure. It can be calculated based on Equation (7.1) by using the book value of equity instead of total assets, and setting D_t to zero. Solving the equation for the growth rate results in:

$$SG = b_t * ROE_0 \tag{7.3}$$

where ROE_0 is the ratio of net income at time t to opening equity.

As previously mentioned, useful information on what financing decisions are taken in a firm in order to realize a certain growth behavior can be derived from the comparison of the actual growth rate with the internal growth level (IG in Equation (7.2)) and the sustainable level (SG in Equation (7.3)). A graphical representation is given in Figure 7.1. A company growing at a rate below or equal to the IG is able to fund its growth by exclusively relying on internally generated financial means (field A). If the realized growth lies in between IG and SG (field B), the firm will need additional external finance like debt to fund its growth. However these firms will use less debt so that their debt/equity ratio will fall below its current level. If higher growth than SG is realized (field C), management can consider different options like issuing new equity, reducing planned profit distributions (dividends) or increasing the anticipated use of debt

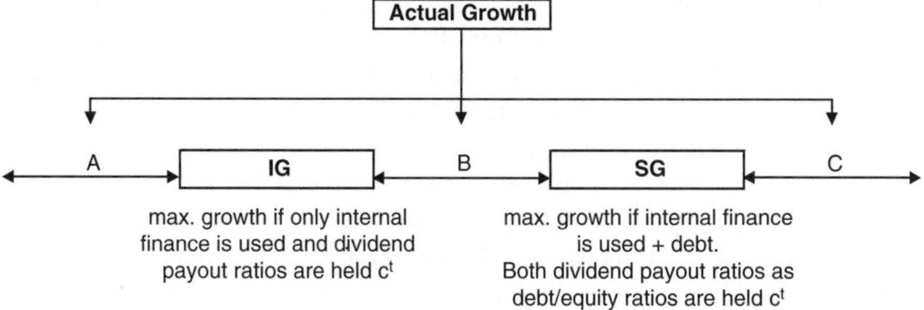

Figure 7.1 Comparison of actual growth and internal/sustainable growth

finance above the current debt/equity ratio, given the enterprise's current financial position and its access to the capital market.[1]

Examples of previous studies that applied the internal and sustainable growth concepts to family businesses are rather scarce. Ward (1987) and Carlock and Ward (2001) however, made reference in their books to this concept as an interesting measure to assess a (family) firm's financial situation. Attention is drawn to the fact that in family firms one of the greatest, but most difficult, challenges lies in the question of how to accommodate the path of growth to the availability of financial resources in order to maintain control within the family. Investment opportunities can arise that need funding beyond the family wealth or beyond the target level of indebtedness. In such situations the choice has to be made between an increased bankruptcy risk or the postponement of the investment project. In this respect the concept of internal/sustainable growth can be used as a measure for risk tolerance.

Referring to the literature on the financing behavior in family firms, and the pecking order theory, it may be clear that management of a family business will try to avoid excessive amounts of debt in its balance structure or the issuance of new external finance, which ultimately results in the abandonment of investment opportunities, and therefore in lower realized growth. With respect to intergenerational difference in family firms, Reid et al. (1999), based on their finding that 'family orientation' becomes more important as family firms develop, postulate that 'family first' firms are more reluctant to use external sources of capital as family control can dilute this, even if it was to support growth. In line with Donckels and Fröhlich (1991), they suggest that these firms will finance growth rather from internal than 'risky' external sources of finance, such as debt or venture capital. Other studies confirm this changing 'risk attitude' and increasing fear of losing control as family firms progress from one generation to the next (for example, Cromie et al., 1995; Kaye and Hamilton, 2004).

Schulze et al. (2003) also describe the changing risk attitude of different generations of family firms, although their results are based on agency theoretical ideas. They start from the fact that there is a high chance in family firms of equity ownership becoming more diffuse with each transition to a next generation. As this can lead to a divergence of interests between shareholders who serve on the boards of these closely held firms they will find it prudent to reduce financial leverage, as increased corporate risk has a direct effect on the safety of their personal investments. The effect of this suboptimal capital structure is that the rate of firm growth is largely limited to the growth rate of internally generated capital.

Referring to Equations (7.2) and (7.3), we are interested to find useful information on the extent to which family firms are willing to take on additional amounts of debt to fund their growth, by comparing the actual growth rate with the internal and sustainable growth levels. For this purpose, only 'fast-growing' family firms are selected, resulting in two subsamples. The first will contain only those firms that grow faster than their internal growth rate, and the second will consist of firms that grow faster than their sustainable growth rate. We expect to find that the absolute differences between the actual growth rate and the internal or sustainable growth levels, respectively, will vary across generations. Therefore our last two hypotheses are:

Hypothesis 3a: The absolute difference between the actual growth rate (AG) and the internal growth rate (IG) in first-generation family firms will be higher compared to second- and third-generation family firms.

Hypothesis 3b: The absolute difference between the actual growth rate (AG) and the sustainable growth rate (SG) in first-generation family firms will be higher compared to second- and third-generation family firms.

DATA AND METHODOLOGY

This research is based both on quantitative and qualitative data in order to investigate intergenerational differences within family firms. The qualitative information was taken from a large-scale written survey sent to the managing directors of 8367 companies in the Flanders region (northern part of Belgium). Based on size, industry and location characteristics of all Flemish firms that have published financial statements over the years 1998–2004, a three-dimensional matrix was designed. This time span of seven years resulted in the exclusion of start-ups in the study as these firms do not have financial information available over the entire period. In a second step 10 per cent of this population was chosen at random according to the percentages of the three-dimensional matrix. Within this group of 21 640 companies, only those with at least five full-time employees received a questionnaire (8367 companies), as micro-firms are expected to behave differently due to the absence of formal management teams. A total of 839 usable responses were received. Besides this survey information, quantitative data were gathered for all of these 839 firms using the Bel-first DVD of Bureau Van Dijk, containing detailed financial information on 304 000 Belgian companies. Using chi-square tests we compared firm size (employment, assets), industry and location (province) between the responding firms and the original 8367 firms of the survey population. With respect to all variables, except firm size, the population of respondents had the same characteristics as the original population of 8367 firms. Respondents were, however, found to be significantly ($p < 1$ per cent) larger than the original 8367 firms. Further statistical analyses on the characteristics of the hundred earliest versus the hundred latest respondents did not reveal the existence of a non-response bias.

The next step concerned a sample reduction owing to the focus in this study on private small- and medium-sized enterprises. Respondents which proved to be listed firms and which employed more than 250 employees were ignored. With regard to identifying family firms within our sample, one can appeal to different definitions used in the literature. In this study a firm is classified as a family firm when the family possesses the majority of the shares and the CEO perceives the firm as a family firm. This classification, which is consistent with Westhead's (1997) definition, resulted in a sample of 613 family businesses.

Finally, family firms were categorized as first-, second- or third-generation-managed companies. For this purpose we relied on the questionnaire that assessed which generation at that moment was actively involved in the management of the firm. The classification was made in correspondence with Sonfield and Lussier (2004), meaning that first-generation family firms were companies still actively managed by the founder. Second- or third-generation family firms did not need to include other members of earlier generations, as they could already be retired from the firm or deceased, meaning that not all generations need to be currently participating in the company. As past studies suggest that it is important to distinguish between family influence from the founding generation and the influence arising from a descendent of the founding generation (for example, McConaughy et al., 2001; Randøy and Goel, 2003), information on founder involvement was also included in the analysis.

Table 7.1 highlights some of the characteristics of the companies included in our study. A total of 168 companies could be identified as first-generation family firms, 250 as second-generation family firms and 143 as third-generation family firms. In about half of the second-generation family firms the founder was still actively involved in the company, whereas this share dropped to 22 per cent in third-generation firms. As expected, a rising pattern in the number of years of operation and the size of the company could be identified when comparing different generations of family firms. On average, first-generation family firms have been in business for 19 years, whereas second- and third-generation family firms have 32 and 56 years of operation, respectively. With regard to the size of the company measured by means of the total assets, we find mean figures ranging from

Table 7.1 Profile of sample firms

Characteristics	1st gen. FF (Mean)	2nd gen. FF (Mean)	3rd gen. FF (Mean)
Number of firms	168 (30%)	250 (45%)	143 (25%)
Firm proportion: founder involvement	100%	50%	22%
Industry: construction	44 (26%)	45 (18%)	29 (20%)
manufacturing	36 (21%)	71 (29%)	50 (35%)
wholesale	31 (19%)	57 (23%)	25 (17%)
retail	19 (11%)	28 (11%)	10 (7%)
services	25 (15%)	26 (10%)	11 (8%)
other	13 (8%)	23 (9%)	18 (13%)
Employment in FTE	19	23	30
Firm age	19	32	56
Mean assets (euro)	2 469 176	2 709 683	3 938 815
Total debt/total assets (mean)	68%	62%	55%
Total cash/total assets (mean)	11%	13%	15%
Assets growth (mean)	9%	8%	4%
Internal growth (mean)	1.99%	0.38%	0.80%
Sustainable growth (mean)	6.67%	3.67%	2.97%
Firm proportion: financing constrained[a]	40%	32%	27%
Retention rate[b] (mean)	65%	77%	83%
Growth objectives: no objective	70 (42%)	99 (41%)	62 (44%)
slow growth	21 (13%)	20 (8%)	20 (14%)
average growth	58 (35%)	100 (41%)	52 (36%)
fast growth	16 (10%)	23 (10%)	8 (6%)

Notes:

[a] The survey included a question assessing whether firms experienced financing constraints in funding their growth.

[b] The retention rate is calculated as 1−(dividend payout ratio).

2.5 million euros to 3.9 million euros. If size is measured by looking at total employment, the same conclusion holds true, as the average number of full-time equivalents increases from 19 to 30 employees. These dissimilarities in age and size proved to be statistically significant at the 5 per cent level. When looking at industry differences, second- and third-generation family firms seem to be more oriented towards the manufacturing sector, whereas first-generation family firms are more concentrated in the construction and services industries. Again, these differences were statistically significant at the 5 per cent level.

As Table 7.1 makes clear, different generations of family firms differ with respect to some business-related variables like age, size and industry. Therefore we control for these variables in order to identify a pure generation effect. In addition, other business characteristics related to growth objectives and financing constraints are included in our analysis. An overview of these variables, together with a short description of how they are calculated, can be found in the Appendix. Corresponding to the work of Rajan and Zingales (1995), Ozkan and Ozkan (2004) and Demirgüç-Kunt and Maksimovic (1998), we further include some other determinants in analyzing a company's level of indebtedness, cash holdings and excess growth, such as, return on assets, fixed assets to total assets, dividend payments to total assets, cash flow to total assets, bank borrowings to total debt and standard deviation of cash flows to average total assets. These variables are also defined in the Appendix.

In this study all hypotheses are tested by relying on multiple regression analysis to identify differences in the financing and growth behavior of first-, second- and third-generation family firms. The whole sample of family firms are taken into consideration for testing Hypotheses 1a, 1b and 2. For Hypotheses 3a and 3b, however, two sub-samples are derived containing 410 and 290 family firms, respectively (either based on firms growing faster than their internal growth rate or their sustainable growth rate). The reason for this approach lies in the fact that we want to investigate how much these internal/sustainable growth rates are exceeded in these companies, as this gives information as to what extent different generations of family firms are willing to take on additional amounts of debt in funding their growth. For all regression analyses, preliminary checks are conducted to ensure that there is no violation of the assumptions underlying this technique. In addition, our model was checked for its robustness against outliers in the sample.

EMPIRICAL RESULTS

As described in Table 7.1, the total debt rate has the tendency to decrease sharply from 68 per cent, to 62 per cent, and to 55 per cent when comparing family firms managed by first-, second- and third-generation family members. Additionally, when examining whether the companies in our sample suffered from any financing constraints (Table 7.1), it could be identified that next-generation family firms experienced less problems (significant at the 5 per cent level) with regard to the availability of bank finance. When integrating this information into our regression analysis, together with business characteristics, results are obtained as described in Table 7.2.

Table 7.2 clearly shows that the identified decrease in the level of indebtedness between different generations of family firms still holds after con-

Table 7.2 Regression analysis (dependent variable: debt/total assets)

Independent Variables	*B*	*Beta*	Significance
(Constant)	0.693		0.000***
Age	0.000	−0.047	0.326
Size (employment)	0.001	0.156	0.000***
2nd versus 1st generation dummy	−0.043	−0.094	0.093*
3rd versus 1st generation dummy	−0.129	−0.252	0.000***
Founder * 2nd generation	−0.017	−0.031	0.522
Founder * 3rd generation	0.109	0.111	0.009***
Financing constrained dummy	0.146	0.305	0.000***
Fixed assets/Total assets	0.258	0.219	0.000***
Profitability	−0.005	−0.199	0.000***
$R^2 = 0.293$ $F = 14.802$			

Notes:
The estimated model is: leverage $= \alpha + \beta_1$Age $+ \beta_2$Size $+ \beta_3$Construction $+ \beta_4$Manufacturing $+ \beta_5$Wholesale $+ \beta_6$Retail $+ \beta_7$Services $+ \beta_8$Generation21 $+ \beta_9$Generation31 $+ \beta_{10}$Founder*Generation21 $+ \beta_{11}$Founder*Generation31 $+ \beta_{12}$Profit $+ \beta_{13}$FA/TA $+ \beta_{14}$Fin.Constr. Estimations are based on OLS Regression. The dependent variable is the mean of total debt to total assets over the period 1999–2004.
***, **, * indicate statistical significance at 1, 5 and 10 per cent respectively.

trolling for several business characteristics. Compared to first-generation firms, next-generation family businesses have a significantly lower debt/total assets ratio. With respect to founder involvement, no dissimilarities in financing behavior exist between second-generation firms in which the founder is still actively involved and those in which the management is solely in the hands of the descendents of the founder. In third-generation family firms this difference seems to become relevant, as founder involvement has the tendency to increase the debt/total assets ratio. One of the explanations could lie in the fact that this small group of founder-managed third-generation family firms proved to be rather young companies, as their mean age averaged around 20. This could indicate that in these firms the evolution towards the third generation did not purely result from succession, but rather from the foundation of the company by multiple generations of family members. In this way, one can expect that the financing behavior of these firms will deviate from their counterparts actively managed by descendents, as the former type of firm will be less characterized by ownership dispersion and conflicts. Further, more profitable firms seem to attract less debt finance, which seems quite logical as these firms have a higher capacity to fund their business internally. A positive significant effect can also be found with respect to the ratio of fixed assets to total assets. The rationale underlying this effect is that tangible assets can serve as collateral, which results in lower agency costs of debt. Finally, firms experiencing financing constraints prove to have higher debt levels. This last positive effect probably results from the fact that companies were questioned about this issue at the end of 2001, meaning that their answer is based on their past and current use of debt, which is exactly measured by the dependent variable in our model.

With respect to Hypothesis 1b, it is already clear from the figures in Table 7.1 that next-generation family firms realize higher cash holdings compared to their first-generation counterparts. Table 7.3 shows that even after controlling for some business characteristics this conclusion still holds, although the difference only proves to be significant when comparing third- and first-generation firms. Again, we find some effect of founder involvement in third-generation family firms. It is further clear that a significant negative effect exists between the rate of dividends to total assets and the total level of cash. Referring to Ozkan and Ozkan (2004), this gives evidence of the idea that firms who pay dividends can raise funds relatively easily by cutting their dividend payout ratio. The same negative effect can

Table 7.3 Regression analysis (dependent variable: cash/total assets)

Independent Variables	*B*	*Beta*	Significance
(Constant)	0.094		0.000***
Age	0.000	0.044	0.376
Size (employment)	0.000	−0.068	0.117
2nd versus 1st generation dummy	0.018	0.070	0.232
3rd versus 1st generation dummy	0.057	0.193	0.001***
Founder * 2nd generation	0.016	0.049	0.327
Founder * 3rd generation	−0.043	−0.076	0.082*
Dividends/Total assets	−0.776	−0.184	0.000***
Cash flow/Total assets	0.160	0.094	0.036**
Bank debt/Total debt	−0.334	−0.324	0.000***
Variability	0.047	0.018	0.646
$R^2=0.223$ $F=9.785$			

Notes:
The estimated model is: cash $= \alpha + \beta_1$Age $+ \beta_2$Size $+ \beta_3$Construction $+ \beta_4$Manufacturing $+ \beta_5$Wholesale $+ \beta_6$Retail $+ \beta_7$Services $+ \beta_8$Generation21 $+ \beta_9$Generation31 $+ \beta_{10}$Founder*Generation21 $+ \beta_{11}$Founder*Generation31 $+ \beta_{12}$Div/TA $+ \beta_{13}$CashFlow/TA $+ \beta_{14}$BankDebt/Debt $+ \beta_{15}$Variability. Estimations are based on OLS Regression. The dependent variable is the mean of total cash and equivalent items to total assets over the period 1999–2004.
***, **, * indicate statistical significance at 1, 5 and 10 per cent respectively.

be found with respect to total bank borrowings. Given that banks fulfill a monitoring and screening role, the existence of bank relationships results in easier access to external finance, which further reduces a firm's need to hold cash. Finally, as expected, firms who realize higher cash flows are able to accumulate more cash. With respect to cash flow volatility, no significant effect can be found. Overall, the above results lead to the acceptance of Hypotheses 1a and 1b stating that next-generation family firms realize lower debt levels but higher cash holdings compared to first-generation family firms. And these are exactly two basic characteristics of financial conservative companies.

In order to test our second hypothesis, which makes assumptions about the realized growth in different generations of family firms, again regression analysis is used. As, in addition to general business characteristics, information was available on the growth objectives of the firms in our sample, this information was also included in the regression analysis. Referring to Table 7.1, no evidence was found that the three types of family firms significantly differ in their growth objectives. In fact, about 42 per cent of all three revealed that growth is not a main issue in the company's objectives. For the remaining 58 per cent of the businesses of different generations, a more or less equal distribution can be identified between firms having slow, average or fast growth ambitions. Results of the regression are included in Table 7.4.

We can derive from Table 7.4 that family firms evolving from the first to the second generation, and subsequently to the third generation, seem to face slower growth in their total assets. A significant effect of more than 4 per cent can be identified between first- and third-generation family firms, even after correcting for business-related variables. It is further clear that realizing high profit figures, and seeking fast growth objectives, is positively related to the realized growth rates in our sample firms. Overall, this results in the acceptance of Hypothesis 2, which states that first-generation family firms will grow faster compared to next-generation family firms.

One of the explanations of the above differences could lie in the relationship that exists between financing and growth behavior. As suggested in the literature, small and medium-sized enterprises in general, and family firms more specifically, have a clear preference for internal funds in financing their activities, indicating a strong dependence on this source of finance in realizing their growth. However, sooner or later, for example due to attractive growth opportunities, family firms will come to a point where their current capital structure and level of indebtedness must be reconsidered. This is where the concepts of internal and sustainable growth become interesting, as they can deliver insights into the extent to which a company is willing to increase its debt rate for seeking growth.

Table 7.4 Regression analysis (dependent variable: assets growth)

Independent Variables	*B*	*Beta*	Significance
(Constant)	0.019		0.467
Age	0.000	−0.043	0.425
Size (employment)	0.000	−0.068	0.151
2nd versus 1st generation dummy	−0.020	−0.077	0.221
3rd versus 1st generation dummy	−0.044	−0.152	0.019**
Founder * 2nd generation	−0.003	−0.010	0.850
Founder * 3rd generation	0.032	0.058	0.222
Profitability	0.003	0.169	0.000***
Slow vs no growth dummy	−0.008	−0.021	0.644
Average vs no growth dummy	−0.002	−0.006	0.903
Strong vs no growth dummy	0.059	0.128	0.005***
$R^2 = 0.101$ $F = 3.746$			

Notes:
The estimated model is: growth $= \alpha + \beta_1$Age $+ \beta_2$Size $+ \beta_3$Construction $+ \beta_4$Manufacturing $+ \beta_5$Wholesale $+ \beta_6$Retail $+ \beta_7$Services $+ \beta_8$Generation21 $+ \beta_9$Generation31 $+ \beta_{10}$Founder*Generation21 $+ \beta_{11}$Founder*Generation31 $+ \beta_{12}$Profit $+ \beta_{13}$SlowGrowth $+ \beta_{14}$AverageGrowth $+ \beta_{15}$StrongGrowth. Estimations are based on OLS Regression. The dependent variable is the mean growth in total assets over the period 1999–2004.
***, **, * indicate statistical significance at 1, 5 and 10 per cent respectively.

For this purpose actual, internal and sustainable growth figures were compared by integrating the absolute differences between these growth rates into a regression analysis. Results are presented in Tables 7.5 and 7.6. Table 7.5 describes the results for a group of 410 family firms that grow faster than their internal growth rate. Table 7.6 shows the results of 290 family firms that grow faster than their sustainable level.

As can be derived from Table 7.5, intergenerational differences can be identified regarding the absolute difference between the actual growth rate and the internal growth rate. For both second- and third-generation family firms the extent to which the internal growth rate is exceeded proves to be lower compared to first-generation companies. However, this effect is only significant for third-generation companies. It is further clear that profitability and the ratio of fixed assets to total assets are significantly correlated with the dependent variable. Less profitable and more capital-intensive firms are more likely to grow at rates that require them to attract external finance.

With respect to Table 7.6, the same conclusions hold true. Results indicate that third-generation family firms exceed their sustainable growth level to a much lower extent compared to first-generation family firms. Therefore Hypotheses 3a and 3b have to be accepted, where it is stated that the

Table 7.5 Regression analysis (dependent variable: absolute difference between AG and IG)

Independent Variables	B	*Beta*	Significance
(Constant)	0.093		0.005***
Age	0.000	−0.044	0.512
Size (employment)	0.000	0.055	0.318
2nd versus 1st generation dummy	−0.019	−0.075	0.334
3rd versus 1st generation dummy	−0.048	−0.168	0.043**
Founder * 2nd generation	0.002	0.008	0.909
Founder * 3rd generation	0.010	0.021	0.728
Profitability	−0.002	−0.147	0.021**
Fixed assets/Total assets	0.101	0.158	0.007***
Dividends/Total assets	−0.242	−0.066	0.271
$R^2 = 0.096$ $F = 2.537$			

Notes:
The estimated model is: $AG\text{-}IG = \alpha + \beta_1 Age + \beta_2 Size + \beta_3 Construction + \beta_4 Manufacturing + \beta_5 Wholesale + \beta_6 Retail + \beta_7 Services + \beta_8 Generation21 + \beta_9 Generation31 + \beta_{10} Founder{*}Generation21 + \beta_{11} Founder{*}Generation31 + \beta_{12} Profit + \beta_{13} FA/TA + \beta_{14} Div/TA$. Estimations are based on OLS Regression. The dependent variable measures the difference between mean annual AG and IG when the firm grows faster than IG over the period 1999–2004.
***, **, * indicate statistical significance at 1, 5 and 10 per cent respectively.

absolute difference between the actual growth rate (AG) and the internal (IG)/sustainable (SG) growth rate in family firms differs according to the generation managing the company.

To summarize, the testing of our last hypotheses revealed that next-generation family firms, and especially third-generation companies, are much more inclined to limit their growth. If they decide to grow beyond their internal level, they restrict the degree to which this level is surpassed, meaning that they avoid large increases in additional external funds. By integrating the sustainable growth rate into our analysis, the same conclusions hold true. Of those family firms that exceed their sustainable growth level, and thus willing to increase the current proportion of debt in their capital structure, firms of the third generation particularly seem to go less far in rising their debt proportion compared to first- and second-generation family firms. In other words, the results in this study provide evidence that third-generation family firms allow for further growth in their company (that is, when $AG > IG$ or $AG > SG$), but to a much lesser degree compared to first-generation family firms in order to avoid irresponsible levels of financial risk. This means that first-generation family firms are more

Table 7.6 Regression analysis (dependent variable: absolute difference between AG and SG)

Independent Variables	*B*	*Beta*	Significance
(Constant)	0.162		0.067*
Age	0.001	0.129	0.098*
Size (employment)	0.000	−0.050	0.438
2nd versus 1st generation dummy	−0.042	−0.071	0.459
3rd versus 1st generation dummy	−0.127	−0.190	0.047**
Founder * 2nd generation	−0.020	−0.029	0.711
Founder * 3rd generation	−0.012	−0.010	0.892
Profitability	−0.009	−0.253	0.001***
Fixed assets/Total assets	0.360	0.251	0.001***
Dividends/Total assets	−0.591	−0.076	0.288
$R^2 = 0.124$ $F = 2.380$			

Notes:
The estimated model is: AG-SG $= \alpha + \beta_1$Age $+ \beta_2$Size $+ \beta_3$Construction $+ \beta_4$Manufacturing $+ \beta_5$Wholesale $+ \beta_6$Retail $+ \beta_7$Services $+ \beta_8$Generation21 $+ \beta_9$Generation31 $+ \beta_{10}$Founder*Generation21 $+ \beta_{11}$Founder*Generation31 $+ \beta_{12}$Profit $+ \beta_{13}$ FA/TA $+ \beta_{14}$ Div/TA. Estimations are based on OLS Regression. The dependent variable measures the difference between mean annual AG and SG when the firm grows faster than SG over the period 1999–2004.
***, **, * indicate statistical significance at 1, 5 and 10 per cent respectively.

prepared to take higher risks, as for this group larger changes in their capital structure could be identified.

DISCUSSION AND CONCLUSION

As highlighted by several researchers in recent studies, family firms are far from one homogeneous group with equal characteristics and behavior. This has to some extent been proven in this study, where this conclusion more specifically holds true with respect to the financing and growth behavior of family firms managed by different generations. Although the empirical literature on intergenerational differences is rather scarce, and earlier attempts to study the sustainable and internal growth concepts are rather limited in small business studies, researchers more or less share the view that it makes a difference whether the founder or other generations of family members manage the family firm. This study provides clear evidence that this so-called generation effect cannot be ignored when studying the growth and financing choices by family-owned businesses.

As has been suggested by our first hypothesis, and clearly confirmed by our results, first-generation family firms realize higher debt levels and lower cash holdings compared to their next-generation counterparts. Between first- and third-generation companies these differences proved to be highly significant, even after correcting for size, industry, age and other business characteristics. In this way, our results correspond to the research of Ward (1987), Miller and Le Breton-Miller (2005; 2006) and Kaye and Hamilton (2004). However, with respect to the idea in the literature on the existence of financing constraints in next-generation family firms (for example, Anderson et al., 2003), our study does not support this point of view. What is more, our sample shows that first-generation companies are the ones that experience higher problems in attracting external finance. Descriptive statistics further indicated that the dividend payout ratio in fact decreases when evolving from one generation to the next. Therefore we assume that this financial conservative behavior in next-generation family firms results rather from a resolute choice of management for creating a healthier capital structure.

A second objective of our study was to look for significant differences in the growth behavior of the various types of family businesses by observing the mean annual realized assets growth rate. Corresponding to our second hypothesis, our results confirmed that first-generation family firms realize higher growth rates in comparison with next-generation companies. The fact that growth objectives were also included in our regression analysis makes us conclude that this 'slower growth behavior' of next-generation family firms does not represent a preference of this type of firm to slow down their development and/or expansion, but rather results from other factors. Based on previous research, our results correspond to those of Dunn (1995), Cromie et al. (1995), Reid et al. (1999) and Miller and Le Breton-Miller (2006), although no proof was found of intergenerational differences in growth objectives.

Probably the most defining feature of the family firm is the will to maintain ownership and control of the company in the hands of a group of people who share family bonds, together with the will to continue doing so in future generations. Partly this desire results from the non-pecuniary benefits of control obtained by the founder or their heirs. Of course, the family owners of the firm will prefer more economic profits to less, but in general it can be assumed that the monetary pay off needed to compensate for loss of control and the loss of non-pecuniary benefits is very high. In that sense, debt is seen as a substitute of equity finance with no decision rights as long as the debt services are satisfied. Family firms can thus be inclined to use debt finance to sustain growth without losing control but, at the same time, if the risk of financial distress is too high, then firms will stop using debt because the likelihood of having to transfer the decision rights to the debt holders becomes too high. Family managers will then choose to strengthen their financial position by lowering their debt levels and increasing their cash holdings in order to further restrict the influence of external capital suppliers and the constraints imposed by them. That is, family firms will limit their growth to keep risks under control. Moreover, in accordance with the view of Reid et al. (1999), Cromie et al. (1995), Kaye and Hamilton (2004) and Schulze et al. (2003) we expect this behavior to strengthen as family firms develop from one generation to the next.

Indeed, as has been identified by testing our last hypotheses, this increased 'family first behavior' seems to have a direct impact on the financing behavior, given the more conservative capital structure decisions, which affect the growth rate that can be realized in the firm. Although ex ante growth objectives do not differ, we do say that next-generation family firms grow at a lower rate as these firms have the tendency of foregoing part of their development rather than losing their independence due to excessive use of 'risky' external capital. This is totally in line with the findings of researchers like Reid et al. (1999). To conclude, we could say that second- and especially third-generation family firms are more constrained in their growth behavior due to a more conservative financial policy. We therefore support the insights from researchers, such as Tsang (2002) and Sharma (2002), who advance the proposition of various family firm typologies. Without claiming that this variety basically lies in the intergenerational differences among family firms, we think that this 'generation issue' will play a considerable role in further attempts to categorize family firms into various groups.

Although interesting conclusions can be derived from this study, we nevertheless have to mention a few shortcomings comprised in this study and suggestions for future research. The fact is that in this study no proof could be found of increased organizational conflict as family firms develop. It would, for example, be interesting to investigate the family situation of the CEO by taking into account the number and age of the children, and the foreseen retirement age of the director. Information on the shareholders' structure would also be useful as it is expected that family firms with many active and passive shareholders will behave differently regarding their dividend and recruitment policy compared to firms managed by only one or two siblings. In this way, a further in-depth exploration into this matter could be useful in order to better understand exactly why it is justifiable to study family firms as a separate research object.

NOTE

1. As the use of external equity financing proved to be extremely exceptional for the firms in our sample seeking external funds, it will be assumed in this chapter that external financial means correspond to debt finance.

REFERENCES

Anderson, R.C., A.S. Mansi and D.M. Reeb (2003), 'Founding family ownership and the agency cost of debt', *Journal of Financial Economics*, **68**(2), 263–85.

Astrachan, J.H., S.B. Klein and K.X. Smyrnios (2002), 'The F-PEC scale of family influence: a proposal for solving the family business definition problem', *Family Business Review*, **15**(1), 45–58.

Becchetti, L. and G. Trovato (2002), 'The determinants of growth for small and medium-sized firms: the role of availability of external finance', *Small Business Economics*, **19**(4), 291–306.

Berger, A.N. and G.F. Udell (1998), 'The economics of small business finance: the roles of private equity and debt markets in the financial growth cycle', *Journal of Banking and Finance*, **22**(6–8), 613–73.

Berggren, B., C. Olofsson and L. Silver (2000), 'Control aversion and the search for external financing in Swedish SMEs', *Small Business Economics*, **15**(3), 233–42.

Bruce, N. and M. Waldman (1990), 'The rotten-kid theorem meets the samaritan's dilemma', *Quarterly Journal of Economics*, **105**(1), 155–65.

Carlock, R.S. and J.L. Ward (2001), *Strategic Planning for the Family Business: Parallel Planning to Unify the Family and Business*, New York: Palgrave.

Chittenden, F., G. Hall and P. Hutchinson (1996), 'Small firm growth, access to capital markets and financial structure: review of issues and an empirical investigation', *Small Business Economics*, **8**(1), 59–67.

Coleman, S. and M. Carsky (1999), 'Sources of capital for small family owned businesses: evidence from the national survey of small business finances', *Family Business Review*, **12**(1), 73–85.

Covin, J.C. and D.P. Slevin (1986), 'The development and testing of an organizational-level entrepreneurship scale', in R. Ronstadt, J.A. Homaday, R. Peterson and K.H. Vesper (eds), *Frontiers of Entrepreneurship Research*, Wellesley, MA: Babson College, pp. 628–39.

Covin, J.G and D.P. Slevin (1989), 'Strategic management of small firms in hostile and benign environments', *Strategic Management Journal*, **10**(1), 75–87.

Cromie, S., B. Stevenson and D. Monteith (1995), 'The management of family firms: an empirical investigation', *International Small Business Journal*, **13**(4), 11–34.

Davis, P. and P. Harveston (1999), 'In the founder's shadow: conflict in the family firm', *Family Business Review*, **12**(1), 311–23.

Demirgüç-Kunt, A. and V. Maksimovic (1998), 'Law, finance, and firm growth', *Journal of Finance*, **53**(6), 2107–37.

Donckels, R. and E. Fröhlich (1991), 'Are family businesses really different? European experiences from STRATOS', *Family Business Review*, **4**(2), 149–60.

Dunn, B. (1995), 'Success themes in Scottish family enterprises: philosophies and practices through generations', *Family Business Review*, **8**(1), 17–28.

Fernández, Z. and M.J. Nieto (2005), 'Internationalization strategy of small and medium-sized family businesses: some influential factors', *Family Business Review*, **18**(1), 77–89.

Gersick, K., J. Davis, M. Hampton and I. Lansberg (1997), *Generation to Generation: Life Cycles of the Family Business*, Boston, MA: Harvard Business School.

Gregory, B.T., M.W. Rutherford, S. Oswald and L. Gardiner (2005), 'An empirical investigation of the growth cycle theory of small firm financing', *Journal of Small Business Management*, **43**(4), 382–92.

Harvey, M. and R.E. Evans (1995), 'Life after succession in the family business: is it really the end of problems?', *Family Business Review*, **8**(1), 3–16.

Higgins, R.C. (1977), 'How much growth can a firm afford?', *Financial Management*, **6**, 7–16.

Jensen, M.C. and W. Meckling (1976), 'Theory of the firm: managerial behavior, agency costs and ownership structure', *Journal of Financial Economics*, **3**(2), 305–60.

Kaye, K. and S. Hamilton (2004), 'Roles of trust in consulting to financial families', *Family Business Review*, **17**(2), 151–63.

Kellermanns, F.W. and K. Eddleston (2004), 'Feuding families: when conflict does a family firm good', *Entrepreneurship Theory and Practice*, **28**(3), 209–28.

Kyd, C.W. (1981), 'Managing the financial demands of growth', *Management Accounting*, **63**(6), 33–41.

Martin, W.L. and G.T. Lumpkin (2003), 'From entrepreneurial orientation to family orientation: generational differences in the management of family businesses', in William D. Bygrave et al. (eds), *Frontiers of Entrepreneurship Research*, Babson Park, MA: Babson College' pp. 309–21.

McConaughy, D.L. and G.M. Phillips (1999), 'Founders versus descendants: the profitability, efficiency, growth characteristics and financing in large, public founding-family-controlled firms', *Family Business Review*, **12**(2), 123–31.

McConaughy, D., C. Matthews and A. Fialko (2001), 'Founding family controlled firms: efficiency, risk, and value', *Journal of Small Business Management*, **39**(1), 31–49.

McMahon, R., S. Holmes, P. Hutchinson and D. Forsaith (1993), *Small Enterprise Financial Management: Theory & Practice*, Sydney: Harcourt Brace.

Miller, D. (1983), 'The correlates of entrepreneurship in three types of firms', *Management Science*, **29**(7), 770–91.

Miller, L. and I. Le Breton-Miller (2005), *Managing for the Long Run: Lessons in Competitive Advantage from Great Family Businesses*, Boston, MA: Harvard Business School Press.

Miller, L. and I. Le Breton-Miller (2006), 'Family governance and firm performance: agency, stewardship, and capabilities', *Family Business Review*, **19**(1), 73–87.

Myers, S. (1984), 'The capital structure puzzle', *Journal of Finance*, **39**(3), 575–92.

Ozkan, A. and N. Ozkan (2004), 'Corporate cash holdings: an empirical investigation of UK companies', *Journal of Banking and Finance*, **28**(9), 2103–34.

Rajan, R.G. and L. Zingales (1995), 'What do we know about capital structure? Some evidence from international data', *Journal of Finance*, **50**(5), 1421–60.

Randøy, T. and S. Goel (2003), 'Ownership structure, founder leadership, and performance in Norwegian SMEs: implications for financing entrepreneurial opportunities', *Journal of Business Venturing*, **18**(5), 619–37.

Reid, R., B. Dunn, S. Cromie and J. Adams (1999), 'Family orientation in family firms: a model and some empirical evidence', *Journal of Small Business and Enterprise Development*, **6**(1), 55–66.

Romano, C.A., G.A. Tanewski and K.X. Smyrnios (2001), 'Capital structure decision making: a model for family business', *Journal of Business Venturing*, **16**(3), 285–310.

Schulze, W.S., M.H. Lubatkin and R.N. Dino (2003), 'Exploring the agency consequences of ownership dispersion among the directors of private family firms', *Academy of Management Journal*, **46**(2), 179–194.

Schwass, J. (2005), *Wise Growth Strategies in Leading Family Businesses*, New York: Palgrave Macmillan.

Sharma, P. (2002), 'Stakeholder mapping technique: toward the development of a family firm typology', Academy of Management Conference Proceedings, 9–14 August, Denver, CO.

Sharma, P. (2004), 'An overview of the field of family business studies: current status and directions for the future', *Family Business Review*, **17**(1), 1–36.

Sogorb-Mira, F. (2005), 'How SME uniqueness affects capital structure: evidence from a 1994–1998 Spanish data panel', *Small Business Economics*, **25**(5), 447–57.

Sonfield, M.C. and R.N. Lussier (2004), 'First-, second-, and third-generation family firms: a comparison', *Family Business Review*, **17**(3), 189–202.

Tsang, E.W.K. (2002), 'Learning from overseas venturing experience: the case of Chinese family businesses', *Journal of Business Venturing*, **17**(1), 21–40.

Ward, J. (1987), *Keeping the Family Business Healthy: How to Plan for Continuing Growth, Profitability and Family Leadership*, San Francisco: Family Enterprise Publishers.

Westhead, P. (1997), 'Ambitions "external" environment and strategic factor differences between family and non-family companies', *Entrepreneurship and Regional Development*, **9**(2), 127–57.

Zahra, S.A. (2005), 'Entrepreneurial risk taking in family firms', *Family Business Review*, **18**(1), 23–40.

APPENDIX

Table 7A.1 Variable description and definitions

Business characteristic	Measurement
Age	Difference between 2001 and the date of foundation
Size	Total employment in 2001 (FTE)
Industry	5 dummy variables corresponding to the construction, manufacturing, wholesale, retail and services sector. 'Other' is used as reference category
Generation	2 dummy variables with first-generation family firms as reference category
Founder	Dummy variable that takes on value 1 if the founder is still actively involved
Financing constrained	Dummy variable that takes on value 1 if the company experiences financing constraints in funding its growth
Growth objectives	3 dummy variables to identify if firms seek weak, average or strong growth. Firms not having growth as one of their main objectives form the reference category
Profitability	Gross return on assets (before tax), averaged over the period 1999–2004
Debt/Total assets	Total debt/total assets, averaged over the period 1999–2004
Cash/Total assets	Total cash and equivalent items/total assets, averaged over the period 1999–2004
Assets growth	Growth in total assets, averaged over the period 1999–2004
Fixed assets/Total assets	Net fixed assets/total assets, averaged over the period 1999–2004
Dividends/Total assets	Total dividends/total assets, averaged over the period 1999–2004
Cash flow/Total assets	Profit (after tax) plus depreciation/total assets, averaged over the period 1999–2004
Bank debt/Total debt	Total bank borrowings/total debt, averaged over the period 1999–2004
Variability	Standard deviation of cash flows/average total assets (1999–2004)

8. The link between family orientation, strategy and innovation in Dutch SMEs: lagged effects

Lorraine M. Uhlaner, Sita Tan, Joris Meijaard and Ron Kemp

INTRODUCTION

In spite of the unmistakable share of family firms in the economy, our understanding of their strategies, behaviour and performance is still quite limited, as are the differences between predominantly family owned and managed and other types of small and medium-sized enterprises (SMEs). Innovativeness is an important determinant of performance; a review of the literature by Capon et al. (1990) finds that in over two-thirds of the studies, a positive relationship between production innovation strategy and firm performance exists, with more recent research confirming this finding for new technology ventures (Li and Atuahene-Gima, 2001). In turn, strategy has been identified as one of the cornerstones of innovation (Cooper and Kleinschmidt, 1995). In linking strategy with innovation, scholars can be divided into two perspectives. The first perspective embraces those scholars who see strategy-making as a deliberate process in which managers, often aided by consultants, customers and others follow a conscious path of action. The other view is that strategy is an emergent understanding, evolving from the cumulative effect of individual operating decisions taken by management (Mintzberg and Waters, 1985). Either way, the two can be seen as linked. In the deliberate view, new products result from the execution of strategy. From the emergent view, innovation is a tangible manifestation of what the strategy of a firm has been.

Previous research has suggested a negative effect of family orientation on innovation (Dekkers, 2003; Gudmundson et al., 1999; Donckels and Fröhlich, 1991; Flören and Wijers, 1996). However, much of the research suggests that links between innovation and performance and, in turn, determinants of innovation may be subject to various contingency effects (Li and Atuahene-Gima, 2001). Another limitation in past research is that family orientation is tested in bivariate tests, without controlling for other aspects of context. However, research suggests that other things being equal, family firms tend to be smaller in terms of total employees in the USA and UK (Coleman and Carsky, 1999; Cromie et al., 1995; Klein, 2000; Daily and Dollinger, 1993; Westhead and Cowling, 1997). Age is a similar variable in that family firms tend to be older, controlling for other variables. Furthermore, family firms may be over- or underrepresented in certain sectors. In the USA family firms have been found to be less likely in the manufacturing industry (Cromie et al., 1995) and in the UK they have been found to be less active in services (Westhead and Cowling, 1996). Family firms may be expected to be overrepresented in the retail and wholesale sectors.

This study aims to overcome these deficiencies in extant research by estimating lagged effects and controlling for context variables. The primary research question is as follows: What are the lagged effects (direct and indirect) of family orientation and of strategy on innovation performance in the SME, after controlling for context variables?

DATA AND METHODS

Key Concepts

In this section we will describe the key concepts of innovation performance, strategy and family orientation in more detail.

Innovation by nature is a rather 'relative' concept (Bellon and Whittington, 1996). The classic Schumpeterian definition of innovation states that innovation is the successful introduction of a new product, a new process or a new organizational model. Innovation can also be defined as the adoption of an idea or behaviour – being a system, a programme, a process, a policy, a device, a product or a service – that is new to the adopting organization (Daft, 1982; Damanpour and Evan, 1984). One may also make a distinction between incremental innovations and radical innovations (for example, Kenny, 2003). Incremental innovations refer to small but useful improvements. They usually entail refinements and extensions of established designs. Substantial price or functional benefits are typically required to define specific change as incremental innovations (Dosi, 1982; Henderson and Clark, 1990; Banbury and Mitchell, 1995). Incremental innovations are relevant to business survival, which depends on the ability to continuously deliver innovations. By being first with incremental innovations, firms can avoid erosion of competitive positions (Banbury and Mitchell, 1995). By contrast, radical innovations are the (incidental) 'life-changers' for the firm and industry which represent complete and often irreversible change in which eventually the whole business environment changes (Bellon and Whittington, 1996).

In this study innovation performance refers to the actual completion of innovations: the introduction of new products and services in the market and/or the actual change of existing systems or processes that lead to them. To avoid possible confounding of the concepts of strategy and innovation, this study defines innovation performance as the end result rather than the process of innovating and/or the strategic choice of creating innovative or new products or processes – the latter is referred to in this chapter as 'innovation differentiation'. Though not measured in the present research, the innovation process is viewed as an important antecedent of the end result, and may be viewed as having several stages. More specifically, the concept of the innovation 'funnel', proposed by Wheelright and Clark (1992), begins with the process of narrowing down a wide range of ideas (Idea-Generation Phase), followed by a screening process – formal or informal – that leads to further development and design of specifications (Concept Development Phase). This is followed, in turn, by either explicit or implicit determination of the innovation's success (Forecasting Phase) and, finally, the actual introduction of the innovation (Ottum, 1996). Strategy, as used in this chapter, has a rather broad meaning, covering a range of concerns describing what the organization wants to do (Griffin and Ebert, 1996). In this study strategy is modelled through the following variables: strategic process, price discounting, differentiation, focus, risk orientation and growth orientation. These variables are explained in more detail below.

'Strategic process' refers to the formality of approach taken towards strategy. The company's leadership may have explicit goals, objectives and targets that it expects to achieve. This directive is typically called the mission or strategy statement (Griffin and Ebert, 1996). In other firms the direction is more informal. Especially among SMEs, many firms lack a formal strategic plan, written or otherwise. The concepts 'price discounting', 'differentiation' and 'focus' are based on an interpretation of Porter's (1985) so-called generic competitive strategies. 'Price discounting' means that the firm offers goods or services at a lower price to improve and retain competitive advantage. This is somewhat narrower in concept than Porter's cost leadership strategy (Porter, 1985). The second generic strategy, 'differentiation', means that the firm offers unique products or services for competitive advantage. The third strategy is 'focus' on a specific market niche – a target group of customers, for instance, or certain distribution channels. In this study exporting is considered an aspect of focus, since this implies a strategy targeting a specific market: that is, customers in a country or countries outside the company's home base.

'Risk orientation' and 'growth orientation' are a more general 'orientation' of a business that may have an influence on more specific strategies chosen by the director of the SME. Risk orientation is a concept that has been previously studied in the context of SME strategy (Verheul et al., 2005). The willingness to take risks ('risk orientation') captures the degree to which management is (or is not) averse to risking money and time in inherently uncertain situations. The willingness to grow ('growth orientation') captures the degree to which management puts priority on growing the firm. Many small firms that may have growth opportunities are nevertheless not interested in taking advantage of these opportunities (Davidsson, 1989).

Defining family orientation is a complex task and the most complete definitions require a mix of criteria. For instance, one of the earliest and still widely adopted structural definitions of family orientation was developed at the London Business School (Stoy Hayward, 1989). According to this definition, a firm is classified as a family business if at least one of the following three criteria is met: more than 50 per cent of shares are owned by one family; at least 50 per cent of management are from one family; and/or a significant number of members of the board are from a single family. The problem, however, is that according to this definition, the vast majority of small firms are classified as family firms (Klein, 2000). For instance, in a recent study over 80 per cent of Dutch SMEs might be classified as family firms (Hulshoff, 2001).

Due to such limitations, more recently developed definitions of family business reflect the acceptance of multiple dimensions as well as the notion that rather than creating a dichotomy, different firms may vary in the extent and manner in which the family is involved with the firm. Thus, for instance, Astrachan et al. (2002) propose the F-PEC scale composed of three dimensions, namely Power, Experience and Culture. The Power dimension, rooted in several family business definitions, reflects the extent to which the family owns, governs and participates in management of the firm (Stoy Hayward, 1989; Westhead et al., 2001; Klein, 2000; Martin and Suarez, 2001). The Experience dimension reflects the degree to which either ownership, governance or management have passed from one generation to the next (Donckels, 1998; Perricone et al., 2001; Cromie et al., 1995; Westhead et al., 2002; Flören and Göbbels, 1995; Flören, 1998). The Culture dimension, derived from Carlock and Ward (2001), captures not so much structure or history of succession as the present influence of family on the firm's strategy and values. In a more recent study by Uhlaner (2005) a multifaceted approach is suggested which combines different dimensions into one scale, using Guttmann scaling techniques. These multiple facets are referred to as family orientation. In this study family orientation captures different dimensions as well (see Appendix).

Research Model

In this section we present the model and hypotheses to be tested in our research. The model proposes that (1) firm strategy has a direct effect on innovation performance, controlling for various context variables, and that (2) family orientation may have both a direct and indirect effect on innovation performance (Figure 8.1).

Hypothesis 1 predicts a direct effect of organization strategy on innovation performance (arrow 1 in Figure 8.1). As explained in the introduction, whether by a deliberate or emergent process, the strategic choices made by management are expected to impact on the degree of innovation in the firm. In particular, firms that are more risk oriented and growth oriented will seek out ways to create new markets by identifying new products or services for their customers. Those firms with a conscious strategy of differentiation or focus are also more likely to pursue activities resulting in new products and services. On the other hand, simple price discounting is a strategy least likely to require innovation, and can be achieved in other ways, including either economies of scale for larger SMEs or lowered administrative costs and flexibility for smaller SMEs. To summarize, Hypothesis 1 can be stated as follows:

Hypothesis 1: Companies following certain approaches to strategy (greater risk orientation, greater growth orientation, more formal strategic process, more focus and innovation differentiation or less emphasis on price discounting) are likely to report a higher level of innovation performance than those who do not follow these approaches. Thus, for example, companies that are more willing to take risks are

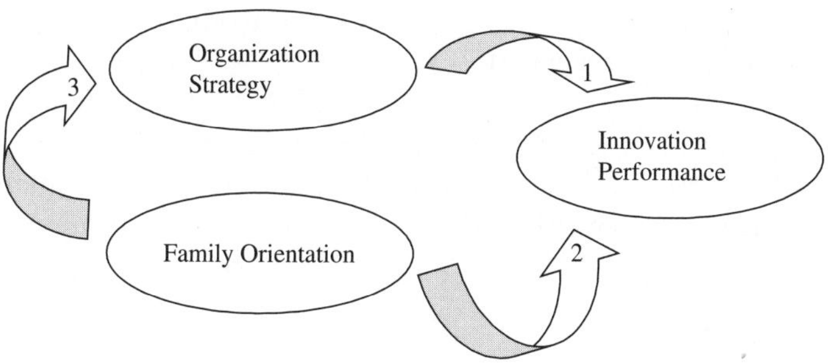

Figure 8.1 Proposed model: influences of family orientation and strategy on innovation performance

likely to report a greater level of innovation performance than companies that are less willing to take risks.

Previous literature suggests that more family oriented firms are less innovative than less family oriented firms (Dekkers, 2003). One explanation for this is that there are differences in strategy: family oriented firms may place such goals as continuity or independence over and above growth in order to preserve the family heritage. Also, a sort of conservatism (doing things the way father did) may be an influence on the strategy of the firm, again, limiting the use of a strategy requiring new product development. In this study we propose to test the two alternative hypotheses as stated in Hypotheses 2 and 3. Hypothesis 2 predicts a direct (negative) effect of family orientation on innovation performance (arrow 2 in Figure 8.1), controlling for strategy variables.

Hypothesis 2: More family-oriented firms, even when controlling for differences in strategy are likely to report fewer innovations than less family-oriented firms (direct effect).

Alternatively, Hypothesis 3 predicts an indirect (negative) relationship between family orientation and innovation performance, controlling for different aspects of strategy (arrows 1 and 2, in combination in Figure 8.1). This hypothesis is consistent with a line of research on family firms carried out by Storey and colleagues, which found that the differences between family and non-family firms often reflect indirect effects based on other intervening factors, such as firm size and sector (Westhead and Cowling, 1996). We state Hypothesis 3 as follows:

Hypothesis 3: More family-oriented firms report fewer innovations than less family-oriented firms due to differences in strategy (indirect effect).

All three hypotheses are tested, controlling for organization context variables and without such controls. Control variables include company size, company age and sector (that is, manufacturing, wholesale and retail and services).

Sample

This study makes use of a subset of a sample tracked longitudinally by EIM Business Policy and Research since 1998. For this particular study, companies were only included where the listed business was a primary company rather than a subsidiary, and directorship had not been transferred in the past three years, in order to eliminate those that had changed hands during the period of data collection. This resulted in an available sample of 338 firms. Data was collected via several rounds of telephone (computer-aided) interviews with the company director between 2001 and 2005. Innovation performance is collected in 2005. All other measures are collected in previous time periods (see Appendix for details). The original telephone interview scales as reported in the Appendix are opposite to those used, with the exception of size and age. These scales are reversed in order to expedite interpretation of results in the tables. Thus a positive correlation is always to be interpreted as a positive relationship between the two variables.

Data Analysis

The variables used in this study are listed in the Appendix. Independent variables include family orientation, different aspects of strategy, including risk orientation, price discounting, focus, innovation differentiation, growth orientation and strategic process. Control variables include company size, age and sector. Factor analyses were carried out within broad categories (for example, all the strategy variables) to assure their independence. Tests for multicollinearity, using VIF scores were carried out. In addition, even when VIF scores were within appropriate ranges, final strategy variables were selected that were least correlated with one another. Variables based on items with scales of the same length were created by taking the mean of different items. Variables that required a combination of items based on items of different lengths made use of the protocol referred to as categorical principal components analysis (CATPCA), executed using the Statistical Package for the Social Sciences (SPSS). Optimal scaling is used in transformation of the variables. In the case of the variables created with the CATCPA program, the Cronbach's alpha reliability coefficient is based on the results of that program. Where means are created for a variable, the Cronbach's alpha is computed on the basis of the original items (see Appendix).

Bivariate relationships are first examined using Pearson product-moment bivariate correlation statistics. A multivariate model is then developed using Ordinary Least Squares multiple regression. Assuming significant relationships between family orientation, strategy and innovation performance – using bivariate tests – direct and indirect effects are tested, according to James and Brett (1984) and Baron and Kenny (1986), by estimating three separate models, all controlling for context:

innovation performance = f(family orientation) (I)
innovation performance = f(strategy) (II)
innovation performance = f(family orientation, strategy) (III)

We assume the presence of an indirect effect of family orientation on innovation performance if family orientation has a significant effect on innovation performance in Model I and family orientation has a non-significant effect on innovation performance in Model III. Likewise, we assume the presence of a direct effect of family orientation on innovation performance in the case of a significant effect of strategy in Model II, in combination with a significant added effect of family orientation on innovation performance in Model III.

RESULTS

Tables 8.1 and 8.2 summarize results for each of the hypotheses proposed in this study. The remaining part of this section discusses the results in relation to each hypothesis.

Hypothesis 1: Effects of Strategy on Innovation

Reviewing the results of both Tables 8.1 and 8.2, the predictions made in Hypothesis 1, relating strategy and innovation, are statistically supported, even when innovation differentiation is added in the all variable model, although the *B* weights drop somewhat for the other strategy variables when it is included. Strategy variables positively predicting innovation performance include greater risk orientation, greater growth orientation, a focus strategy, an innovation differentiation strategy and a more formal strategic process. The only strategy negatively associated with innovation performance is price discounting.

Hypothesis 2: Testing for the Direct Effects of Family Orientation on Innovation

Reviewing the results of Table 8.2, the direct negative effect of family orientation on innovativeness is supported. This means that the higher the family orientation, the less innovative a company will be. However, the effect is rather small: family orientation explains only 2–3 per cent of the total variation in innovativeness. Even in the bivariate analysis, when not controlling for control variables, the effect is very small, since the square of 0.17 is only about 3 per cent.

Table 8.1 Pearson correlations between all variables for the total sample ($n = 338$)

	1	2	3	4	5	6	7	8	9	10	11	12
1. Innovation performance	1											
2. Family orientation	−0.17[b]	1										
3. Company size	0.36[c]	−0.03	1									
4. Company age	0.06	0.06	−0.29[c]	1								
5. Manufacturing sector	0.03	−0.01	−0.03	−0.05	1							
6. Retail sector	−0.03	−0.08	0.11	0.04	−0.30[c]	1						
7. Focus	0.27[c]	−0.01	0.18[c]	0.01	−0.06	−0.08	1					
8. Risk orientation	0.30[c]	−0.04	0.20[c]	−0.04	0.01	0.01	0.10	1				
9. Strategic process	0.37[c]	−0.18[c]	0.29[c]	0.05	0.02	−0.07	0.20[c]	0.20[c]	1			
10. Growth orientation	0.34[c]	−0.04	0.28[c]	0.06	0.11[a]	−0.02	0.25[c]	0.18[c]	0.17[b]	1		
11. Price discounting	−0.09	−0.00	0.06	0.08	0.09	−0.11[a]	0.02	−0.05	−0.04	0.02	1	
12. Innovation differentiation	0.48[c]	−0.18[c]	0.22[c]	−0.09	0.04	−0.07	0.24[c]	0.24[c]	0.30[c]	0.20c	−0.09	1
MEAN	1.45	0.03	2.49	27.72	0.34	0.15	–0.01	0.00	1.75	1.31	2.23	2.13
STD. DEVIATION	0.39	1.45	1.53	26.92	0.47	0.35	0.88	0.99	0.35	0.46	0.77	0.67

Note: [a] $p < 0.05$; [b] $p < 0.01$; [c] $p < 0.001$, two-tailed tests of significance.

Table 8.2 Regressions of family orientation, context and strategy on innovation performance (n = 338)

Explanatory Variables[b]		Model I Context B (t-value)	Model II Context/FO B (t-value)	Model III Strategy excl. ID B (t-value)	Model IV Context/FO/ Strategy excl. ID B (t-value)	Model V All variables B (t-value)	ΔR^2 [a]
Context							0.14***/0.03**
	Company size	0.10 (−7.20)***	0.10 (−7.18)***		0.05 (−3.96)***	0.04 (−3.24)***	
	Company age	−0.00 (0.87)	−0.00 (0.64)		−0.00 (–0.06)	0.00 (−0.86)	
	Manufacturing	0.02 (0.46)	0.02 (0.38)		0.02 (0.38)	0.01 (0.27)	
	Retail	−0.06 (−1.06)	−0.08 (−1.35)		−0.04 (–0.74)	−0.02 (−0.30)	
Family	Family Orientation		−0.05 (−3.26)***		−0.03 (−2.56)*	−0.02 (−1.79) #	0.03**/0.01#
Strategy							0.36***/0.23***
	Focus			0.07 (3.03)**	0.06 (2.84)**	0.04 (2.03)*	
	Risk orientation			0.07 (3.88)***	0.06 (3.42)***	0.05 (2.68)**	
	Strategic process			0.29 (5.29)***	0.21 (3.74)***	0.16 (2.89) **	
	Growth orientation			0.20 (4.69)***	0.16 (3.71)***	0.14 (2.47) ***	
	Price discounting			−0.04 (−1.70)***	−0.05 (−2.19)*	−0.04 (−1.66)#	
Strategy excluding innovation differentiation							0.28***/0.09***
	Innovation differentiation					0.18 (6.20)***	0.23***/0.07***
R-squared		0.14	0.17	0.28	0.32	0.40	
Adjusted *R*-squared		0.13	0.15	0.27	0.30	0.37	
F-statistic (df1, df2)		13.50 (4.333)***	13.23 (5.332)***	25.29 (5.332)***	15.63 (10.327)***	19.33 (11.326) ***	

Notes:
*** Significant at the 0.001 level; ** significant at the 0.01 level; * significant at the 0.05 level; # significant at the 0.1 level.
[a] Change in R^2 when adding this variable first/last to the model (including all variables).
[b] *B*-values refer to the unstandardized coefficients of the explanatory variables.

Hypothesis 3: Testing for the Indirect Effects of Family Orientation on Innovation

Alongside the evidence of direct effects, there is also some evidence of indirect effects of family orientation on innovation (Table 8.2). The change in *R* squared drops from 0.03 to 0.01, suggesting that 2 per cent of the variation explained may be due to an indirect effect. Regarding the relation between family orientation and strategy, our findings suggest that more family-oriented companies have a less formal strategic process. However, no link is found with risk orientation or growth orientation. Likewise, family-oriented companies are not less likely to follow a focus strategy. More family-oriented firms appear less likely to follow a differentiation strategy, developing unique products or services.

DISCUSSION

Comparison with Previous Research

We found a relationship between strategy and innovation. Strategy has been identified as an important determinant of innovation earlier (Cooper and Kleinschmidt, 1995; Huang and Brown, 1998). Past research on Dutch SMEs also found a positive relationship between innovation performance and various aspects of strategy, including risk orientation, growth orientation, focus and differentiation and, on the other hand, a negative relationship between innovation performance and price discounting (Dekkers, 2003).

We found a negative effect of family orientation on innovativeness. This is supported by other research (Dekkers, 2003; Gudmundson et al., 1999; Donckels and Fröhlich, 1991; Flören and Wijers, 1996). Different possible explanations are given for this prediction, including possible differences in risk orientation, growth orientation, focus strategy and differentiation strategy. We will expand on each of these possible explanations below. However not all writers predict a negative relationship between family orientation and innovation. For instance, family-oriented firms may be positively linked to innovation because they are typically found to rely to a lesser degree on the use of formal internal control systems. This may increase innovation, also through the employees' personal commitment and involvement to the company (Daily and Dollinger, 1993). Another reason may be that family-oriented firms typically stick to a combined function of owner and manager. In both first- and multi-generation firms, ownership and control will typically not be separated. Family control is maintained through proportional increases in family representation on the board of directors (Flören and Wijers, 1996; Westhead et al., 2002). When the owner-manager carries out their responsibilities adequately, the business is less likely to experience agency conflicts, which, in turn, enhances innovation (Westhead and Cowling, 1997). The greater the functional integrity of the family system, the smaller the tension due to business issues will be. This smaller tension may result in more success in general through responsiveness and more focus (Danes et al., 1999). This may also concern innovation goals.

We did not find a difference in risk orientation between more and less family oriented firms, although this is consistent with other research. Daily and Dollinger (1993), for example, find that neither risk taking nor new product introductions differ between more and less family-oriented firms. In fact, family firms were found to be aggressive in protecting their market position. When controlling for size, age and sector, Dekkers (2003) also finds no effect of family orientation on risk orientation. Nevertheless, the view still lingers that family-oriented firms are more risk averse and, in turn, less innovative. For instance, perhaps the emotional element that is linked to family commitment ('culture') may cause tension between business and family interests leading to decisions that are more risk averse (Flören and Wijers, 1996; Donckels, 1998).

We also did not find a link between family orientation and growth orientation, contradicting earlier studies (Donckels, 1998; Donckels and Fröhlich, 1991; Gomez-Mejia et al., 1987; Martin and Suarez, 2001; Janszen, 2000). Past research also suggests that in order to preserve their wealth, family firms are more likely to follow less growth-oriented strategies than non-family firms (Donckels and Fröhlich, 1991; Gomez-Mejia et al., 1987). As a result, there might be a slower growth path (Harris et al., 1994), which is supported by more recent research by Martin and Suarez (2001). They show that smaller size stems from less aggressive growth policies, due to so-called 'wealth effects'. In order to maintain control, families do not raise the external capital needed to finance (optimal) growth.

As mentioned earlier in the chapter, Carlock and Ward (2001) suggest that family businesses are more likely to serve a niche market than are non-family firms, benefiting from the special knowledge of the family. However, we find no differences between family and non-family-oriented companies regarding their likelihood of following a focus strategy. We found that more family-oriented firms appear less likely to follow an innovation differentiation strategy. This is in agreement with past literature, which suggests that family firms are more likely to maintain a tradition of providing quality and value to the customer (value for money), thereby diminishing the likelihood that a differentiation strategy is followed. The innovativeness of the firm may be negatively affected if the family name and reputation are linked to a particular product and service (Hodgetts and Kuratko, 1982; Daily and Dollinger, 1993; Davis, 1983; Neubauer and Lank, 1998).

Another explanation of differences in innovation is given by Flören and Wijers (1996) and Davis (1983), who suggests that family firms emphasize goals of long-term viability rather than short-term profits. These goals of long-term viability can be referred to as a priority of continuity (as opposed to profitability and growth), which, again, may be related to greater aversion to risk and strategic choices that limit radical change. However, these suggestions are not tested empirically.

The finding that family orientation and strategy may be linked is consistent with the strategic choice paradigm (Child, 1972; Entrialgo, 2002), which postulates that key decision-makers have considerable control over an organization's future direction. Moreover, the finding may be traced back even further to research by behavioural theorists (Cyert and March, 1963; March and Simon, 1958). However, previous research using this model generally tends to focus on the personality of individual CEOs (Miller et al., 1982) rather than on the characteristics of multiple family owners. Nevertheless, the notion that managerial characteristics may influence strategy is grounded in this theory.

Limitations

Owner-managers formed the sources of data for this study. Future studies on this subject could deal with the multi-level problem by interviewing more than one respondent from the same company. Furthermore, this study only tests for the possible mediating effects of strategy in the relationship between family orientation and innovation performance. There may be other intervening or mediating variables between family orientation and innovation performance (organizational structure, for instance) that might also help to explain away the direct effect. The results of the current study could also be tested on a broader sample, not only with respect to company size, but also country representation. The family orientation variables of this study could also be used to predict other aspects of firm performance, like sales revenue, employment growth, productivity and net profit.

Considering the limitations of the study further, it should be pointed out that by focusing on the firm as the unit of analysis, it is possible that the level of innovation is understated. For instance, it may be appropriate in future studies to consider the effects of habitual entrepreneurship. Thus the establishment of a new firm by an existing entrepreneur and/or entrepreneurial family may itself reflect an innovation that would not be captured by measuring within-firm innovation. The current study also fails to capture the complexities of holding firms that may have multiple subsidiaries owned by the same individual or owning family. These issues are common to most studies within the field of entrepreneurship which focus on the firm as the unit of analysis rather than the owning family or entrepreneur. Sampling on the basis of owners versus firms, however, presents a special set of problems given the fact that most publicly available databases are organized on the basis of firms rather than owning groups. However, qualitative studies might explore some of these issues in more detail.

CONCLUSION

The results of this study allow us to conclude that family orientation has a very small negative impact, if any, on innovation performance of SMEs. Although this conclusion implies that family orientation may indeed be an obstacle for innovation as was predicted by some earlier studies (Flören and Wijers, 1996; Donckels and Fröhlich, 1991; Gudmundson et al., 1999), most of this effect can be explained by differences in strategy. In particular, companies, regardless of family orientation, that are more risk oriented, more focused on a specific market niche, more oriented to an innovation differentiation strategy and less reliant on a price discount strategy, are almost as innovative as their non-family counterparts. Although not tested directly as a hypothesis, company size is also a strong predictor of innovation performance, consistent with some, but not all, other studies on size and innovation, but consistent with a resource-based view that larger firms have more resources available for new product development (Huang and Brown, 1998).

We found that more family-oriented firms are likely to report fewer innovations than less family-oriented firms, even when controlling for size, age, sector and differences in strategies. Furthermore, we found that family firms report less innovation due to differences in strategy followed by those firms. However, the effects of family orientation on innovation performance are very small. We also found that companies following certain approaches to strategy (that is, greater risk orientation, greater growth orientation, more formal strategic processes, more focus, greater innovation differentiation, and less emphasis on price discounting) are likely to report a greater level of innovation performance than those who do not, even after controlling for size, age and sector and on a lagged basis for a period of up to four years.

REFERENCES

Astrachan, J.H., S.B. Klein and K.X. Smyrnios (2002), 'The F-PEC scale of family influence: a proposal for solving the family business definition problem', *Family Business Review*, **15**(1), 45–58.

Banbury, C. and W. Mitchell (1995), 'The effect of introducing important incremental innovations on market share and business survival', *Strategic Management Journal*, **16** (special issue), 161–82.

Baron, R.M. and D.A. Kenny (1986) 'The moderator-mediator variable distinction in social psychological research: conceptual, strategic, and statistical considerations', *Journal of Personality and Social Psychology*, **51**(6), 1173–82.

Bellon, B. and G. Whittington (1996), *Competing through Innovation*, Dublin: Oak Tree Press.

Capon, N., J. Farley and S. Hoenig (1990), 'Determinants of financial performance: a meta-analysis', *Management Science*, **36**, 1143–59.

Carlock, R.S. and J.L.Ward (2001), *Strategic Planning for the Family Business Parallel Planning to Unify the Family and Business*, New York: Palgrave.

Child, J. (1972), 'Organization structure, environment, and performance: the role of strategic choice', *Sociology*, **6**, 1–22.

Coleman, S. and M. Carsky (1999), 'Sources of capital for small family-owned businesses: evidence from the national survey of small business finances', *Family Business Review*, **7**(1), 73–85.

Cooper, R.G. and E.J. Kleinschmidt (1995), 'Benchmarking firms: new product performance and practice', *Engineering Management Review*, **23**, 112–20.

Cromie, S., B. Stevenson and D. Monteith (1995), 'The management of family firms: an empirical investigation', *International Small Business Journal*, **13**(4), 11–34.

Cyert, R.M. and J.G. March (1963), *A Behavioural Theory of the Firm*, Englewood Cliffs, NJ: Prentice Hall.

Daft, R.L. (1982), 'Bureaucratic versus non-bureaucratic structure of the process of innovation and change', in S. Bacharach (ed), *Research in the Sociology of Organizations*, Greenwich: JAI Press, pp. 129–66.

Daily, C.M. and M.J. Dollinger (1993), 'Alternative methodologies for identifying family versus non-family businesses', *Journal of Small Business Management*, **31**(2), 79–90.

Damanpour, F. and W. Evan (1984), 'Organizational innovation and performance: the problem of organizational lag', *Administrative Science Quarterly*, **29**, 392–409.

Danes, S.M., V. Zuiker, R. Kean and J. Arbuthnot (1999), 'Predictors of family business tension and goal achievement', *Family Business Review*, **12**(3), 241–51.

Davidsson, P. (1989), 'Continued entrepreneurship and small firm growth', Dissertation, Economic Research Institute, Stockholm School of Economics, Stockholm.

Davis, P. (1983), 'Realizing the potential of the family business', *Organizational Dynamics*, **12**(1), 47–56.

Dekkers, E.J.M. (2003), 'Innovation in Dutch family-orientated firms: The direct and indirect effects of family orientation on innovation', Master's (doctorandus) programme, Management of Innovation, Rotterdam School of Management, Erasmus University Rotterdam, the Netherlands.

Donckels, R. (1998), 'Ondernemen in het familiebedrijf', in D.P. Scherjon and A.R. Thurik (eds), *Handboek Ondernemers en Adviseurs in het MKB*, Deventer: Kluwer Bedrijfsinformatie, pp. 161–83.

Donckels, R. and E. Fröhlich (1991), 'Are family businesses really different? European experiences from STRATOS', *Family Business Review*, **4**(2), 149–60.

Dosi, G. (1982), 'Technological paradigms and technological trajectories: a suggested interpretation of determinants and directions of technological change', *Research Policy*, **2**, 147–62.

Entrialgo, M. (2002), 'The impact of the alignment of strategy and managerial characteristics on Spanish MEs', *Journal of Small Business Management*, **40**(3), 260–70.

Flören, R.H. (1998), 'The significance of family business in the Netherlands', *Family Business Review*, **11**(2), 121–34.

Flören, R.H. and M.W. Göbbels (1995), 'De partner van de directeur en het familiebedrijf', Walgemoed Accountants and Advisors, Breukelen, Centre for Entrepreneurship, Nijenrode University.

Flören, R.H. and E.J. Wijers (1996), 'Handboek van het familiebedrijf', Walgemoed Accountants and Advisors, Breukelen, Nijenrode University.

Gomez-Mejia, L.R., H. Tosi and T. Hinkin (1987), 'A managerial control, performance and executive compensation', *Academy of Management Journal*, **30**, 51–70.

Griffin, R. and R. Ebert (1996), *Business*, New Jersey: Prentice Hall International Editions.

Gudmundson, D., E.A. Hartman and C.B. Tower (1999), 'Strategic orientation: differences between family and non-family firms', *Family Business Review*, **12**(1), 27–39.

Harris, D., J. Martinez and J.L. Ward (1994), 'Is strategy different for the family-owned business?', *Family Business Review*, **7**(2), 159–74.

Henderson, R. and K. Clark (1990), 'Architectural innovation: the reconfiguration of existing product technologies and the failure of established firms', *Administrative Science Quarterly*, **35**, 9–30.

Hodgetts, R.M. and D.F. Kuratko (1982), 'Understanding the family business', in R.M. Hodgetts and D.F. Kuratko (eds), *Effective Small Business Management*, Orlando, CA: Dryden Press.

Huang, X. and A. Brown (1998), 'Innovation management and contemporary small enterprise research', Proceedings of the International Council for Small Business World Conference, 8–10 June, Singapore, www.sbaer.uca.edu/research/icsb/1998/pdf/125.pdf (accessed 27 March 2008).

Hulshoff, H. (2001), 'Strategic study; family business in the Dutch SME-sector, definition and characteristics', Zoetermeer, EIM Business and Policy Research, the Netherlands.

James, L.R. and J.M. Brett (1984), 'Mediators, moderators, and tests for mediation', *Journal of Applied Psychology*, **69**(2), 307–21.

Janszen, F. (2000), *The Age of Innovation*, London: Prentice Hall Financial Times.

Kenny, J. (2003), 'Effective project management for strategic innovation and change in an organizational context', *Project Management Journal*, **34**(1), 43–54.

Klein, S. (2000), 'Family business in Germany: significance and structure', *Family Business Review*, **13**(3), 157–74.

Li, H. and K. Atuahene-Gima (2001), 'Product innovation strategy and the performance of new technology ventures in China', *Academy of Management Journal*, **44**(6), 1123–34.

March, J.G. and H.A. Simon (1958), Organizations, New York: Wiley.

Martin, J.J.S. and K.C. Suarez (2001), 'Behaviour and performance of listed family companies versus listed non-family companies', Proceedings of the Family Business Network Conference, Rome, Italy, pp. 436–53.

Miller, D., M.F.R. Kets de Vries and J.-M. Toulouse (1982), 'Top executive locus of control and its relationship to strategy-making, structure, and environment', *Academy of Management Journal*, **25**(2), 237–53.

Mintzberg, H. and J. Waters (1985), 'Of strategies, deliberate and emergent', *Strategic Management Journal*, **3**, 257–72.

Neubauer, F. and A.G. Lank (1998), *The Family Business, it's Governance for Sustainability*, New York: Routledge.

Ottum, B. (1996), 'Focus groups and new product development', *Marketing News*, **30**(12), H26.

Perricone, P.J., J.R. Earle and I.M. Taplin (2001), 'Patterns of succession and continuity in family owned businesses', *Family Business Review*, **14**(2), 105–20.

Porter, M.E. (1985), *Competitive Strategy: Techniques for Analyzing Industries and Competitors*, New York: Free Press.

Stoy Hayward (1989), *Staying the Course: Survival Characteristics of the Family Owned Business*, London: Stoy Hayward.

Uhlaner, L.M. (2005), 'The use of the Guttman scale in development of a family orientation index for small-to-medium-sized firms', *Family Business Review*, **43**(1), 41–56.

Verheul, I., L.M. Uhlaner and A.R. Thurik (2005), 'Business accomplishments, gender and entrepreneurial self-image', *Journal of Business Venturing*, **20**(4), 483–518.

Westhead, P. and M. Cowling (1996), 'Demographic contrasts between family and non-family unquoted companies in the UK', CSME working paper 32, Warwick Business School, University of Warwick, Coventry.

Westhead, P. and M. Cowling (1997), 'Performance contrasts between family and non-family unquoted companies in the UK', *International Journal of Entrepreneurial Behaviour and Research*, **3**(1), 30–52.

Westhead, P., M. Cowling and C. Howorth C. (2001), 'The development of family companies: management and ownership imperatives', *Family Business Review*, **14**(4), 369–84.

Westhead, P., C. Howorth and M. Cowling (2002), 'Ownership and management issues in first and multi-generation family firms', *Entrepreneurship and Regional Development*, **14**, 247–69.

Wheelright, S. and K. Clark (1992), *Revolutionizing Product Development; Quantum Leaps in Speed, Efficiency, and Quality*, New York: Free Press.

APPENDIX

Table 8A.1 Description of variables[1]

Name of Variable	Description of Variable
Innovation Performance	
Innovation Performance $\alpha = 0.46$	For innovation performance, the mean of the following two questions was computed at time 't'(2005): 1. Has the company introduced new products, services or production processes to the market in the last 3 years? 2. Has the company introduced new products or services to the market in the last 3 years? (1 = 'no'; 2 = 'yes')
Family Orientation	
Family Orientation $\alpha = 0.83$	This scale was created by combining answers to the following 12 questions using the CATPCA technique (see text). Measured in time 't-3' years (2002). 1. What is the share of ownership within a single family? (1 = < 50%; 2 = 50%; 3 = > 50% but < 100;4 = 100%) The following were answered with the following scale: (1 = 'yes'; 2 = 'no') 2. Two or more owners are related to each other? 3. Two or more generations of the same family are owners? 4. Members of one family own the company for at least two generations? 5. Owner plans to retain ownership within one family? 6. Two or more managers are related to each other? 7. Two or more generations of the same family are managers? 8. Would you describe your company as a family business? The scales for the following items are indicated below each question or set of questions: 9. What is the likelihood of management transfer to family member or owner? (1 = 'probably not'; 2 = 'maybe'; 3 = 'probably') 10. To what extent do family members determine strategy? 11. To what extent do family members determine culture? (1 = 'not or to a very limited extent'; 2 = 'to some extent'; 3 = 'to a very large extent') 12. Is the predecessor of the CEO related to the (current) owners?

Table 8A.1 (continued)

Name of Variable	Description of Variable
	(1 = 'predecessor from outside the family'; 2 = 'no predecessor' 3 = 'predecessor within family')
Context	
Company Size	Computed as the natural logarithm of the response to the following question at time 't-2' years (2003). How many persons does the company employ? (Respondents and co-working family members included, part-timers count for their part-time)
Company Age	Computed based on the difference between founding year and 2003 (measured at time 't-2' years (2003).
Manufacturing Sector	Whether the company is operating in a manufacturing sector. Question: Is the company operating in either the industrial sector or in construction? (1 = 'no'; 2 = 'yes')
Retail and Wholesale Sector	Whether the company is operating in the retail and wholesale sector. Question: Is the company operating in retail and wholesale? (1 = 'no'; 2 = 'yes')
Strategy	
Focus $\alpha = 0.82$	The company follows a 'Focus' competitive strategy, on a particular target market (t-4; 2001 and on going). This scale was based on two items, combined using the CATPCA method: 1. Is the statement relevant/true for the company: To beat our competition, we focus on a specific target group of customers. (1 = 'not relevant at all'; 2 = 'partly relevant'; 3 = 'very relevant') 2. Does your company export goods and/or services outside the country? (1 = 'no'; 2 = 'yes')
Risk Orientation $\alpha = 0.75$	Whether the company is willing to take business risks (t-3; 2002). This scale was based on four items, combined using the CATPCA method. 1. If you have to choose, which of the following descriptions best fits your business? (1 = There is a preference to make decisions with little risk, where the expected yield is 'normal' and known in advance; 2 = There is a preference to make decisions with reasonable to great risk, where the expected returns are variable but high)

Table 8A.1 (continued)

Name of Variable	Description of Variable
	2. Which of the following better describes the philosophy of your firm? (1 = Working cautiously in a step-by-step manner; 2 = A preference for daring decisions as opposed to cautious actions) 3. Which type of decisions does your business take in situations of uncertainty? (1 = An anticipatory approach to avoid costly decisions; 2 = A proactive strategy to exploit different possibilities) 4. How much risk does the company take compared to other companies? (1 = 'very little risk to no risk'; 2 = 'very little risk'; 3 = 'some risk'; 4 = 'relatively much risk', 5 = 'much risk')
Strategic Process $\alpha = 0.53$	This scale is based on a mean of the following two items: (t-4; 2001). 1. Is the competitive strategy for your business written down? (1 = 'no'; 2 = 'yes') 2. Do you approach strategy systematically? (in a planned manner) (1 = 'no'; 2 = 'yes')
Growth Orientation	Whether the desire or wish to grow is present in the company (t-4; 2001). Question: Do you want to let the company grow? (1 = 'no'; 2 = 'yes')
Price Discounting	The company follows a 'Price discounting' competitive strategy (t-1; 2001). Is the statement relevant/true for the company: To beat our competition, we keep our prices as low as possible. (1 = 'not relevant at all'; 2 = 'partly relevant'; 3 = 'very relevant')
Innovation Differentiation $\alpha = 0.75$	The company follows an 'Innovation differentiation' competitive strategy (t-4; 2001). This scale is based on a mean of the following two items: 1. How much thought have you given in the past 3 years to the following means to compete? 'Bringing new products to the market'. 2. How much thought have you given in the past 3 years to the following means to compete? 'Developing new products.' (1 = 'none at all'; 2 = 'little thought'; 3 = 'much thought')

Note: 1. As presented, all scales are reversed from what was originally measured, with the exception of company size and age. This is to expedite interpretation of signs in the tables. Thus, for instance, for innovation performance, originally 1 = yes, 2 = no and so on.).

PART IV

Performance of New Ventures

9. New venture teams: the relationship between initial team characteristics, team processes and performance

Daniela A. Almer-Jarz, Erich J. Schwarz and Robert J. Breitenecker

INTRODUCTION

New and young ventures advance employment, innovation and competitiveness (Jungbauer-Gans, 1993; Schwarz and Grieshuber, 2003). There is evidence that young ventures founded by two or more persons (team foundations) have higher success prospects than their solo entrepreneurial counterparts (Cooper and Bruno, 1977; Picot et al., 1989; Mellewigt and Späth, 2002). Team foundations are likely to possess higher economic, cultural and social capital. As a consequence, they have better starting and development conditions (Lechler and Gemünden, 2003). However, there are only a limited number of studies concerning new venture teams (NVT) (Francis and Sandberg, 2000; Ensley and Pearce, 2001; Chandler et al., 2005) which examine the aspect of new venture performance in particular (Vyakarnam et al., 1999).

Within the literature on NVT and new venture performance two main lines of studies have emerged. One line of studies addresses demographic characteristics of the founders. These studies concentrate on such aspects as team size, heterogeneity, previous experience and education (Teach et al., 1986; Ensley et al., 1998; Amason et al., 2006). The other line of studies focuses on team processes, for example, conflicts or cohesion within the team (Watson et al., 1995; Ensley et al., 2002). For both, team characteristics (Teach et al., 1986) and process variables (Ensley et al., 2002), significant effects on new venture performance have been found. Both approaches disregard the existing relationship between team characteristics and team processes. The simultaneous analysis of team characteristics and team processes is necessary (Smith et al., 1994; Camelo-Ordaz et al., 2005 (for top management teams)). Only few studies consider both aspects of newly founded ventures simultaneously (Lechler and Gemünden, 2003).

The aim of this chapter is to investigate the influence of team characteristics (size, heterogeneity and educational level of the team members) and characteristics of the team process (communication, work norms and fluctuation) on new venture performance. This chapter is based on the data of a longitudinal study of young Austrian SMEs. For the structural model we use the Partial Least Squares-method (PLS-method).

The chapter is structured as follows. It starts with a literature analysis of previous research on new venture performance of NVTs. The need for simultaneous analysis of demographic and process characteristics is outlined. Afterwards the hypotheses are developed and tested on the basis of a structural model. The chapter ends with a discussion of the results and scientific and practical implications.

DEMOGRAPHIC CHARACTERISTICS AND TEAM PROCESSES AS INFLUENCING FACTORS FOR NEW VENTURE PERFORMANCE

Definition of New Venture Teams

In previous literature on new venture teams a variety of team definitions exists, which makes comparison of the results difficult (Birley and Stockley, 2000). These definitions have in common the fact that a founder team has to consist of at least two individuals. This broad quantitative approach disregards qualitative aspects of the team. Within the literature on groups the qualitative aspects are stressed. Therefore it is quite common to differentiate between the concept of team and the concept of group (Katzenbach and Douglas, 2003). Teams in a narrower sense are seen as special groups which are more closely connected, stand up for one another and are characterized by engagement and commitment. They can be characterised in the following way: (1) pursuit of common goals, (2) working together in the venture and (3) commitment (Katzenbach and Douglas, 2003).

Differentiation between founder teams in a broader and a narrower sense is of paramount importance. Only teams in a narrower sense have numerous characteristics, which are discussed as advantageous for new venture performance (for example, variety of perspectives within the decision making process). In this chapter we analyse teams in a narrow sense. Our definition is that: a founder team has to consist of at least two individuals, all team members have to be shareholders (bearing risks), they must participate actively in the venture (work together) and make concerted decisions (corporative goals).

Theoretical Background

Studies indicate that top management teams in large companies have high impact on organizational performance (Hambrick and Mason, 1984). Following the upper echelon theory organizational outcomes can be seen as reflections of the values and cognitive bases of powerful actors in the organization. Early studies on teams and performance based on the upper echelon theory concentrated on the demographic characteristics of the founder team, for example, team size, educational level, measures of heterogeneity (Hambrick and Mason, 1984) Most of these studies are aware of the fact that the use of proxies is only of 'methodological convenience' (Carpenter et al., 2004). They require the influence of team processes to be analysed directly, stating that there is a need to explore the 'black box' (Birley and Stockley, 2000).

It can be assumed that a founder team has more influence on the development of a venture than a top management team in a large enterprise. Top management teams in established organizations have strict routines, a set of rules, (in)formal structure of power and less scope to be creative (Greiner, 1998). Therefore the upper echelon perspective has also been applied for new venture teams (Birley and Stockley, 2000; Ensley et al., 2002).

In the context of new ventures, for example, the size of the founder team can be seen as an indicator for competences, such as problem solving (Birley and Stockley, 2000), or a higher degree of homogeneity leads to better outcomes when considering satisfaction (Chowdhury, 2005). Demographic variables take on the role of proxies for team process outcomes. Thereby, no explicit statements of the mode of action of the proxies are given (Birley and Stockley, 2000). The second line of literature emphazises the importance of investigating the processes in teams (Ensley et al., 2002; Spieker, 2004). For example, Ensley et al. (2002) found that affective conflicts have a negative influence on new venture performance. In addition, a positive correlation between decision quality and new venture performance was reported (Spieker, 2004).

Only few studies concerning top management teams in established organizations give equal consideration to demographic and process characteristics (Smith et al., 1994). In the context of NVTs only the study of Lechler and Gemünden exists (2003).

Previous research does not analyse demographic characteristics and team process characteristics simultaneously. Theoretically, we continue the efforts of Ensley and Pearson (2005) and Ensley et al. (2002) to extend the upper echelon perspective, with elements from theories of group behaviour. By doing so, we analyse how demographic characteristics affect new venture performance via team processes. We will use elements from the signalling theory and also from theories on group behaviour (for example, theories about work norms and communication). Firstly, we will analyse how demographic variables cause direct and indirect effects on new venture performance. For example, a larger founder team can raise more resources and so gain advantages in capacity (Lechler and Gemünden, 2003). A higher education level of the founder team could, according to the signalling theory (Arrow, 1973), foster the trust of capital providers and customers. A heterogeneous team also has access to broader networks, which overlap each other less (for the network approach, see Brüderl and Preisendörfer, 1998). All the effects of demographic variables mentioned affect new venture performance directly. At the same time, a larger founder team affects the outcomes of team processes. For example, the team size has a direct influence on the communication quality of the team and this again affects new venture performance (indirect effect) (Figure 9.1).

Secondly, we will also analyse the effects of team processes on new venture performance. In this chapter work norms, communication and fluctuation are discussed. 'Norms are rules of conduct which specify appropriate behaviour in a given range of social contexts. A norm either prescribes a given type of behaviour or forbids it. All human groups follow definite types of norms, which are always backed by sanctions of one kind or another – varying from informal disapproval to physical punishment or execution' (Giddens, 1997, p. 538). Social norms (work norms) are a basic element of group processes. In the context of team foundations work norms have not been investigated so far, but their relevance has been proven in the research of work groups (Cohen and Bailey, 1997). Similar assumptions can be stated for communication. Communication can be defined as 'the transmission of information from one individual or group to another. Communication is the necessary basis of all social interaction' (Giddens, 1997, p. 581). Therefore it is also a basic element of group processes. To date, communication has been neglected in nearly all entrepreneurship literature, but there are studies in the context of work teams, which support the importance of high quality of communication in teams. Fluctuation is described as the exit and entry of new members in the entrepreneurial team. Changes in the entrepreneurial founder team are very common. Cooper and Bruno (1977) recount that in 48 per cent of high technology firms they investigated at least one founder had left the surveyed ventures. Similar observations have been made by Gumbert (1983) and Timmons (1990, cited by Ucbasaran et al., 2003). The issue of management fluctuation has been well recognized within larger established firms. The studies provide support that longer organizational tenure leads to less effective teams in organizations that need to make strategic shifts (Cohen and Bailey, 1997).

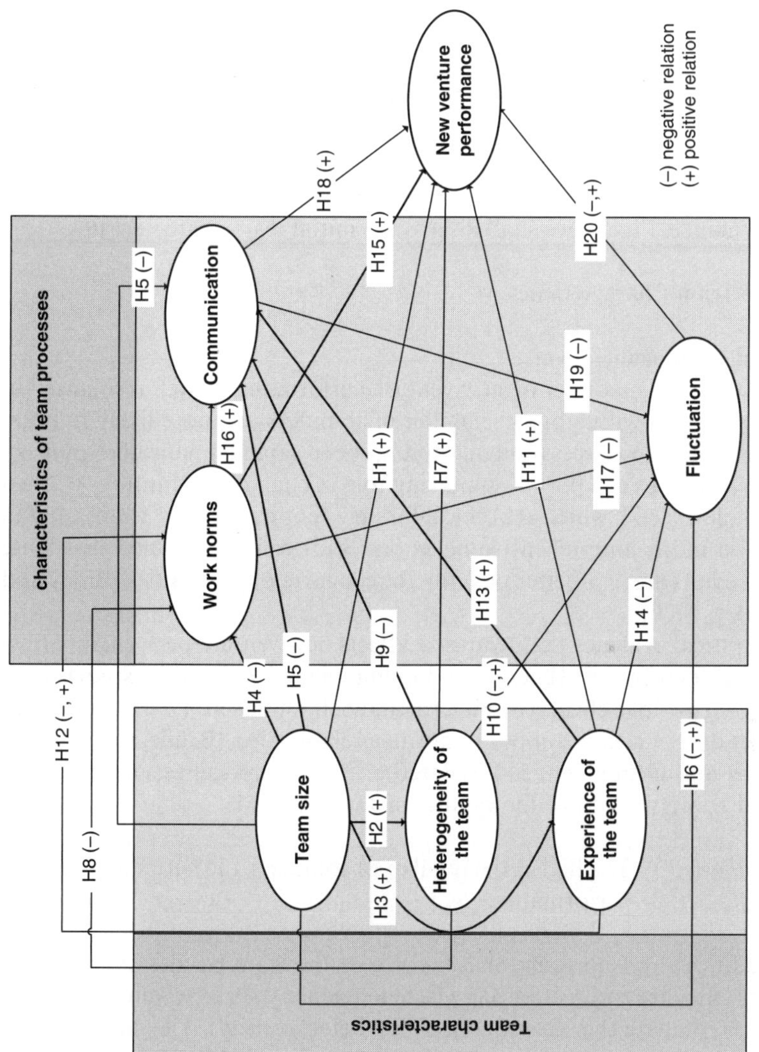

Figure 9.1 *Theoretical model*

But the relationships found in top management teams in larger established firms may not necessarily hold for founder teams. Through the less stable structure in newly founded ventures a change of the NVT can cause existential crisis. So the effect of fluctuation could be negative to new venture performance.

DEVELOPMENT OF THE HYPOTHESES

We developed twenty hypotheses on how the selected initial team characteristics and the characteristics of the team processes can affect new venture performance. Firstly, we shall discuss the initial team characteristics.

Initial Team Characteristics

Size of the founding team

Team size as a predictor of new venture performance is well recognized in studies. Teams with a higher number of founders are more likely to bring in worthwhile resources (human capital, social capital, financial resources). These resources can play a supporting role in changing conditions (Cohen and Bailey, 1997), which are typical for new ventures. Larger teams can fall back on more comprehensive networks. So it can be assumed that these larger teams are in a better position to recognize opportunities (Birley and Stockley, 2000).

Empirical evidence that team size affects new venture performance positively is inconsistent (Lechler and Gemünden, 2003). Some studies have identified positive effects (Eisenhardt and Schoonhoven, 1990), while other studies do not clearly support a positive relationship (Brüderl et al., 1996; Lechler and Gemünden, 2003). Based on the theoretical assumptions presented above we assume the validity of Hypothesis 1.

Hypothesis 1: The higher the number of founders, the better new venture performance.

Additionally, we assume that the size of the team besides having direct effects also has indirect effects via heterogeneity on new venture performance (compare the section concerning heterogeneity). The more individuals founding a new venture, the higher the likelihood is that these individuals differ more when it comes to age, experience and other factors.

Hypothesis 2: The larger new venture teams, the more heterogeneous the team.

The larger the team the higher the likelihood is that at least one person has a higher level of education, therefore the team size should be controlled within the analysis of experience and new venture performance.

Hypothesis 3: The larger new venture teams, the higher their amount of experience.

The phenomenon of social loafing emerges in groups. Social loafing is the tendency for individuals to expend less effort when working collectively than when working individually. The first observation that suggests a possible decrease in individual motivation as a result of working in a group was conducted at the beginning of the twentieth century. Male volunteers were asked to pull on a rope (tug-of-war), as hard as they could in groups of varying size. The rope was connected to a strain gauge that measured the group's total effort. The result indicated that as the group size increased, group effort was increasingly lower than would be expected by a single addition of individual performance. For this phenomenon two explanations were suggested. On the one hand, there is the possibility that this reduction of effort is because of a coordination loss. On the other hand, the reason could be a loss of motivation. Various experiments have supported the second assumption. Since that time the term social loafing in literature stands for the discouraging affect of working in groups. To date, the concept has been widely empirically tested in a great variety of tasks (Karau and Williams, 1993). The phenomenon of social loafing can also occur in new venture teams. The more team members, the more there is a danger to neglect the promise that all founders will work with equal work commitment, each founder operates at full capacity to achieve the business objectives and all team members get equally involved in the process of goal attainment (work norms)

Therefore we can assume that there is a negative relation between team size and work norms. Additionally, in larger teams it is more difficult to agree upon collective goals. Collective goals are important for the coordination within a group. Without coordination division of labour is not possible.

Hypothesis 4: The larger new venture teams, the worse the quality of work norms.

The size of the founding team influences communication and work norms negatively (Lechler and Gemünden, 2003). The more persons there are who have to communicate with each other, the less direct contact is possible (Smith et al., 1994; Wahren, 1994). This can have effects on the accuracy of the transfer of information which can cause delayed decisions. Therefore we assume that the size of the venture team effects communication negatively.

Hypothesis 5: The larger new venture teams, the worse the quality of communication.

Whether the size of the founder team affects the fluctuation positively or negatively is controversial. Ucbasaran et al. (2003), who differentiated between team member entry and team member exit, postulated different directions of influence. Regarding team member entry they postulated that the team size is negatively linked with subsequent team member entry. For the team member exit they assume that the size of the founding team was positively associated with subsequent team member exit. Only the second assumption could be upheld (Ucbasaran et al., 2003).

We do not distinguish between team member entry and team member exit. We have defined fluctuations as changes within the team. It can be assumed that larger teams have less problems with fluctuation than smaller teams, because they are more able to compensate the situation if a person leaves the team. They are in a better position to exchange team members because of their broader networks. It could also be assumed that smaller teams have more need to strengthen their team by integrating new members. So we formulate an undirected hypothesis.

Hypothesis 6: The size of the founder team affects the fluctuation of the team.

Heterogeneity

The analysis of heterogeneity of founder teams concerning industry and leadership experience, age and other characteristics is important when identifying factors which support new venture performance (Chowdhury, 2005). The mode of action of heterogeneity on new venture performance is not quite clear. In the literature heterogeneity is therefore characterized as a 'double edged sword' (Milliken and Martins, 1996).

A venture team with varying abilities and experiences should be in a better position to handle new situations and problems (Ensley et al., 1998). There are varied new tasks to handle, especially in the start-up phase; therefore it can be assumed that heterogeneity has a positive effect on new venture performance. Further more, demographic heterogeneity could lead to a wide cognitive spectrum which supports the process of finding new strategies and creative solutions. Empirical findings support a positive relation between heterogeneity of industry experience and new venture performance (Eisenhardt and Schoonhoven, 1990; Lechler and Gemünden, 2003).

Following the social capital approach, social networks are of paramount importance for opportunity recognition and subsequently for the exploitation of opportunities, but also for the legitimating of the new business (Granovetter, 1973; Schwarz et al., 2005). In the process of opportunity recognition the founders use primarily weak ties, which provide a wide base of different information (Bloodgood et al., 1995, cited by Elfring and Hulsink, 2003). To exploit these opportunities resources have to be acquired. The help of friends and relatives (strong ties) is thereby important (Landström and Winborg, 1995; Taub and Gaglio, 1995). The number of network partners will be higher if the size of the founder team is larger. The breadth of the network depends on how much the networks of the founders overlap. If team members have different career and personal backgrounds (heterogeneous founder teams), the founder team has access to a broad and highly differentiated network.

In the context of team foundations we assume, based on theoretical arguments and previous empirical findings, positive direct effects of team heterogeneity and new venture performance.

Hypothesis 7: The higher the heterogeneity of the NVT, the better the new venture performance.

The relationship between heterogeneity and work norms has not been investigated so far in the context of entrepreneurial teams. The literature in the field of work teams and top management teams is also scarse. Empirical results regarding work teams suggest that homogeneous groups have more stable cooperative norms than heterogeneous groups (Chatman and Flynn, 2001). According to Goldthorpe's 'action' approach, workers define and interpret their current work situation based on subjective assumptions which are minted by previous experiences (Goldthorpe's thesis, cited by Mikl-Horke, 2000). Hence previous work experience (leadership experience, industry experience) have concrete influence on the team work. It can be assumed that heterogeneous teams, in terms of different work experience, have different opinions on how to organize work that can have negative effects on the development of cooperative work norms. According to this, it can be assumed that teams with high age heterogeneity have different conceptions of lifestyle and different forms of habitus (in the sociological sense). Also, age can be a proxy for psychological and physical capacity. Therefore it can be assumed that high differences in age can lead to a situation in which not all team members provide the same work effort. We formulate:

Hypothesis 8: The higher the heterogeneity of the NVT, the worse the quality of work norms.

Team work needs communication. But communication processes also have a risk potential of misunderstandings and misinterpretations. These risks arise, for example, from the differing previous work experiences of the team members. Comprehensibility of communication is a key of success within innovation teams (Hauschildt and Salomo, 2007). Research on demographic diversity of top management teams stresses that heterogeneity can have a negative impact on communication. People have a tendency to place individuals into social categories based on demographic characteristics. Often they perceive their own category as superior and tend to stereotype members of other categories, which can lead to a hostile atmosphere and ineffective communication results (Chowdhury, 2005).

Hypothesis 9: The higher the heterogeneity of the NVT, the worse the communication quality.

Demographic heterogeneity has the potential to produce emotional conflicts (Eisenhardt et al., 1997). Arising distrust and problems within the team work can lead to decisions where team members exit and leave the new venture. On the other hand, based on arguments of the human capital theory, heterogeneity in the team leads to an ideal situation concerning the balance and compensations of skills and abilities within the team. There is no need to receive new members into the team and also no need for someone to leave. We have formulated an undirected hypothesis:

Hypothesis 10: The heterogeneity of the founder team affects fluctuation.

Experience

In general, a positive influence of previous experience and new venture performance is predicated (Cooper et al., 1994; Sapienza and Grimm, 1997). The theoretical basis for this assumption is based on the human capital theory and the theory of social capital. The human capital theory postulates that human capital affects the productivity of labour positively (Becker, 1964). The human capital perspective is used in a broader sense in entrepreneurship literature. Here it is assumed that human capital, for example industry experience and the educational level of the individuals, influence new venture performance. Founders with a wide background of experiences are able to handle new information in a better way. They are better in identifying opportunities ('entrepreneurial alertness') (Ardichvili et al., 2003). Social capital is defined as the ability of individuals to extract benefits from their social structures, networks and memberships (Hitt and Ireland, 2005). In the field of entrepreneurship the social relations of the founders are discussed as an important source of gaining essential resources (Brüderl et al., 1996). Social ties are important when getting information about potential employees, customers and venture capital. Previous work experience provides valuable contacts which are also useful for finding new opportunities. Bhidé reports that 70 per cent of business ideas of founders or founder teams of the Inc. 500, a fast growing group of new ventures in the USA, were developed in previous employment (Bhidé, 2000).

Individuals who had already started a venture in the past gained experiences, regardless of whether the venture was successful or not. It can be assumed that these 'habitual entrepreneurs' are less naive and have a clearer picture about their new business idea. They have also gained managerial experiences, which can be useful within the new venture (Wright et al., 1998).

Previous empirical studies do not give a clear answer about the effect of human capital and new venture performance (for an overview, see Kennedy and Drennan, 2001). Based on theoretical assumptions we assume positive effects.

Hypothesis 11: The higher the amount of experience, the better new venture performance.

Experience may effect work norms positively and negatively. On the one hand, persons with leadership experience are familiar with modern leadership concepts, which are normally more cooperative than authoritarian. On the other hand, persons with leadership experience are used to delegate operative tasks. Now, in the role of the founder, they have to do many tasks on their own, because most newly founded ventures have (if any) only a small number of employees (Schwarz and Grieshuber, 2003). This new role may lead to conflicts which can effect work norms negatively. Also, entrepreneurial experience (if it was not acquired in a team) could indicate that these persons do not have much experience in team-oriented work approaches. Because of these conflicting arguments we formulate the hypothesis as non-directional.

Hypothesis 12: The amount of experience affects the quality of work norms.

Mintzberg (1971) described management tasks as strongly related to communication competences. Especially in the context of interpersonal management roles, for example the manager as figurehead, as external liaison and leader, but also in his function as the nerve centre of the organization's information system, communication competences are essential. Communication competences are learned within the process of socialization (for an overview of socialization theory, see Zimmermann, 2003). We assume that persons with higher leadership experience have more communication experiences, because in their previous work situation they were able to gain a variety of experience on how to communicate effectively and how to avoid and solve conflicts.

Entrepreneurial experience, which will be the second dimension of experience in our model, effects the quality of communication positively. In the context of entrepreneurship it is necessary to gather information and also to hand over information punctually. Persons who have had entrepreneurial experience in the past have learned to use their time efficiently.

Hypothesis 13: The more experienced the team members, the better the quality of communication.

If a team has a lot of experience it can be assumed that there is no need for someone new to join the team. It is also in the interest of the team that all qualified team members stay within the newly founded venture (Ucbasaran et al., 2003). To sum up, less experience could lead to fluctuation because it makes sense for new members to join the team to support and complement the original founder team. If there is a high level of experience it can be assumed that there will be no changes within the structure of the founder team. We formulate Hypothesis 14.

Hypothesis 14: The more experienced the team members, the higher the fluctuation.

Characteristics of Team Processes

Work norms

In a newly founded venture it is essential that there is an agreement within the team that the work has to be divided. The division of responsibilities within the founder team needs coordination. Coordination reduces waiting time overlapping, double work or to tasks being forgotten. Especially in young ventures there are situations which have to be coped with without a predefined work flow. In such a situation norms, which describe appropriate behaviour in a given range of social contexts (Hillmann, 1994), can be an instrument for coordination. If the team has developed cooperative work norms, team members can make decisions faster.

The advantages of NVTs only yield fruit if the team members trust each other and know that everyone is motivated to give his/her best. A shared understanding of how the team members act in standard and non-standard situations through the compliance with work norms also strengthens the cohesion of the team. If the team members are proud to be a part of the team, the work performance increases (Cohen and Bailey, 1997). Also the shared visions, which are represented within the cooperative work norms, can be related to venture performance (Ensley et al., 2002). Therefore we assume that:

Hypothesis 15: The higher the quality of work norms, the better new venture performance.

For the coordination of the work, accurate and timely communication is essential. An agreement in the team on how the work should be divided can reduce potential conflicts. If the team members are cooperative about goals, for example, if all team members get equally involved in the process of goal attainment, they will, as a matter of course, transfer the information (punctually and accurately) to other team members. Therefore we assume that there is a direct relation between work norms and communication.

Hypothesis 16: The higher the quality of work norms, the better the quality of communication.

It can be assumed that if the team members are pleased with the coordination of team work, nobody will leave the team. Also if team members are satisfied about the quality of work norms they do not wish that someone else will join the team. If a new team member enters the team, costs of adaptation emerge. It takes time until new team members share the work norms of the original team.

Hypothesis 17: The higher the quality of work norms, the lower the fluctuation.

Communication

A strength of NVTs is that they can divide up all activities which occur in the venture. Especially in cases where the team members have different skills, all can benefit from the advantages of specialization. In order to divide and coordinate duties the team members have to communicate. This means they have to exchange reciprocal information.

In the early development stage of the venture multiple tasks have to be managed and all has to be done in time. Most of these tasks are strongly correlated to each other. Communication plays a crucial rule in handling these jobs. Each day the team faces unexpected occurrences, for example, in terms of changes in supply or customers or financing, which need coordination within the team. Frequent communication within the team is therefore necessary. The aspect of punctuality and accuracy is also important for the development of the new venture because there are strong interdependences within the work process. For project teams Keller found that communication of the team was positively related to managers' assessment of performance (Keller, 1994, cited by Cohen and Bailey, 1997, p. 264). For top management teams Smith investigated informal communication and communication frequency (Smith et al., 1994). For both aspects the authors found, contrary to their hypothesis, negative effects.

Hypothesis 18: The higher the quality of communication, the better new venture performance.

For the relation between communication and fluctuation we also assume effects. It can be proposed that if the team members evaluate the quality of communication highly, they are satisfied with the team culture and will stay in the team. It can be assumed that if team members like the way the team communicates they do not want new persons to join. If a new member enters the team, costs of adaptation emerge until the new team member learns how the formal and informal communication works in the original team. Therefore we assume that communication affects fluctuation negatively.

Hypothesis 19: The higher the quality of communication, the lower the fluctuation.

Fluctuation

Fluctuation can be defined as changes in the founder team over a specified period (Daily and Dalton, 1995; Krishnan, Miller and Judge, 1997, cited by Ucbasaran et al., 2003, p. 108). Most research has been made in the field of top management teams. Within the investigation of newly founded ventures the investigation of fluctuation has been neglected.

Therefore the direction of the influence of fluctuation on new venture performance is quite unclear. On the one hand, it can be assumed that if a founder person leaves the venture it can lead to bottle necks, and advantages which emerged from the reciprocal complementation of abilities and skills get lost. But fluctuation can also have positive effects. For example, when a team member that does not fit into the team leaves the venture, this can effect the development of the venture positively. A further example of a positive effect of fluctuation is if there are changes in strategy. It can be assumed that if the venture has made strategic change within the first years, and maybe a team member cannot contribute to the development of the venture because of these changes, an exit could also be positive for the development of the new venture. It could be also positive should a new person enter the team who is able to contribute to the development of the new venture. In addition, an exit may be positive when there are important differences concerning the strategy of the venture, or differences relating to the daily work process or personal conflicts.

Because we have measured fluctuation in terms of entry and exit, we cannot make any assumptions on what effects entry or exit will cause. We can investigate if changes in the NVT have an effect on new venture performance. We assume that:

Hypothesis 20: Fluctuation affects new venture performance.

EMPIRICAL ANALYSIS

Sample

The study is based on the population of 22 000 ventures of the founding cohort 1999. The data are from the Austrian Chamber of Commerce. This database includes 80 per cent of all ventures founded in 1999. In the first cross section (2002), data of 729 ventures were collected by random sample (including solo foundations and team foundations). Then, from personal interviews the new ventures were differentiated into solo ventures and team foundations. One hundred and eighty-two of these ventures (25 per cent) were founded by more than one person (teams in a broader sense). In a second cross section (2005), 130 of these team foundations were interviewed again (ventures founded by at least two persons).

In this study only team foundations in a narrower sense are investigated (see definition of 'team' above). All new ventures which are not founded by at least two persons, and all ventures where not all team members are involved in important decision processes of the venture, are excluded. Thus ventures where only one founder works in the venture and the other members only participate financially are excluded. Additionally, foundations by spouse and near family were excluded because they could not give objective and reliable information about the team processes in the firm. Twelve founding teams refused to be interviewed and six of those questioned had to be excluded because of missing data. Finally, 62 new ventures were analysed. The average team size is 2.92 persons. The maximum team size is 6 persons. Fifty-six per cent of the ventures are stable in terms of fluctuation. Forty-four per cent of the ventures have fluctuation, which can be divided as follows: in 63 per cent of the cases of fluctuation, a founder person has left the team and no one has entered the team; in 33 per cent of the cases of fluctuation somebody has left the team but a new team member has joined; and in one case only a new team member has entered.

In terms of sector distribution 54.8 per cent of the ventures are in the service sector, 21 per cent in the retail industry, 11.3 per cent are in manufacturing industry and a similar amount (9.7 per cent) operates in the building sector. The remaining 3.2 per cent of the ventures are in the transport sector or other sectors.

Measurement

The literature suggests different ways of measurement of new venture performance (NVP) (Ford and Gioia, 1995; Delmar, 1997). In this study we used the growth of employees and the turnover (growth in percentages). Profit is not used as a performance indicator in this study because above all innovative growth-oriented young ventures have to invest. They resign early profits to gain profits in the future (Schmidt, 2002). In addition, the number of employees and the change of this indicator is easier to survey than to determine the average of return, because the latter indicator is much more confidential (Frank et al., 1995).

When analysing team characteristics as exogenous variables, the size of the founder team, indicators for heterogeneity and experiences are used. The size of the founder team is measured by the number of founders who founded the venture, those working in the venture and those engaged in decision making processes. The heterogeneity is measured by age, amount of industry experience and leadership experience. As the indicator for heterogeneity the standard deviation within the team is used (Bortz, 1999). Experience is made up of leadership experience and entrepreneurial experience. In the analysis we consider the maximum experience in the team. Fluctuation is measured in the change of the founder team within the first six years. Change means team member entry and/or exit. Within the analysis of process communication and work norms each were measured in three items (Lechler and Gemünden, 2003) (Table 9.1).

Method

In this study in addition to direct effects of team characteristics and the characteristics of team processes, indirect effects of team characteristics on

Table 9.1 Measurement of the constructs

	Label (number of items)	Description	Scale
NVP	new venture performance (2)	growth of employees	metrical
		growth of turnover (percentages)	metrical
team characteristics	size of the founding team	number of founders	metrical
	heterogeneity (3)	heterogeneity of age	metrical
		heterogeneity of industry experience	metrical
		heterogeneity of leadership experience	metrical
	experience (2)	length of time of leadership experience (max. team)	metrical
		length of time of entrepreneurship experience (max. team)	metrical
team processes characteristics	fluctuation	team member entry and/or exit	dichotomous
	communication (3)	frequency of communication	ordinal
		punctuality of information	ordinal
		accurate transfer of communication	ordinal
	work norms (3)	all founders work with equal work commitment	ordinal
		each founder operates at full capacity to achieve the business objectives	ordinal
		all team members get equally involved in the process of goal attainment	ordinal

new venture performance are also assumed (structural model). Constructs are used as well which are not observable and which have to be operationalized through measurement models. To investigate simultaneous complex relations between constructs, structural models are adequate instruments (SEM) (Nachtigall et al., 2003).

In this study we have used the Partial Least Square Method (PLS), because this method does not have a specific assumption of distribution. Also PLS is based on variances and therefore this method needs less cases than covariance based SEM methods (Albers and Hildebrandt, 2006). The analysis is carried out with the statistical software package Smart PLS (Ringle et al., 2005). To evaluate the quality of the model we discuss in a first step the measurement model and in a second step the structural model. Because there are no distribution assumptions, resampling methods (bootstrapping methods) are used to state if results are significant (Ringle, 2004).

RESULTS

Evaluation of the Reflective Measurement Model

A fit measure for the reflective measurement models is the item reliability. The reliability of items revealed on the variance of the items can be explained by the latent construct (composite). Loadings of more than 0.7 are acceptable (Krafft et al., 2005). Except for the loading of age heterogeneity with 0.697 all items are satisfactory (Table 9.2). On the basis of the t-values of the bootstrapping, each with 62 cases from 500 drawings, all loadings are significant (on a level under 1 per cent).

For the construct (composites) there are two fit measures. The construct is well developed if the AVE explains at least 50 per cent of the variance of the construct. In this study all AVEs are adequate (Table 9.2). A further criterion is the composite reliability. Krafft states that the loadings should be at least 0.7 (Krafft et al., 2005). All measurement models are satisfactory,

Table 9.2 Information concerning the fit of the measurement model

Composite	Indicator	Loading of indicator	t-values of the composite	Composite-reliability	AVE
work norms	commitment	0.890	25.076***	0.923	0.800
	work load	0.914	23.755***		
	goals	0.880	18.890***		
heterogeneity	het. of age	0.697	6.103***	0.818	0.600
	het. of industry experience	0.770	6.147***		
	het. of leadership experience	0.850	9.517***		
communication	frequency	0.794	12.694***	0.861	0.675
	accuracy	0.809	5.334***		
	punctuality	0.859	13.526***		
experience	entrepreneurial experience	0.875	12.488***	0.803	0.672
	leadership experience	0.761	3.904***		
new venture	growth of employees	0.747	5.279***	0.695	0.533
performance	growth of turnover (percentages)	0.713	4.675***		

Note: Significance α (probability of error): *** $\alpha < 0.01$.

Table 9.3 Root of AVE and correlation matrix of the latent constructs

	1	2	3	4	5	6	7
1. NVP	**0.730**						
2. heterogeneity	−0.025	**0.775**					
3. experience	−0.228	0.585	**0.819**				
4. communication	0.218	−0.321	−0.378	**0.813**			
5. size	0.356	0.221	0.162	−0.110	**1.000**		
6. work norms	−0.006	−0.485	−0.470	0.475	−0.262	**0.895**	
7. fluctuation	0.096	0.003	−0.034	−0.150	0.367	−0.057	**1.000**

except the measurement model of new venture performance, but with 0.695 it is near to the minimum threshold (Table 9.2).

Additionally, the discriminant validity should be proven. Therefore we have to test whether the root of the AVE is larger than the correlation between the latent variables (Krafft et al., 2005). This criterion is satisfactory (Table 9.3).

Fit Measures of the Structural Model

A central fit measure is the coefficient of determination R^2. R^2 of about 33 per cent is classified as average and values about 19 per cent are classified as weak (Chin, 1998). In this study 25.1 per cent of the variance of new venture performance, 30.1 per cent of the variance of work norms, 23.2 per cent of communication and 16.8 per cent of the variance of fluctuation are explained. Therefore the coefficient of determination can be ranked as average through weak. The strength of the relation between the constructs is reflected in the path coefficient. Paths under the value of 0.1 are not considered within the model (Krafft et al., 2005), as such paths are not significant. If a path is excluded, the hypothesis is not supported (Krafft et al., 2005). To prove if paths are significant, bootstrapping is conducted (Bollen and Stine, 1993; Efron and Tibishirani, 1993). In this analysis bootstrapping was conducted with 62 cases and 500 drawings (Table 9.4). Significant positive relations are between: size and new venture performance (NVP), communication and NVP, work norms and communication, size and fluctuation. Negative relations are between: experience and NVP, experience and work norms, heterogeneity and work norms.

The direct and indirect effects can be summed up to the total effects of the latent exogenous variable. An indirect effect can be calculated from the product of the path coefficients from a latent exogenous to a latent

Table 9.4 Path coefficients of the structural model (direct effects)

Path Coefficients	Estimated	Bootstrap Mean	Standard Deviation	t-statistics	
size -> NVP	0.390	0.379	0.133	2.925	***
experience -> NVP	−0.276	−0.265	0.154	1.797	*
communication -> NVP	0.221	0.229	0.092	2.393	**
work norms -> NVP	−0.134	−0.120	0.165	0.813	n.s.
experience -> communication	−0.189	−0.216	0.121	1.555	n.s.
work norms -> communication	0.364	0.366	0.176	2.071	**
size -> work norms	−0.153	−0.154	0.114	1.348	n.s.
experience -> work norms	−0.274	−0.260	0.161	1.702	*
heterogeneity -> work norms	−0.288	−0.302	0.158	1.821	*
experience->fluctuation	−0.155	−0.168	0.115	1.343	n.s.
communication->fluctuation	−0.166	−0.180	0.150	1.104	n.s.
size->fluctuation	0.375	0.372	0.106	3.528	***

Note: Significance α (probability of error): * $\alpha<0.1$; ** $\alpha<0.05$; *** $\alpha<0.01$; not significant = n.s.

endogenous variable. In this analysis eight total effects are significant. There exists a significant positive total effect between communication and team size and new venture performance and a significant negative effect between experience and new venture performance. We can report further total effects between heterogeneity and work norms (negative), between experience and communication (negative), between experience and work norms (negative), between team size and fluctuation (positive) and between work norms and communication (positive) (Table 9.5).

Evaluation of the Structural Model

All fit measures for the structural model as well as the criteria for the measurement models are satisfactory. So the validity of the model is given (Figure 9.2).

DISCUSSION OF THE HYPOTHESES

Direct effects can be extracted from the path coefficients of the structural model. Table 9.6 lists which hypotheses have been supported. To complete the interpretation of the structural model the indirect effects have to be discussed as well.

Table 9.5 Total effects in the structural model

Total Effects	Estimates	Bootstrap Mean	Standard Deviation	t–statistics	
heterogeneity->NVP	0.016	0.011	0.055	0.282	n.s.
heterogeneity -> communication	−0.105	−0.118	0.090	1.168	n.s.
heterogeneity ->work norms	−0.288	−0.302	0.158	1.821	*
heterogeneity ->fluctuation	0.017	0.015	0.022	0.798	n.s.
experience-> NVP	−0.303	−0.312	0.125	2.421	**
experience ->communication	−0.288	−0.310	0.118	2.450	**
experience -> work norms	−0.274	−0.260	0.161	1.702	*
experience ->fluctuation	−0.107	−0.111	0.116	0.925	n.s.
communication-> NVP	0.221	0.229	0.092	2.393	**
communication -> fluctuation	−0.166	−0.180	0.150	1.104	n.s.
size-> NVP	0.398	0.386	0.127	3.137	***
size ->communication	−0.056	−0.054	0.050	1.121	n.s.
size -> work norms	−0.153	−0.154	0.114	1.348	n.s.
size -> fluctuation	0.384	0.379	0.106	3.629	***
work norms -> NVP	−0.054	−0.038	0.167	0.322	n.s.
work norms -> communication	0.364	0.366	0.176	2.071	**
work norms -> fluctuation	−0.060	−0.045	0.059	1.026	n.s.

Note: Significance α (probability of error): * $\alpha<0.1$, ** $\alpha<0.05$; *** $\alpha<0.01$; not significant =n.s.

Beginning with the team characteristics, the most important team characteristic is the size of the NVT. A positive relation was found to exist between the size of the founder team and new venture performance. The direct effect of team size and NVP is significantly positive (H1) (consistent with Ahlstrom and Bruton, 2002; Chandler et al., 2005). The result supports the assumption that team size influences NVP not only through team processes but mainly via direct effects, such as signalling or through extended resources. Indirect effects via the team process outcomes could only be partly confirmed in the model. Neither work norms nor communication (H4 and H5) are affected by the team size. There is a strong positive influence of team size and fluctuation (H6). By fluctuation we mean that in most of our cases someone has left the team (66 per cent of the cases) and in 44 per cent of the cases fluctuation means that team members have left the venture but that simultaneously somebody has entered. Only seldom does fluctuation mean that someone has entered the team without anybody leaving beforehand. The results of the structural model show us that larger teams have more changes within the team structure. Larger teams are more likely to reduce the team size or exchange somebody.

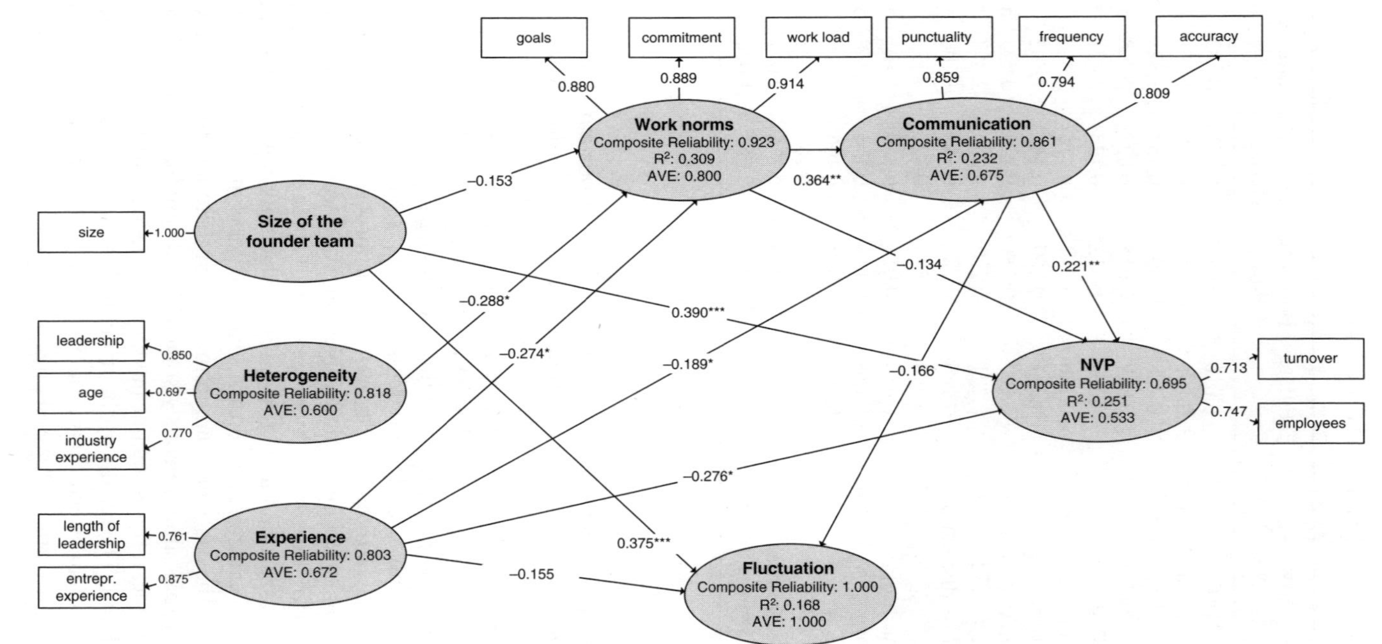

Note: Significance α (probability or error): * $\alpha < 0.1$; ** $\alpha < 0.05$; *** $\alpha < 0.01$.

Figure 9.2 Structural model

Table 9.6 *Results*

Hypotheses	Relation	Expected relation	Direction of paths	Sign. paths
H1	size of the founder team (size) and new venture performance (NVP)	+	+	***
H2	size and heterogeneity	+	p.d.	n.s.
H3	size and experience	+	p.d.	n.s.
H4	size and work norms	–	–	n.s.
H5	size and communication	–	p.d.	n.s.
H6	size and fluctuation	–,+	+	***
H7	heterogeneity and NVP	+	p.d.	n.s.
H8	heterogeneity and work norms	–	–	*
H9	heterogeneity and communication	–	p.d.	n.s.
H10	heterogeneity and fluctuation	–,+	p.d.	n.s.
H11	experience and NVP	+	–	*
H12	experience and work norms	+/–	–	*
H13	experience and communication	+	–	n.s.
H14	experience and fluctuation	–,+	–	n.s.
H15	work norms and NVP	+	–	n.s.
H16	work norms and communication	+	+	**
H17	work norms and fluctuation	–	p.d.	n.s.
H18	communication and NVP	+	+	**
H19	communication and fluctuation	–	–	n.s.
H20	fluctuation and NVP	–,+	p.d.	n.s.

Note: Significant α (probability of error): * $\alpha<0.1$; ** $\alpha<0.05$; *** $\alpha<0.01$; not significant = n.s.; path deleted (under 0.1) = p.d.

Against our assumption, there is no relation between team size and heterogeneity or experience, which were the other team characteristics we tested. So Hypotheses 2 and 3 are not confirmed. This indicates that further team members are not chosen on the aspect of heterogeneity.

Concerning the second team characteristic, heterogeneity, the direct relation between heterogeneity and NVP could not be supported (H7). This indicates that the compensation of strengths and weaknesses in heterogeneous teams or the extended networks of those teams do not have a significant influence on NVP. This is an astonishing result because the team research to date stresses the importance of heterogeneous teams. As assumed there is a significant negative relation between heterogeneity and work norms (H8). The relation between heterogeneity and communication is not supported in the model (H9). The team composition in terms of age, leadership and industry experience does not affect the quality of communication. Demographic heterogeneity is not related to fluctuation either (H10). Maybe heterogeneity should also be measured in terms of personality heterogeneity. As Chowdhury states, demographically similar people may differ in their thinking style as well. Teams lacking demographic diversity may have access to a diverse scope of cognitive attributes (Chowdhury, 2005). The same can also be stated for demographically dissimilar teams.

The third team characteristic that we included in the model was the experience of the founder team. Following the human capital theory, we proposed a positive relation between experience and NVP. This effect could not be supported (H11). On the contrary, we found a weak negative direct influence of experience and new venture performance. A possible explanation for this finding is that leadership experience and entrepreneurial experience correlate with the age of the founder persons. The literature suggests that older founders are more averse to risk and less able to work under pressure, which has a negative influence on NVP (Tversky and Kahneman, 1991; Bhidé, 2000). Experience does not affect communication and fluctuation. So Hypotheses 13 and 14 have to be rejected. But there is, as assumed, a negative influence of experience on work norms (H12). Experience is repressive for the development of cooperative norms. Here too we can stress the age of the founder person. Long work experience may lead to less compromise orientation and stronger individual work structuring. Continuing coordination is not desired by these experienced persons. It can be assumed that the entrepreneurial experience was collected as solo entrepreneur (80 per cent of all new ventures in Austria are founded by one person). So these persons are used to working on their own without team orientation.

With regard to the team processes, we investigated work norms, communication and fluctuation. The most important influences lead via the path of communication. Communication has a strong positive influence on NVP (H18). This supports the idea that a frequent exchange of information, as well as punctuality and accuracy of information, assist new venture development positively. The relation of communication and fluctuation is not significant (H19). The expected positive path between work norms and new venture performance could not be supported. So we had to reject Hypothesis 15. There is also no significant effect of work norms and fluctuation (H17), whereas there is a strong positive influence of work norms on communication (H16). A positive influence of work norms on new venture performance leads via the path of communication. An explanation for the fact that we did not discover a relation between work norms and new venture performance could be that it is not enough to find out whether the team shares common goals and whether all team members are trying to achieve them. The problem may lay in the nature of the goals. This study did not consider whether growth is desired by the founder team. If the team has other goals, for example to attain an acceptable income, no effect of work norms on NVP can be expected.

The last factor we did consider in the model was fluctuation. As discussed in the section on hypotheses, subsequent personal changes within the newly founded teams have been identified (Cooper and Bruno, 1977). In our sample 44 per cent of the teams have gone through a change within the founder teams. The investigation of fluctuation has been badly neglected within the investigation of newly founded ventures. We proposed an undirected hypothesis, because we assumed that, on the one hand, if a founder person leaves the venture it can lead to bottlenecks and the loss of advantages which emerge from the fact that abilities and skills complement each other. But fluctuation can also have positive effects. For example, when a team member that does not fit into the team leaves the venture this can affect the development of the venture positively. However, we did not find any proof that fluctuation has a direct influence on NVP (H20).

The paths of work norms and fluctuation, and communication and fluctuation are not significant. The reason may be because of the small sample size.

CONCLUSION

Even though the high potential of venture teams is emphasized in literature, there is still a small number of studies regarding NVTs and new venture performance (Vyakarnam et al., 1999). The intent of this study was to investigate the relationship between initial team characteristics, in particular team size, heterogeneity and experience of the founder team and the outcome of team processes, such as work norms, communication and fluctuation. The study is based on the upper echelon approach, which assumes a strong linkage between top management team characteristics and organizational performance (Hambrick and Mason, 1984). Recent literature emphasizes that the mechanism between team characteristics and organizational performance has to be explored (Birley and Stockley, 2000). For example, the integration of concepts of behavioural science (Ensley et al., 2002) and also the transfer of the upper echelon perspective from large organizations to young ventures are recommended. 'The Upper Echelon perspective fits best into the arena of new ventures, which are themselves crucibles where managerial choice drives organizational performance most directly' (Ensley et al., 2002, p. 381).

The primary contribution of the study is to extend the upper echelon theory for teams and organizational performance. In this study we have discussed a model which proposes that team characteristics and team processes have to be analysed simultaneously. We were able to show that the contribution of approaches of behavioural science can enrich the investigation on new venture teams. We wanted to integrate new aspects in the analyses. Communication, work norms and fluctuation are process outcomes which have scarcely been investigated within the top management team and venture team literature.

The results clearly indicate that there are relations between team characteristics and work norms, communication and fluctuation. Through simultaneous analysis we could gain results which reflect the complex structure of team characteristics and process outcomes and new venture performance, and thus draw conclusions for the development process of young ventures founded in teams.

Beginning with the team characteristics, a central finding of this study is that team size has a direct influence on new venture performance, and team size affects the fluctuation of the founder team. Larger teams more often undergo a change when someone leaves the team and another person enters. There are, however, no affects of team size on communication and work norms. The results of the direct path (team size and NVP) indicate the assumed signalling effects. The results suggest that larger founder teams seem to inspire more confidence in stakeholders (banks, customers, suppliers). The consequence for the venture teams is that they should emphasize their team size more strongly in their information and communication policy. Concerning the heterogeneity, we have concentrated on age, industry and leadership heterogeneity. A direct relation of heterogeneity and new venture performance could not be supported. This suggests that the recommendation of advisory literature, that teams should be composed of different professionals, is maybe not that effectual. Other criteria of heterogeneity, for example heterogeneity of personality, should be included in further studies. There is some evidence that an indirect link of heterogeneity may run through the path of work norms and communication, which suggests that in the process of team compositions attention should be given to the development of team work. The results suggest that agreement in the team about work norms and communication structures is more important than the advantages of specialization (team composition).

Concerning the team process outcomes, the results indicate that the communication quality (frequency, punctuality and accuracy) is a central element in predicting new venture performance. This result indicates that in the development process the team should be aware of the importance of information and communication supporting instruments. Communication schoolings and coaching can be recommended too. The fluctuation (changes in the team structure) does not have any impact on new venture performance. Of all investigated relations between fluctuation and other elements, only the path of team size and fluctuation is significant. This would lead to the argument that neither the addition nor the departure of members of the founder team has any impact on new venture performance. But we are not sure about this conclusion. The results reached by Chandler et al. (2005) are also contradictory, but indicate more probably that fluctuations matters. They report 'that adding team members during start-up through the first five years of the business is detrimental except in highly dynamic environments. In contrast, dropping team members during start-up does not appear to be detrimental, and dropping them after start-up during the first five years of operation appears to be significantly beneficial' (Chandler et al., 2005, p. 722). In our sample all ventures are of the same age and have been operating five years on the market. Maybe we did not find support for the importance of fluctuations because of the way of measuring. Due to the fact that we did not differ between entry and exit, effects may have been weakened and are not measurable. That leads us to the discussion of shortcomings and limitations of our study.

Firstly, our study is based on a small number of cases. A larger number of cases should have given more solid results. If we had had more cases we would have been able to differentiate within the model between team member entry and team member exit. In addition, there are some steps which could help to improve the measurement. For example, heterogeneity could also include sociology or psychological heterogeneity.

Most of the present results about new venture teams are from US samples. As with Chandler et al. (2005), we think there are differences in culture, environment and venture structure between European ventures (Austrian ventures) and large US new ventures. In the future such differences should be given more consideration.

The structural model has given important insights, but the results also clearly indicate that further research is needed. Interesting questions would be why heterogeneity in founder teams does not play such an important role as it does in larger established firms. Another interesting aspect would be to make a group comparison between founding teams with fluctuation and founding teams without fluctuation.

REFERENCES

Ahlstrom, D. and G.D. Bruton (2002), 'An institutional perspective on the role of culture in shaping strategic actions by technology-focused entrepreneurial firms in China', *Entrepreneurship Theory and Practice*, 53–69.

Albers, S. and L. Hildebrandt (2006), 'Methodische Probleme bei der Erfolgsfaktorenforschung – Messfehler, formative versus reflektive Indikatoren und die Wahl des Strukturgleichungs-Modells', *Zeitschrift für Betriebswirtschaftliche Forschung*, **58**(1), 2–33.
Amason, A.C., R.C. Shrader and G.H. Tompson (2006), 'Newness and novelty: relating top management team composition to new venture performance', *Journal of Business Venturing*, **21**(1), 125–48.
Ardichvili, A., R.N. Cardozo and S. Ray (2003), 'A theory of entrepreneurial opportunity identification and development', *Journal of Business Venturing*, **18**(1), 105–23.
Arrow, K.J. (1973), 'Higher education as a filter', *Journal of Public Economics*, **2**(3), 193–216.
Becker, G.S. (1964), *Human Capital – A Theoretical and Empirical Analysis, with Special Reference to Education*, New York, London: Columbia University Press.
Bhidé, A.V. (2000), *The Origin and Evolution of New Businesses*, New York: Oxford University Press.
Birley, S. and S. Stockley (2000), 'Entrepreneurial teams and venture growth', in D.L. Sexton and H. Landström (eds), *The Blackwell Handbook of Entrepreneurship*, Oxford: Blackwell Business, pp. 287–307.
Bollen, K.A. and R.A. Stine (1993), 'Bootstrapping goodness-of-fit measures in structural equation models', in K.A. Bollen and J.S. Long (eds), *Testing Structural Equation Models*, Newbury Park: Sage, pp. 111–35.
Bortz, J. (1999), *Statistik für Sozialwissenschaftler*, Berlin: Springer.
Brüderl, J. and P. Preisendörfer (1998), 'Network support and the success of newly founded businesses', *Small Business Economics*, **10**(3), 213–25.
Brüderl, J., P. Preisendörfer and R. Ziegler (1996), *Der Erfolg neugegründeter Betriebe – Eine empirische Studie zu den Chancen und Risiken von Unternehmensgründungen*, Berlin: Duncker & Humblot.
Camelo-Ordaz, C., A.B. Hernández-Lara and R. Valle-Cabrera (2005), 'The relationship between top management teams and innovative capacity in companies', *Journal of Management Development*, **24**(8), 683–705.
Carpenter, M.A., M.A. Gelekanycz and W.G. Sanders (2004), 'Upper echelons research revisited: antecedents, elements, and consequences of top management team composition', *Journal of Management*, **30**(6), 1–39.
Chandler, G.N., B. Honig and J. Wiklund (2005), 'Antecedents, moderators, and performance consequences of membership change in new venture teams', *Journal of Business Venturing*, **20**(5), 705–25.
Chatman, J.A. and F. Flynn (2001), 'The influence of demographic heterogeneity on the emergence and consequences of cooperative norms in work teams', *Academy Management Journal*, **44**(5), 956–74.
Chin, W.W. (1998), 'The partial least squares approach to structural equation modeling', in G.A. Marcoulides (ed.), *Modern Business Research Methods*, Mahwah, NJ: Lawrence Erlbaum Associates, pp. 295–336.
Chowdhury, S. (2005), 'Demographic diversity for building and effective entrepreneurial team: is it important?', *Journal of Business Venturing*, **6**(20), 727–46.
Cohen, S.G. and D.E. Bailey (1997), 'What makes teams work: group effectiveness research from the shop floor of the executive suite', *Journal of Management*, **23**(3), 239–90.
Cooper, A.C. and A.V. Bruno (1977), 'Success Among high-technology firms', *Business Horizons*, **20**(2), 16–22.

Cooper, A.C., J.F. Gimeno-Gascon and C.Y. Woo (1994), 'Initial human and financial capital as predictors of new venture performance', *Journal of Business Venturing*, **9**(5), 371–95.

Delmar, F. (1997), 'Measuring growth: methodological considerations and empirical problems', in R. Donckels and A. Miettinen (eds), *Entrepreneurship and SME Research: On its Way to the Next Millenium*, Aldershot, Hants, UK: Ashgate, pp. 199–215.

Efron, B. and R. Tibishirani (1993), *An Introduction to the Bootstrap*, New York: Chapman and Hall.

Eisenhardt, K.M. and C.B. Schoonhoven (1990), 'Organizational growth – linking founding team, strategy, environment, and growth among U.S. semiconductor ventures, 1978–1988', *Administrative Science Quarterly*, **35**(3), 504–29.

Eisenhardt, K.M., J.L. Kahwajy and L.J. Bourgeois (1997), 'How management teams can have a good fight', *Harvard Business Review*, 77–85.

Elfring, T. and W. Hulsink (2003), 'Networks in entrepreneurship: the case of high-technology firms', *Small Business Economics*, **21**(4), 409–22.

Ensley, M.D. and C.L. Pearce (2001), 'Shared cognition in top management teams – implications for new venture performance', *Journal of Organizational Behavior*, **22**(2), 145–60.

Ensley, M.D. and A.W. Pearson (2005), 'An exploratory comparison of the behavioral dynamics of top management teams in family and nonfamily new ventures: cohesion, conflict, poteny and consensus', *Entrepreneurship Theory and Practice*, **29**(3), 267–84.

Ensley, M.D., J.W. Carland and J.C. Carland (1998), 'The effect of entrepreneurial team skill heterogeneity and functional diversity on new venture performance', *Journal of Business Entrepreneurship*, **10**(1), 1–14.

Ensley, M.D., A.W. Pearson and A.C. Amason (2002), 'Understanding the dynamics of new venture top management teams. Cohesion, conflict, and new venture performance', *Journal of Business Venturing*, **17**(4), 365–86.

Ford, C.M. and D.A. Gioia (1995), *Creative Action in Organizations – Ivory Tower Visions and Real World Voices*, Thousand Oaks, CA: Sage.

Francis, D.H. and W.R. Sandberg (2000), 'Friendship within entrepreneurial teams and its association with team and performance', *Entrepreneurship Theory and Practice*, **25**(5), 5–25.

Frank, H., J. Mugler and H. Wanzenböck (1995), 'Entwicklungspfade von geförderten Unternehmensgründungen–Beendigungsquoten und Wachstumsdynamik', *Journal für Betriebswirtschaft*, **45**(1), 5–20.

Giddens, A. (1997), *Sociology*, Cambridge, UK: Polity Press.

Granovetter, M. (1973), 'The strength of weak ties', *American Journal of Sociology*, **78**(6), 1360–80.

Greiner, L.E. (1998), 'Evolution and revolution as organizations grow', *Harvard Business Review*, **50**(4), 55–69.

Hambrick, D.C. and P. Mason (1984), 'Upper echelons: the organization as a reflection of its top managers', *Academy of Management Review*, **9**(2), 193–206.

Hauschildt, J. and S. Salomo (2007), *Innovationsmanagement*, München: Vahlen.

Hillmann, K.-H. (1994), *Wörterbuch der Soziologie*, Stuttgart: Kröner.

Hitt, M.A. and R.D. Ireland (eds) (2005), *Entrepreneurship*, Malden, Oxford, Victoria: Blackwell.

Jungbauer-Gans, M. (1993), *Frauen als Unternehmerinnen*, Frankfurt am Main u.a.: Peter Lang.

Karau, S.J. and K.D. Williams (1993), 'Social loafing: a meta-analytic review and theoretical Integration', *Journal of Personality and Social Psychology*, **65**(4), 681–706.

Katzenbach, J.R. and K.S. Douglas (2003), *Teams. Der Schlüssel zur Hochleistungsorganisation*, Frankfurt, Wien: Ueberreuther.

Kennedy, J. and J. Drennan (2001), 'A review of the impact of education and prior experience on new venture performance', *International Journal of Entrepreneurship and Innovation*, **2**(3), 153–69.

Krafft, M., O. Götz and K. Liehr-Gobbers (2005), 'Die validierung von strukturgleichungsmodellen mit hilfe des partial-least-squares (PLS) – ansatzes', in F. Bliemel, A. Eggert and J. Henseler (eds), *Handbuch PLS-Pfadmodellierung. Methode, Anwendung, Praxisbeispiele*, Stuttgart: Schäffer-Poeschel, pp. 71–86.

Landström, H. and J. Winborg (1995), 'Small business managers' attitudes towards and use of financial sources', in W.D. Bygrave, B.J. Bird, S. Birley, N.C. Churchill, M.G. Hay, R.H. Keeley and W.E. Wetzel, Jr (eds), *Frontiers of Entrepreneurship Research 1995*, Babson Park, MA: Babson College, pp. 172–86.

Lechler, T. and H.G. Gemünden (2003), *Gründerteams. Chancen und Risiken für den Unternehmenserfolg*, Heidelberg: Physica.

Mellewigt, T. and J.F. Späth (2002), 'Entrepreneurial teams – a survey of German and US empirical studies', *ZfB – Ergänzungsheft*, 5107–125.

Mikl-Horke, G. (2000), *Industrie- und Arbeitssoziologie*, München, Wien: Oldenbourg.

Milliken, F.J. and L.L. Martins (1996), 'Searching for common threads: understanding the multiple effects of diversity in organizational groups', *Academy of Management Review*, **21**(2), 402–34.

Mintzberg, H. (1971), 'Managerial work: analysis from observation', *Management Science*, **18**(2), 97–110.

Nachtigall, C., U. Kröhne, F. Funke and R. Steyer (2003), '(Why) should we use SEM? Pros and cons of structural equation modeling', *MPR-Online*, **8**(2), 1–22.

Picot, A., U.-D. Laub and D. Schneider (1989), *Innovative Unternehmensgründungen – eine ökonomisch-empirische Analyse*, Berlin: Springer.

Ringle, C.M. (2004), 'Gütemaße für den Partial Least-Squares-Ansatz zur Bestimmung von Kausalmodellen', in *Industrielles Management*, Arbeitspapier no. 16, Hamburg: Universität Hamburg.

Ringle, C.M., S. Wende and A. Will (2005), '*SmartPLS 2.0*', Hamburg: University of Hamburg, available at http://www.smartpls.de (accessed 30 May 2008).

Sapienza, H.J. and C.M. Grimm (1997), 'Founder characteristics, start-up process, and strategy, industry structure variables as predictors of shortline railroad performance', *Entrepreneurship Theory and Practice*, **22**(1), 5–20.

Schmidt, A.G. (2002), 'Indikatoren für Erfolg und Überlebenschancen junger Unternehmen', *Zeitschrift für Betriebswirtschaft*, **5** (Ergänzungsheft), 21–53.

Schwarz, E.J. and E. Grieshuber (2003), *Vom Gründungs – zum Jungunternehmen. Eine explorative Analyse*, Wien, New York: Springer.

Schwarz, E.J., D.A. Almer-Jarz and R.J. Breitenecker (2005), 'Geschlechtstypische Unterschiede im Bereich des Wachstums von jungen Unternehmen und mögliche Erklärungsansätze', in H. Klandt, L. Koch and K.-I. Voigt (eds), *Jahrbuch Entrepreneurship*, Berlin: Gründungsforschung und Gründungsmanagement, pp. 305–21.

Smith, K.G., K.A. Smith, J.D. Olian, H.P. Sims and D.P. O'Bannon (1994), 'Top management team demography and process: the role of social integration and communication', *Administrative Science Quarterly*, **39**(3), 412–38.

Spieker, M. (2004), *Entscheidungsverhalten in Gründerteams – Determinanten, Parameter und Erfolgsauswirkungen*, Wiesbaden: Deutscher Universitätsverlag.
Taub, R.P. and C.M. Gaglio (1995), 'Entrepreneurship and public policy: beyond solving the credit crunch', in W.D. Bygrave, B.J. Bird, S. Birley, N.C. Churchill, M.G. Hay, R.H. Keeley and W.E. Wetzel, Jr (eds), *Frontiers of Entrepreneurship Research 1995*, Babson Park, MA: Babson College, pp. 437–44.
Teach, R.D., F.A. Tarplay and R.G. Schwartz (1986), 'Software venture teams', in R. Ronstadt, J.A. Hornaday, R. Peterson and K.H. Vesper (eds), *Frontiers of Entrepreneurship Research 1986*, Wellesley, MA: Babson College, pp. 546–62.
Tversky, A. and D. Kahneman (1991), 'Loss aversion in riskless choice: a reference dependent model', *Quarterly Journal of Economics*, **106**(4), 1039–61.
Ucbasaran, D., A. Lockett, M. Wright and P. Westhead (2003), 'Entrepreneurial founder teams: factors associated with member entry and exit', *Entrepreneurship Theory and Practice*, **28**(2), 107–27.
Vyakarnam, S., R. Jacobs and J. Handelberg (1999), 'Exploring the formation of entrepreneurial teams: the key to rapid growth business?', *Journal of Small Business and Enterprise Development*, **6**(2), 153–65.
Wahren, H.-K.E. (1994), *Gruppen- und Teamarbeit in Unternehmen*, Berlin, New York: Walter de Gruyter.
Watson, W.E., L.D. Ponthieu and J.W. Critelli (1995), 'Team interpersonal process effectiveness in venture partnerships and its connection to perceived success', *Journal of Business Venturing*, **10**(5), 393–411.
Wright, M., P. Westhead and J.E. Sohl (1998), 'Habitual entrepreneurs and angel investors', *Entrepreneurship Theory and Practice*, **22**(4), 5–21.
Zimmermann, P. (2003), *Grundwissen Sozialisation*, Opladen: Leske/Budrich.

10. Entrepreneurs' human capital and early business performance

Espen John Isaksen

INTRODUCTION

The creation of new businesses and the various outcomes linked to new businesses are of interest to practitioners, policy-makers and researchers. The interest relates to societal level issues, such as job-generation (Reynolds et al., 1994) and more efficient use of resources (Acs and Storey, 2004). In addition, at the individual level, starting new businesses may constitute a viable and interesting career alternative. In this study the focus is on entrepreneurs' human capital reported at the time of new business registration and subsequent early business performance.

While several studies have investigated factors related to performance in existing businesses, there still seems to be a lack of studies focusing on newly started businesses. Studies identifying factors associated with firm performance using samples of young businesses have clearly made contributions to the entrepreneurship field of research. However, there is also a need to explore factors associated with outcomes in very new businesses. This is important since factors previously found to be related to superior performance in young firms need not be the same as those factors associated with superior performance in new firms. The lack of studies exploring performance in new firms may be related to problems associated with identifying samples of new businesses. This study is based on a large representative sample of businesses over two points in time. Efforts were made to approach the businesses when they were still very new. The founders provided information concerning factors presumed to be associated with new business performance, shortly after the businesses had entered a Norwegian businesses register. The dependent variable, early business performance, was temporally separated from the presumed explanatory factors by approximately 19 months. This research design issue addresses calls and recommendations made from several scholars urging entrepreneurship studies to a larger extent to utilize longitudinal data sets of entrepreneurs and businesses (for example, Chandler and Lyon, 2001;

Ucbasaran et al., 2001). To temporally separate presumed causes from presumed effects should be useful since new insights can be gained regarding initial founding variables influencing later business performance (Cooper, 1993). The sample of new businesses seems to constitute a particular appropriate context for a study of early business performance. The fact that the entrepreneurs responded to the first survey close to business registration implies that information was collected at the time of an important event in the business start-up process.

In this study human capital theory is utilized to guide the development of a research model of factors assumed to be associated with superior performance in new small businesses. According to the human capital perspective (see, for example, Becker, 1993) the business founders' investments in key attributes (for example, education and training) are linked to competencies and skills that may improve business performance. The human capital framework refers to explanatory factors at the individual level of analysis. To focus at the individual level of analysis should be useful when exploring new business performance. This in particular is related to the fact that it is reasonable to assume that the entrepreneur and the new business are closely linked (Chandler and Hanks, 1994; Cooper et al., 1994). Hence using a theoretical perspective that illuminates the business founder's contribution to the new business is regarded as appropriate and important.

The human capital framework has been used explicitly and implicitly in several entrepreneurship and small business studies. Individuals' human capital attributes have been linked to various outcomes including business survival (Brüderl et al., 1992; Cooper et al., 1994), entry into self-employment (Bates, 1995), opportunity identification (Ucbasaran et al., 2003a), new venture employment growth (Cooper et al., 1994), firm growth in terms of sales (Chandler, 1996) and new business profits (Bosma et al., 2004). An important idea within the human capital framework is the distinction between general and specific human capital. General human capital relates to factors expected to increase the individual's productivity for a wide range of job alternatives (Gimeno et al., 1997), whereas specific human capital are assumed only to be applicable to a specific domain (Westhead et al., 2005).

Increased levels of human capital attributes are generally expected to be associated with increased levels of skills and competencies. While the entrepreneurs' levels of skills and competencies are generally hypothesized to be positively associated with superior early business performance, it is likely that some human capital attributes are more important than others with regard to superior early business performance. Hence the following research question will be explored:

Which of the business founders' human capital attributes are associated with subsequent superior early business performance?

As indicated by the research question, the aim is to identify initial human capital factors associated with subsequent performance in small new independent businesses. Based on previous conceptual and empirical research relevant general and specific human capital variables assumed to be related to early business performance will be selected. The dependent variable selected for the study, early business performance, is a summated scale and consists of the elements: (1) sales turnover, (2) invested capital and (3) employment. While other performance dimensions are interesting to study, these three indicators of performance should be regarded relevant in relation to new businesses. The indicators relate to both financial (sales turnover and invested capital) and non-financial new business outcomes.

DERIVATION OF HYPOTHESES

As previously noted, an important contribution within the human capital framework is the distinction among different categories of human capital investments. In this study a distinction is made between general human capital and specific human capital. It is generally assumed that specific human capital compared with general human capital is more likely to contribute to entrepreneurial success. Variables included in the general human capital category include work experience, management experience and education. With regard to specific human capital the following variables are included: business ownership experience, parental self-employment and business similarity.

General Human Capital Variables

Watson et al. (2003) suggested that work experience is related to the tacit knowledge critical for devising strategy, acquiring resources and other necessities associated with venture performance. Among empirical studies using business survival as the outcome variable, both Brüderl et al. (1992) and Boden and Nucci (2000) found that work experience had a positive significant influence on the business's survival chances. However, Bosma et al. (2004) found no significant effect on firm survival. While these studies together indicate that work experience is a relevant variable concerning business performance, the more relevant outcome variable with respect to the present study are empirical studies of firm growth and/or business volume. Bosma et al. (2004), using a sample of 758 Dutch start-up firms, reported that experience as an employee had a significant positive effect on cumulative employment in the firms (from 1994 to 1997). Watson et al. (2003) found in a sample of 175 small businesses operated by two partners (350 respondents) that respondents with more work experience perceived their firms to be more successful in terms of growth than respondents with less work experience. Based on this discussion, the following hypothesis is suggested:

Hypothesis 1a: Business founders reporting more years of work experience are more likely to report superior early business performance.

Castanias and Helfat (2001, p. 662) suggested that 'managers acquire and perfect their skills in part through prior work experience'. Hence managerial work experience is considered an important empirical indicator of managerial human capital (Castanias and Helfat, 2001; Ucbasaran et al., 2003b). However, prior management experience should not only be viewed as productive in the context of existing firms, it should be possible to transfer this experience to new businesses. Cooper et al. (1994) suggested that the level of prior management experience may serve as a proxy for greater motivation and problem solving ability. However, in their longitudinal study of 1053 new ventures they found that prior management level was neither significantly related to marginal business survival nor to business growth in terms of employment. Duchesneau and Gartner (1990) collected both quantitative data and qualitative data from 26 small young firms (13 classified as successful and 13 classified as unsuccessful or failed) in a single industry (distribution of fresh juice). They found that the successful entrepreneurs were likely to have a broad range of previous managerial experience. While the Cooper et al. (1994) and the Duchesneau and Gartner (1990) studies were concerned with the level and the breadth of management experience, respectively, other studies have investigated the effect of the length (that is, the number of years) of prior management experience. Pẽna (2004) conducted analyses on a sample of 114 Basque start-up firms participating in a business assistance programme. They detected that years of management experience had a significant positive impact on employment growth but did not have a significant impact on sales growth. Nevertheless, most empirical evidence suggests the following hypothesis:

Hypothesis 1b: Business founders reporting more years of management experience are more likely to report superior early business performance.

Cooper and Gascon (1992) claimed that education is one of the most widely studied entrepreneurship variables. And Watson et al. (2003, p. 148) suggested 'education provides the knowledge base and analytic and problem-solving skills to more effectively deal with the demands of entrepreneurship'. Further, Kangasharju and Pekkala (2002) argued that self-employed people with higher education should improve the growth opportunities of their businesses due to high education probably being associated with improved ability to comprehend market prospects, hence resulting in better exploitation of demand in the market. Hence it could be expected that individuals with a high level of education will own firms that perform better. However, Cooper and Gascon (1992) argued that it is uncertain how level of education may influence business performance since it is not clear whether scholarly knowledge is enough to achieve success.

With reference to a literature review, Cooper and Gascon (1992) detected that 10 out of 17 studies reported a positive relationship between prior level of education and superior firm performance. Thus, while these results showed inconsistency, they indicated a positive association between the two variables. Kangasharju and Pekkala (2002) used a sample of Finnish self-employed persons in order to investigate longitudinally the effect of education on the closure rates of firms, as well as the firm growth probability in terms of sales turnover. The analysis indicated that firms run by highly educated people had higher growth probability than firms run by the less educated self-employed people. The Cooper et al. (1994) study reported that level of education contributed both to marginal survival and achieving high employment growth among new businesses. However, the influence on high growth was weakly positively significant. Pẽna (2004) found that entrepreneurs at a higher education level were more likely to report sales and employment growth. Bosma et al. (2004) found that entrepreneurs with higher education owned more profitable firms. Conversely, the study detected no relationship between education level and cumulative employment growth or business survival. The discussion suggests the following hypothesis:

Hypothesis 1c: Highly educated business founders are more likely to report superior early business performance.

Specific Human Capital Variables

As previously noted, three specific human capital variables are considered in this study: (1) business ownership experience, (2) parental self-employment/business ownership and (3) business similarity (similarity between previous job/business and the current business).

Business ownership experience may indicate that an individual has acquired abilities and skills especially appropriate for starting and managing a small business. Moreover, Ucbasaran et al. (2003b, p. 234) noted that previous business ownership experience may be related to access to a variety of resources (for example, enhanced reputation and broader social and business networks). The research interest associated with this variable relates to opportunity identification (Ucbasaran et al., 2003a) as well as to exploitation of opportunities (manifested in such business performance dimensions as, for example, venture-implementation (Alsos and Kolvereid, 1998) and employment and profits (Bosma et al., 2004)). Hence business ownership experience may be considered a key aspect explaining variance in new business performance.

MacMillan (1986) emphasized the fact that some entrepreneurs start more than one business and make a habit of starting new businesses. Hence these entrepreneurs were named habitual entrepreneurs. This phenomenon has been verified empirically. Studies (Birley and Westhead, 1993; Kolvereid and Bullvåg, 1993; Ronstadt, 1988) have revealed that a relatively large percentage of business founders are not one-shot entrepreneurs but have been involved in several businesses.

Ronstadt (1988) suggested that the act of starting the first business opens windows of new and potentially more attractive opportunities not previously open to the first business start-up attempt. This was labelled 'the corridor principle', implying that as the new venture corridor opens, more is known or discovered about relevant contacts. These relevant contacts include reliable suppliers, viable markets, product availability, competitive resources and response time. Ronstadt (1988) suggested that habitual business founders acquire specific knowledge regarding how to start and manage new businesses. In addition, the act of starting a business provides the business founder with valuable information concerning the external environment. With regard to the habitual founders, Birley and Westhead (1993, p. 40) suggested the definition: 'habitual founders had established at least one other business prior to the start-up of the current new independent new venture'. Hence, according to this definition, habitual founders in contrast to novice founders have acquired prior experience from founding at least one prior business. Further, a distinction has been made between two different types of habitual founders, serial and portfolio business founders (see, for example, Alsos and Kolvereid, 1998; Westhead and Wright, 1998). The research on the differences between habitual founders and novices (for example, Birley and Westhead, 1993; Kolvereid and Bullvåg, 1993) as well as the research on differences among novice founders, serial founders and portfolio founders (for example, Alsos and Kolvereid, 1998; Westhead and Wright, 1998) can be viewed as an effort to perform more fine-grained analyses with regard to previous entrepreneurial experience (business ownership experience and/or business founding experience). Hence these studies have taken into account at least some of the heterogeneity existing among business founders. With regard to the effect of previous start-up experience on subsequent business performance, Starr and Bygrave (1991) observed that there have been mixed findings. They suggested that the outcomes of prior start-up experience can be regarded as both an asset and a liability to subsequent ventures. Starr and Bygrave (1991) stressed that previous success may be especially detrimental to subsequent business outcomes. They suggested that three potentially detrimental factors operate with regard to subsequent businesses: (1) biases and blind spots, (2) strong ties and (3) success syndrome. Biases and blinders relate among other things to a successful business founder typically relying on rules of thumb in order to deal with diverse tasks. However these rules of thumb that were appropriate to the prior business may not be appropriate to the current business. Strong ties may have the effect that business founders are stuck in routine patterns of network relationships, hindering their ability to change and see new opportunities. Finally, the success syndrome relates, according to Starr and Bygrave (1991, p. 222), to 'an entrepreneur with a track record of prior success(es) may be particularly vulnerable to the hazard of success'. The previous successful business founder may be over-confident in their own ability and doubt the capability of alternative approaches. The existence of such factors operating in relation to subsequent businesses could explain inconsistency in the empirical findings.

The effects of previous business ownership experience[1] on business performance have been investigated in several studies. Stuart and Abetti (1990) detected that entrepreneurial experience (defined as the number of previous new venture involvements and the role played in the ventures by the entrepreneur) was the most significant factor explaining performance in a sample of 52 new technical ventures. Duchesneau and Gartner (1990) reported that the lead entrepreneur in successful firms has had more prior start-up experience. Other studies (Birley and Westhead, 1993; Bosma et al., 2004; Kolvereid and Bullvåg, 1993; Westhead and Wright, 1998) have failed to detect evidence that entrepreneurs with prior business ownership experience reported superior levels of business performance.

As noted above, according to Starr and Bygrave (1991), acquired knowledge and abilities from previous entrepreneurial experience may not always be advantageous to subsequent businesses. Hence for some business founders the liabilities of prior experience may outweigh the assets acquired during prior business ownership experience. However, in spite of the chance that such effects operate with regard to early business performance, it is expected that business ownership experience is positively associated with superior early business performance.

Previous research indicates that prior business ownership experience is a key variable with regard to reaching milestones in the business start-up process (Rotefoss, 2001) and is positively related to the probability of venture implementation (Alsos and Kolvereid, 1998). Rotefoss (2001) reported that individuals with current entrepreneurial experience (the founders were currently self-employed or owner/manager of a business) and persons with previous entrepreneurial experience (the founders had previously been self-employed or owner/manager of a business) were more likely to become an aspiring entrepreneur, a nascent entrepreneur and a business founder. Alsos and Kolvereid (1998) reported that parallel entrepreneurs (individuals who had started at least one previous business and had retained a previous business) had a higher probability of venture implementation than novices and serial entrepreneurs (individuals who had previously owned a business). The fact that the outcome variable in this study relates to performance in very new businesses strengthens the hypothesized relationship. Hence this discussion suggests the following hypothesis:

Hypothesis 2a: Business founders reporting previous business ownership experience are more likely to report superior early business performance.

Parents may act as role models for their children (Gimeno et al., 1997). Individuals with parents who are or have been self-employed and/or business owners may be more likely to view entrepreneurship as a viable career alternative (Cooper et al., 1994; Gimeno et al., 1997). Scott and Twomey (1988) suggested that the influence of self-employed parents is twofold. First, the parents can act as occupational role models for their children. Second, they can provide resources. Moreover, it may be reasonable to expect that individuals from the latter background put more effort into the business start-up process. Consequently, these individuals benefiting from role models may own businesses that report superior business performance. Parents with business ownership experience may encourage their children to utilize more diverse social and business networks in order to gain access to critical resources.

Cooper et al. (1994) detected that business survival was associated with having parents who owned a business. However, parental role models had no significant effect on high growth in terms of employment. They suggested that a possible explanation related to this finding is that business founders with the latter background may be satisfied with lifestyle businesses that do not experience much growth. Duchesneau and Gartner

(1990) found, in the comparisons of unsuccessful and successful lead entrepreneurs, that successful entrepreneurs were more likely to come from entrepreneurial families (that is, parents owned a business). They explained this finding with 'that previous family business experience appears to provide entrepreneurs with more realistic expectations from self-employment and the kinds of attitudes and behaviors necessary for surmounting the crises of entrepreneurship' (Duchesneau and Gartner, 1990, p. 306). It is possible that business founders with this kind of background have an advantage also with regard to early business performance. This discussion suggests the following hypothesis:

Hypothesis 2b: Business founders drawn from a parental background with prior self-employment/business ownership experience are more likely to report superior early business performance.

The degree of similarity between previous businesses/jobs and the new business should be a relevant aspect with regard to early business performance. Individuals can leverage their prior industry knowledge or know-how (Cooper et al., 1994). Gimeno et al. (1997) argued that the similarity between the new business and prior involvements (experience) may make the business founder able to build on prior relationships with the relevant stakeholder, reducing the 'liability of newness'. According to Cooper et al. (1994, p. 379), who referred to Stinchcombe (1965), 'the liability of newness arises because of lack of stable suppliers and customer relationships, inadequately developed internal processes and problems in acquiring resources'. Hence entrepreneurs reducing the liability of newness may be more likely to overcome the barriers associated with starting a new business. Consequently, the latter business founder may be in a position to own businesses that at an early stage perform better.

Gimeno et al. (1997) detected, with reference to a sample of 1547 entrepreneurs of new businesses, that business closure was negatively associated with entrepreneurs reporting similar businesses (a composite measure of similarity between present and previous businesses in terms of product/services, customers and suppliers). Further, they reported that this relationship was driven by a strong positive impact on economic performance (money taken out from the business). Cooper et al. (1994) reported that their measure of business similarity had significant positive influence on marginal survival as well as employment growth. In relation to this finding, they suggested that similar business may lessen the 'liability of newness' of the ventures and is therefore associated with less 'trial and error' as the business gets started. Following this line of reasoning, it is hypothesized that business similarity contributes to early business performance. This discussion suggests the following hypothesis:

Hypothesis 2c: Business founders reporting higher levels of business similarity (similarity between the present business and previous jobs or businesses) are more likely to report superior early business performance.

METHOD

The sampling frame for this study consists of businesses that entered a Norwegian business register during four weeks in May/June 2002. Four legal forms were included in the sampling frame: sole traders, partnerships with mutual responsibility, partnerships with shared responsibility and unlisted limited liability companies. These four legal forms constituted 98 per cent of all new registrations in 2002 (Statistics Norway, 2005). A questionnaire was mailed in four rounds to all the 3121 businesses entering the register during the four weeks. The questionnaire was sent to the businesses not more than two weeks after they entered the register. A reminder with a new copy of the questionnaire was sent three weeks after the initial mailing. Of the 3121 businesses approached, 126 questionnaires were returned unreachable, while 1048 respondents returned a completed questionnaire, giving a response rate of 35 per cent.

Follow-up data relating to the dependent variable in this study, early business performance, was collected approximately 19 months after the initial mailing (weeks 5–8 2004). A professional survey agency telephoned the respondents that had participated in the postal survey. However, only 980 respondents were approached since 29 businesses had deregistered from the register, 6 respondents had more than 50 per cent missing data in the initial survey and, finally, 33 respondents were not listed in any available telephone directory. Of the 980 respondents approached, 275 were inaccessible and 54 refused to participate. A total of 3924 telephone calls were carried out in order to collect information from a total of 651 business founders, constituting a response rate of 66.4 per cent of the respondents on the list.

Several requirements were used with regard to the final sample for the analysis of variables associated with early business performance. First, only businesses reported to be started from scratch were included. Second, respondents reporting not to be responsible for starting the businesses were excluded from the sample. These requirements reduced the initial 1048 respondents to 862. Further, the following five requirements reduced the final sample to 261 businesses. Respondents were excluded if: (1) the postal questionnaire was not returned within 90 days after business registration, (2) they did not respond to the follow-up telephone interview, (3) the businesses were deregistered or reported not to be in operation in 2004, (4) the respondents reported in 2004 that they were not alone or were with partners/owner of the business or (5) the respondents did not submit complete data sets for the selected dependent variable, independent variables and control variables.

In order to examine the possibility of response bias, chi-square tests and t-tests were conducted. The tests related to the 862 businesses constituting the sample after post stratification (excluding acquisitive entries and excluding respondents reporting not being responsible for establishing the businesses). The 264 businesses in the final sample were compared with the 698 non-respondents with regard to independent and control variables. No differences were detected between the respondents and non-respondents at the 0.01 level of statistical significance. These tests give no reason to suspect that the sample is not representative of Norwegian independent business start-ups.

Measures

Early business performance

The early business performance variable is a summated scale consisting of the three indicators: (1) sales turnover in 2003, (2) invested financial capital (reported in February 2004) and (3) employment (total number of hours worked in the business per week reported in February 2004). Responses to the three indicators were first categorized in 11 categories and then added together and divided by three. The Cronbach's alpha value for the early business performance variable is 0.80.

General human capital variables

Three variables are used to reflect the business founders' general human capital: years of work experience, years of management experience and level of education. Because both the work experience variable and the management experience variables deviated from the normal distribution, both variables were transformed by taking the square root of the number of years of experience.

In this study the level of education was originally measured using five categories. Respondents were asked to report their highest level of education: (1) elementary/primary school, (2) junior high school, (3) senior high school, (4) university/college one to three years and (5) university/college 4 years or more. The variable was transformed to a dummy variable consisting of two categories: 1 = 'high education' (education at university level, at least one year at university) and 0 = 'middle or low education' (education at high school or compulsory school level).

Specific human capital variables

Business ownership experience, parental self-employment and business similarity were used to measure specific human capital. The business ownership experience variable was operationalized based on whether or not the business founders were portfolio or serial entrepreneurs at the time of new business registration. Portfolio entrepreneurs are generally defined as individuals that at the time of the start-up of a new business own and manage another business. Serial entrepreneurs are those that at the time of the start-up report have previously owned and managed another business. In this study it is deemed sufficient to identify whether or not the business founders have previously attained business ownership experience. That is, if the new business founders are either classified as portfolio entrepreneurs or as serial entrepreneurs according to the definitions above, they are assumed to have acquired business ownership experience. Hence, based on two questions concerning portfolio entrepreneurs and serial entrepreneurs, a dummy variable was created where 1 = 'business ownership experience' and 0 = 'no business ownership experience'.

With regard to the parental self-employment, studies (Brüderl et al., 1992; Cooper et al., 1994) have considered parental self-employment or parents that owned a business as a human capital variable. In this study parental self-employment/business ownership was operationalized as follows: the variable was assigned a value of 1 if the business founder reported that one or both parents were or are self-employed or business owners. Otherwise the variable was assigned a value of 0.

The final variable included in the human capital model is labelled business similarity. This is a construct that is assumed to capture aspects of the business founder's knowledge of the context in which the new business operates (Chandler, 1996; Gimeno et al., 1997). Cooper et al. (1994) operationalized similar businesses as the similarity to previous organizations in terms of a three-item scale: similarity of services, customers and suppliers. This study adopted measures of business similarity developed by Chandler and Jansen (1992). The five-item measure refers to their business similarity scale, that is, the similarity of: (1) customers, (2) suppliers, (3) competitors, (4) products and (5) technology. Respondents were asked to report how similar (1 = very different and 7 = very similar) the newly registered business was to previous jobs/businesses with regard to the five items. The responses to the five statements were added together and then divided by five. Cronbach's alpha for the variable is 0.94.

Control variables

Based on Murphy et al. (1996) recommendations, five control variables are selected for this study. Murphy et al. (1996) suggested that business size, age of the business, risk and industry are particularly relevant control variables to entrepreneurship and small business studies. The first control variable included in the study, employment, is used as an indicator of business size at registration. A dummy employment variable was calculated with a value of 1 for businesses that had employed persons, otherwise the businesses were denoted a value of 0.

Since the businesses are of the same age (all registered in May/June 2002) business age is not a relevant control variable. Instead of age the stage in the development of products or service is measured. The business founders were asked if the business product or service technology was: (1) already completed, (2) would be completed during one year, (3) would be completed during one to two years or (4) more than two years of development was needed. The product/service development variable was operationalized as a dummy variable, where the value of 1 indicates that the development of the product or service was completed at business registration (option 1). The value of 0 indicates that the development was not yet completed (option 2, 3 or 4).

While Murphy et al. (1996) did not include gender in their list of key control variables, the variable is considered in this study. This relates to those studies (for example, Cooper and Gascon, 1992) that have suggested that gender is associated with variance in firm performance.

With regard to risk, a variable named perceived financial risk is included. The business founders were asked to indicate the level of financial risk associated with the new businesses on a 7-point scale (1 = very small risk, 7 = very large risk). Since the variable was highly skewed, it was transformed by calculating the logarithm of each response.

Concerning industry, a distinction is made among businesses in service industries (transportation, financial services, personal services, professional services and others) and businesses in other industries. A dummy variable was created where 1 = 'service industries' and 0 = 'other industries'.

RESULTS

Descriptive statistics, variance inflation factor (VIF) scores and correlations among variables are shown in Table 10.1. Inspection of the correlation coefficients and the VIF scores suggest that multicollinearity will not seriously distort the regression models.

Table 10.1 Descriptive statistics, VIF scores and correlation coefficients

	Mean	Standard deviation	VIF scores	1	2	3	4	5	6	7	8	9	10	11
Control variables														
1. Employment	0.14		1.093	1.00										
2. Product/ service dev. (completed)	0.70		1.066	0.056	1.00									
3. Gender (male)	0.78		1.104	0.035	0.013	1.00								
4. Perceived financial risk (log)	0.61	0.57	1.092	0.054	−0.022	0.083	1.00							
5. Industry (services)	0.69		1.251	−0.121	−0.188	−0.158	−0.116	1.00						
General human capital														
6. Work experience (sq. root)	3.86	1.40	1.982	0.134	0.003	0.071	0.092	−0.105	1.00					
7. Management experience (sq. root)	1.91	1.68	2.226	0.157	−0.066	0.194	0.196	0.042	0.645	1.00				
8. High education	0.60		1.300	−0.104	−0.097	−0.024	−0.142	0.352	−0.176	0.085	1.00			
Specific human capital														
9. Business ownership experience	0.31		1.271	0.071	−0.110	0.143	0.136	−0.004	0.310	0.395	−0.094	1.00		

Table 10.1 (continued)

	Mean	Standard deviation	VIF scores	1	2	3	4	5	6	7	8	9	10	11
10. Parental self-employment	0.37		1.060	0.042	0.023	−0.009	0.006	−0.128	−0.042	−0.027	−0.106	0.138	1.00	
11. Business similarity	4.10	2.22	1.075	0.193	0.109	0.091	0.009	−0.038	0.063	0.006	0.014	−0.032	0.039	1.00
Performance														
12. Early business performance	4.01	2.30		0.275	0.178	0.245	0.346	−0.234	0.116	0.191	−0.126	0.193	−0.017	0.314

Note: Correlations greater than ±0.121 are significant at $p<0.05$ (two-tailed tests); correlations greater than ±0.158 are significant at $p<0.01$ (2-tailed); $n=264$.

Table 10.2 Regression results on early business performance

	Model 1	Model 2	Model 3
Control variables			
Employment	0.230***	0.216***	0.168**
Product/service dev. (1 = completed)	0.149***	0.153***	0.141**
Gender (1 = male, 0 = female)	0.192***	0.174**	0.134*
Perceived financial risk (log)	0.308**	0.289***	0.276***
Industry (1 = services)	−0.112*	−0.120*	−0.137*
General human capital variables			
Work exp. (sq. root)		−0.037	−0.088
Management exp. (sq. root)		0.107	0.098
High education		−0.017	−0.027
Specific human capital variables			
Business ownership exp.			0.144*
Parental self-employment			−0.080
Business similarity			0.259***
R^2	0.269	0.276	0.354
Adjusted R^2	0.255	0.253	0.326
ΔR^2		0.007	0.078***
F-value	18.993***	12.126***	12.543***

Notes: Standardized regression coefficients (betas) are displayed in the table.
Level of statistical significance: * indicates $p < 0.05$; ** indicates $p < 0.01$;
*** indicates $p < 0.001$ (2-tailed); $n = 264$.

The hypotheses are formally tested using hierarchical regression. As shown in Table 10.2 variables are entered in three blocks into the regression analysis. First, the five control variables are entered, then the three general human capital variables are included and, finally, the three specific human capital variables are entered into the analysis. The increments of the explained variance (that is, ΔR square) and the standardized betas for individual variables will be considered when testing the hypotheses.

Model 1 is the base model where the five control variables are considered. The base model is statistically significant at the 0.001 level and has an adjusted R square of 0.255. The five control variables are all associated with early business performance at the 0.05 level of significance.

In order to test the hypotheses relating to the entrepreneurs' general human capital (H1a, H1b and H1c), the three variables referring to work experience, management experience and education were added to the base model. The results are displayed in Model 2. The improvement in R square of 0.007 is not statistically significant. Moreover, none of the general human capital variables are significantly associated with early business performance. Hence Hypotheses 1a, 1b and 1c are not supported.

Hypotheses 2a, 2b and 2c concern the specific human capital attainments of the business founders. To test the hypotheses the three specific human capital variables were added to control variables and general human capital variables. Results reported in Model 3 show that the inclusion of specific human capital variables make a statistically significant contribution. The explained variance increase from 0.276 to 0.354 (ΔR square = 0.078). The improvement is statistically significant at the 0.001 level. Two out of the three specific human capital variables are statistically significant associated with superior early business performance. Business founders reporting business ownership experience are more likely to report superior early business performance ($p < 0.05$). Hypothesis 2a is therefore supported. Hypothesis 2b suggested that business founders drawn from a parental background with prior self-employment or business ownership experience are likely to report superior early business performance. The hypothesis is not supported since the variable is negatively and not statistically significantly associated with the dependent variable. The business similarity variable is positively and significantly associated with early business performance ($p < 0.001$). Hence Hypothesis 2c is supported.

DISCUSSION

The present research has utilized a human capital model to explore early performance differences among new independent Norwegian businesses. The composite dependent variable, early business performance, relates to sales turnover, invested capital and employment. Guided by previous empirical and conceptual research, relevant variables were selected and hypotheses relating to the entrepreneurs' human capital were developed. The hypotheses were presented relating to a representative sample of 264 new businesses surveyed over two points. Regression analysis was used to test the presented hypotheses.

The presented research question focused on the relationship between entrepreneur's human capital attributes and subsequent superior early businesses performance. It is assumed that individuals with more human capital will own businesses that report superior levels of early business performance. A distinction has been made between general human capital and specific human capital. Selected general human capital variables relates to years of work and management experience and the level of education and selected specific human capital variables relates to business ownership experience, parental self-employment/business ownership and business similarity. General human capital is considered beneficial for a wide range of employment alternatives. Specific human capital, however, may be solely relevant to business ownership contexts. Due to the limited scope of application, specific human capital may be of a special value to business start-up processes and early business performance.

The present study found that two out of three specific human capital variables were associated with superior early business performance. Business ownership experience and business similarity were positively and significantly associated with superior early business performance. General human capital variables were, however, not linked to the dependent variable. The results reported in this research suggest that studies need to make a distinction between specific and general human capital.

There may be several explanations relating to the lack of support for hypotheses referring to general human capital. A possible explanation is that while general human capital contributes to firms' economic performance, the entrepreneur's threshold of performance is also raised (Gimeno et al., 1997). Hence business founders with high levels of general human capital may raise expectations with regard to business outcomes. If expectations are not met, individuals may be inclined to switch to full-time or part-time employment and consequently exert less effort on the new business. An alternative or complementary explanation relates to the measurement of general human capital. Measuring prior experience using number of years does not directly address the specific skills or expertise obtained from previous experience (Cooper et al., 1994; Reuber et al., 1990). If better measures were constructed that more directly reflect entrepreneur's competencies obtained from prior experience, relationships between general human capital and early business performance may have been detected.

With regard to specific human capital, the study failed to find support for the hypothesized relationship between parental self-employment/business ownership and superior early business performance. Hence entrepreneurs having this kind of background seem not to be more likely to report superior early business performance. The hypotheses relating to business similarity and business ownership experience were supported. Policy-makers and practitioners seeking to encourage superior new business performance may have a role in honing business founders' skills with regard to industry knowledge and business ownership.

A strength associated with this study is the analysis of a large representative sample of respondents over two points in time and that the human capital factors are temporally separated from the outcome variable, early business performance. Moreover, the sample of new business registration has enabled a study of performance in very new businesses making a contribution to the literature on human capital and business performance.

The combination of human capital variables and control variables explained 35 per cent of the variation in early business performance. Even if this result is acceptable, a substantial proportion of variation in the dependent variable remains unexplained. Using several theoretical perspectives and more than one level of analysis may contribute to a larger share of explained variance in early business performance. It is acknowledged that the time-lag between human capital variables, on the one hand, and subsequent business performance, on the other hand, is short. Future research should investigate if key variables are associated with longer term business performance.

NOTE

1. A distinction with respect to prior ownership experience is appropriate. Dyke et al. (1992) distinguished between (1) previous experience in a small business and (2) participation in previous business start-ups (start-up experience). While these two aspects of ownership experience are likely to be strongly correlated, some business founders with prior business ownership experience will have acquired entrepreneurial experience but not obtained business start-up experience. This subgroup would then typically have purchased or inherited their previous business(es). In this study the concept of business ownership experience is applied. Accordingly, this concept refers to previous experience in a small business but not necessary to prior start-up experience.

REFERENCES

Acs, Z.J. and D.J. Storey (2004), 'Introduction: entrepreneurship and economic development', *Regional Studies*, **38**(8), 871–7.

Alsos, G.A. and L. Kolvereid (1998), 'The business gestation process of novice, serial, and parallel business founders', *Entrepreneurship Theory and Practice*, **22**(4), 101–14.

Bates, T. (1995), 'Self-employment entry across industry groups', *Journal of Business Venturing*, **10**(2), 143–56.

Becker, G.S. (1993), *Human Capital: A Theoretical and Empirical Analysis with Special Reference to Education* (3rd edn), Chicago, IL: University of Chicago Press.

Birley, S. and P. Westhead (1993), 'A comparison of new businesses established by "novice" and "habitual" founders in Great Britain', *International Small Business Journal*, **12**(1), 38–60.

Boden, R.J. and A.R. Nucci (2000), 'On the survival prospects of men's and women's new business ventures', *Journal of Business Venturing*, **15**(4), 347–62.

Bosma, N., M. van Praag, R. Thurik and G. de Wit (2004), 'The value of human and social capital investments for the business performance of startups', *Small Business Economics*, **23**, 227–36.

Brüderl, J., P. Preisendörfer and R. Ziegler (1992), 'Survival chances of newly founded business organizations', *American Sociological Review*, **57**(2), 227–42.

Castanias, R.P. and C.E. Helfat (2001), 'The managerial rents model: theory and empirical analysis', *Journal of Management*, **27**, 661–78.

Chandler, G.N. (1996), 'Business similarity as a moderator of the relationship between pre-ownership experience and venture performance', *Entrepreneurship Theory and Practice*, **20**(3), 51–65.

Chandler, G.N. and S.H. Hanks (1994), 'Founder competence, the environment, and venture performance', *Entrepreneurship Theory and Practice*, **18**(3), 77–89.

Chandler, G.N. and E. Jansen (1992), 'The founders self-assessed competence and venture performance', *Journal of Business Venturing*, **7**(3), 223–36.

Chandler, G.N. and D.W. Lyon (2001), 'Issues of research design and construct measurement in entrepreneurship research: the past decade', *Entrepreneurship Theory and Practice*, **25**(4), 101–13.

Cooper, A.C. (1993), 'Challenges in predicting new firm performance', *Journal of Business Venturing*, **8**(3), 241–53.

Cooper, A. and F. Gascon (1992), 'Entrepreneurs, processes of founding, and new-firm performance', in D.L. Sexton and J.L. Kasarda (eds), *The State of the Art of Entrepreneurship*, Boston, MA: PWS-Kent Publishing.

Cooper, A.C., F.J. Gimeno-Gascon and C.Y. Woo (1994), 'Initial human capital and financial capital as predictors of new venture performance', *Journal of Business Venturing*, **9**(5), 371–95.

Dyke, L.S., E.M. Fischer and A.R. Reuber (1992), 'An inter-industry examination of the impact of owner experience on firm performance', *Journal of Small Business Management*, **30**(4), 72–87.

Duchesneau, D.A. and W.B. Gartner (1990), 'A profile of new venture success and failure in an emerging industry', *Journal of Business Venturing*, **5**(5), 297–312.

Gimeno, J., T.B. Folta, A.C. Cooper and C.Y. Woo (1997), 'Survival of the fittest? Human capital and the persistence of underperforming firms', *Administrative Science Quarterly*, **42**(4), 750–83.

Kangasharju, A. and S. Pekkala (2002), 'The role of education in self-employment success in Finland', *Growth and Change*, **33**(2), 216–37.

Kolvereid, L. and E. Bullvåg (1993), 'Novices versus experienced founders: an exploratory investigation', in S. Birley, I. MacMillan and S. Subramony (eds), *Entrepreneurship Research: Global Perspectives*, Amsterdam: Elsevier Science Publishers, pp. 275–85.

MacMillan, I.C. (1986), 'Executive forum: to really learn about entrepreneurship, let's study habitual entrepreneurs', *Journal of Business Venturing*, **1**(3), 241–3.

Murphy, G.B., J.W. Trailer and R.C. Hill (1996), 'Measuring performance in entrepreneurship research', *Journal of Business Research*, **36**, 15–23.

Pẽna, I. (2004), 'Business incubation centers and new firm growth in the Basque country', *Small Business Economics*, **22**, 223–36.

Reuber, A.R., L.S. Dyke and E.M. Fischer (1990), 'Experientially acquired knowledge and entrepreneurial venture success', in L.R. Jauch and J.L. Wall (eds), *Academy of Management Best Papers Proceedings*, San Francisco, CA, USA, pp. 69–73.

Reynolds, P., D. Storey and P. Westhead (1994), 'Cross-national comparisons of the variation in new firm formation rates', *Regional studies*, **28**(4), 443–56.

Ronstadt, R. (1988), 'The corridor principle', *Journal of Business Venturing*, **3**(1), 31–40.

Rotefoss, B. (2001), 'A resource based approach to the business start-up process – a longitudinal study', PhD. thesis, Brunel University/Henley Management College.

Scott, M.G. and D.F. Twomey (1988), 'The long-term supply of entrepreneurs: students career aspirations in relation to entrepreneurship', *Journal of Small Business Management*, **26**(4), 5–13.

Starr, J.A. and W.D. Bygrave (1991), 'The assets and liabilities of prior start-up experience: an exploratory study of multiple venture entrepreneurs', in N.C. Churchill, W.D. Bygrave, J.G. Covin, D.L. Sexton, D.P. Slevin, K.H. Vesper and W.E. Wetzel (eds), *Frontiers of Entrepreneurship Research*, Wellesley, MA: Babson College, pp. 213–28.

Statistics Norway (2005), 1 July, available at: http://www.ssb.no (accessed 1 July 2005).

Stinchcombe, A.L. (1965), 'Organizational and social structure', in J.G. March (ed.), *Handbook of Organizations*, Chicago, IL: Rand-McNally, pp. 142–93.

Stuart, R.W. and P.A. Abetti (1990), 'Impact of entrepreneurial and management experience on early performance', *Journal of Business Venturing*, **5**(3), 151–62.

Ucbasaran, D., P. Westhead and M. Wright (2001), 'The focus of entrepreneurial research: contextual and process issues', *Entrepreneurship Theory and Practice*, **25**(4), 57–80.

Ucbasaran, D., P. Westhead and M. Wright (2003a), 'Human capital based determinants of opportunity identification', in W.D. Bygrave, C.G. Brush, P. Davidsson, J. Fiet, P.G. Greene, R.T. Harrison, M. Lerner, G.D. Meyer, J. Sohl and A. Zacharakis (eds), *Frontiers of Entrepreneurship Research*, Wellesly, MA: Babson College, pp. 430–44.

Ucbasaran, D., M. Wright, P. Westhead and L.W. Busenitz (2003b), 'The impact of entrepreneurial experience on opportunity identification and exploitation: habitual and novice entrepreneurs', in J.A. Katz and D.A. Shepherd (eds), *Advances in Entrepreneurship, Firm Emergence and Growth, Volume 6: Cognitive Approaches to Entrepreneurship Research*, Oxford: Elsevier Science, pp. 231–63.

Watson, W., W.H. Steward and A. BarNir (2003), 'The effects of human capital, organizational demography, and interpersonal processes on venture partner perceptions of firm profit and growth', *Journal of Business Venturing*, **18**, 145–64.

Westhead, P. and M. Wright (1998), 'Novice, portfolio, and serial founders: are they different?', *Journal of Business Venturing*, **13**(3), 173–204.

Westhead, P., D. Ucbasaran and M. Wright (2005), 'Experience and cognition. Do Novice, serial and portfolio entrepreneurs differ?', *International Small Business Journal*, **23**(1), 72–98.

11. Direct and indirect effects of entrepreneurial and market orientations on the international performance of Spanish and Belgian international new ventures

María Ripollés, Andreu Blesa, Diego Monferrer and Ysabel Nauwelaerts

INTRODUCTION

An important body of research in international entrepreneurship has focused on the determination of the main factors that may explain the exceptional speed with which certain new ventures internationalize (Westhead et al., 2001; Zahra and George, 2002; Rialp et al., 2005; Oviatt and McDougall, 2005). However, the research on how international new ventures can develop positional advantages and grow in foreign markets has not attracted the same attention in the literature. According to Day and Wensley (1988, p. 1), positional advantage generally refers to what is observed in the market: 'a positional superiority in relation to a few targets of competitors'. Some authors have examined how speed of market entry (Autio et al., 2000) and technical knowledge influence international growth in new ventures (Autio et al., 2000; Oviatt and McDougall, 1997; 2004; Congcong and Khavul, 2005). Others have examined how business networks contribute to success and international growth in new ventures (Chetty and Campbell-Hunt, 2003; Autio et al., 2005; Fernhaber and McDougall, 2005; Congcong and Khavul, 2005). But, in order to overcome the liabilities of newness and foreignness (Stinchcombe, 1965; Hymer, 1976) and to develop a positional advantage in international markets, new ventures must develop tacit market knowledge (Autio et al., 2005; Oviatt and McDougall, 2005). Adopting the resource based view of the firm and its extension the dynamic capability theory, tacit market knowledge comes from the way in which the firm manages market information and translates it into specific actions to bridge the interface between the firm and its international markets (Knight and Liesch, 2002; Autio et al., 2005). As tacit market knowledge is firm-specific knowledge, it is not easily transferable, imitable and replicable (Teece et al., 1997); it therefore results in positional advantages in the foreign market (Barney, 1991; Grant, 1991).

Bearing in mind that internationalization from inception is becoming increasingly widespread, due largely to changing industry and market conditions and to the internationalization of competition (Oviatt and McDougall, 1994), and that the analysis of factors influencing positional advantages would allow us to improve the understanding of the international competitiveness and performance of these firms, future research is recommended in this direction (Autio et al., 2005; Zahra, 2005). So, the main aim of this chapter is to analyse how international new ventures acquire, interpret and translate foreign market knowledge into actions to achieve a better competitive position in international markets. A brief analysis is made of how the development of an entrepreneurial orientation and a market orientation influence the way international new ventures manage foreign market information and contribute to the generation of positional competitive advantages and to the international performance of these firms.

The relationship between entrepreneurial orientation and market orientation and its implications for business competitiveness and performance have been studied by many scholars (see Wiklund and Shepherd, 2003 or Bhuian et al., 2005 for a review), but with inconclusive results. The diversity of approaches in the literature indicates that the combined effects of market orientation and entrepreneurial orientation on company performance are undoubtedly complex and need more research (Bhuian et al., 2005), especially in the international arena and with international new ventures in which the above relationships have not been sufficiently investigated (Knight and Cavusgil, 2004). This chapter analyses how both entrepreneurial orientation and market orientation can influence the way international new ventures manage international market information to generate tacit market knowledge, and how both orientations can influence competitiveness and performance in international new ventures.

The remainder of the chapter starts with a review of the background literature to justify the hypotheses making up our theoretical model. The methodology of the empirical study is therefore divided into two parts: first, the measuring instruments used are presented, and then the results obtained among Spanish and Belgian international new ventures are compared to the hypotheses. Next, the results are discussed on the basis of the body of theory that shapes entrepreneurship and international marketing, bearing in mind the limitations of the study. Finally, the paper closes with conclusions, implications and future research developments.

ENTREPRENEURIAL ORIENTATION AND THE COMPETITIVENESS OF INTERNATIONAL NEW VENTURES

The definition of entrepreneurial orientation that has been most widely accepted in the specialized literature is the one popularized by Miller (1983). This author defined entrepreneurial orientation as a strategic construct whose conceptual domain includes the inter-relationship of three characteristics of managerial attitude: innovation, a predisposition to assume high but controlled risks and proactivity (Miller, 1983).

The innovation related to entrepreneurial orientation is not necessarily innovation involving creative destruction – in the words of Schumpeter (1934) – associated with the creation of new resources. It also includes minor innovations resulting from new ways of combining existing resources (Zahra et al., 1999; Shane, 2003). The key factor in being able to identify an innovation as enterprising is that it involves the search for new relationships between resources and/or existing products (Shane and Venkataraman, 2000; Eckhardt and Shane, 2003). Proactive orientation involves a constant effort to take initiative and anticipate competitors' movements (Covin and Slevin, 1989; Lumpkin and Dess, 1996; 1997). This dimension of entrepreneurial orientation has been developed mainly from the works of Stevenson and his collaborators, who analyse proactivity as an organizational process aimed at searching for new business opportunities and not at optimizing the resources already held (Stevenson and Gumpert, 1985; Stevenson and Jarillo, 1990). Proactivity therefore requires business people to be constantly scanning the environment so they can identify new enterprise opportunities and capitalize on them before their competitors. Finally, an entrepreneurial orientation involves taking moderate to high risks in strategic decisions. As might be expected, the acceptance of risks in managerial decision-making is inevitable in innovative and proactive behaviours (Covin and Slevin, 1989; Lumpkin and Dess, 1996; 1997).

Research on the nature, antecedents and effects of entrepreneurial orientation has mainly been aimed at studying its relationship with business performance (Zahra et al., 1999). In this sense it has been proven that entrepreneurial orientation has a direct effect on the economic performance of new ventures (Wiklund, 1999; Zahra and George, 2002; Dimitratos et al., 2004; Jantunen et al., 2005; Hughes and Morgan, 2006). Recently, this relationship has been extended to international competition (McDougall and Oviatt, 2000). Entrepreneurial orientation is closely linked to firms' international activities because internationalization can only occur through brokering, leveraging and risk-taking practices (Zahra and Garvis, 2000;

Lu and Beamish, 2001; Fletcher, 2004; Jantunen et al., 2005). Knight and Cavusgil (2004) have argued that entrepreneurial orientation should be instrumental in the development and performance of key organizational routines in order to succeed in international markets.

However, it has recently been pointed out that, besides the direct effect of entrepreneurial orientation on companies' international performance, an indirect effect also exists through the positional advantages that this orientation provides (Knight and Cavusgil, 2004). A positional advantage can be conceptualized as a superior marketplace position that captures the provision of superior customer value and the achievement of lower relative costs (Day and Wensley, 1988). Firms sustain a positional advantage if rivals are unable to acquire and deploy a similar or substitute mix of resources and capabilities (Mahoney and Pandian, 1992). A high level of entrepreneurial orientation enhances the ability of the organization to recognize and create opportunities through its conduct and actions (Shane, 2003). In order to take advantage of these opportunities, companies must develop new capabilities to transform their low-value resources and to reshape their processes and structures. In a recent study Zahra et al. (2006) state that entrepreneurial companies develop and apply different capabilities when faced by changes in the environment, to reshape their basic resources, changing invalid or unusable resources (Sirmon and Hitt, 2003), or recombining resources in an innovative way to be able to develop new substantive capabilities in current or new markets (Sirmon et al., 2007). Moreover, a strong emphasis on innovation moves companies to enter new markets, to renew their presence where they are already present and to explore new possibilities (Garud and Nayyar, 1994; Hult and Ketchen, 2001; Cho and Pucik, 2005; Hughes and Morgan, 2006). In addition, Calantone et al. (2002) demonstrate that business innovation contributes to the achievement of competitive advantages, facilitating creative thought in organizational learning activities. Furthermore, Carbonell and Rodriguez (2006) empirically show a positive relationship between speed of innovation and a positional advantage. In this sense, the capability to introduce innovations in the market quickly ensures that the new products contain the ideas of the market and more recent technological innovations in comparison with competitors' products (Atuahene-Gima, 2003) and, consequently, these products may be perceived by the consumers as more modern than those of competitors. In fact, Kessler and Bierly (2002) demonstrate that rapid innovation is related to greater perception of product quality.

Proactive companies are also used to market changes and trends, which make it easier for them to understand latent needs when faced with competition (Hamel and Prahalad, 1990). Thus, by means of anticipation and active preparation for change, companies with proactive values are in a better position to take rapid control of a greater market share when the change takes place. Proactive new ventures can mobilize resources earlier than their rivals.

Finally, tolerance of risk orientates companies towards action and makes them more used to uncertain atmospheres. At the same time, taking risks is associated with speed in making strategic decisions. As a consequence, both factors bring the possibility of obtaining better positioning (Eisenhardt, 1989). Thus risk-oriented companies combine a behaviour of searching for opportunities with a constructive predisposition towards risk, intending to generate means of exploration and operation (Lumpkin and Dess, 1996). This prevents the company from acquiring positions of inert calm, inactivity or sticking to traditions (Busenitz and Barney, 1997). So, managers who take risks normally take advantage of the opportunities the market offers and jeopardize resources before fully understanding the actions that should be taken (Covin and Slevin, 1991). Such an approach aims at obtaining advantages in evolutionary situations, taking advantage of the fact that markets are rarely stable for long.

In accordance with the above reasoning, it could be stated that the development of an entrepreneurial orientation provides new ventures with a crucial ability to understanding positional advantages in international activities. Thus we propose the following hypotheses:

Hypothesis 1: The entrepreneurial orientation of international new ventures positively influences their international economic performance.

Hypothesis 2: The entrepreneurial orientation of international new ventures positively influences their international positional advantages.

ENTREPRENEURIAL ORIENTATION AND MARKET ORIENTATION OF INTERNATIONAL NEW VENTURES

Following the two most relevant market orientation approaches (Kohli and Jaworski, 1990; Narver and Slater, 1990) and gathering the integrative definitions of them (for a review, see Bigné and Blesa, 2002) a market-oriented organization can be defined as one that develops behaviours coordinating the different company functions addressed towards searching for and gathering information from consumers, competitors and the environment. It disseminates this information across the company and designs and implements a reaction depending on the information obtained, based on identifying and constructing distinctive capabilities of the organization in order to satisfy consumers by providing them with superior value.

Some empirical studies suggest that a firm's market orientation (the coordinated behaviour of the different functions of the organization aimed at developing a response in accordance with the information from consumers, competitors and the environment with a view to providing customers with greater value) can improve the relationship between entrepreneurial orientation and performance (Atuahene-Gima and Ko, 2001; Blesa and Ripollés, 2004; Bhuian et al., 2005). The reason is that market orientation provides not only market information but also market intelligence processes that help new ventures obtain the advantages of an entrepreneurial orientation; that is, the reconfiguration produced by market orientation on existing entrepreneurial orientation can explain the performance of new ventures. In international new ventures this reconfiguration may occur because, in order to be innovative in international markets, they need to develop searching processes, as well as analysing market information to redesign innovation according to the different needs and characteristics of international markets. Moreover, market orientation of entrepreneurial firms contributes to their proactiveness through scanning and sharing information activities (Slater and Narver, 1995; 1998). Market-oriented businesses carry out much wider explorations, adopt a long-term approach and are far more likely to take on a generative learning process (Slater and Narver, 1998). This takes the form of a commitment to understanding both the expressed and unexpressed needs of their customers and their competitors' plans and capabilities through the processes of acquiring and evaluating market information in a systematic and anticipatory way. Finally, a way of reducing the risk involved in entrepreneurial orientation is developing a market orientation that provides information about the market needs. Thus the following hypothesis is proposed:

Hypothesis 3: The entrepreneurial orientation of international new ventures positively influences their market orientation.

MARKET ORIENTATION AND THE COMPETITIVENESS OF INTERNATIONAL NEW VENTURES

Market knowledge and market competition are fundamental to the performance and competitiveness of international new ventures (Oviatt and McDougall, 1994). International new ventures need information and knowledge to overcome the liabilities of newness and foreignness (Knight and Liesch, 2002). But, in addition, these companies must process and integrate this information into their existing knowledge to generate tacit market knowledge and marketing capabilities (Cohen and Levinthal, 1990; Huber, 1991; Zahra and George, 2002). Market orientation can play a decisive role in this process (Cadogan et al., 2001; 2002; 2003; 2006; Álvarez et al., 2005). The processes of market information, which are at the heart of market orientation, help to define marketing capabilities that allow the company to develop distinguishing activities and improve its economic performance (Day 1994; Vorhies and Harker, 2000; Tsai and Shih, 2004; Bhuian et al., 2005; Mazaira et al., 2005).

In addition, market orientation can lead new ventures to advantageous positioning for the company. Market-oriented companies are focused on intelligence generation and, through this, they constantly improve and update their values and abilities for organizational learning (Liu et al., 2002). This relationship is strengthened by the fact that market orientation contributes to generating sustainable advantages which protect and help to increase the company's market share (Lambin, 1996). With the implementation of market orientation, companies create lasting positional advantages that allow them to offer more value to their customers and obtain better results than the average for their sector. A particularly important element in achieving these advantages is the amount and quality of information that companies have. So, the fact of obtaining and processing information related to customers, competitors and the company itself receives fundamental importance in the process of constructing competitive advantages (Gordon, 1989). Also, the generation of tacit market knowledge, inherent in market orientation and its application in order to provide better value to the consumer, helps the company to develop the basis for a positional advantage (Narver and Slater, 1990).

As the main responsibility of marketing is to meet customers' long-term needs, it can be deduced that market-oriented companies will be best prepared to obtain those abilities or resources, making it possible to achieve real positional advantages. Specifically, Mazaira et al. (2005) confirm that the delivery of greater value to the customer, which characterizes market-oriented companies, involves the development of a greater capacity to understand the market in order to develop responses and capabilities to adapt to it and to maintain relationships with customers. Additionally, as Vila and Küster (1998) indicate, this orientation could be considered a strategic capability if a company adopts and implements this culture all over the organization, as a market-oriented company is in a better position to identify positional advantages using the resources and abilities necessary to obtain them (Vázquez et al., 1998). In this sense, Martín (1995) empirically demonstrates that the resources and capabilities theory allows an explanation of business competitiveness, considering market orientation as an internal company factor that could explain its positional competitiveness. So, in this study we assume that:

Hypothesis 4: The market orientation of international new ventures positively influences their international positional advantages.

Hypothesis 5: The market orientation of international new ventures positively influences their international economic performance.

INTERNATIONAL POSITIONAL ADVANTAGES AND INTERNATIONAL PERFORMANCE IN INTERNATIONAL NEW VENTURES

The relationship between positional advantages and performance is one of the pillars on which modern strategic management theory is based. So, different studies carried out since Porter's contributions and those shaping resources and capabilities theory (Wernerfelt, 1984; Peteraf, 1993; Grant, 1996 among others) are based on that relationship. Morgan et al. (2004) have shown that positional advantages also influence export performance. Positional advantages are direct antecedents of export venture performance because the relative superiority of a venture's value offering determines target customers' buying behaviour and the outcomes of this behaviour (Morgan et al., 2004). From the resource-based view and dynamic capabilities theories, both the possibilities of reinvestment of the funds generated to get new resources and capabilities and the organizational learning derived from positional advantages are the main arguments to justify the relationship between positional advantages and international performance (Morgan et al., 2004). Thus it can be posited that:

Hypothesis 6: The international positional advantages of international new ventures positively influence their economic international performance.

Figure 11.1 shows the model to be analysed.

METHODOLOGY

To test these hypotheses, data were gathered from samples of new international ventures from Spain and Belgium operating in several indus-

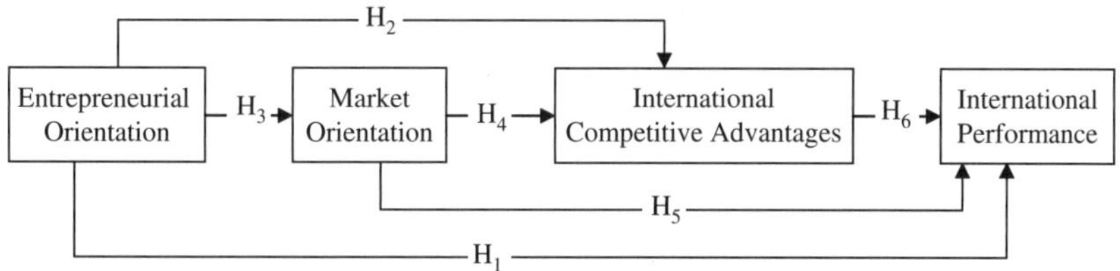

Figure 11.1 Model of effects of entrepreneurial and market orientations on international performance of Spanish and Belgian international new ventures

tries. Spanish firms were selected from the Duns and Bradstreet (2002) database, which contains references on 850 000 Spanish firms in terms of turnover. Belgian firms were selected from the 'Gewestelijke Ontwikkelingsmaatschappij' (GOM, 2005) database of Flemish enterprises containing 15 000 Flemish firms. The firms belonging to an industrial group were eliminated from both databases to ensure that they took their own decisions. Three criteria were used to select the companies for the survey. Firstly, the companies had to be recently established; in this sense, the requirement set for the sample was that the firms should have been set up after 1997. Secondly, the companies had to be engaged in international activities, considering that those businesses whose level of exports was more than 25 per cent of their annual sales could be considered as having a consolidated international presence. Thirdly, they could not be subsidiary or affiliate companies. The field research was carried out during the last quarter of 2005. After these selection procedures our sample consisted of 537 Spanish and 382 Belgian international new ventures. For the field research, interviewee collaboration was requested, together with confirmation of the e-mail address. After the questionnaire had been sent out, follow-up contact was made by telephone to increase the response rate. The questionnaire was posted on the Internet and an e-mail with a link to it was sent to each manager. A total of 135 Spanish companies (25.14 per cent) and 72 Belgian companies (18.85 per cent) completed the questionnaire. The average age of Spanish companies was 4.38 years old (std. dev. 1.68) and they had had international activity for 3.9 years (std. dev. 1.61). Moreover, these companies had an average number of 25.91 employees. Their annual turnover was below 800 000 euros for 22.6 per cent of the firms, between 800 000 and 5 000 000 euros for 45.9 per cent and over five million euros for the remaining 25.7 per cent. Regarding the Belgian firms, they were 4.55 years old (std. dev. 2.31), had had international activity for 4.04 years (std. dev. 1.70) and had an average number of 46.81 employees.

In addition, 22.7 per cent of Belgian firms had a turnover of below 800 000 euros, 54.6 per cent of between 800 000 and 5 000 000 euros and 22.7 per cent of over five million euros.

Measuring Instruments

In this study we consider the concept of entrepreneurial orientation defined by Miller (1983) as the inter-relationship of three basic characteristics: innovative attitude, willingness to take controlled risks and proactiveness, and we use Miller's scale as extended in the specialized literature (Covin and Slevin, 1989). This measure has been used in a wide variety of research settings and has shown high levels of reliability and validity in numerous studies (Barringer and Bluedorn, 1999; Becherer and Maurer, 1997;

BOX 11.1 MEASUREMENT OF ENTREPRENEURIAL ORIENTATION

1. The top managers of my company favour a strong emphasis on R&D, technological leadership, and innovations. (Entrepr.1)
2. My business has recently entered into new activities and/or launched new products. (Entrepr.2)
3. My business frequently carries out significant changes in product lines or services. (Entrepr.3)
4. My business only undertakes actions in the sector after knowing the movements of competitors. (Entrepr.4)
5. My business undertakes actions in the sector which are later followed by competitors. (Entrepr.5)
6. My business is a pioneer in developing new products, administrative techniques or technologies. (Entrepr.6)
7. My business avoids direct confrontation when faced with actions by competitors. (Entrepr.7)
8. Due to the dynamism of the environment, my business prefers to start with small investments and to gradually enlarge its commitment of resources. (Entrepr.8)
9. My business prefers to undertake high-risk investment projects. (Entrepr.9)
10. When my business is faced with a decision involving a certain degree of uncertainty, we adopt a prudent position. (Entrepr.10)

Dickson and Weaver, 1997; Kreiser et al., 2002). This entrepreneurial orientation scale has three sub-dimensions (Box 11.1).

Market orientation was measured with the eclectic scale developed by Blesa and Bigné (2005). The dimensions of this scale were based on the MARKOR (Kohli et al., 1993) and MKTOR scales (Narver and Slater, 1990), although its structure made it necessary to move some of the items from their place on the original scale. Repeated items were also removed and items from other scales, referring to aspects not reflected in the above scales, were included, such as price policies, discussion of market trends

BOX 11.2 MEASUREMENT OF MARKET ORIENTATION

1. We hold an inter-departmental meeting at least once a quarter to discuss market trends and development. (Coordina.1)
2. The staff of all our firm's departments hold periodic meetings to jointly plan responses to changes occurring in the environment. (Coordina.2)
3. We periodically meet some of our customers to ascertain their current needs and the products they will be needing in the future. (Search1)
4. We systematically gather information on the problems distributors may have when marketing our products. (Search2)
5. We periodically collect information on distributor satisfaction. (Search3)
6. The information on end-user satisfaction is systematically distributed to all sections of our firm. (Disemin.1)
7. Sales or marketing staff dedicate a great deal of their time to debating potential future needs of customers, both among themselves and with the rest of the staff. (Disemin.2)
8. High-level managers discuss the strengths and weaknesses of our competitors with the other managers in the firm. (Disemin.3)
9. When a firm staff member has important information on our competitors, they quickly alert other departments in the firm. (Disemin.4)
10. Any information coming from the market is distributed to all sections in the firm. (Disemin.5)
11. We periodically review our products to make sure they match end-user needs. (Desing1)

12. Our firm makes its market strategy compatible with our distributors' objectives. (Desing2)
13. We offer full information to our end-users for better use of our products. (Implem.1)
14. We provide relevant information to our distributors on our marketing strategy. (Implem.2)
15. We carry out actions to convince our distributors of the advantages of working with us. (Implem.3)
16. We participate actively in actions that show the social usefulness of our sector to the general public. (Implem.4)

(Deshpandé et al., 1993), identification of emerging segments, appearance of new products, information exchange stimulation, environmentally-directed strategies and information flow to consumers (Box 11.2). This procedure was similar to that applied by Matsuno et al. (2000) to refine the MARKOR scale.

To measure the international positional advantages the entrepreneurs were asked for the position of their business in its main foreign market with respect to its main competitors in that market for different competitive areas, such as products, services, price and communication (Box 11.3).

In this study it has been decided to consider three general indicators of business results. Specifically, the managers were asked about the position of their company in the main foreign market with respect to the main competitors in that market with respect to the profitability (ROI), the net profit (Zahra and Garvis, 2000) and the market share (Knight and Cavusgil, 2004). These represent the three most common types of performance used in the literature and, in practice, they represent, respectively, the financial results, effectiveness results and operational results (Álvarez et al., 2005). We used a three-item Likert type of five points (1 = far below or worst; 5 = very superior or leader).

To support the validity of the scaling content used, all the items were taken from a review of the related literature. We also attempted to ensure that they meet the conceptual definition and reflect all the relevant dimensions.

The technique most frequently used by social researchers to evaluate convergent validity is the confirmatory analysis. Since the aim of our analysis is to describe the validity of indicators as measuring instruments of the different scales, the different initial models were adjusted following the indications of Jöreskog and Sörbom (1993). The following criteria were applied: each indicator had to reach a lambda of 0.4 to ensure its continuity on the scale, and the t-value had to be significant. Following these criteria, in the Spanish sample we eliminated the items Entrepr.4 and Entrepr.7 from the

BOX 11.3 MEASUREMENT OF INTERNATIONAL POSITIONAL ADVANTAGES

1. Developing new products. (IntComAd1)
2. Adapting export product design style. (IntComAd2)
3. Meeting export product quality standards/specifications. (IntComAd3)
4. Meeting export packaging/labelling requirements. (IntComAd4)
5. Providing technical/after sales service. (IntComAd5)
6. Price policies. (IntComAd6)
7. Accessing export distribution channels. (IntComAd7)
8. Maintaining control over foreign middlemen. (IntComAd8)
9. Personal selling. (IntComAd9)
10. Advertising. (IntComAd10)
11. Promotion. (IntComAd11)

entrepreneurial orientation scale and the item Implem.4 from the market orientation scale. Only item IntComAd6 had to be eliminated from the international positional advantages scale in the Belgian sample. For better comparison of our model in the two countries, these items were eliminated from the Spanish and Belgian samples. The results of the full measurement model and reliability analyses are described in Tables 11.1 and 11.2.

One risk indicator in the entrepreneurial orientation scale was slightly above the threshold of 0.4 in both samples (0.36 and 0.38, respectively) but we decided to maintain it in order to have at least two indicators of each construct (Jöreskog and Sörbom, 1993). In addition, although the indicator IntComAd6 was under the threshold, as it was the only indicator of price we decided not to eliminate it.

Although some indicators of extracted variance are under the generally suggested value of 0.5 (dissemination and international positional advantage in the Spanish sample and risk, search and design in the Belgian one), the index of compound reliability was good in all these cases.

RESULTS AND DISCUSSION

Structural equation models have proved to be particularly useful when the aim of the research is to establish the direct causal contribution of one

Table 11.1 Results of measurement model analysis

Spanish sample							
Scale							Parameters
Entrepreneurial orientation							0.36–0.78
Market orientation							0.43–0.89
International positional advantages							0.44–0.76
International performance							0.68–0.79
Measurements of quality of fit							
χ2/fd =	RMSR =	GFI =	AGFI =	NFI =	CFI =	IFI =	RFI =
2.72	0.072	0.95	0.94	0.94	1.00	1.00	0.92
Belgian sample							
Scale							Parameters
Entrepreneurial orientation							0.38–0.57
Market orientation							0.50–0.89
International positional advantages							0.34–0.88
International performance							0.69–0.91
Measurements of quality of fit							
χ2/fd =	RMSR =	GFI =	AGFI =	NFI =	CFI =	IFI =	RFI =
3.56	0.084	0.94	0.93	0.93	1.00	1.00	0.92

variable to another in a non-experimental situation (Jöreskog and Sörbom, 1993). This type of analysis was used in the present study. Table 11.3 shows the results of the estimation of the relationship model with the SEM. To simplify the model, the market orientation measurement scale was narrowed down to five indicators, which corresponded to its dimensions. To do this, the items making up each dimension were averaged.

Not all the relationships proposed were statistically corroborated in both samples. As expected, positive and significant relationships were found between entrepreneurial orientation and market orientation ($\gamma = 0.68/0.91$, $t = 14.89/9.37$), thus confirming Hypothesis 3 in both samples. This relationship was also found by Matsuno et al. (2002), who established that the greater the level of entrepreneurial proclivity, the greater the level of market orientation. This result confirms entrepreneurial orientation as an antecedent of market orientation, thereby corroborating previous empirical results (Blesa and Ripollés, 2004) in international new ventures and in different countries.

The link between international positional advantages and international performance ($\gamma = 0.38/0.86$, $t = 2.12/3.18$) was also positive and significant, confirming Hypothesis 6 in both analyses. Thus, as expected, the advantages obtained from using a company's resources and capabilities in its plans and actions improve the international new venture's performance. This result is also along the same lines as those obtained in previous works

Table 11.2 Results of the analyses of reliability of the measurement models

Spanish Sample					
Scale	Entrepreneurial orientation				
Dimensions	Innovation		Proactiveness		Risk
CR*	0.83		0.66		0.78
EV**	0.63		0.50		0.69
Scale	Market orientation				
Dimensions	Interfunctional coordination	Search	Dissemination	Design	Implementation
CR	0.90	0.84	0.81	0.68	0.75
EV	0.78	0.64	0.47	0.51	0.51
Scale	International positional advantages			International performance	
CR	0.82			0.77	
EV	0.43			0.52	
Belgium Sample					
Scale	Entrepreneurial orientation				
Dimensions	Innovation		Proactiveness		Risk
CR	0.79		0.69		0.68
EV	0.57		0.55		0.43
Scale	Market orientation				
Dimensions	Interfunctional coordination	Search	Dissemination	Design	Implementation
CR	0.93	0.63	0.88	0.68	0.70
EV	0.57	0.46	0.57	0.42	0.50
Scale	International positional advantages			International performance	
CR	0.83			0.95	
EV	0.50			0.76	

Notes: * CR: Compound reliability; ** Extracted variance.

(Homburg et al., 2002; Wiklund and Shepherd, 2003; Blesa and Ripollés, 2005; Vorhies and Morgan, 2005) but our findings allow us to generalize this to an international level.

Furthermore, positive and significant relationships were found between entrepreneurial orientation and international performance ($\gamma = 0.38$, $t = 2.54$), thus confirming Hypothesis 1 in the Spanish sample. This result confirms those obtained in previous studies (Lumpkin and Dess, 2001; Liu et al., 2002; Wiklund and Shepherd, 2003; Blesa and Ripollés, 2005; Wiklund and Shepherd, 2005). Moreover, in Spanish international new ventures entrepreneurial orientation has positive effects on international

Table 11.3 Results of estimating standardized parameters for the model of effect of entrepreneurial and market orientations on international performance of new ventures

Spanish Sample				
Entrepreneurial orientation – International performance	0.38	2.54 ($p<0.05$)	H_1	Accepted
Entrepreneurial orientation – International positional advantages	0.068	1.21	H_2	Rejected
Entrepreneurial orientation – Market orientation	0.68	14.89 ($p<0.01$)	H_3	Accepted
Market orientation – International positional advantages	0.47	4.65 ($p<0.01$)	H_4	Accepted
Market orientation – International performance	0.069	–0.25	H_5	Rejected
International positional advantages - International performance	0.38	2.12 ($p<0.05$)	H_6	Accepted

Measurements of quality of fit

$\chi 2$/fd = 3.78	RMSR = 0.080	GFI = 0.96	AGFI = 0.93	NFI = 0.94	CFI = 0.98	IFI = 0.98	RFI = 0.91

Belgian sample				
Entrepreneurial orientation – International performance	0.18	0.68	H_1	Rejected
Entrepreneurial orientation – International positional advantages	0.21	0.48	H_2	Rejected
Entrepreneurial orientation – Market orientation	0.91	9.37 ($p<0.01$)	H_3	Accepted
Market orientation – International positional advantages	0.37	0.47	H_4	Rejected
Market orientation – International performance	−0.27	−0.41	H_5	Rejected
International positional advantages - International performance	0.86	3.18 ($p<0.01$)	H_6	Accepted

Measurements of quality of fit

$\chi 2$/fd = 2.40	RMSR = 0.094	GFI = 0.94	AGFI = 0.94	NFI = 0.91	CFI = 1.00	IFI = 1.00	RFI = 0.88

performance in direct and indirect ways. So, to the direct relationship found, the analysis adds one indirect relationship in which market orientation, fostered by entrepreneurial orientation, promotes the international positional advantages that improve international performance.

A positive and significant relationship was found between market orientation and international positional advantages ($\gamma=0.47$, $t=4.65$), confirming Hypothesis 4 in this sample. However, this is not the case with Belgian international new ventures. Although the analysis shows a positive and significant relationship between entrepreneurial orientation and market orientation and between international positional advantages and international performance, there is no relationship between these strategic orientations and international positional advantages. In order to determine whether this absence of relation concerns all the dimensions of the international positional advantages or whether, on the contrary, it is only related to some of them, a new model was tested which distinguishes four dimensions of international positional advantages: those related to the product (IntComAd1, IntComAd2, IntComAd3 and IntComAd4); those related to the service and the price (IntComAd5 and IntComAd6); those related to the distribution channel (IntComAd7 and IntComAd8) and, finally, those related to communication activities (IntComAd9, IntComAd10 and IntComAd11).

The new analysis in this sample allowed us to discover positive and significant relationships between entrepreneurial orientation and international positional advantage based on the product ($\gamma=0.29$, $t=2.67$); based on service and price ($\gamma=0.23$, $t=2.47$) and based on communication ($\gamma=0.30$, $t=9.27$). Furthermore, we found a significant but negative relationship between market orientation and international positional advantage based on the product ($\gamma=-0.24$, $t=-2.22$) and on communication ($\gamma=-0.28$, $t=-8.98$). This result does not allow us to generalize the positive effects of entrepreneurial and market orientations to the international arena and seems to show that factors related to the environment of the company's country of origin might affect the relationship between these orientations and their international positional advantages. In this sense, it has been considered that companies with entrepreneurial orientation are more successful in dynamic environments, where they are more prepared for searching for new products/markets (Covin and Slevin, 1989; Lumpkin and Dess, 2001; Gotteland and Boulé, 2006), which would explain the positive relationship between this orientation and the international positional advantages based on the product and on service/price.

In addition to this, it has also been suggested that the dimensions of both orientations could have an effect on other variables that negatively influence the company's performance in the short term. For example, the effects of innovation on the company's costs would negatively affect the relationship between entrepreneurial orientation and international performance. In the same sense, seeking market information contributes to increasing company costs, which would negatively affect international positional advantages. Further research is needed to detect whether the difference in the results from both samples is explained by the way managers from different countries are implementing their strategic orientations.

Finally, the relationships between entrepreneurial orientation and international positional advantages and between market orientation and international performance were not significant in both samples, rejecting Hypotheses 2 and 5. Again, the presence of intermediate variables could explain these results (Weerawardena and O'Cass, 2004). In the case of Spanish international new ventures entrepreneurial orientation requires the participation of market orientation to generate international positional advantages, but this is not the case in the Belgian sample. This result points out the need for further research explaining the origin of international positional advantages in Belgian international new ventures.

In relation to the absence of an effect of market orientation on international performance, the literature has not reached an agreement about this relationship and, consequently, it is possible to find studies which do not support the above relationship (Agarwal et al., 2003; Sandvik and Sandvik, 2003). The absence of a direct effect of market orientation on performance is an indicator which shows us that this orientation offers an effective way of providing superior value to the consumer which allows the company to develop new products, to fix higher prices or to improve the channel relations. These activities will have a positive effect on the performance of the organization (Blesa and Bigné, 2005; Sandvik and Sandvik, 2003). In fact, in the Spanish sample market orientation has a positive effect on international performance through the generation of positional advantages.

CONCLUSIONS AND IMPLICATIONS

The results obtained in this study allow us to move forward in the analysis of the factors that may explain the competitiveness of new international ventures. In brief, from this research it can be suggested that international positional advantages can act as a mediating force in the relationship between market and entrepreneurial orientations and the performance of Spanish and Belgian international new ventures. However, in light of the results obtained in the empirical analysis, different conclusions are obtained depending on the country we consider.

In broad terms this study confirms the positive relationship between entrepreneurial orientation and market orientation. Thus the uncertainty that is generated in international new ventures by the fact that they enter international markets from their early days will require the development of market-oriented activities in order to understand, in a systematic and anticipated way, both the expressed and latent needs of customers, as well as their competitors' plans and capabilities through processes of acquiring and evaluating information. One way of reducing the risk associated with entrepreneurial behaviour is to adopt a market orientation.

Additionally, international positional advantages show a positive influence on international performance. In the case of Spanish international new ventures, managers who promote entrepreneurial orientation can enhance international performance if their companies adopt a market orientation. In this respect, the entrepreneurs of these companies have to be proactive, focused on innovation and undertaking high-risk projects and, in addition, they have to develop mechanisms of information processing in order to know precisely the future and present needs of their clients, the strengths and weaknesses of their competitors and the most influential factors of their environments. By doing this, international new ventures will obtain international advantages with regard to their main international rivals, which, in turn, will be translated into better international results.

However, this does not hold true in the case of Belgian international new ventures, as no relationship was found between market orientation and international positional advantages. Belgian managers need to identify the sources of their international positional advantages in order to know where to direct their efforts to improve their international performance.

Although the specialized literature assumes that a positive relation exists between entrepreneurial and market orientations and economic performance, it is also considered that this relationship depends on the environmental conditions which characterized the sample studied. The results obtained support the need to consider other factors to analyse the above relationship. In fact, the direct relationship between these orientations and performance has not been proved in any of the samples studied.

Limitations and Future Lines of Research

The use of cross-sectional data is a limitation of this study in order to make causal inferences. However, as the main explanatory variables of the proposed model (entrepreneurial and market orientation) are path-dependent and time-consuming activities embedded in organizational routines and processes (Lumpkin and Dess, 1996; Jantunen et al., 2005), it might be reasonable to assume a causal explanation structure, as has just been done, in which entrepreneurial and market orientation have a positive impact on the generation of international positional advantages, which implies obtaining better international performance.

In addition, our empirical study has been based on the answers of a single respondent from each of the companies from our samples. This procedure raises the question of whether just one respondent can adequately report for the entire firm. In this sense, as our study is based on new ventures, the entrepreneur is the appropriate respondent to provide information about the strategic orientations of new ventures and the results associated with them (Davidsson, 2004). Taking into account the above limitations, future research should study the proposed relationships using longitudinal data.

Chetty and Campbell-Hunt (2004) analyse the extent to which international new ventures deviate from the conventional internationalization model. Their research suggests that many of the phenomena believed to distinguish the born-global internationalization path are also characteristic of firms that began their internationalization in the traditional way. In this sense, it is suggested that future research should analyse how these two business situations differ (Bell et al., 2004; Chetty and Campbell-Hunt, 2004; Laanti et al., 2007). Further studies are needed to study whether the relationships put forward in this study are characteristic of international new ventures or whether they also exist in companies that follow a slower internationalization process.

From the resource-based view and dynamic capabilities theories, the relevance of entrepreneurial and market orientations in determining both positional advantages and international performance of international new ventures is based on the learning created by the development of these orientations. Blomstermo et al. (2004) concluded that international new ventures show a different absorption capacity structure to firms which have five years or more domestic existence before the first foreign assignment. However, our research has not studied in depth the way in which this learning effect is generated or how the development of market and entrepreneurial orientations affects the absorption capability of these companies. In this sense, new research is recommended in order to thoroughly study the learning processes that these companies develop and the way in which this learning is translated into specific entry strategies in new markets (Chetty and Campbell-Hunt, 2004).

ACKNOWLEDGEMENTS

The authors gratefully acknowledge the support of Institut Valencià d'Investigacions Econòmiques, S.A. for the Study of Market Orientation as Determinant of new Ventures Internationalisation (06i108.01/1). This study is part of the 'Analysis of Factors that Influence on Competitiveness and Business Performance of Global New Ventures' (GV/2007/102) research project, financially supported by the Valencian Government's Ministry of Business, Universities and Science. The authors thank Carlos Ocampo and Ilke Van Beveren from the Lessius University College (Antwerp, Belgium) for their cooperation in the Belgian fieldwork.

REFERENCES

Agarwal, S., M.K. Erramilli and C. Dev (2003), 'Market orientation and performance in service firms: role of innovation', *Journal of Services Marketing*, **17**, 68–82.

Álvarez, L.I., M.L. Santos and R. Vázquez (2005), 'Escalas de medida del concepto de orientación al mercado. Revisión crítica de su contenido y de sus propiedades psicométricas', *ESIC Market*, (**April**), 161–202.

Atuahene-Gima, K. (2003), 'The effects of centrifugal and centripetal forces on product development speed and quality: how does problem solving matter?', *Academy of Management Journal*, **46**, 359–73.

Atuahene-Gima, K. and A. Ko (2001), 'An empirical investigation of the effect of market orientation and entrepreneurship orientation alignment on product innovation', *Organization Science*, **12**(2), 54–74.

Autio, E., H. Sapienza and J. Almeida (2000), 'Effects of age of entry, knowledge intensity and imitabilitiy on international growth', *Academy of Management Journal*, **43**, 909–24.

Autio, E., H.J. Sapienza and P. Arenius (2005), 'International social capital, technology sharing, and foreign market learning in internationalizing entrepreneurial firms', *Advances in Entrepreneurship, Firm Emergence and Growth*, **8**, 9–42.

Barney, J. (1991), 'Firm resources and sustained competitive advantage', *Journal of Management*, **17**(1), 99–120.

Barringer, B.R. and A.C. Bluedorn (1999), 'The relationship between corporate entrepreneurship and strategic management', *Strategic Management Journal*, **20**, 421–44.

Becherer, R.C. and J.G. Maurer (1997), 'The moderating effect of environmental variables on the entrepreneurial and marketing orientation of entrepreneur-led firms', *Entrepreneurship Theory and Practice*, **22**(1), 47–59.

Bell, J., D. Crick and S. Young (2004), 'Small firms internationalization and business strategy', *International Small Business Journal*, **22**(1), 23–56.

Bhuian, S.N., B. Menguc and S.J. Bell (2005), 'Just entrepreneurial enough: the moderating effect of entrepreneurship on the relationship between market orientation and performance', *Journal of Business Research*, **58**, 9–17.

Bigné, J.E. and A. Blesa (2002), 'Una concepción ecléctica de la orientación al mercado y su escala de medición', *Revista Española de Investigación de Marketing-Esic*, **6**(2), 33–58.

Blesa, A. and E. Bigné (2005), 'The effect of market orientation on dependence and satisfaction in dyadic relationships', *Marketing Intelligence and Planning*, **23**(3), 249–65.

Blesa, A. and M. Ripollés (2004), 'Orientación emprendedora, orientación al mercado y rendimiento empresarial', *The Entrepreneur and Starting Up New R&D&I Business*, Valencia, Universitat de València, pp. 59–70.

Blesa, A. and M. Ripollés (2005), 'Relación entre la orientación al mercado y la orientación emprendedora: su influencia en el rendimiento de la empresa', *Revista Europea de Dirección y Economía de la Empresa*, **14**(3), 165–80.

Blomstermo, A., K. Eriksson, A. Lindstrand and D.D. Sharma (2004), 'The perceived usefulness of network experiential knowledge in the internationalizing firm', *Journal of International Management*, **10**, 355–73.

Busenitz, L. and J. Barney (1997), 'Differences between entrepreneurs and managers in large organizations', *Journal of Business Venturing*, **13**(4), 295–316.

Cadogan, J.W., N. Paul, R.T. Salminen, K. Puumalainen and S. Sundqvist (2001), 'Key antecedents to export market-oriented behaviours: a cross-national empirical examination', *International Journal of Research in Marketing*, **18**(3), 261–82.

Cadogan, J.W., A. Diamantopoulos and J.A. Siguaw (2002), 'Export market-oriented activities: their antecedents and performance consequences', *Journal of International Business Studies*, **33**(3), 615–26.

Cadogan, J.W., C.C. Cui and E.K. Yeung Li (2003), 'Export market-oriented behaviour and export performance: the moderating roles of competitive intensity and technological turbulence', *International Marketing Review*, **20**(5), 493–513.

Cadogan, J.W., C.C. Cui, R.E. Morgan and V.M. Story (2006), 'Factors facilitating and impeding the development of export market-oriented behaviour: a study of Hong Kong manufacturing exporters', *Industrial Marketing Management*, **35**, 634–47.

Calantone, R.J., S.T. Cavusgil and Y. Zhao (2002), 'Learning orientation, firm innovation capability, and firm performance', *Industrial Marketing Management*, **31**(6), 515–24.

Carbonell, P. and A.I. Rodríguez (2006), 'The impact of market characteristics and innovation speed on perceptions of positional advantage and new product performance', *International Journal of Research in Marketing*, **23**, 1–12.

Chetty, S. and C. Campbell-Hunt (2003), 'Explosive international growth and problems of success amongst small to medium-sized firms', *International Small Business Journal*, **21**(1), 5–27.

Chetty, S. and C. Campbell-Hunt (2004), 'A strategic approach on internationalization: a traditional versus a "born-global" approach', *Journal of International Marketing*, **12**(1), 57–81.

Cho, H. and V. Pucik (2005), 'Relationship between innovativeness, quality, growth, profitability, and market value', *Strategic Management Journal*, **26**(6), 555–75.

Cohen, W.M. and D.A. Levinthal (1990), 'Absorptive capacity: a new perspective on learning and innovation', *Administrative Science Quarterly*, **35**, 128–53.

Congcong, Z. and S. Khavul (2005), 'Capability development, learning and growth in international entrepreneurial firms: evidence form China', in D. Sheperd and J. Katz (eds), *International Entrepreneurship*, Oxford: Elsevier, pp. 273–96.

Covin, J.G. and D.P. Slevin (1989), 'Strategic management of small firms in hostile and benign environments', *Strategic Management Journal*, **10**, 75–87.

Covin, J.G. and D.P. Slevin (1991), 'A conceptual model of entrepreneurship as firm behavior', *Entrepreneurship Theory and Practice*, **16**(1), 7–25.

Davidsson, P. (2004), 'Scott Shane, a general theory of entrepreneurship: the individual–opportunity nexus', *International Small Business Journal*, **22**(2), 206–9.

Day, G.S. (1994), 'The capabilities of market-driven organizations', *Journal of Marketing*, **58**(4), 37–52.

Day, G.S. and R. Wensley (1988), 'Assessing advantage; a framework for diagnosing competitive superiority', *Journal of Marketing*, **52**(2), 1–20.

Deshpandé, R., J. Farley and F. Webster (1993), 'Corporate culture, customer orientation, and innovativeness in Japanese firms: a quadrate analysis', *Journal of Marketing*, **57**(1), 23–37.

Dickson, P. and K. Weaver (1997), 'Environmental determinants and individual-level moderators of alliance use', *Academy of Management Journal*, **40**, 404–25.

Dimitratos, P., S. Lioukas and S. Carter (2004), 'The relationship between entrepreneurship and international performance: the importance of domestic environment', *International Business Review*, **13**(1), 19–41.

Eckhardt, J. and S. Shane (2003), 'Opportunities and entrepreneurship', *Journal of Management*, **29**(3), 333–49.

Eisenhardt, K.M. (1989), 'Building theories from case study research', *Academy of Management Review*, **14**(4), 532–50.

Fernhaber, S.A. and P.P. McDougall (2005), 'New ventures growth in international markets: the role of strategic adaptation and networking capabilities', *Advances in Entrepreneurship, Firm Emergence and Growth*, **2**, 111–36.

Fletcher, D. (2004), 'International entrepreneurship and the small business', *Entrepreneurship and Regional Development*, **16**, 289–305.

Garud, R. and P. Nayyar (1994), 'Transformative capacity: continual structuring by inter-temporal technology transfer', *Strategic Management Journal*, **15**, 365–85.

Gordon, I. (1989), *Beat the Competition*, Oxford: Basil Blackwell.

Gotteland, D. and J.M. Boulé (2006), 'The market orientation – new product performance relationship: redefining the moderating role of environmental conditions', *International Journal of Research in Marketing*, **23**(2), 171–85.

Grant, R.M. (1991), 'The resource-based theory of competitive advantage: implication for strategy formulation', *California Management Review*, **33**(3), 114–35.

Grant, R.M. (1996), 'Prospering in dynamically-competitive environments: organizational capability as knowledge integration', *Organizational Science*, **7**, 375–87.

Hamel, G. and C.K. Prahalad (1990), *Competing for the Future*, Boston, MA: Harvard Business School Press.

Homburg, C., W. Hoyer and M. Fassnacht (2002), 'Service orientation of a retailer's business strategy: dimensions, antecedents, and performance outcomes', *Journal of Marketing*, **66**, 86–101.

Huber, G. (1991), 'Organizational learning: the contributing process and the literatures', *Organisational Science*, **2**, 88–115.

Hughes, M. and R.E. Morgan (2006), 'Deconstructing the relationship between entrepreneurial orientation and business performance at the embryonic stage of firm growth', *Industrial Marketing Management*, **36**(5), 651–61.

Hult, G.T. and D.J. Ketchen (2001), 'Does market orientation matter?: a test of the relationship between positional advantage and performance', *Strategic Management Journal*, **22**(9), 899–906.

Hymer, S. (1976), *The International Operations of National Firms: A Study of Direct Investment*, Boston, MA: MIT Press.

Jantunen, A., K. Puumalainen, S. Saarenketo and K. Kyläheiko (2005), 'Entrepreneurial orientation, dynamic capabilities and international performance', *Journal of International Entrepreneurship*, **3**, 223–43.

Jöreskog, K. and D. Söbom (1993), *LISREL 8: Structural Equation Modeling With the Simplis Command Language*, Chicago, IL: Scientific Software International.

Kessler, E.H. and P.E. Bierly (2002), 'Is master really better? An empirical test of the implication of innovation speed', *Transactions on Engineering Management*, **49**(1), 2–12.

Knight, G.A. and T. Cavusgil (2004), 'Innovation, organizational capabilities, and the born-global firm', *Journal of International Business Studies*, **35**, 124–41.

Knight, G.A. and P.W. Liesch (2002), 'Information internalisation in internationalising the firm', *Journal of Business Research*, **55**, 981–95.

Kohli, A.K. and B.J. Jaworski (1990), 'Market orientation: the construct, research propositions and managerial implications', *Journal of Marketing*, **54**(2), 1–18.

Kohli, A.K., B.J. Jaworski and A. Kumar (1993), 'MARKOR: a measure of market orientation', *Journal of Marketing Research* (November), 467–77.

Kreiser, P.M., L.D. Marino and K.M., Weaver (2002), 'Assessing the psychometric properties of the entrepreneurial orientation scale: a multi-country analysis', *Entrepreneurship Theory and Practice*, **26**, 71–92.

Laanti, R., M. Gabrielsson and P. Gabrielsson (2007), 'The globalization strategies of business-to-business born global firms in the wireless technology industry', *Industrial Marketing Management*, **36**(8), 1104–17.

Lambin, J.J. (1996), 'The misunderstanding about marketing, today, marketing is too important to be left to sale marketing function. An empirical study in the private insurance sector', *CEMS Business Review*, **1**(1/2), 37–56.

Liu, S.S., X. Luo and Y.Z. Shi (2002), 'Integrating customer orientation, corporate entrepreneurship and learning orientation in organizations-in-transition: an empirical study', *International Journal of Research in Marketing*, **19**(4), 367–82.

Lu, J.W. and P.W. Beamish (2001), 'The internationalization and performance of SMEs', *Strategic Management Journal*, **22**, 565–86.

Lumpkin, G.T. and G.G. Dess (1996), 'Enriching the entrepreneurial orientation construct – a reply to Entrepreneurial Orientation or pioneer advantage', *Academy of Management*, **21**(3), 605–7.

Lumpkin, G.T. and G.G. Dess (1997), 'Proactiveness versus competitive aggressiveness: teasing apart key dimensions of an entrepreneurial orientation', *Frontiers for Entrepreneurship Research*, Wellesley, MA: Babson College, pp. 47–58.

Lumpkin, G.T. and G.G. Dess (2001), 'Linking two dimensions of entrepreneurial orientation to firm performance: The moderating role of environment and industry life cycle', *Journal of Business Venturing*, **16**(5), 429–51.

Mahoney, J.T. and J.R. Pandian (1992), 'The resource-based view within the conversation of strategic management', *Strategic Management Journal*, **13**, 363–80.

Martín, E. (1995), 'Rentabilidad y orientación al mercado', Summer Workshop on Business Market Orientation, May, Castelló, Spain.

Matsuno, K., J.T. Mentzer and J.O. Rentz (2000), 'A refinement and validation of the MARKOR scale', *Journal of the Academy of Marketing Science*, **28**(4), 527–40.

Matsuno, K., J.T. Mentzer and A. Özsomer (2002), 'The effects of entrepreneurial proclivity and market orientation on business performance', *Journal of Marketing*, **66**(3), 18–32.

Mazaira, A., A. Dopico and E. González (2005), 'Incidencia en el grado de orientación al mercado de las organizaciones empresariales en el desarrollo de las capacidades estratégicas de marketing', *Revista Europea de Dirección y Economía de la Empresa*, **14**(3), 181–208.

McDougall, P.P. and B.M. Oviatt (2000), 'International entrepreneurship: the intersection of two research paths', *Academy of Management Journal*, **43**(5), 902–6.

Miller, D. (1983), 'The correlates of entrepreneurship in three types of firms', *Management Science*, **29**, 770–91.

Morgan, N.A., A. Kaleka and C.S. Katsikeas (2004), 'Antecedents of export venture performance: a theoretical model and empirical assessment', *Journal of Marketing*, **68**, 90–108.

Narver, J.C. and S.F. Slater (1990), 'The effect of market orientation on business profitability', *Journal of Marketing*, **54**(4), 20–35.

Oviatt, B.M. and P.P. McDougall (1994), 'Toward a theory of international new ventures', *Journal of International Business Studies*, **25**(1), 45–64.

Oviatt, B.M. and P.P. McDougall (1997), 'Challenges for internationalization process theory: the case of international new ventures', *Management International Review*, **37** (special issue 2), 85–99.

Oviatt, B.M. and P.P. McDougall (2004), 'The internationalization of entrepreneurship', *Journal of International Business Studies*, **36**(1), 2–8.

Oviatt, B.M. and P.P. McDougall (2005), 'Defining international entrepreneurship and modeling the speed of internationalization', *Entrepreneurship Theory and Practice*, **29**(5), 537–53.

Peteraf, M. (1993), 'The cornerstones of competitive advantage: a resource-based view', *Strategic Management Journal*, **13**, 363–80.

Rialp, A., J. Rialp and G. Knight (2005), 'The phenomenon of early internationalizing firms: what do we know after a decade (1993–2003) of scientific inquiry?', *International Business Review*, **14**(2),147–66.

Sandvik, I.L. and K. Sandvik (2003), 'The impact of market orientation on product innovativeness and business performance', *International Journal of Research in Marketing*, **20**(4), 355–76.

Schumpeter, J.A. (1934), *The Theory of Economic Development*, Cambridge, MA: Harvard University Press.

Shane, S. (2003), *A General Theory of Entrepreneurship: The Individual-Opportunity Nexus, New Horizons in Entrepreneurship*, Cheltenhan, UK and Northampton, MA, USA: Edward Elgar Publishing.

Shane, S. and S. Venkataraman (2000), 'The promise of entrepreneurship as a field of research', *Academy of Management Review*, **25**(1), 217–26.

Sirmon D.G. and M.A. Hitt (2003), 'Managing resources: linking unique resources, management and wealth creation in family firms', *Entrepreneurship Theory and Practice*, **27**(4), 339–58.

Sirmon, D.G., M.A. Hitt and R.D. Ireland (2007), 'Managing firm resources in dynamic environments to create value: looking inside the black box', *Academy of Management Review*, **32**(1), 273–92.

Slater, S.F. and J.C. Narver (1995), 'Market orientation and the learning organization', *Journal of Marketing*, **59**, 63–74.

Slater, S.F. and J.C. Narver (1998), 'Customer-led and market-orientated: let's not confuse the two', *Strategic Management Journal*, **19**(10), 1001–6.

Stevenson, H. and D. Gumpert (1985), '*The Heart of Entrepreneurship*', *Harvard Business Review* (**March–April**), 85–94.

Stevenson, H. and J.C. Jarillo (1990), 'A paradigm of entrepreneurship: entrepreneurial management', *Strategic Management Journal*, **11**, 17–27.

Stinchcombe A. (1965), 'Social structure and organizations', in J. March (ed.), *Handbook of Organizations*, Chicago, IL: Rand McNally, pp. 142–93.

Teece, D.J., G. Pisano and A. Shuen (1997), 'Dynamic capabilities and strategic management', *Strategic Management Journal*, **18**, 509–33

Tsai, M. and C. Shih (2004), 'The impact of marketing knowledge among managers on marketing capabilities and business performance', *International Journal of Management*, **21**(4), 524–30.

Vázquez, R., M.L. Santos and M.J. Sanzo (1998), *Estrategias de Marketing para Mercados Industriales*, Madrid: Civitas.

Vila, N. and I. Küster (1998), '*Recursos y capacidades y posicionamiento producto-mercado: su relación con el rendimiento y la rivalidad empresarial*', XII Encuentro de Profesores Universitarios de Marketing, September, Santiago de Compostela.

Vorhies, D.W. and M. Harker (2000), 'The capabilities and performance advantages of market-driven firms: an empirical investigation', *Australia Journal of Management*, **25**(2), 145–73.

Vorhies, D.W. and N.A Morgan (2005), 'Benchmarking marketing capabilities for sustainable competitive advantage', *Journal of Marketing*, **69**, 80–94.

Weerawardena, J. and A. O'Cass (2004), 'Exploring the characteristics of the market-driven firms and antecedents to sustained competitive advantage', *Industrial Marketing Management*, **33**(5), 419–28.

Wernerfelt, B. (1984), 'A resource-based view of the firm', *Strategic Management Journal*, **5**, 171–80.

Westhead, P., M. Wright, D. Ucbasaran and F. Martin (2001), 'International market selection strategies of manufacturing and services firms', *Entrepreneurship and Regional Development*, **13**, 17–46.

Wiklund, J. (1999), 'Entrepreneurial orientation as predictor of performance and entrepreneurial behaviour in small firms – longitudinal evidence', *Frontiers for Entrepreneurship Research*, available: http:www.babson.edu/entre/fer (accessed 11 March 2008).

Wiklund, J. and D. Shepherd (2003), 'Knowledge-based resources, entrepreneurial orientation, and the performance of small and medium-sized businesses', *Strategic Management Journal*, **24**, 1307–14.

Wiklund, J. and D. Shepherd (2005), 'Entrepreneurial orientation and small business performance: a configurational approach', *Journal of Business Venturing*, **20**, 71–91.

Zahra, S.A. (2005), 'A theory of international new ventures: a decade of research', *Journal of International Business Studies*, **36**(1), 20–8.

Zahra, S.A. and D.M. Garvis (2000), 'International corporate entrepreneurship and firm performance: the moderating effect of international environmental hostility', *Journal of Business Venturing*, **15**(5/6), 469–92.

Zahra, S.A. and G. George (2002), 'International entrepreneurship: the current status of the field and future research agenda', in M.A. Hitt, R.D. Ireland, S.M. Camp and D.L. Sexton (eds), *Strategic Entrepreneurship: Creating a New Mindset*, Oxford: Blackwell, pp. 255–88.

Zahra, S.A., D.F. Jennings and D.F. Kuratko (1999), 'The antecedents and consequences of firm-level entrepreneurship: the state of the field entrepreneurship', *Entrepreneurship Theory and Practice*, **24**(2), 45–66.

Zahra, S.A., H.J. Sapienza and P. Davidsson (2006), 'Entrepreneurship and dynamic capabilities: a review, model and research agenda', *Journal of Management Studies*, **43**(4), 917–55.

PART V

Processes and Entrepreneurship

12. Emergency entrepreneurship: creative organizing in the eye of the storm

Bengt Johannisson and Lena Olaison

INTRODUCTION

Entrepreneurship is an elusive phenomenon that does not just appear as new business venturing in the market. Within the public sector there is a call for more entrepreneurial bureaucrats (du Gay, 2001) and entrepreneurship is entering the business schools as well as the educational system at large from the university to the compulsory school (Hjorth and Johannisson, 2007) with the political ambition to make all of Europe more entrepreneurial (Lambrecht and Pirnay, 2005). Accordingly, studies on different entrepreneurial endeavours tend to end up with prefixes, such as team entrepreneurship (Stewart, 1989), collective entrepreneurship (Johannisson, 2003), community entrepreneurship (Johannisson and Nilsson, 1989; Johnstone and Lionais, 2004), social entrepreneurship (Steyaert and Hjorth, 2006) and public entrepreneurship (Hjorth and Bjerke, 2006). This suggests that it is not possible to conclusively generate models and/or conceptualize entrepreneurship once and for all. Nonetheless, two perspectives on entrepreneurship are frequently used in the literature, namely entrepreneurship as a special kind of management – from Mintzberg (1973) to Shane (2003), and entrepreneurship as forms of social creativity (Hjorth et al., 2003; Gartner et al., 2003). In this chapter entrepreneurship is approached as a societal phenomenon practising creative organizing.[1] We especially associate entrepreneurship with imaginative ways of dealing with ruptures in the everyday life context. The 'prosaic view' of entrepreneurship as suggested by Steyaert (2004) is then interesting to relate to.

With this brief review of optional images of entrepreneurship in mind, we want to invite the reader to the drama that the Hurricane Gudrun enacted in Sweden in 2005. Late on the evening of 8 January a heavy storm struck Kronoberg County and its neighbouring region in the south of Sweden, causing blocked roads, tearing power lines into pieces, destroying property and incapacitating institutions responsible for the infrastructure. Hitting 5 per cent of the forestry area of Sweden, Gudrun tore down 80 million cubic metres, equal to one year's lumbering for the entire Swedish forestry industry. In total 253 000 households and organizations were left without power because of Gudrun, the majority also without any telephone connection. Gudrun caused by far the greatest damage ever to the elaborate Swedish infrastructure. The public institutions and other formal market organizations did not have the resources, capabilities or power to cope with the crisis, especially in the rural areas. Instead, a number of initiatives were taken by civic organizations, communities and individuals that were tied to the place.

It is here, in the in betweens of different organizational settings, that our story takes place. We propose that ruptures such as the one caused by Gudrun may initiate processes that uncover and (re)produce entrepreneurship which remain invisible when 'business as usual' rules in society. The purpose of this chapter is thus to enquire into localized creative organizing in the face of (natural) catastrophes and to conceptualize 'emergence entrepreneurship' accordingly. Next we elaborate upon our understanding(s) of entrepreneurship and how this relates to organization/organizing. In the following section we present the methodology that is practised in the field studies and then the empirical accounts are described. Revisiting the images of entrepreneurship and other understandings of organizing in dramatic settings, we close our discourse in the last section with a tentative conceptualization of 'emergency entrepreneurship'.

ALTERNATIVE IMAGES OF ENTREPRENEURSHIP

Mainstream research presents entrepreneurship, here addressed as 'opportunity-driven', as a proactive rational economic activity, a strategy aiming to systematically identify and evaluate existing opportunities, preferably radical innovations, on the market and allocate the resources needed in such a way that the opportunities chosen are efficiently exploited. This strictly instrumental view of entrepreneurship suggests that boundaries in social space are intentionally crossed by, for example, the proactive introduction of new products or processes or by the opening up of new product or factor markets (for example, Schumpeter [1911], 1934). Bounded rationality due to lack of information concerning available opportunities and resources, though, means that entrepreneurial venturing is associated with risk. Reputation/trustworthiness and legitimacy are in this perspective considered as means of accessing resources that would otherwise not be available, a rationale that Starr and MacMillan (1990) address as 'social

Table 12.1 Three modes of entrepreneurship – generic features

Aspect	Opportunity-driven entrepreneurship	Enactive entrepreneurship	Prosaic entrepreneurship
Origin of initiative	Existing opportunities in the market	Coincidences and enacted environments	Challenges in everyday life
Process characteristics	'Boundedly rational' exploitation of opportunities	Playful experimentation	Casual coping with problems/ opportunities
Generic coping	Proactive risk-taking	Interaction aiming at exploiting ambiguity	Interaction in order to keep uncertainty at bay
Role and sources of social capital	Resourcing relying on calculated trust	Relating through mutual commitment to dialogue	Reproducing by way of collective identity and blind trust
Organizing rationale	New means-ends framework	Social creativity	Daily activity and interaction

contracting'. This concern for systematic renewal and change, organized in a new means-end framework (Shane, 2003), is what makes entrepreneurship stand out and yet remain in the management family. Table 12.1 summarizes the generic aspects of entrepreneurship that we have illustrated with the opportunity-driven view.

A contrasting image of entrepreneurship, here labelled 'enactive entrepreneurship', associates entrepreneurship with social creativity on other arenas besides the market. Whatever the setting, new opportunities are in this perspective interactively enacted, instigated by coincidences and chance, yet ultimately shaping new worlds for many (Spinosa et al., 1997). In a socially constructed world of becoming (Chia, 1995) entrepreneurship implies coping with ambiguity (Johannisson, 1992; Weick, 1995). Entrepreneurial processes are initiated by curiosity, organized by spontaneity and intrinsically driven by passion and joy (Hjorth and Steyaert, 2003; Hjorth et al., 2003). Opportunities to explore and associate tactics to exploit them emerge in parallel (Gartner et al., 2003). This perspective on entrepreneurship shifts the focus from organization to organizing, from formal structure to emergent process (Gartner et al., 1992). Ventures crystallize out of personal networks, constituted by genuine relations based on trust and defined as much existentially as instrumentally, used as much for crafting individual and collective identity as for actualizing new business

(Johannisson, 2000). Entrepreneurship is accompanied by a general belief in the good will of others and their commitment to participating in dialogues for negotiating new realities.

Yet another, third, image of entrepreneurship is following Steyaert (2004) 'prosaic entrepreneurship'. Steyaert argues that 'the everydayness of entrepreneurship refers as much to a mundane, and – why not – even a boring posture as to a literary connotation where a prosaic – as in the novel – addresses the actuality of becoming, its ongoing becoming effected through conversational processes' (p. 9). Prosaic or mundane views on entrepreneurship focus, not on model building or general concepts, but acknowledge the importance of 'the everyday and the ordinary, the familiar and the frequent, the customary and the accustomed, the mediocre and the inferior' (Steyaert, 2004, p. 9). All entrepreneurial processes certainly, however path breaking, include routine activities just as all human beings as adults occasionally engage in entrepreneurial processes. 'Prosaic' entrepreneurship at the firm and societal level, for example, appears in the industrial district as a localized small-firm cluster. Westlund and Bolton (2003) systematically dissect the concept of 'localized social capital', defined as 'spatially defined norms, values, knowledge, preferences, and other social attributes or qualities that are reflected in human relations' (p. 79), and its relation to entrepreneurship. Entrepreneurship as organizing is then continuous and carried by the district as a socially embedded collective of business units, that is, not by individual firms (Johannisson, 2003). As traditional family businesses, the latter are neither willing nor able to practise innovativeness and growth.

However complex networking, interaction and organizing as conceptual constructs present themselves, their (metaphorical) use obviously contributes to our understanding of why and how entrepreneurship may be practised. While opportunity-driven and enactive entrepreneurship both associate entrepreneurship with dramatic events that are instigated by strategically and tactically alert individuals, prosaic entrepreneurship is hidden behind the apparent uniformity of everyday life. In spite of this wide range of images of entrepreneurship none of them, though, tells us what creative organizing may be triggered by if communities which appear as dormant are challenged by an external shock, an artificial or natural disaster like Gudrun.

EXPERIENCING AND STUDYING A NATURAL DISASTER

The empirical study was carried out over a ten-month period. In February and March 2005, that is immediately after the disaster, the junior author jointly with fellow master students interviewed ten persons involved in organizing in the wake of the hurricane. We were looking for organizations, temporary or formal, that became visible through their achievements in the restoration work. The aim of the conversations was to find out what kind of organizing the dramatic event had triggered: who got engaged, how, after whom and after what resources the activities patterned themselves.

We think that there is a need for a narrative approach and contextually sensitive accounts when trying to grasp how existing formal and informal structures may enforce or hinder potential entrepreneurial initiatives in the face of disaster. Soon enough we understood that our informants in the immediate aftermath of the hurricane could provide no systematically reflected insights, 'only' stories. Czarniawska (2004), though, argues that narratives represent modes of knowing and communicating and, what is more, they may guide the enactment of the storytellers' future lives.

Listening to stories through the media and our personal networks we used our personal contacts in the region to get access to local agents (civic associations, authorities and small firms), national incorporated structures and also intermediary organizations which bridge between the other two categories. It so happens that all our ten interviewees are men. This bias does not only reveal that the authors' personal networks are dominated by men, but also that there were mainly men working with the restoration after the hurricane. Obviously, we have silenced some of the stories that might have been told by women.[2]

In October and November 2005 the authors of this chapter together revisited five of the original informants for further conversations. The informants were then encouraged to reflect upon their own stories told in the aftermath of Gudrun. We thus used quotations from the original interview to create a conversation with the interlocutor concerning how they had experienced the event back then and again ten months later. Since our conversations concerned issues that were (and are) emotionally loaded, we allow our interlocutors to speak when we communicate our field experiences.

Our interpretation of the agents' immediate and retrospective experiences of the hurricane was organized as follows. First, the two authors independently read the raw interview texts in order to identify statements that reflected (creative) coping with the dramatic events and consequently contributed to the construction of entrepreneurship in such a setting. These primary interpretations were then, according to each category of informants, jointly reflected upon by us. The stories as presented and interpreted are subsequently analyzed further by bringing in Lanzara's (1983) notion of 'ephemeral organizations' and formal (project organization and crisis management) organizations. Our conceptual and empirical work and the images of temporary organizations are used to craft our notion of 'emergency entrepreneurship'. Our methodology obviously both resembles and contrasts the Eisenhardt (1989) idea of generating theory out of case/qualitative material. We stay with a proposed conceptualization of 'emergency entrepreneurship' that may inspire refinement by way of additional theoretical and empirical work.

TALES OF THE FIELD – COPING WITH CHAOS IN EVERYDAY LIFE

The stories told by the informants are organized into five subsections according to what agency they represent. We shortly summarize their stories accordingly. First, we introduce a spokesman for a civic association representing a rural community and experience how he dealt with the dramatically imposed rupture in his everyday life. Then we listen to representatives of the public organizations which are formally responsible for organizing and governing territorial space, namely the financially strong Swedish municipalities. In the following two subsections we encounter representatives of business organizations: a local small firm and an external corporate structure, for which the area struck by Gudrun is part of their market. Finally, we listen to the stories told by the spokesmen for two intermediary organizations, which, due to their organizing tactics and way of doing business, created new tasks for themselves, enforcing their roles as bridges between different structures. The voices of each group of agents are systematically reflected upon with respect to their way of organizing and will be echoed in the last section for further analysis.

Civic Associations Taking Charge

Anders Malmqvist, one of the organizers of an informal community group that locally dealt with the emergency, has many stories to tell. On the morning after the hurricane Malmqvist immediately joins other residents from his village who were trying to make their way through the giant jackstraws of trees caused by Gudrun. They keep working intensively, knowing that if they fail there will be no way out of the village. In the evening, when they are about to give up, they hear the persistent sound of a tractor somewhere from the other side of the enormous mess of trees. Now convinced that somebody is trying to reach them, they get energized and continue to work their chainsaws in the growing darkness.

When the main roads are clear Malmqvist starts to discuss the restoration work with a retired electrician from E.ON (the dominant power company in the South of Sweden, a corporation that we will encounter again):

> We asked ourselves: what do we need? We need to establish an information centre, where we can collect information and co-ordinate resources; we must open the gas station to secure fuel and reparations and we need to make sure that everyone working can eat at least every four hours.

Malmqvist describes the organizing as an arena for acute problem-solving: 'We had no right to make decisions, and we didn't. What we could do was to identify a problem and bring together those who had resources to come up with solutions.' Through the residents' personal networks they could enact measures even if these were not compatible with the formal norms: 'I know that we broke some regulations and maybe a law or two to get what we needed, but what could we do?'

Reflections

The stories about the first initiatives after the hurricane tell us about spontaneous and immediate organizing. There was no time to discuss or reflect upon the situation, since people were often both literally and metaphorically working in the dark, whether coping day and night with the jam of fallen and broken trees or trying to muddle through in corporate and public decision-making structures. A kind of push-triggered collective (social) entrepreneurship emerged, which released the same kind of creativity that is associated with pull-triggered individual/team commercial entrepreneurship: acting upon gut feeling, using previous experiences to cope with the new situation and network intensely.

The Moment of Truth for the Municipality

When we meet Claes Göran Carlsson, mayor of Ljungby municipality, at the beginning of March 2005, our conversation largely concerns what can be learnt from one chaotic situation to the next. In the summer of 2004, six months before Gudrun hit the same area, the main streams in Ljungby municipality flooded. During the flooding the municipal executive board, together with appropriate technical units, created a structure to cope with the acute situation:

> You need to act directly and on a large scale; create a staff so you can speed up the decision-making process. You have to down size the formal processes and move to execution. But the municipal staff have to know that they have the politicians behind them in their decisions. Generally, institutions are afraid to act because of the costs and the risk of being criticized for unauthorized action. But it's better to be criticized for doing too much than for doing nothing.

When revisiting Carlsson in November 2005 we bring up the learning experiences. He then tells us that immediately after the flooding he and the rescue leader were invited to other municipalities and asked to share their lessons with them. After Gudrun these kinds of requests have increased: 'We are quite satisfied with our achievement. I know we can do it again if necessary.' Coping with Gudrun enforces the importance of established relations:

> Not just having the contacts, but knowing that you can work together. When you reorganize and create space for action, you can draw as many organization maps you want, but if the [personal] relationships are not working, nothing can help you in an emergency situation. The social capital is decisive, you need to build the foundation, share the same values, before you have to deal with the emergent situation, both inside and outside the organization.

Reflections

Ljungby municipality appears as a role model for organizational learning aiming at flexibility and preparedness for emergencies. Natural disasters vary with respect to their surprise effect and have to be dealt with accordingly. In order to create space for action information has to be rationed – a unique case in an otherwise indifferent and democratic Swedish society. A dual municipal order is practised – one that copes with everyday routine operations and one that enters the scene in case of emergency. These parallel structures seem to jointly infuse entrepreneurship into a public structure. Even more important, trust is tightly connected with previous experiences and reveals itself only when the community faces an emergency. Learning and knowledge creation come from hands-on experience, but also from telling stories to others, sharing experiences. Repeated reflections on one's own action enforces self-identity and increases the willingness to act again. Mayor Carlsson recognizes the role of emotion and commitment in the making of organized efforts. The language he then uses is more of an entrepreneurial voice, relieved from the bureaucratic vocabulary that public structures are usually associated with.

Small Businesses – Disconnected from their Customers

In this section we meet Roland Axelsson, responsible for retail at Rottne Industry Ltd. The company is one of the leading manufacturers of logging vehicles, with its markets in Europe, North America and Australia.

On the Monday morning when Gudrun had left southern Sweden, Rottne Industry Ltd immediately starts to mobilize. Emergency organizations, forestry entrepreneurs and forestry owners turn to the company asking for vehicles and drivers. 'Several organizing solutions have been created in our community to facilitate the reconstruction after Gudrun. They are provisional and will probably dissolve and disappear when they have fulfilled their mission', says Roland Axelsson. Rottne Industry Ltd also takes an active part in the recovery work. Even though the company uses retailers when business is as usual and never deals with used machinery, they now take advantage of their well established network to gather and disseminate information, search for subcontractors from Europe, and even to work as mediators for second-hand machinery and logging machinery of other brands.

Reflections

The hurricane makes Rottne Industry Ltd reconsider what constitutes an important customer, opening up a field between commercially and socially important actions. Self-centredness was replaced with a need to call attention to what heroic contributions have been made by others in the local context. In the face of Gudrun, action is not triggered by emerging business opportunities but by a necessity to contribute to the reconstruction of the everyday life they share with their fellow citizens.

Incapacitated Corporate Structures

Gudrun's impact on the infrastructure in the region, for example E.ON, the major regional power provider, is devastating. When we first meet immediately after Gudrun, Sven Ruther at E.ON is busy organizing the recovery work. He explains that they got reinforcement not just from other power companies in Sweden and Europe but also from local networks. In the 1960s Sydkraft, E.ON's predecessor, created 'LRF-supportive groups' (developed in collaboration with the Federation of Swedish Farmers – LRF) in the rural areas, enacting the ambition to always being able to have staff available locally. Where these groups are still active E.ON uses them to cope with the damages that Gudrun has caused. In other places they re-emerge: 'Without means of communication you need to have people from the area that can guide electricians, and first, before you can even start to organize the restoration work, you need to clear blocked roads and wires.'

When we meet again with Sven Ruther he is responsible for customer contacts at E.ON. He explains his new assignment to us:

> E.ON has an emergency organization that gets activated in case of a crisis. Since I live in Älmhult, I know the area and the industrial plants. I was working in Älmhult as early as in the 60s so I know the people personally. In these situations you gain a lot if you know your way around and if they know you.

In the aftermath of Gudrun E.ON has learnt about the importance of preserving local knowledge, and the corporation has re-established LRF-supportive groups in every municipality where it operates.

Reflections

Corporations such as E.ON have realized the need for a dual structure, one for routine operations and one to implement in case of emergencies, the former increasingly global, the latter increasingly local. Thus a 'glocal' matrix organizational structure emerges. A related lesson from E.ON's experience is the importance of being close, physically as well as mentally and socially. Knowledge originating in everyday local life turned out to be a major source for entrepreneurship in the emergency situation created by the hurricane. That is, coping with Gudrun also exposed collective tacit knowledge and entrepreneurship.

Intermediators in Broken Structures

Smaland Airport Ltd is a minor regional airport with limited operations in the middle of the area struck by Gudrun. Like any airport, Smaland Airport Ltd is strictly controlled by laws and security rules, but Jan Fors, its managing director, can also tell many stories about creative organizing. Realizing that the airway is the only operating exit from or entry into the region, he and his staff jointly decide that they are going to keep the airport open round the clock until they know that all land roads have been cleared:

> The regional actors have not been able to get organized; not even once did they contact us to see if we were all right or if we had the resources needed to keep the airport open. We managed to do it, but isn't that worth finding out?

When we revisit Jan Fors in November 2005 he summarizes what he and his staff have learnt from dealing with Gudrun:

> The initiative and strength come from individuals; they have the commitment and the wish to help one another. And personally I have learnt to understand life in the countryside. My staff lives there, we talked a lot about their situation and I have realized that we sometimes forget about that kind of life.

According to Jan Fors, hands-on action is the most important thing when coping with a crisis, experience and also good relations to people you need to deal with: 'When there is an emergency, you don't have time to establish something new, you use what you've got, even though it is in new forms'.

Our interviewees often have difficulties communicating how they came to organize the way they did. Revisiting Mats Folkesson, coordinator at Farmers' Services, a kind of rural co-operative employment and staffing agency set up by farmers and bridging between corporate structures and civic society, again tries to explain:

> I don't know how it all started, things just began to move. First it was a question of survival, to reach the main road. We started to work three and three, and as we progressed we began to gather more and more people. We never had a discussion about money or whether we should get involved or not.

Since Farmers' Services normally deal with corporate structures, such as E.ON, the National Swedish Road Administration and business firms, they could mediate between the formal structures and the private initiatives. In order to be close to where the action was Farmers' Services temporarily moved their administration from their town office to a garage in the rural area.

Reflections

From coping with the hurricane we once again get proof that large 'well-structured' organizations run into problems when surprised by (literally) path-breaking events. Smaller informal organizations, in contrast, quite easily adapt their organization to the new situation. At Smaland Airport Ltd Gudrun even triggers new perspectives on its own organization, recognizing the employees as both goals and means for bridging their core business activities and the societal context. Jan Fors's stories underline that trust appears when needed actions are embedded in long-term relationships.

The crisis situation made visible the need for recombining existing competencies according to need: individuals like Mats Folkesson brought together people and resources at hand and created solutions to problems as they emerged. Because of Gudrun Farmers' Services were suddenly offered a task environment that was begging for their way of organizing. They were the ones trained to connect between different actors, since their staff were trusted both among local residents and formal structures. Such temporary organizing demonstrates a form of entrepreneurship that is driven by emergency and practised through immediate (inter)action.

SEARCHING THE ROOTS OF EMERGENCY ENTREPRENEURSHIP

In this section we shall further analyse our field accounts and search for the origins of the proposed features of what we here, inspired by, among others, Gartner (1993), name 'emergency entrepreneurship'. We argue that studies of extreme situations will not only reveal entrepreneurial forces that remain hidden under 'normal' circumstances, cf. Weick (1990), but generally enrich our understanding of organization/organizing as including entrepreneurship as well as management. Therefore we first tentatively position emergency entrepreneurship in the context of the other images of entrepreneurship introduced above. Since issues associated with coping with surprises and dramas appear in the literature on management as well as on entrepreneurship we then provide a general, yet simple, model for structuring different ways to deal with turbulent environments. We especially elaborate on this theme by juxtaposing the conceptual lessons from our empirical research with Lanzara's (1983) notion of 'ephemeral organization'. After that we see a need to qualify Lanzara's understanding of formal organization and therefore we review the 'project organization' and 'crisis management' as institutionalized ways of dealing with temporary challenges and/or surprises in the environment.

Revisiting Proposed Modes of Entrepreneurship

The stories about localized creative organizing in a region facing a natural disaster as related and interpreted above call for a different understanding of entrepreneurship than those presented in Table 12.1. First, it is in our case obvious that there was no omnipotent actor who could practise 'opportunity-based entrepreneurship'. The hurricane and the needs for reconstruction that it made obvious may possibly be seen as an instant opportunity, but the belief in calculated trust seems alien in a situation which has no precedents. Our notion of 'enactive entrepreneurship' also seems inappropriate, since coping with a disaster certainly is not about playful experimentation instigated by a subject in order to joyfully enact new environments out of ambiguous surroundings. The triggering initiative does not belong to the agent, and the experimentation needed to cope with the emergent situation is characterized by genuine uncertainty: what needs to be done first – restoring physical structures – is more than obvious, but the feasibility of alternative action tactics is totally unknown. The notion of 'prosaic entrepreneurship' obviously brings limited understanding to how to deal with a natural catastrophe that undermines the everydayness of life. In the case of emergency all initiatives aim at the reconstruction of everyday life, not, as in the case of prosaic entrepreneurship, using everyday life as a basis for instigating (ad)ventures.

Our tentative understanding of emergency entrepreneurship is, nevertheless, in some respects related to the other modes of entrepreneurship according to Table 12.1. With opportunity-based entrepreneurship our notion of emergency entrepreneurship shares the importance of social capital in resourcing the measures taken to cope with challenges on their arrival (although emergency entrepreneurship needs bonding rather than bridging social capital; see Johannisson and Olaison, 2007 cf. Davidsson and Honig, 2003). Experimentation was certainly called for as much as in enactive entrepreneurship when dealing with Gudrun, but that was since the situation was out of control and since people desperately asked for more information. That is, uncertainty, not ambiguity, prevailed. Passivity, even paralysis, facing the devastating effects of the hurricane, though, soon enough turned into intense local interaction in order to find ways to reconstruct basic everyday life. Commitment to place and collective identity associated with the territory as a physical and social space encompassing everyday life activated the social capital needed to practise mundane, yet creative, organizing, the hallmark of prosaic entrepreneurship.

Organizing Under Pressure

In order to come to grips with ways of dealing with unexpected events that call for (at least) temporary solutions, we have to go one step back and conceptualize a shared ground for entrepreneurship and management, certainly ways of organizing that are different in kind (cf. Hjorth et al., 2003). Here two simple dichotomies are used in order to illustrate qualitative differences between entrepreneurship and management in this context. The two dimensions are 'structure' and 'ways of coping with the environment' (Figure 12.1). As indicated, organizational structures may be permanent or temporary. Organizations may relate to environmental change proactively or reactively. Typically, entrepreneurship, as well as management, appears in and/or as permanent structures that operate proactively. Incorporated rescue organizations, for instance, are permanent organizations which are managed in such a way that they can, reactively yet professionally, deal with environmental rupture. Even bread-and-butter family businesses which are pushed into existence are entrepreneurial while still emerging, but the entrepreneurial spirit usually vanishes once established reactive behaviour dominates their coping.

Our focus here, though, is on the temporary structures. Looking first at entrepreneurship as more or less a proactive, strategic activity, habitual entrepreneurship comes to the fore. The entrepreneurial career may be looked upon as the enactment of a bundle of temporary ventures, cf., for example, Westhead and Wright (1998). Larson and Starr (1993) and Johannisson (2000) look upon entrepreneuring as the flow of (temporary) ventures which sediment out of the personal network of the entrepreneur. Within the field of management 'project organizing' is a well-established proactive practice to which we shall return below. We shall also elaborate on 'crisis management', that is, routinized ways of reacting to dramatic environmental change. We obviously propose the notion of 'emergency entrepreneurship' as an image of entrepreneurship that makes it triggered by external events and calls for immediate and temporary reaction.

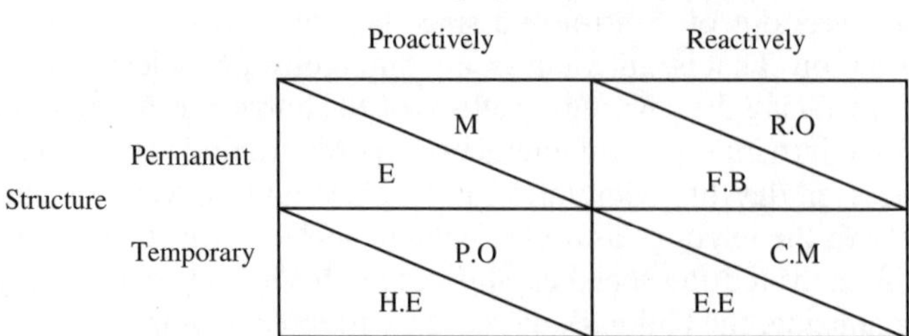

Notes: M – Management (dominant view); E – Entrepreneurship (dominant view); R.O – Rescue Organization; F.B – Family Business; P.O – Project Organization; H.E – Habitual Entrepreneurship; C.M – Crisis Management; E.E – Emergency Entrepreneurship.

Figure 12.1 Entrepreneurial and managerial ways of structuring activities and coping with the environment

Enquiring into the 1980 earthquake in southern Italy, Lanzara (1983) tells the story about volunteers who immediately entered the region being hit. There they organized their support as temporary ventures, only to exit after a few days when they were succeeded by rescue teams set up 'from above' by the public authorities. An institutional order thus soon enough replaced the original spontaneous rescue operations with their 'ephemeral' structure, lacking a history as well as a future. Since these two support structures are organized in radically different ways they have, according to Lanzara (1983), to be separated in time. Our story, in contrast, tells of how a disaster was originally dealt with from below and from the inside, that is, by collaborating local and regional agents, involving citizens as well as formal institutions. That is, the notion of emergency entrepreneurship reports on organizational endeavours, where spontaneous organizing and institutionalized structures emerged into collaboration founded in a shared history and with the prospects of a jointly built future.

Recently, it has been argued, other forms of temporary organization, such as the project organization, offer a new paradigm in the management field (Turner and Keegan, 1999), where it is usually applied to intra-organizational structuring. Research in the field usually focuses on projects within the boundaries of existing organizations (Heller, 1999). Projects are then broadly defined as 'organizational processes of planning, organizing, directing, and controlling resources for a relatively short-term objective established to complete specific goals and objectives' (Shenhar, 2001, p. 241). Peterson (1981), as early as a quarter of a century ago, used the notion of 'operative adhocracy' to present presumably dynamic corporations as bundles of projects. 'Adhocracy' was later appropriated by

Mintzberg (1988) and Storper (1989), for example, when researching the alleged creative Canadian and American (film) industries. However it has also been argued that firms in the film industry constituted as hosts for projects, in fact, are themselves lacking innovativeness and entrepreneurship (Davenport, 2006). The industry invites to repeatable structures, not to originality. Projects are: (1) set up either in order to proactively exploit creative people (for example, in the film industry) or in order to implement standardized measures more efficiently (for example, in the construction industry), not in order to reactively deal with devastating environmental change; (2) arenas where the participants are expected to use their unique individual competencies, not to demonstrate collective concerns; and (3) settings where creativity, spontaneity and improvization are used to craft new social and mental structures, not in order to restore physical ones.

The crisis management literature also appears paradoxical regarding structure and planning. We see this literature as divided into two parts. The first one is concerned with preparing companies for potential crises, predominantly financial crises, by creating temporary structures that can be put in place to restabilize organizations (Loosemore and Hughes, 2001) and possibly use the crisis to develop them further. The second part of the crisis management literature concerns itself with planning for and managing natural disasters, using models primarily from public management and project management (inter alia Moe and Pathranarakul, 2006). These primarily empirical studies repeatedly indicate that local governments (McEntire and Myers, 2004) as well as small businesses lack plans or organizational structures aimed at coping with disasters (Runyan, 2006; Spillan and Hough, 2003). Studies also report that it is citizen responses and personal and social networks that 'save the day' (Helsloot and Ruitenberg, 2004; Ok Choi and Brower, 2006; Pardasani, 2006). Nevertheless, crisis-management research tries to fill the gap between formal plans and the way networks in a crisis actually work (Ok Choi and Brower, 2006) with models for systematically building preparedness (McEntire and Myers, 2004). We thus state that project organizations and crisis management are settings where the 'ad hocness' is very much designed as a tool for management. In Table 12.2 we juxtapose, on the one hand, the project organization and crisis management with Lanzara's notion of 'ephemeral organization', on the other, with our emerging concept of 'emergency entrepreneurship'.

Only marginal adjustments are needed when making Lanzara's general image of formal structures also include the project organization and crisis management. Lanzara (1983) states that in a formal (project) organization, internal and external boundaries are distinct, while in an ephemeral organization the boundaries are fuzzy. Further, in crisis management the boundaries are distinct, since it aims at a pre prepared plan for a specific need. As a

Table 12.2 Alternative structures for temporary organizing

Feature	Project organizations/crisis management	Ephemeral organizations	Emergency entrepreneurship
Boundaries	Distinct	Fuzzy	Spatially distinct, socially/mentally fuzzy
Leadership	Central, shifting	Shifting, lacking	Local and multiple
Organizational structure	Formal, hierarchical	Informal, spontaneous	Loosely coupled and local
Information flow	Vertical	Horizontal	Lateral
Performance criterion	Economic efficiency/ restabilizing	Practical effectiveness	Restoration of everyday life

Source: Inspired by Lanzara (1983), Table 1, p. 88.

territorial phenomenon, emergency entrepreneurship is enacted in a context where the space boundaries are unambiguous to all concerned. General time restrictions tie people and their everyday practices to a place. Many public organizations are also organized by physical space. In case of an emergency the social boundaries inside and between the private and public spheres/sectors, however, dissolve on the micro/individual as well as on the organizational level. General commitment to place triggers residents to take initiatives also in the interest of other local residents – *homo economicus* turns into *homo curans*. The dramatically changed natural and social environments produce an ambiguity that invites, or rather requests, people to turn coincidences into opportunities, calling for hidden professional strengths and dormant entrepreneurial capabilities. As a bridging force between organizational structures and individual and local initiatives, emergency entrepreneurship reminds us of 'situational altruism' which 'motivates people to help in ways that are not mentioned in contingency plans. This creates opportunities for organizations and helps let [*sic*] them work more actively' (Helsloot and Ruitenberg, 2004, p. 103).

Devastating events, such as natural catastrophes, trigger and force everybody to take their own initiatives, since residents in the area struck by the disaster can neither exit nor just stay placid or give voice (Hirschman, 1974). Practising a 'heterarchical order' (cf. Grabher, 2001), leadership in one's own field of competence appears as everybody's right and obligation. The very tactics used for coping with the effects of Gudrun meant instigating initiatives in as many contexts as possible, even in the borderland between the legal and the illegal, trusting others to make similar efforts and believing in spontaneous co-ordination, in self-organizing. Ephemeral organizing, as illustrated by Lanzara (1983), is initiated from the outside by people driven by general humanitarian concerns. Elsewhere we argue that sustainable development, energized by the making of a collective identity, can only be achieved if organized from below and formed inside (Hjorth and Johannisson, 2003). Even if leadership is shifting (Kasvi et al., 2002), paying special attention to success criteria (Westerveld, 2003), leadership in the project management and crisis management literature is concerned with producing general techniques for the leaders from above/outside in order to make possible the centralized control of an ambiguous situation (Moe and Pathranarakul, 2006). Leadership in the context of emergency entrepreneurship is about taking charge of one's own as well as other people's lives. Even if the leadership that our stories communicate was local and fragmented, it was appropriate.

In case of emergencies of the Gudrun magnitude any established organization structure appears obsolete by definition. There was no need to break out of existing structures, an issue often discussed in the literature on organizational learning and innovation. The structures themselves broke down, indicating a need for a more flexible order. In our case 'loose coupling' was practised as a generic organizing principle in the region at large, with local task forces operating autonomously yet interdependently (Weick, 1976, cf. also Heller, 1999). Community-based project organizations adopt a similar structure (Skutle et al., 2002). Further empirical accounts from coping with natural disasters report the same insights (Helsloot and Ruitenberg, 2004), indicating that loose coupling is feasible for a broad mobilizing of resources. The need for immediate action and temporary restructuring calls attention to the image of 'organized anarchy' (March and Olsen, 1976), where problems and solutions are dating each other. While project/temporary formal organizations, like the permanent organization, carry a formalized administration, there was no time for planning or structuring in the Gudrun case. 'Glocal' organizing, implying core local action cells that take advantage of distant (global) resources by way of networking associated with bonding social capital, appears as a generic organizing feature of emergency entrepreneurship.

The enormous need for information reflects the huge uncertainty that most people experienced during and after Gudrun. That uncertainty could only be reduced by intense (social) (inter)action and an unrestricted, 'lateral' information flow. The sociality of the social capital that embeds economic activity has itself to be pulled out of the bed. In an emergency situation even the dark side of personal networking, the risk that it may violate democratic values and processes, has to be accepted, as much as the idea that civil disobedience may be the only way to cope in critical situations where institutions fail.

For all residents in the rural part of the region that Gudrun struck it was more than obvious that on the morning of Sunday 9 January something concrete had to be done. No other performance, but local commitment and general responsiveness to the existential and practical challenges would do (cf. Stryjan, 1987). This immediate need, though, soon enough turned into a demand for specific and certainly localized services. Activating previous hands-on experiences, individuals in local organizations were taking action far from the formal structures framing their normal routines (cf. Sauri et al., 2003). Ephemeral organizing and emergency entrepreneurship share a pragmatic concern, while project organizations are primarily driven by decontextualized economic efficiency (Halman and Braks, 1999; Davenport, 2006). Crisis management aims at restabilizing and 'managing disaster with a basic goal to minimize effectively the impact of disaster' (Moe and Pathranarakul, 2006, p. 398).

CONCLUSIONS: TOWARDS A DEFINITION OF EMERGENCY ENTREPRENEURSHIP

Contemporary dominant views on entrepreneurship propose, albeit using different ontological assumptions and vocabularies and relating to different spaces for boundary-spanning (inter)action, that entrepreneurship is about the creative non-routine organizing of people and resources. Exploring unknown domains makes (business) venturing intrinsically experiential, whether global challenges are exploited in a way that change people's everyday practices (Spinosa et al., 1997) or, as in the case of emergency-triggered entrepreneurship, established practices have to be reconstructed.

Again, entrepreneurial initiative is certainly not just driven by self-interest and concerned with (economic) growth. The Gudrun story tells us that spontaneously organized multi-skilled rural citizens both restored old relations and created new social trails in a physical landscape that had completely changed due to the disaster. The lesson told is that entrepreneurship is also closely associated with generalized responsibility and that 'common sense' is important as a means for taking on surprises and challenges and not only as being itself the target for change. The importance of localized social capital with its strong bonds, which promise solidarity and trigger action when most needed, is re-established as well.

As indicated, an entrepreneurial career can be described as a set of interrelated project/ventures embedded in the personal networking of the entrepreneur (Johannisson, 2000). The role of personal initiatives is made visible in Lanzara's notion of 'ephemeral organization'. Such organizations are instigated by an individual who sees a natural disaster as an opportunity to 'display his capacity and [that] at the same time the opportunity "creates" the actor, shapes his system of representation, and enhances his capacity for action' (Lanzara, 1983, p. 73). Obviously, the notion of 'ephemeral organization' connects what we address as enactive, prosaic and emergency entrepreneurship. This is hardly surprising, considering that a disaster breaks down the socially constructed barrier between private and public lives, forcing a new structure to be built from below. Early on, Katz and Kahn (1966) told the story about how the municipal fire brigade emerged out of voluntary collaboration between residents in a community, whenever property was on fire, and successively formalized into its present structure (cf. also Christoplos, 1998). In the absence of a public organization local solidarity and responsiveness to challenges were self-evident.

When the everyday physical world is turned upside down by a major disaster, entrepreneurial action, then meaning maintaining and re-establishing everyday practices, has to be instigated. It means immediacy and hands-on (inter)action, evoking the embodied knowledge needed for operatively coping with concrete challenges that leave little time for reflection. In parallel, people locally have to re-establish and activate existing bonds and create new relations to incorporated private and public organizations. Together they have to try to integrate their own measures with those of existing public and market structures (cf. Sauri et al., 2003). Relating then means taking the trustworthiness of others for granted. Research into how people cope with (natural) disasters also suggests that trust becomes personal (Gephart, 1984; Christoplos, 1998; Hurlbert et al., 2000; Sauri et al., 2003), neither organizational nor institutional (Sanner, 1997).

We can now conclusively conceptualize the proposed notion of 'emergency entrepreneurship' in the perspective of our introductory three images of entrepreneurship. Above, we already briefly stated that the emergency entrepreneurship is different in kind to them. Regarding the aspects presented in Table 12.3, we first state that the triggering event, the initiative, is external to those concerned, appearing as a natural and/or artificial disaster that creates a rupture in everyday life. The entrepreneurial process is characterized by the need for immediate (inter)action in the face of non-negotiable conditions that put important material conditions and existential values at stake. Once the external shock is recognized, local interaction with the situation at hand appears as generic coping. The roles of social capital, the major potential resource, are multiple: a trigger, a lubricant and a safeguard in spontaneous organizing. Local commitment, instrumental

Table 12.3 Emergency entrepreneurship – generic features

Aspect	Emergency Entrepreneurship
Origin of initiative	Rupture in everyday life
Process characteristics	Immediate (inter)action
Generic coping	Local interplay with the situation at hand
Role and sources of social capital	Organizing based on local commitment and swift trust
Organizing rationale	Social bricolage

Note: Compare also Table 12.1.

in such a situation, acknowledges the need for and facilitates the use of 'swift' trust (Meyerson et al., 1996) when action has to be taken instantly and incessantly. The organizing rationale appears as a kind of 'social bricolage'. While the (artisan) bricoleur, according to Lévi-Strauss [1968] (1971), brings together redundant artefacts/resources in order to compose local responses to problems as they present themselves (cf. also Baker and Nelson, 2005), social bricolage means combining and locally – in time as well as in space – integrating chunks of everyday routines according to the events that the drama produces. This indeed means practising an ontology of becoming, according to Chia (1995).

Some may argue that it is unnecessary, even inappropriate, to offer yet another image of entrepreneurship in an academic community already swarming with proposed understandings of the evasive phenomenon. However, in an increasingly globalized world, social and economic changes will create sudden and radical emergencies in many local settings, as suggested by chaos theory. As a matter of fact, the most popular demonstration of that theory is that a butterfly's movement of its wings may cause a hurricane on the other side of the globe! Our lessons from how Gudrun was locally dealt with not only bring insights about how common people may practise their entrepreneurial capabilities. Our research also communicates the potential of the 'glocal' tactics adopted by emergency entrepreneurship as a generic means for locally taking on global challenges and thus enriching our general understanding of organization/organizing.

ACKNOWLEDGEMENTS

We are grateful to FSF (the Swedish Foundation for Small Business Research) for their financial support of the research reported here.

NOTES

1. In previous work we have enquired into the interface between entrepreneurship and social capital as reflecting/reflected in reputation/mutual trust and a rationality based on care (see Johannisson and Olaison, 2007).
2. This is not to argue that women were not involved in the recovery process, but that their roles remained less visible and that our approach did not invite them. For a discussion about the representation of women in research and media reporting after natural disasters, see Childs (2006).

REFERENCES

Baker, T. and R. Nelson (2005), 'Creating something from nothing: resource construction through entrepreneurial bricolage', *Administrative Science Quarterly*, **50**(3), 329–66.

Chia, R. (1995), 'From modern to postmodern organizational analysis', *Organization Studies*, **16**(4), 579–604.

Childs, M. (2006), 'Not through women's eyes: photo-essays and the construction of a gendered tsunami disaster', *Disaster Prevention and Management*, **15**, 202–12.

Christoplos, I. (1998), 'Humanitarianism and local service institutions in Angola', *Disasters*, **22**, 1–20.

Czarniawska, B. (2004), *Narratives in Social Science research*, London: Sage.

Davidsson, P. and Honig, B. (2003), 'The role of social and human capital among nascent entrepreneurs', *Journal of Business Venturing*, **18**, 301–31.

Davenport, D. (2006), 'UK film companies: project-based organizations lacking entrepreneurship and innovativeness?', *Creativity and Innovation Management*, **15**(3), 250–57.

du Gay, P. (2001), *In Praise of Bureaucracy – Weber, Organization, Ehtics*, London: Sage.

Eisenhardt, K.M. (1989), 'Building theories from case study research', *Academy of Management Review*, **14**(4), 532–50.

Gartner, W.B. (1993), 'Words lead to deeds: towards an organizational emergence vocabulary', *Journal of Business Venturing*, **8**, 231–39.

Gartner, W.B, B.J. Bird and J.A. Starr (1992), 'Acting as if: differentiating entrepreneurial behaviour from organizational behaviour', *Entrepreneurship Theory and Practice*, **16**(3), 13–30.

Gartner, W.B., N.M. Carter and G.E. Hills (2003), 'The language of opportunity', in C. Steyaert and D. Hjorth (eds), *New Movements in Entrepreneurship*, Cheltenham, UK and Northampton, MA, USA: Edward Elgar, pp. 103–24.

Gephart, R.P. (1984), 'Making sense of organizationally based environmental disasters', *Journal of Management*, **10**(2), 205–25.

Grabher, G. (2001), 'Ecologies of creativity: the village, the group, and the heterarchic organization of the British Advertising Industry', *Environment and Planning A*, **33**, 351–74.

Halman, J.I.M. and B.F.M. Braks (1999), 'Project alliancing in the offshore industry', *International Journal of Project Management*, **17**(2), 71–6.

Heller, T. (1999), 'Loosely coupled systems for corporate entrepreneurship: managing the innovation project/host organization interface', *Entrepreneurship Theory and Practice*, **24**(2), 25–32.

Helsloot, I. and A. Ruitenberg (2004), 'Citizen response to Disasters: a Survey of Literature and some practical implications', *Journal of Contingencies and Crisis Management*, **12**, 98–111.

Hirschman, A.O. (1974), *Exit, Voice and Loyalty. Responses to Decline in Firms, Organizations and States*, Cambridge, MA: Harvard University Press.

Hjorth, D. and B. Bjerke (2006), 'Public entrepreneurship: moving from social/consumer to public/citizen', in C. Steyaert and D. Hjorth (eds), *Entrepreneurship as Social Change: A Third New Movements in Entrepreneurship Book*, Cheltenham, UK and Northampton, MA, USA: Edward Elgar.

Hjorth, D. and B. Johannisson (2003), 'Conceptualising the opening phase of regional development as the enactment of a "collective identity" ', *Concepts and Transformation*, **8**(1), 69–92.

Hjorth, D. and B. Johannisson (2007), 'Learning as an entrepreneurial process', in A. Fayolle (ed.), *Handbook of Research in Entrepreneurship Education*, Cheltenham, UK and Northampton, MA, USA: Edward Elgar.

Hjorth, D. and C. Steyaert (2003), 'Entrepreneurship beyond (a new) economy: creative swarms and pathological zones', in C. Steyaert and D. Hjorth (eds), *New Movements in Entrepreneurship*, Cheltenham, UK and Northampton, MA, USA: Edward Elgar, pp. 286–305.

Hjorth, D., B. Johannisson and C. Steyaert (2003), 'Entrepreneurship as Discourse and Life style', in B. Czarniawska and G. Sevón (eds), *The Northern Lights: Organization Theory in Scandinavia*, Malmö, Copenhagen, Oslo: Liber/Copenhagen Business School Press, Abstrakt, pp. 91–110.

Hurlbert, J.S., V.A. Haines and J.J. Beggs (2000), 'Core networks and tie activation: what kinds of routine networks allocate resources in nonroutine situations?', *American Sociological Review*, **65**(4), 598–619.

Johannisson, B. (1992), 'Entrepreneurship – the management of ambiguity', in T. Polesie and I-L. Johansson (eds), *Responsibility and Accounting – The Organizational Regulation of Boundary Conditions*, Lund: Studentlitteratur, pp. 155–79.

Johannisson, B. (2000), 'Networking and entrepreneurial growth', in D.L. Sexton and H. Landström (eds), *Handbook of Entrepreneurship*, Oxford: Blackwell, pp. 368–86.

Johannisson, B. (2003), 'Entrepreneurship as a collective phenomenon', in E. Genescà, D. Urbano, J. Capelleras, C. Guallarte and J. Vergès (eds), *Creación de Empresas – Entrepreneurship*, Barcelona, Spain: Servei de Publicacions de la Universitat Autònoma de Barcelona, pp. 87–109.

Johannisson, B. and A. Nilsson (1989), 'Community entrepreneurship – networking for local development', *Entrepreneurship and Regional Development*, **1**(1), 1–19.

Johannisson, J. and L. Olaison (2007), 'The moment of truth – reconstructing entrepreneurship and social capital in the eye of the storm', *Review of Social Economy*, **LVX**(1), 55–78.

Johnstone, H. and D. Lionais (2004), 'Deleted communities and community business entrepreneurship: revaluing space trough place', *Entrepreneurship and Regional Development*, **16**, 217–33.

Kasvi, J., M. Vartiainen and M. Hailikari (2002), 'Managing knowledge and knowledge competences in projects and project organizations', *International Journal of Project Management*, **21**, 571–82.

Katz, D. and R.L. Kahn (1966), *The Social Psychology of Organizations*, New York: Wiley.

Lambrecht, J. and F. Pirnay (2005), 'An evaluation of public support measures for private external consultancies to SMEs in the Walloon Region of Belgium', *Entrepreneurship and Regional Development*, **17**, 89–108.

Lanzara, G.F. (1983), 'Ephemeral organizations in extreme environments: emergence, strategy, extinction', *Journal of Management Studies*, **20**(1), 71–95.

Larson, A. and J.A. Starr (1993), 'A network model of organization formation', *Entrepreneurship Theory and Practice*, **17**(2), 5–15.

Lévi-Strauss, C. (1971), *Det Vilda Tänkandet* (*The Savage Mind*), Stockholm: Bonniers. Cf. Lévi-Strauss, C. (1968), *The Savage Mind (Nature of Human Society)*, Chicago, IL: University of Chicago Press.

Loosemore, M. and W.P. Hughes (2001), 'Confronting social defence mechanisms: avoiding disorganization during crisis', *Journal of Contingencies and Crisis Management*, **9**, 73–87.

March, J.G. and J.P. Olsen (1976), *Ambiguity and Choice in Organizations*, Oslo: Universitetsforlaget.

McEntire, D.A. and A. Myers (2004), 'Preparing communities for disasters: issues and processes for government readiness', *Disaster Prevention and Management*, **13**, 140–52.

Meyerson, D., K.E. Weick and R.M. Kramer (1996), 'Swift trust and temporary groups', in R.M. Kramer and T.R. Tyler (eds), *Trust in Organizations: Frontiers of Theory and Research*, Thousands Oaks, CA: Sage, pp. 166–95.

Mintzberg, H. (1973), *The Nature of Managerial Work*, New York: Harper and Row.

Mintzberg, H. (1988), 'The adhocracy', in J.B Quinn (ed.), *The Strategy Process*, Englewood Cliffs, NJ: Prentice Hall, pp. 607–27.

Moe, T.L. and P. Pathranarakul (2006), 'An integrated approach to natural disaster management: public project management and its critical success factors', *Disaster Prevention and Management: An International Journal*, **15**(3), 396–413.

Ok Choi, S. and R.S. Brower (2006), 'When practice matters more than government plans', *Administration and Society*, **37**, 651–78.

Pardasani, M. (2006), 'Tsunami reconstruction and redevelopment in the Maldives – a case study of community participation and social action', *Disaster Prevention and Management,* **15**, 79–91.

Peterson, R.A. (1981), 'Entrepreneurship and organization', in P.C. Nystrom and W.H. Starbuck (eds), *Handbook of Organizational Design*, vol. 1, Oxford: Oxford University Press, pp. 65–83.

Runyan, R.C. (2006), 'Small business in the face of crisis: identifying barriers to recovery from a natural Disaster', *Journal of Contingencies and Crisis Management*, **14**, 12–26.

Sanner, L. (1997), *Trust Between Entrepreneurs and External Actors. Sensemaking in Organizing New Business Ventures*, Uppsala: Uppsala University.

Sauri, D., V. Domingo and A. Romero (2003), 'Trust and community building in the Doñana (Spain) toxic spill disaster', *Journal of Risk Research*, **6**(2), 145–62.

Schumpeter, J.A. [1911] (1934), *The Theory of Economic Development*, Cambridge, MA: Harvard University Press.

Shane, S. (2003), *A General Theory of Entrepreneurship. The Individual-Opportunity Nexus*, Cheltenham, UK and Northampton, MA, USA: Edward Elgar.

Shenhar, A. (2001), 'Contingent management in temporary, dynamic organizations: the comparative analysis of projects', *Management Research*, **12**, 239–71.

Skutle, A., E. Iversen and T. Bergan (2002), 'A community-based prevention program in western Norway: organization and progression model', *Addictive Behaviours*, **27**, 977–88.

Spillan, J. and M. Hough (2003), 'Crisis planning in small businesses: importance, impetus and indiffenence', *European Management Journal*, **21**, 398–407.

Spinosa, C., F. Flores and H.L. Dreyfus (1997), *Disclosing New Worlds: Entrepreneurship, Democratic Action, and the Cultivation of Solidarity*, Cambridge, MA: MIT Press.

Starr, J.R. and I.C. MacMillan (1990), 'Resource cooptation via social contracting: resource acquisition strategies for new ventures', *Strategic Management Journal*, **11**, 79–92.

Stewart, A. (1989), *Team Entrepreneurship*, London: Sage.

Steyaert, C. (2004), 'The prosaics of entrepreneurship', in D. Hjorth and C. Steyaert (eds), *Narrative and Discursive Approaches in Entrepreneurship*, Cheltenham, UK and Northampton, MA, USA: Edward Elgar, pp. 8–21.

Steyaert, C. and D. Hjorth (2006), 'What is social in social entrepreneurship?', in C. Steyaert and D. Hjorth (eds), *Entrepreneurship as Social Change: A Third New Movements in Entrepreneurship Book*, Cheltenham, UK and Northampton, MA, USA: Edward Elgar, pp. 1–20.

Storper, M. (1989), 'The transition to flexible specialization in the US film industry; external economies, the division of labour, and the crossing of industrial divides', *Cambridge Journal of Economics*, **13**, 273–305.

Stryjan, Y. (1987), *Impossible Organizations. On Self-management and Organizational Reproduction*, Uppsala: Uppsala University.

Turner, J.R. and A. Keegan (1999), 'The versatile project based organization: governance and operational control', *European Management Journal*, **17**(3), 296–309.

Weick, K.E. (1976), 'Educational organizations as loosely coupled systems', *Administrative Science Quarterly*, **21**, 1–19.

Weick, K.E. (1990), 'Social behavior in organizational studies', *Journal for the Theory of Social Behavior*, **20**(4), 323–46.

Weick, K.E. (1995), *Sensemaking in Organizations*, California: Sage.

Westerveld, E. (2003), 'The project excellence model: linking success criteria and critical success factors', *International Journal of Project Management*, **21**, 411–18.

Westhead, P. and M. Wright (1998), 'Novice, portfolio, and serial founders: are they different?', *Journal of Business Venturing*, **13**, 173–204.

Westlund, H. and R. Bolton (2003), 'Local social capital and entrepreneurship', *Small Business Economics*, **21**, 77–113.

13. On the role of academic staff as entrepreneurs in university spin-offs: case studies of biotechnology firms in Norway

Olav R. Spilling

INTRODUCTION

Over the last decades, an increasing interest has developed in the field of technology transfer from academic institutions, and as part of this a growing awareness of the importance of university spin-offs and academic entrepreneurship has evolved. The purpose of this chapter is to focus on university spin-offs and analyse the role of academic staff in the processes of developing new firms spinning out from universities. While the concept of academic entrepreneurship may be perceived as a fairly wide concept, including all types of entrepreneurial activity conducted by academic people, the concept of university spin-off focuses more narrowly on the businesses starting up based on new knowledge developed in a university department or a related research institute (Shane, 2004). In this chapter focus is on the fairly complicated processes that may follow in the attempts of developing a new business based on research results and, in particular, focus is on the role of academic staff in such processes and how academic staff may contribute as entrepreneurs in the formation of new spin-off businesses.

The literature on academic entrepreneurship, commercialization of research based knowledge and university spin-offs is fairly rich. However, much of the literature is based on a simple stage model approach for analysing processes of commercialization, and there are tendencies to overlook how complicated such processes may be. Furthermore, although there are some important contributions to the discussion of the various roles academic staff may take as entrepreneurs, there are tendencies to provide a very simple picture of what the role of academic staff may be.

The reason for this may be that much research in the field is based on surveys and cross-sectional approaches, which do not provide opportunities for following how the processes of commercialization evolve over time and to go into details about the complexity of such processes. Neither will these approaches provide good opportunities for discussing the variety in how academic staff may contribute to the commercialization process.

In this chapter the analysis is based on a longitudinal case study approach. Four spin-off firms have been selected for study; all four cases belong to the biotechnology sector and they are part of an emerging cluster of firms developing in the area around one specific university located in a city on the Norwegian coast. Based on the examination of the story of these four spin-offs and the entrepreneurs starting and developing the firms, the purpose of the chapter is to develop more qualitative insights in processes of commercialization and the role of academic staff in such processes.

Although the main focus is on the entrepreneurial processes per se, it is important to analyse entrepreneurship as a contextualized phenomenon which is under the influence of a number of factors (Spilling, 2008). Generally, a number of institutions exist which are of importance in order to support the formation of university spin-offs. Particularly during the later years a number of new institutions have been developed in order to stimulate the creation of technology based firms and firms spinning out from universities. Although these institutions may be of some importance for the processes we are studying in this chapter, they will not be our primary focus. Our main emphasis will be on the entrepreneurial processes per se, and the role of various support mechanisms will only be briefly commented on to the extent that they are reflected through the stories of the case entrepreneurs.

COMMERCIALIZATION

The main purpose of any process of spin-off and technology transfer is that of commercial exploitation of the new knowledge. Therefore we start the literature review by discussing the concept of commercialization, which may be identified as the process of transferring and transforming theoretical knowledge (Chiesa and Piccaluga, 1998) as existing in an academic institution into some kind of commercial activity. Based on a framework developed by Jolly (1997) commercialization can be defined as the process that starts with the techno-market insight and ends with the sustaining functions of the market-competent product. The problems of commercialization include links between technological discoveries and opportunities, demonstration of technology to opinion leaders, incubation of technology, resources for successful demonstration, market acceptance and transfer of benefits, and selection of proper business tools.

This definition invites us to think of the processes of commercialization in terms of a stage model. Such models generally starts with the technology-driven basic development of new knowledge in terms of technology based discoveries and inventions. The models are followed up with the incubation process in which the business opportunities and business concepts are more systematically explored and developed, and end with the established business activity positioned in the market.

In the literature one will find a number of different approaches to describe stage models. For instance, Virtanen and Laukkanen (2002), in their discussion of commercialization strategies, have distinguished between the following stages: (1) invention/discovery, (2) proof of principle, (3) demonstration unit/model, (4) working prototype, (5) marketable product, (6) product palette and (7) established market position.

An alternative version is provided by Ndonzuau et al. (2002) who distinguish between the following four stages:

1. Generate business ideas from research
2. Finalize new venture projects out of ideas
3. Launch spin-off firms from projects
4. Strengthen the creation of economic value by spin-off firms.

One important aspect of the stages, as outlined above, is that the process of commercialization will undergo a shift from a mainly technology-driven process to a process which is mainly market-driven. In the early stages it is the opportunities identified based on technological knowledge that are the main driving forces, and which motivate the actors in their work. During the process there will gradually be a shift towards more emphasis on market opportunities and how these may be exploited by developing products or services which will meet some needs in the market. In the final stages the main emphasis will be on market opportunities and how the business concept and the business strategy may be designed in order to fully exploit these opportunities. It may also be important to recognize the process of commercialization as a 'transformation process' (Chiesa and Piccaluga, 1998; Fontes, 2003; 2005), as scientific concepts and principles are turned into viable technologies and products or services, which means that knowledge is transformed from one mode to another.

When describing the commercialization process in terms of stage models, it inevitably invites us to think in terms of linearity; that is, the process goes smoothly through the various stages one by one. This may be taken as a support for the traditional linear model of innovation, which has mostly been rejected by the development of the interactive innovation model (Lundvall, 1992). However the point here is not to advocate a simplistic understanding of innovation processes as 'linear'. As will be shown by the case studies of this chapter, such processes may be very complex. Thus the purpose here, by referring to the stage model approach, is rather to point at a way of structuring and provide a basis for analysis. By this we identify stages in the process which may differ from others regarding what kind of knowledge, skills and activities are important, and this may in turn provide a basis for developing a framework for analysis (Ndonzuau et al., 2002).

This is not to neglect the fact that processes generally are complicated, and do not necessarily follow the 'linear' pattern indicated by the stage model. Actors may partly go back and forth between the stages, they may partly combine elements from different stages simultaneously or important elements from different stages may come in a different order. Furthermore, the actors will also depend on interaction and communication with a number of other actors belonging to the business community as well as the research community. So, interaction across stages and organizational boundaries are most important for the process. Using this background, the innovation process may be termed as 'chaotic' and as an 'innovation journey' (Van de Ven et al., 1999).

However a basic feature of commercialization of R&D is that it implies some kind of 'linearity' in the sense that the process necessarily will take the existing knowledge base as its point of departure, and the new project will start out based on the existing knowledge base.

ACADEMIC SPIN-OFFS

The main focus of this chapter is on spin-offs from universities or research institutions, and our concern is about the entrepreneurial processes related to spin-offs and the role of academic staff in these processes. A commonly applied definition of a spin-off is a company that is created based on knowledge resources in a parent organization, and which is organized independently, or at least partially independently, of the parent organization (Birley, 2002; Carayannis et al., 1998; Dahlstrand, 1999; 2000; Nicolaou and Birley, 2003; Shane, 2004; Steffensen et al., 1999). Different concepts may be applied, like academic spin-offs, university spin-offs or R&D spin-offs, and also the concept of 'spinout' is applied synonymously with spin-off. The spin-off is originated in an academic institution, and the entrepreneurs generally have a background as scientists in the organization. The new venture is based on the intellectual assets of the parent organization (Birley, 2002), and the process is typically characterized by an employee leaving this organization in order to start the new company based on these assets (Carayannis et al., 1998; Steffensen et al., 1999). To qualify for a spin-off, the new business must be based on a business idea which originated in the previous organization (Dahlstrand, 2000); the new business is based on intellectual property developed in the parent organization (Birley, 2002; Carayannis et al., 1998) and may include the transfer of rights (IPR) related to this.

Pirnay et al. (2002) state that any phenomenon can be qualified as a spin-off when it fulfils the following three conditions:

- It takes place within an existing organization, generally known as the 'parent organization'.
- It involves one or several individuals, whatever their status and function are within the 'parent organization'.
- These individuals leave the 'parent organization' to create a new one.

While much of the literature is focused on spin-offs resulting in wholly new firms, the concept may also include cases in which the new business activity is developed in an existing firm by way of selling licenses for obtaining the rights to exploit commercially the new technology (Shane, 2002; Hill, 1995). This is also a common way of organizing technology transfer. The main point is not whether the spin-off ends up in a new firm, but that the result of the process is the creation of a new business activity, and independent of it is organized as a new legal business unit or adopted by an incumbent firm which organizes the new business activity internally. However in this chapter we only focus on cases which involve the start-up of wholly new ventures.

The literature on spin-offs provides many aspects of these processes. According to Roberts and Malone (1996) and Carayannis et al. (1998), four types of actors may be distinguished that will all play important roles in the process; that is, the parent organization, the technology originator, the entrepreneur and the venture investor (cf. summary in Table 13.1). Carayannis et al. (1998) apply the concept of role rather than actor, but here we prefer to use the concept of actor as this gives a better identification than the concept of role.

The classical way of organizing a spin-off is that one or more of the scientists who have contributed to developing the technological innovation organize the new business and leave the parent organization when the new venture is started. This is what Birley (2002) describes as an 'orthodox' spin-off, which is characterized by a 'clean break', that is, the scientists previously employed by the parent organization leave to start the new business. This implies, referring to the types of actors summarized in Table 13.1, that the scientist initially has the role as technology originator, and then follows up by taking the role as entrepreneur.

Table 13.1 Main actors and their primary roles in the spin-off process

Actor	Examples	Primary role
Parent organization	University department, research laboratory	Host and organize R&D activities to create technological innovations. May also serve as a facilitator for spin-off processes
Technology originator	Individual or group of engineers or scientists	Bring the technological innovation through the innovation-development process; bring the process to the point where technology transfer is possible
Entrepreneur	Engineers, scientists; 'external' person with business knowledge	Identify the business idea and develop the new business venture based on the technological innovation; take the technology to create a new venture from it
The venture investor	Venture capital organization, business angles, informal investors	Provide the financial resources to develop the new venture; may also provide needed business management expertise

Source: Based on Roberts and Malone (1996) and Carayannis et al. (1998).

In addition to the orthodox spinout, Birley (2002) has introduced two other categories of spinouts (she applies the concept of spinout rather than spin-off); the technology spinout and the hybrid spinout. In the case of the technology spinout an outside actor (investor, manager or company) buys or leases the rights of exploiting commercially the technological innovation. The academic staff continue in their roles as scientists and technology originators, while the entrepreneurial function of developing the new business activity is taken care of by external actors. Here, there is no overlap of personnel, the scientists remain as employees in the parent organization, although they may contribute to the new venture development on a minor basis, for instance, as consultants and equity holders. The third category, the hybrid spinout, represents a combination of the two previous categories; the new venture is based on a joint organization of external and internal actors.

A number of other authors have contributed to the discussion of spin-offs and academic entrepreneurship and focused on different aspects of such processes (Dickson et al., 1998; Fontes, 2003; Jones-Evans, 1997; Radosevitch, 1995), and some typologies are summarized in Table 13.2.

The typology suggested by Fontes (2003) is quite similar to that of Birley (2002). While Birley has distinguished between orthodox,

Table 13.2 Spin-offs and entrepreneurial roles

Author	Typology of spin-offs/ entrepreneurial roles	Definitions/comments
Birley (2002)	Orthodox spinout	Scientist(s) leave to form the new company – 'clean break'
	Technology spinout	Outside actor organizes the commercial exploitation
	Hybrid spinout	Combination of inside and outside actors
Fontes (2003)	Insider conducted commercialization	Insiders of the research organization (RO) exploring knowledge originating from RO
	Outsider conducted commercialization	Outsiders who establish relationships to gain access to an RO to assist development of business ideas
	Intermediary conducted commercialization	Outsiders or (more rarely) insiders who operate as intermediaries in technology transfer as a business
Radosevitch (1995)	Inventor entrepreneur model	Scientist(s)/inventor(s) organize the new venture
	Surrogate entrepreneur model	External actor with entrepreneurial experience organizes the new venture
Dickson et al. (1998)	Academic entrepreneur	Scientists who engage in entrepreneurial endeavours, but maintain their identity as academic scientists
	Entrepreneurial scientist	Scientists operating full-time in the new business essentially dedicated to scientific interests
	Scientific entrepreneur	Integration of scientific and business interests, utilizing a high level of scientific intelligence to identify new business opportunities
Jones-Evans (1997)	Research technical entrepreneur Producer technical entrepreneur User technical entrepreneur Opportunist entrepreneur	Terminology based on the background of the entrepreneur

technology and hybrid spin-offs, Fontes has distinguished between insider and outsider conducted commercialization and intermediary conducted process as the third category. The insider conducted process corresponds to the orthodox spin-off as it is the scientific staff – the insiders – who conduct the process, while the technology spin-offs corresponds to the outsider conducted process. However, while the orthodox spin-off as defined by Birley implies that the scientific staff involved in the process leave the university – it is a 'clean break' – this is not the primary focus in the typology of Fontes; her emphasis is on who conducts the process whether they maintain their relationships with the research organization or not. Furthermore, there is also a difference in the way the third category is defined. While Birley regards the hybrid type as a mixture of the orthodox and technology spin-off, the third category, in the case of Fontes, focuses explicitly on intermediary organizations as potential actors in the process of commercialization.

A similar typology is also suggested by Radosevitch (1995) who has distinguished between two models for commercialization of public sector technology; the inventor entrepreneur model in which the scientist takes the role as entrepreneur and organizes the new venture, and the surrogate entrepreneur model in which an external actor takes the role as entrepreneur. The advantage of the first model is that the technology originators organize the entrepreneurial process, and in this way provide greater technical capacity and have commitment to the technology and good relationships with the technology source. On the other hand, this model implies disadvantages in terms of less experience from entrepreneurial activities and less business knowledge (Radosevitch, 1995). The champion of the business idea is seldom the best to manage (Clarysse and Moray, 2004). The advantages and disadvantages of the second model, the surrogate entrepreneur model, go in the opposite direction. Advantages are related to entrepreneurial experience and good contacts with the business community, while relationships with the technology originators will be less developed.

A somewhat different framework is suggested by Jones-Evans (1997) who in his studies of technology-based entrepreneurs has distinguished between types of entrepreneurs according to their background; that is, in research or as producer, user or opportunist. The first category will coincide with the inventor entrepreneur model, while the other three relate to the surrogate entrepreneur model in which the process is organized by external actors with backgrounds from different positions in the business community.

THE ROLE OF ACADEMIC STAFF

It follows from the previous discussion that the role of academic staff may represent a great variety, both in terms of what functions they are taking care of in the new venture, to what extent they get involved in the new venture and to what extent they combine activity in the new firm with continued activity in the university or research organization.

One of the main issues is to what extent academic staff are involved in the role as entrepreneur or not. In the case of the orthodox spin-off, academic staff play a role as entrepreneurs and, obviously, they have to combine this role with their roles as researchers devoted to further development of the technology. The same is the situation in the cases of insider conducted commercialization and the inventor entrepreneur model. In the other models – the technology spin-off, outsider conducted commercialization or surrogate models – there are other actors recruited from outside that take care of the entrepreneurial role, and which means that the academic staff involved in the business may concentrate on the R&D related part of the venture development.

Another issue is to what extent academic staff combine their role in the new venture with a role in the university or research organization, and in what ways their academic position and activities are maintained. In most of the categories of spin-offs referred to in Table 13.2 this is not clear. An exception is the category 'orthodox spin-off' which per definition implies that the academic staff leave the academic institution and work full time in the new venture.

Furthermore, the typology suggested by Dickson et al. (1998) is interesting in this respect as it distinguishes between academic entrepreneur, entrepreneurial scientist and scientific entrepreneur. The 'academic entrepreneur' is the scientist who engages in entrepreneurial endeavours, but retains their identity as academic scientist by maintaining the affiliation with the university or research organization. In contrast to this, the 'entrepreneurial scientist' operates full time in the new venture, but is essentially dedicated to scientific interests. The third category, the 'scientific entrepreneur', is somewhat more unclear, but the point made by the authors is that this type of actor integrates 'scientific and business interests' and makes important decisions related to the future development of the business based on 'scientific intelligence to identify new business opportunities' (Dickson et al., 1998, p. 36). Although their use of concepts are not intuitively fully clear, and is also in conflict with the normally much broader concept of academic entrepreneurship, the distinctions inherent in the typology are interesting for the further discussion of the role of academic staff in processes of commercialization.

The issue of to what extent academic staff combine their role in the new venture with a role in the university or research organization has been investigated by Samson and Gurdon (1993). Their conclusion is that in a significant majority of the cases they studied the academics worked full time in the new ventures and maintained no relationships with the university. A smaller share of the academic staff combined part-time affiliation with the new venture with full-time activity in the university, and in just one case the academic remained in the university without maintaining any contact with the new venture.

The variety of roles of academic staff in the new venture is illustrated by a case described by Birley (2002), in which the roles of the different academics participating in the team varied from full-time participators as entrepreneurs to part-time or temporary involvement as consultants, board members, members of advisory boards and so on. An alternative may also be that the scientist works with the new venture for some time, for instance during the incubation phase, and then returns to their original position in the parent organization.

THE INSTITUTIONAL AND SYSTEMIC CONTEXT FOR SPIN-OFFS

As a result of the growing awareness of the importance of university spin-offs, over the last decades a number of institutions and programmes have been developed in order to facilitate processes of commercializing academic knowledge in most European countries, such as science parks, innovation centres and incubators (Albert et al., 2002; Dahlstrand, 1999; Dahlstrand and Klofsten, 2003; Stankiewicz, 1998). Typically, these institutions are located in the vicinity of universities and R&D institutions, often on the university campus. Furthermore, the role of universities and other institutions for higher education has been addressed in many ways, for instance, by organizing industrial liaison offices (ILO) and technology transfer offices (TTO), and by launching specific programmes in order to facilitate commercialization processes (Rasmussen, 2006; Rasmussen et al., 2006).

The spin-off process takes place in the interface between the university or research organization and industry, and the process will to a significant extent depend on specific features of the university environment and milieu as well as the more general industrial and socio-cultural environment (Virtanen and Laukkanen, 2002; Spilling, 2008). The ability to identify and develop business opportunities will depend on a number of factors in this environment, including the entrepreneurial culture of the academic milieu, and so will the further processes of commercialization.[1] The key driving force, however, is the ability of the entrepreneurs to identify and develop business opportunities, and as part of this to exploit resources available in the environment and organize partnerships or develop other forms of networks with important actors. The institutional set-up may facilitate these processes, and in our analyses we shall briefly comment on these aspects. Our main focus, however, will be on how the process of commercialization evolves and the role of academic staff in these processes.

METHOD AND DATA

This study is based on a qualitative case study approach in which four cases, all belonging to the biotechnology industry in the same geographical area, have been selected for study. All cases are part of an emerging cluster formed around a university located in a city on the Norwegian coast.

The research has been organized in two steps; first, the development of the whole cluster has been mapped, mostly based on analysis of secondary data, including data available in public data sources.[2] Also, some key data about the firms and their entrepreneurship stories have been collected from the individual firms by e-mail contact. Furthermore, as the actual cluster is fairly small with some 15–20 companies, and it has a secretariat which organises a website with an overview of the participating firms, it has been fairly easy to collect information about the evolution of the whole cluster.

The second step was to select four cases which seemed of interest to illustrate different roles of academic staff. The main criteria for selecting cases were that they should belong to the biotechnology cluster, they should be regarded as spin-offs from the university or a related research organization located on campus and they should represent variety. However, as there were problems in establishing contacts with some of the firms, we also had to be pragmatic and select among the firms with which we obtained contact.

The four case companies have all been visited, and the main entrepreneur or actor in the process has been interviewed. In three cases the interview lasted for an hour, while in the fourth case, we had two interviews with a total duration of four hours. Data collected through the interviews have been supplemented with other available data of the firms, like accounting data and annual reports. For two of the cases, we tried to organize follow-up interviews, but without success.

The interviews were conducted as open and unstructured; the only structuring element was the process of commercialization and the entrepreneurship story related to this, and different events of importance to the development of the firms. However, entrepreneurial processes are often very complicated, and it takes a lot of time to map all details and to understand the story and the role of different actors. Given the short time available for most of the interviews, many details may be missing, and our main emphasis has been on illustrating the most important events of the entrepreneurship stories.

CASES

In the following sections we give a descriptive presentation of the four case firms and their entrepreneurs, here called BioX (the professor entrepreneur), BioLab (the laboratory manager), BioPhD (the research based entrepreneurs) and BioGroup (the industrial entrepreneur). As outlined above, all firms belong to the biotechnology sector and are part of an emerging cluster formed around a university. Three of the firms started in the field of marine biotechnology, the part of biotechnology related to life in the sea, while the third company started up in pharmaceuticals. All four firms have evolved in the local area around the university, two of them even in the science park located on campus. To a significant extent, the cluster has developed in close interaction with the academic milieu of the university, and the university may be regarded as the main provider of the scientific knowledge base of the cluster.

While the first company, BioX, started in the mid 1980s and may be regarded as one of the pioneering firms of the cluster, the other firms are of later origin with start-ups during the 1990s and around the turn of the twenty-first century. From one point of view, the cases may be regarded as fairly homogeneous, as they belong to the same sector, are based on the same type of knowledge and are even located in the same geographical area. On the other hand, as will be shown by the descriptions that follow, the four cases also represent significant variety, both in terms of patterns of development and the ways academics have been involved.

Case A: The Professor Entrepreneur

This is the story of one of the most successful university spin-offs within the field of biotechnology in Norway. The company, here called BioX, was established in 1984 in collaboration between a university professor and four of his students. The company was reorganized in 1990, and experienced a steady growth during the 1990s. The company was listed on the Oslo Stock Exchange during autumn 2005, and reported 56 employees and a turnover of 73 million NOK in 2006.

However, in order to understand this story, it is necessary to go back to 1972 when the main person, the professor, was employed at the university as professor in the Department of Biotechnology. From the very beginning, he was concerned about the industrial exploitation of biotechnology based knowledge, in particular related to fish farming and the health of fish. He was a pioneer in developing fish vaccines; he also contributed to the development of other technologies which were successfully exploited in the fish industry. When BioX started in 1984, the business idea was to develop technologies, including vaccines, for the fish farming and fish processing industry. The professor was the main entrepreneur of the company and 'orchestrated' the whole business. However, he did not take the role as manager. This role was left to one of the participating students – candidate A – while he himself took the position as board chairman and research director. He also maintained his position as professor, the first years in full position, later in an adjunct position.

BioX had a good start and was profitable from the very beginning. However, the development was fairly unpredictable. The market for one of their business activities collapsed after a few years, while other markets developed very well. In particular, the team successfully developed a nutrition ingredient which turned out to be very favourable to the fish farming industry, and this triggered an interesting development partly based on research collaboration with an international company.

Towards the end of the 1980s, a new owner took over the majority share of the company. After some time, however, the new owner went bankrupt, and the professor and his team had to buy back the full ownership of BioX. After a short period of collaboration with another local firm, an exchange of business areas was organized in 1990, and from then on BioX has focused on pharmaceutical products and developed its business activities within this field. During the 1990s, the company's development was characterized by steady growth; one VC company was involved during the mid 1990s, another VC was involved towards the end of the 1990s when BioX became a public company and prepared for the stock exchange, but due to the recession and the development in the capital market during the early 2000s, the listing on the stock exchange was postponed until 2005.

Over almost the whole lifetime of BioX the professor has held the role as chairman of the board and worked as research director of the company. He has also, until recently, held his position as adjunct professor at the university. His students have also been involved. Candidate A had the role as manager for the first years of the company, then candidate B took over the role as manager after some years. In the mid 1990s candidate B left the company and is now the managing director of another company. Candidate C, who had followed BioX all the time, then took over as managing director, and has been in this position until recently (2006) when he moved to another company in the biotechnology sector. Both the professor and candidates B and C are still shareholders of BioX.

An interesting aspect of the role of the professor is his role as serial entrepreneur, as he has been involved in some other start-ups. However, this will not be discussed further here.[3]

Case B: The Research Based Entrepreneurs

The story of this company, which we call BioPhD, may be traced back to 1992 when two doctoral students started a research project to test a protein with a very high level of anti-bacterial activity, and identified a field with great potential for further development and commercialization. Contacts were established with a national pharmaceutical company, joint research activities were organized with the company as lead partner, and up to 2001 about 50 million NOK were spent on these research activities which resulted in five patents.

However, the pharmaceutical company restructured and changed strategy, and left the project. BioPhD was then established in 2003 with the two previous doctoral students as co-founders, and the rights to the developed IPR were transferred to their company.

The company is organized with a small staff of four people, including the two co-founders who are combining their work in BioPhD with half-time positions as professor and assistant professor, respectively, at the university. The company is still (2007) in its early stage of development; its main activity includes further testing of products, and this is estimated to continue for another 2–3 years. Basic funding has been provided by private placements, first in two rounds in 2004–05, and then a follow-up round in 2006 of NOK 20 million, which was heavily oversubscribed.

An option for the future may be to look for an industrial partner in order to organize a joint venture, but licensing may also be an alternative.

Case C: The Laboratory Manager

The story of this company, which we call BioLab, started in 1993 when a research institute, which we call RI, located on campus of the actual university, was visited by a Japanese person interested in kitosan, which is an important ingredient in cosmetics. The contact revealed that RI had the capacity for producing kitosan of very good quality. However, due to various reasons, the contact with the Japanese did not lead to any form of collaboration.

In 1994, RI started collaboration with a German company, and a joint research project was organized. In 1995 a new company, which we call

Company C, was started jointly by the two parties in order to exploit the commercial opportunities which were expected to develop based on the research activities. A patent was obtained. It was owned 50:50 by RI and the German company – and was licensed to Company C.

In 1998 BioLab was established. It was owned jointly by the German company and Company C. BioLab was originally staffed with a manager with background from the UK, and with two staff from RI in charge of the research activities and the operation of laboratory facilities. A new production plant was set up not far away from campus, and all its produced kitosan was delivered to the German company, which sold it to their customers. However, the Germans faced market problems. Only parts of the production capacity of BioLab were exploited, and a very complicated story followed. Eventually, Company C gave up their involvement in BioLab and the German company started a process of restructuring. It sold out all their business activities related to ingredients, which were taken over by another company that we call 'Int-C Scandinavia', which is the Scandinavian branch of a European company.

Since then, Int-C Scandinavia has hired RI to manage the production activity of BioLab, which is still operating in 2007 on a modest scale. Two people are employed in the production facilities and the role of production manager is contracted to RI with one of their research directors in charge.

Case D: The Industrial Entrepreneurs

This company, which started as BioNutra and later was restructured into BioGroup, was established in 2000 by two founders with various backgrounds in biotechnology related research and industrial experience. One of the founders was originally an economist with a background in industrial activity and also research activities at a centre for fishery research; the other has a background in marine biotechnology and has also previous experience as an entrepreneur.

Based on their industrial experience, they developed a very ambitious strategy for starting a new company in the consumer and animal food ingredients industry. The first development was based on collaboration with an American company. BioNutra obtained a license to sell one of the American company's products worldwide. They started planning a production facility in Norway, and the American company acquired the majority of the shares of BioNutra. However the relationship between the American company and the Norwegian founders did not work very well. A very complicated story followed, the end of which was that the founders acquired back the full ownership of their company.

A period of reconsidering their strategy followed. They reorganized their business activities into the new company, BioGroup. A private placement was successfully organized in 2004, and a rapid development has followed with the integration of other companies, among them a production facility located in the region. BioGroup was by 2007 probably the fastest growing biotech company in the region, and planned to be listed on the Oslo Stock Exchange during 2007.

The reported sales in 2006 were more than 70 million NOK, and the company employed around 55 people.

PROCESSES OF COMMERCIALIZATION AND FIRM DEVELOPMENT

The four cases illustrate that processes of commercialization may be complicated and turbulent, and they may last for many years, even several decades. This is in contrast to the simple pictures provided by most stage models. To illustrate this, we have summarized some characteristics of the evolution of the cases in Table 13.3.

To the extent that these cases are representative, there is no simple way from research to a successful, viable company. In the case of BioX (case A), which so far seems to be the most successful company, it took more than 20 years from the initial start until the full fledging company was listed on the stock exchange. The company is still in its early stages of development, it is still investing heavily in R&D and it has reported significant deficits in the last years. Furthermore, the initial years of the development of BioX were characterized by a high level of turbulence, with the need to reorganize the business activities several times before finding a sustainable structure of the company.

In the case of BioPhD (case B), the initial research period lasted for more than ten years, and the company has so far not earned money and has a long way to go to complete the process of commercialization. Thus the way from research based knowledge to an operative business may be very long.

In case C (BioLab), the time horizon has been shorter, as the actual product basically was developed when contact was established with the industrial partner. However, in spite of this, the start-up of the new production facility was based on five years' collaborative research activities.

In case D, the pattern of development is quite different. The main focus of the new company, BioNutra, was to organize production of ingredients that were fairly well developed and more ready for the market than in the other cases. R&D activity was less important in this case, and the company was profitable after a few years in business.

Table 13.3 Stages in the processes of commercialization of case companies

	Case A The professor entrepreneur Company: BioX	**Case B** The research based entrepreneurs Company: BioPhD	**Case C** The laboratory manager Company: BioLab	**Case D** The industrial entrepreneurs Company: BioNutra/ BioGroup
Pre start-up development	1972–80 Various research activities at the Department of Biotechnology at the university in collaboration with various companies; developing and implementing new technologies.	1992–2001 Extensive research activities over several years organized in collaboration between the university and a leading national pharmaceutical company (NPC), with the company as the lead partner, E.	1993– Research activities in the field of marine biotechnology, organized at a research institute (RI) located on campus. Research collaboration with a German company on applying kitosan in cosmetics.	1990s The two entrepreneurs have various backgrounds from research activities at the university and larger companies in Norway and abroad, one of them also with background as the entrepreneur in a regionally based biotech firm.
Entrepreneur(s)	Professor at the Department of Biotechnology in collaboration with some of his students.	Two PhD candidates from the university (Department of Medicine and Department of Chemistry).	German company in collaboration with RI and a local company.	Two co-founders; (a) a candidate from the university and (b) an economist educated abroad.
Triggering factor for start-up	The professor and some of his students identified new opportunities for commercialization.	NPC restructured their business activity and focused on other fields.	RI contacts with industry representatives interested in their kitosan.	Ambitions to start a fast growth biotech company.

Table 13.3 (continued)

	Case A The professor entrepreneur Company: BioX	**Case B** The research based entrepreneurs Company: BioPhD	**Case C** The laboratory manager Company: BioLab	**Case D** The industrial entrepreneurs Company: BioNutra/ BioGroup
Start-up year/ firm	1984: BioX	2003: BioPhD	1998: BioLab	2000: BioNutra / 2003: BioGroup
Field of business	Fish vaccines Fish food ingredients Enzyme technology.	Development of pharmaceutical products – anti-cancer drugs.	Production of kitosan. All production sold to the German company.	Consumer and animal food ingredients.
Early development	1984–90 Developed and launched various products, turbulent market development: • BioX was acquired by another company which experienced economic problems • BioX was acquired back by the entrepreneurs • Collaboration with a local company, exchange of business areas	2003– The company is heavily involved in developing anti-cancer drugs, and is still in the stage of testing out various molecules. Funding of activity by private investors – two private placements organized in 2003–04, and a new placement in 2006. Additional funding by public research programmes.	1998–2004 Market problems, only a smaller part of the production capacity was utilized. Turbulent development; was taken over by the Scandinavian branch of an international company in 2004.	2000–03 Collaboration with an American partner, obtained license for producing one of their products, majority ownership taken over by the partner. Production facility opened in 2002. Turbulent development, partnership cancelled, the founders got back full ownership of their company.

	• Research collaboration with a leading international company.			
Later development	1990– BioX was restructured and established in its current form in 1990 with focus on pharmaceutical products. • Steady growth, two emission during the 1990s • Organized as public company in 2000 • Listed on Oslo Stock Exchange in 2005.	The company is still in its early development.	2004– The company is operated on a low level activity; approx. one-third of the production capacity is exploited. The production facility is managed by the staff of RI.	2003– Reorganizing of company, steady growth in own business activities and expansion through investments in other companies, building a company group. Plans to be listed on Oslo Stock Exchange during 2007.
Status 2006 (million NOK)	No of employees: 56 Turnover: 73 Profit: −40 R&D activity: 35	Employees: 4 Turnover: 2.8 Profit: −4.2	Two people employed in production, two academic staff sharing the role as manager.	Employees; 55 Turnover: about 72 Profit: 5.2

What really seems to complicate the process of commercialization are the relations between the emerging new businesses and their industrial partners. In the case of BioX alliances with another company were important in the early stages in order to get access to capital, and also to technology and markets. However, when their partner faced economic problems, it threatened the whole development of the company, which had to restructure its activities. In the case of BioPhD, the initial strategy was to develop the new business in collaboration with one of the leading, national pharmaceutical companies, and extensive research activities were organized. A potential outcome of this process might be that the new pharmaceuticals were included in the company's product portfolio. However, the company changed strategy and defined its core business in other fields. The development of the new business activity was threatened, and this necessitated the start-up of the new company, BioPhD.

In cases C and D the evolution has been even more turbulent. The industrial partners have faced very significant economic problems related to the market. In the case of BioLab their partner reorganized, and a new partner has been involved. In the case of BioNutra the relationship between the entrepreneurs and their partner turned out to be very problematic, the relationship was ended, and the entrepreneurs redefined their strategy, which led to a new start and the reorganization of their business activity into BioGroup.

Although the cases are not necessarily representative for the whole cluster, impressions based on summary information about the other companies of the cluster may indicate that the four stories are not unique. A common feature of the evolution of this type of biotechnology firms seems to be the long time horizon of their development and that the outcomes of the processes are less predictable. There is a long way to go from the initial research results and to the new, commercially viable business being established (Hine and Kapeleris, 2006). Thus the cases support our earlier comments that simple stage models may be less adequate to describe the complexity and turbulence of the processes. It seems to be a quite common phenomenon that projects have to be redefined and reorganized, and support the view that such processes often may be chaotic (Van de Ven et al., 1999).

THE SPIN-OFF PROCESSES

To facilitate our further discussion, we have summarized some characteristics of the spin-off processes in Table 13.4. Our point of departure is that all four cases may be classified as university spin-offs as they have developed

Table 13.4 Characteristics of the spin-off processes

	A. BioX	B. BioPhD	C. BioLab	D. BioGroup
Parent organization	University department (Department of Biotechnology)	University department in collaboration with a national pharmaceutical company (NPC)	Research Institute (RI) located on university campus	No specific parent organization
Technology originator	The professor and some of his students	Two PhD candidates in collaboration with the R&D department and NPC	The Research Institute Institute	No specific technology originator; based on already developed technology
Entrepreneur(s)	The professor and some of his students	The two PhD candidates	Industrial partner (German company)	Two academic candidates with supplementary industrial and entrepreneurial background; also some background in research
Type of spin-off	Insider conducted	Insider conducted	Outsider conducted	Indirect spin-off Outsider conducted
Role of academic staff	Entrepreneurial, with combined focus on R&D and business development	Entrepreneurial, but with main focus on R&D	Production management	Entrepreneurial from an outsider position
Location of company	Headquarters and laboratories located in the city close to campus; also an office in Oslo	In the science park on campus	Production facilities located a few kilometres outside campus	Headquarters located in science park on campus, production facilities located elsewhere in the region

Table 13.4 (continued)

	A. BioX	**B. BioPhD**	**C. BioLab**	**D. BioGroup**
Venture investors	Start-up: the entrepreneurs Next stages: • Industrial partners • National venture capital firms • IPO (listed on Oslo Stock Exchange 2005)	Start-up: the entrepreneurs Next stages: • Private placements	Industrial partner	Start-up: the entrepreneurs Next stages: • Private placements • Planned IPO (Oslo Stock Exchange) in 2007
Public research funding?	Yes, extensively	Yes, extensively	No	Yes, moderate
Support from Innovation Norway?	No	Yes, start-up grant	No	No
Public seed capital?	No	Yes, regional seed capital fund	No	Yes, regional seed capital fund

in close relationship with the university or related research institutes. However, the form of this relationship varies between the four cases.

Cases A and B are similar in the sense that the point of departure for the development were research activities conducted at the university. In case A the new firm was initiated by the professor in collaboration with some of his students, and the new start-up was directly based on knowledge developed in the university department. Thus the university department may be regarded as the parent organization, the professor and his students were the technology originators and the spin-off process may be classified as an insider conducted process; insiders were in charge of the process of commercialization in the early stages of development.

Similarly, in case B the development of the new venture was triggered by the research activities of the two PhD candidates. However their original research was only a point of departure for extensive further research, which was organized over several years in a national pharmaceutical company, and when the new company eventually was started by the two PhD candidates, the spin-off may be said to have originated from the national company rather than the university. However, the link back to the university is quite clear as the initial research activities started there, and the follow-up research was organized in collaboration with the company and the university. So this may also be classified as an insider conducted university spin-off, although the links are more indirect than in the previous case.

The third case, BioLab, is different in the sense that the main entrepreneurial actor in the commercialization process was an international company, and the spin-off may be regarded as an outsider conducted spin-off. However, the scientific knowledge was developed on campus.

The fourth case, BioGroup, comes in a different category in terms of how the specific knowledge for commercialization has originated, and what role the academic staff have taken in the process. First, it is not possible to identify a specific parent organization of the research the company is based on. The basis for developing the company has mostly been already developed or semi-developed nutrition products, and the company has to a significant extent evolved through acquisition and expansion of existing production processes. Second, the founders of the firm have started from a position as outsiders; based on their previous industrial and entrepreneurial experiences, they developed their new business idea and so far have succeeded in developing a fast growing company.

Although their links to the university are not as clear as in the other cases, the links seem strong enough to classify the company as a university spin-off. The two founders have significant relationships with the university; one of them as a graduate (master candidate) from the university, while the other was employed as research fellow at one of the research institutes. Furthermore, the company headquarters is located in the science park on campus, and the company is now conducting R&D in part funded by a R&D programme organized in order to stimulate the development of the biotech cluster around the university. It seems quite obvious that BioGroup would never have been established in the area if it had not been for the local knowledge base and the emerging cluster formed around the university. However, it may be adequate to classify this case as an indirect university spin-off.

THE ROLE OF INSTITUTIONS

The four cases belong to an emerging industrial cluster located in a fairly marginal region facing some significant problems related to industrial development. For several decades, the region has pursued a systematic strategy for regional development. One of the main elements in its strategy has been the development of the university and to provide education and develop research activities in areas with a high potential for industrial development. As a part of this strategy, a diversified structure for facilitating technology transfer and university spin-offs has been developed; research centres have been established in order to specialize in areas like fishery and marine biotechnology, a science park and related incubator facilities was established in the mid 1990s, and a specific research programme focusing on marine biotechnology has been organized to stimulate commercialization and interaction between the academic institutions and industry. Furthermore, regionally based seed capital funds have been organized, the university has organized its technology transfer office, and a process for developing a forum and network to support the cluster development has been organized in collaboration with many parties over the last years.

In Table 13.4 we have briefly shown to what extent the case companies have taken advantage of the various support mechanisms. This may be summarized in the following points:

- The most important factor is the research activities organized at the university, and the quality and entrepreneurial orientation of the research staff. This has been an important basis for establishing all four companies.
- Two cases are located in the science park on campus.
- Three cases have obtained funding from national and regional R&D programmes.

- Mostly, the four cases have been based on private risk capital obtained through private placements and public offerings. Local seed capital is involved in two of the cases, and as a part of this representatives for the seed capital fund are on the boards of these companies.
- Start-up grant is obtained from the national innovation agency in one case.

Using this background it may be concluded that there are some working support mechanisms that may be of importance for the evolution of the cluster.[4] However, when talking with the actors involved in the new ventures, their main concern is about all the challenges related to the organizing and strategic development of their company. Various support mechanisms may facilitate this; however, the main driving force is the entrepreneurs themselves.

THE ROLE OF ACADEMIC STAFF

The role of the academic staff varies between the four cases, and we will now discuss in some detail their roles in developing the new venture, in particular, how they have been involved as entrepreneur, and how they have conbined their role in the new venture with their role at the university or the research institute.

BioX (case A): The professor was the main entrepreneur and took the role of 'orchestrating' the whole business while combining the position of research director with the position as chairman of the board, a position he has held continuously until recently. During the whole period he has also maintained close contacts with the university. During the first years he kept his position at the university in combination with part-time involvement in the company. Later he was working full time in the company as research director and combined this with a part-time position as adjunct professor at the university, a position he held until the turn of the twenty-first century. As part of this he has also been the supervisor for PhD students.

With his main focus on 'orchestrating' the development of the new venture, the professor may be characterized as very entrepreneurial. Based on the framework suggested by Dickson et al. (1998), he may be characterized as a 'scientific entrepreneur'. He has been 'utilising a high level of scientific intelligence to identify new business opportunities' (Dickson et al., 1998, p. 35), and during most of his life long career, he has been able to combine his role as entrepreneur with his position as professor at the university.[5]

BioPhD (case B) has to some extent followed the same pattern of development as BioX. The main focus of the two entrepreneurs has been on

R&D. They were involved in research projects at the university, identified interesting opportunities for commercialization and established collaboration with a national company which organized more research in the field. When the company changed strategy, the IPR was transferred to the research fellows who started their new business in which they continued their R&D activities related to developing new anti-cancer drugs. Both founders combine their activities in the company with half-time positions at the university. However, what distinguishes this approach from that of BioX is that they still have a long way to go to develop the commercial potential, and they have not yet clarified what will be the future commercial model of the company. They also seem to have a stronger focus on R&D and disciplinary matters than on the commercial issues which they leave to other members of the team.

BioLab (case C) represents a very different story as the academic staff have not taken the lead role in the entrepreneurial process, but rather have had a supportive function to the external partner that has organized the new business. The main focus of the research institute and the two research fellows involved in the process has been that of supporting their industrial partner in developing the production facilities, while they have not been involved in other functions related to the new business. When the new business eventually was operating, their main task has been that of managing the production process on a contract basis.

BioGroup (case D) represents another and quite different story. The two entrepreneurs both have backgrounds as academics – one as a business economist who graduated from a university in the USA, the other as a biologist who graduated from the university – and both have some academic experience in research related to fishing and the marine sector. However their main background is industrial as they have worked with larger industrial companies for some years. One of the entrepreneurs also has previous experience as an entrepreneur as during the 1990s he was one of two cofounders of a biotechnology firm in the region.

The approach of the two founders has been very entrepreneurial. Their business idea was to organize the commercial production of consumer and animal food ingredients that basically were developed. Their main focus has been on exploiting business opportunities in this field, and they are pursuing a very ambitious growth strategy. Based on the previous framework, they are operating as actors who are external to the university and the research institutes, they are the 'surrogate entrepreneurs' (Radosevitch, 1995) and, with their strong emphasis of industrialization, it may be adequate to characterize them as 'industrial entrepreneurs'.

The four cases illustrate that the approaches in the entrepreneurial processes may be rather diverse. To some extent, this diversity may be explained by differences in types of knowledge that are exploited in the process of commercialization, and thus the role of R&D is very different. In cases A and B continued R&D activity is a basic precondition for the commercialization process, and actually the R&D activity is the most important part of the business, at least in the early stages. Naturally, then, the academic staff may take a leading role in organizing the new venture.

In case C R&D activities were important in the early stages, and were related to testing out the use of a specific ingredient for a cosmetic product controlled by their industrial partner. The role of the research institute was basically that of testing out the product and developing the production facilities, while knowledge related to the final consumer product and marketing was controlled by the partner. In this case it was a natural solution to hire the research institute and their staff for managing the production process.

In case D the products were mostly developed prior to start-up. The start-up was based on a licence agreement, and an important task was to set up production facilities. It has also been an important part of the company's strategy to integrate other businesses in the group. Thus their primary activities have been less research based. It is the entrepreneurial process and knowledge related to this that has been most essential when organizing this venture.

When processes of development are in the early stages of development and a high level of R&D activity is still required, this will naturally give much more opportunities for academic staff than commercialization processes focusing on more developed areas. Both cases A and B are examples of early stage processes in which there is a long way to go to be in the market with their products. Case D represents the opposite situation; the commercialization process is close to the market, other types of competences are more essential and this gives room for the 'surrogate' entrepreneurs.

In order to structure our understanding of the roles of academics in spin-off processes, we have set up a matrix based on two dimensions, research commitment and entrepreneurial commitment, and the typology derived from this is displayed in Table 13.5.

'The entrepreneurial professor' mainly focuses on the overall development of the business and works continually to develop the commercial activity. They combine a high level of entrepreneurial commitment with a high level of commitment in research. The basis for this is their scientific merits, and in order to maintain the high level of scientific quality it is important to combine their role in the company with a continued position at the university. In the specific case of BioX the professor has maintained such close relationships throughout his whole career, although during the last decade he worked full time in the company.

Table 13.5 Typology of the role of academic staff in spin-off ventures

		Research Commitment	
		High	Low
Entrepreneurial	High	The entrepreneurial professor Continued focus on developing new commercial activities based on a high level of scientific commitment (BioX)	The industrial entrepreneur Main task to organize and develop the new business, strong focus on market opportunities and industrialization (BioGroup)
Commitment	Low	The research oriented entrepreneur Main focus on research and disciplinary activities in the new firm, involvement in business activities is balanced with the academic career (BioPhD)	The production manager The role in the company mainly devoted to manage routine tasks, no R&D activity involved. Keeps the main position in the university or research institute (BioLab)

'The industrial entrepreneur' is highly committed to entrepreneurial activities, and is less committed to research and disciplinary activities. This also means that links to the university are weaker, although their background as an academic with knowledge in a specific field is important and may be a key precondition for conducting the role as entrepreneur in an adequate way. In the case of BioGroup the entrepreneurs have important industrial and entrepreneurial backgrounds, which provided a platform for starting up one of the most dynamic and fast growing biotech companies in the actual cluster.

The next category is 'the research oriented entrepreneur' who starts a new business to develop commercial activity based on their own research. Although this type of entrepreneur contributes to start new businesses which may have a high potential, the main focus of the academic is on research and disciplinary matters. This category is close to what Dickson et al. (1998) denote as 'entrepreneurial scientist' with a main focus on scientific issues, while other aspects of the entrepreneurial function are left to other members of the team. In the case of BioPhD the company is organized with a small team, and important functions related to the commercial development are delegated to other team members, while the two founders dedicate much of their time for their work in the university.

The fourth category is called 'the production manager', and points to a situation in which the academic staff who have contributed to the start-up of the new venture have a rather limited role in new business in terms of R&D. Their main role is confined to routine management activities. In the case of BioLab the staff have continued in their ordinary positions in the parent organization (the Research Institute) and serve as managers for the new production facility on a part-time basis.

CONCLUSION

This study has provided some important insights regarding processes of commercialization and the role of academic staff in commercialization processes.

First, it is important to recognize that processes of commercialization may be characterized by complexity, turbulence and a high level of uncertainty. While the literature is based on simple stage model approaches, evidence presented here indicates that processes may be very complex, sometimes chaotic, and there may often be a need for redefining and reorganizing the project. Processes of commercialization are often less predictable, and when planning such processes – to the extent that planning is possible – it is important to have an open and flexible approach and be prepared to redefine and start the project in a new way. It may be of great importance that academics involved in such projects acknowledge these aspects of processes of commercialization.

Second, academic staff may take different roles in processes of commercialization, and there may be different routes from the academic position in the university to the new venture where the academics may be involved in various ways. Based on the two dimensions of academic and entrepreneurial commitment, we have developed the following typology of roles of academics in processes of commercialization:

- The entrepreneurial professor with a high commitment in entrepreneurial tasks as well as research
- The industrial entrepreneur with a high commitment in entrepreneurial tasks while less commitment in research
- The research oriented entrepreneur with a high commitment in research activities and less in entrepreneurial tasks
- The production manager with a low commitment in research as well as in the entrepreneurial tasks of the firm, but still with an important role in managing the production of the new company.

The typology may provide a framework for a more differentiated discussion of the role of academic staff in spin-offs. While much of the literature does not discuss the various roles that academics may take in such processes, this framework may provide a basis for a more differentiated discussion, and for further development of knowledge in the field.

In academic milieus there are often perceived conflicts between academic and commercial activities, and there may be significant barriers to develop a more entrepreneurial culture. And pointing at 'the entrepreneurial professor' as the ideal role may even increase the barriers, as this role will be unrealistic to most academic staff. Probably, there are few academics that are able to take this role, as it requires a very unique combination of scientific and entrepreneurial skills. In this context the suggested framework may be of importance to point at different ways that academic staff may contribute in developing new ventures and to contributing to the development of a more entrepreneurial university.

The suggested typology is the result of explorative research, and as the empirical evidence so far is limited, it would be interesting to test out the typology, and possibly develop it further with follow up studies.

ACKNOWLEDGEMENT

The chapter is based on the research project 'Barriers to commercialization of knowledge' funded by the Norwegian Research Council. A previous version of the study was presented at the RENT XX Conference in Brussels. The author is grateful for very valuable comments received at the conference and from an anonymous reviewer.

NOTES

1. For a systematic account of how different system related factors may influence on the commercialization process, see Spilling and Godø (2007).
2. In Norway all companies are obliged to report to a public data register, the 'Firm Register', from which general information about the business is publicly available. For limited companies and public companies key accounting data and annual reports are also available.
3. For a discussion of the whole story related to BioX and the professor entrepreneur, see Spilling (2007).
4. For a more systematic account of factors influencing the commercialization process, see Spilling and Godø (2007).
5. The professor is widely recognized as a pioneer in developing industrial applications based on marine biotechnology, and he was in 2005 appointed Doctor of Honour by the university.

REFERENCES

Albert, P., M. Bernasconi and L. Gaynor (2002), *Incubators: The Emergence of a New Industry*, Sophia Antipolis, CERAM Sophia Antipolis.

Birley, S. (2002), 'Universities, academics, and spinout companies: lessons from Imperial', *International Journal of Entrepreneurship Education*, **1**(1), 1–21.

Carayannis, E.G., E.M. Rogers, K. Karihara and M.M. Allbritton (1998), 'High-technology spin-offs from government R&D laboratories and research universities', *Technovation*, **18**(1), 1–11.

Chiesa, V. and A. Piccaluga (1998), 'Transforming rather than transferring scientific and technological knowledge – the contribution of academic "spin out" companies: the Italian way', in R. Oakey and W. During (eds), *New Technology-Based Firms in the 1990s*, vol. V, London: Paul Chapman, pp. 15–31.

Clarysse, B. and N. Moray (2004), 'A process study of entrepreneurial team formation: the case of a research-based spin-off', *Journal of Business Venturing*, **19**, 55–79.

Dahlstrand, Å.L. (1999), 'British and Swedish science parks and incubators for small technology-based firms', in R. Oakey, W. During and S.-M. Mukhtar (eds), *New Technology-Based Firms in the 1990s*, vol. VI, Amsterdam: Pergamon, pp. 246–62.

Dahlstrand, Å.L. (2000), 'Large firm acquisitions, spin-offs and links in the development of regional clusters of technology-intensive SMEs', in D. Keeble and F. Wilkinson (eds), *High-Technology Clusters, Networking and Collective Learning in Europe*, Aldershot: Ashgate, pp. 156–81.

Dahlstrand, Å.L. and M. Klofsten (2003), 'Growth and innovation support in Swedish science parks and incubators', in R. Oakey, W. During and S. Kauser (eds), *New Technology-Based Firms in the New Millennium*, vol. II, Amsterdam: Pergamon, pp. 31–46.

Dickson, K., A.-M. Coles and H.L. Smith (1998), 'Science in the market place: the role of the scientific entrepreneur', in W. During and R. Oakey (eds), *New Technology-Based Firms in the 1990s*, vol. IV, London: Paul Chapman, pp. 27–37.

Fontes, M. (2003), 'A closer look at the process of transformation of scientific and technological knowledge as conducted by academic spin-offs', in R. Oakey, W. During and S. Kauser (eds), *New Technology-Based Firms in the New Millennium*, vol. II, Amsterdam: Pergamon.

Fontes, M. (2005), 'The process of transformation of scientific and technological knowledge into economic value conducted by technology spin-offs', *Technovation*, **25**, 339–47.

Hill, D.D. (1995), 'University-industry entrepreneurship: the organization and management of American university technology transfer units', *Higher Education*, **29**, 369–84.

Hine, D. and J. Kapeleris (2006), *Innovation and Entrepreneurship in Biotechnology – An International Perspective*, Cheltenham, UK and Northampton, MA, USA: Edward Elgar.

Jolly, V.K. (1997), *Commercializing New Technologies. Getting from Mind to Market*, Boston, MA: Harward Business School Press.

Jones-Evans, D. (1997), 'Technical entrepreneurship, experience and the management of small technology-based firms', in D. Jones-Evans and M. Klofsten (eds), *Technology, Innovation and Enterprise*, New York: St Martin's Press, pp. 11–60.

Lundvall, B.Å. (1992), 'Introduction', in B.Å. Lundvall (ed.), *National Systems of Innovation. Towards a Theory of Innovation and Interactive Learning*, London: Pinter Publisher, pp. 1–19.
Ndonzuau, F.N., F. Pirnay and B. Surlemont (2002), 'A stage model of academic spin-off creation', *Technovation*, **22**, 281–89.
Nicolaou, N. and S. Birley (2003), 'Academic networks in a trichotomous categorisation of university spinouts', *Journal of Business Venturing*, **18**, 333–59.
Pirnay, F., B. Surlemont and F. Nlemvo (2002), 'Toward a typology of university spin-offs', *Small Business Economics*, **21**(4), 355–69.
Radosevitch, R. (1995), 'A model for entrepreneurial spin-offs from public technology sources', *Technology Management*, **10**(7/8), 879–93.
Rasmussen, E. (2006), *Facilitating University Spin-off Ventures – An Entrepreneurship Process Perspective*, Bodø: Bodø Graduate School of Business, p. 273.
Rasmussen, E., Ø. Moen and M. Gulbrandsen (2006), 'Initiatives to promote commercialization of university knowledge', *Technovation*, **26**(4), 518–33.
Roberts, E.B. and D.E. Malone (1996), 'Policies and structures for spinning off new companies from research and development organizations', *R&D Management*, **26**(1), 17–48.
Samson, K.J. and M.A. Gurdon (1993), 'University scientists as entrepreneurs: a special case of technology transfer and high-tech venturing', *Technovation*, **13**(2), 63–71.
Shane, S. (2002), 'Selling university technology: patterns from MIT', *Management Science*, **48**(1), 122–37.
Shane, S. (2004), *Academic Entrepreneurship. University Spinoffs and Wealth Creation*, Cheltenham, UK and Northampton, MA: Edward Elgar.
Spilling, O.R. (2008), 'Entrepreneurship and heterogeneity', in E.G. Carayannis, A. Mariussen and A. Kaloudis (eds), *Diversity in the Knowledge Economy and Society: Heterogeneity, Innovation and Entrepreneurship*, Cheltenham, UK and Northampton, MA: Edward Elgar, pp. 140–64.
Spilling, O.R. (2007), 'Team entrepreneurs, serial entrepreneurs and entrepreneurial chains. A case study of an entrepreneurial team in the biotechnology industry in Norway', paper presented at the ICSB World Conference, Turku, Finland, 13–15 June.
Spilling, O.R. and H. Godø (2007), 'Barriers to commercialisation of knowledge in emerging technological regimes – a comparison of marine biotechnology and mobile commerce in Norway', paper presented at 6th Triple Helix, Singapore, 16–18 May.
Stankiewicz, R. (1998), 'Science parks and innovation centers', in H. Etzkowitz, A. Webster and P. Healey (eds), *Capitalizing Knowledge*, Albany, NY: State University of New York Press, pp. 133–47.
Steffensen, M., E.M. Rogers and K. Speakman (1999), 'Spin-offs from research centers at a research university', *Journal of Business Venturing*, **15**, 93–111.
Van de Ven, A.H., D.E. Polley, R. Garud and S. Venkataraman (1999), *The Innovation Journey*, New York and Oxford: Oxford University Press.
Virtanen, M. and M. Laukkanen (2002), 'Towards HEI-based new venture generation: the business lab of University of Kuopio', *Industry & Higher Education*, **16**(3), 159–66.

14. Innovation at the intersection of market strategy and technology: a study of digital marketing adoption among SMEs

Vladimir Vanyushyn

INTRODUCTION

The opportunities inherent in the digitization of marketing and selling activities are substantial. Going on-line can lead to more efficient business processes, round the clock operations, flexible pricing, rapid internationalization, increased market reach, cost reduction and better targeting of products – just to name a few (Bengtsson et al., 2007; Sultan and Rohm, 2004; Sharma and Tzokas, 2002). For manufacturing firms, e-business may lead to higher profits as the reseller's margin no longer applies. Early studies conducted in the mid-1990s suggested that Internet technology would open up new opportunities for the smaller firms and level up the playing field against large incumbent competitors (Kotler, 2000; Poon and Jevons, 1997; Haynes et al., 1998).

The growing importance of and academic interest in digital business has produced a voluminous literature. Many researchers, however, conclude that Internet and e-commerce research is at the embryonic stage (BarNir et al., 2003), and point out the lack of integrative frameworks (Jeyaraj et al., 2006; Kim and Malhotra, 2005) and reliable measures (Wu et al., 2003). In the area of small business research most of the studies reported are conceptual, normative or qualitative (for example, Houghton and Winklhofer, 2004), and there is a recognized need for empirical research focusing on e-business adoption by smaller firms (Fillis and Wagner, 2005).

Against this background, this study aims to identify and examine antecedents of digitization of marketing and sales by smaller manufacturing firms. To do so, three partially overlapping, but nonetheless conceptually and empirically distinct groups of studies, are reviewed and integrated. The first group of studies, common in mainstream management and marketing journals, approached the digitization from the innovation perspective. The second group, represented mostly by information and management science publications, is grounded in technology acceptance models that evaluate the perceived usefulness and ease of use of an IT application. The third approach examines the digitization from the product-market strategy perspective. These three approaches are rather compartmentalized and have been weakly integrated in the literature. Innovation studies rarely consider perceived usefulness, technology acceptance studies rarely include innovation antecedents, and links between product-market strategy and digitization are few and far between. Furthermore, the relationship between firm size and the adoption of IT innovation has been a subject of debate. In this context the more specific objectives pursued in this study are as follows: (1) to operationalize the digitization of marketing and sales, (2) to identify predictors that can explain the digitization of marketing and sales, (3) to empirically test alternative models incorporating various combinations of these predictors and (4) to suggest and test an integrative model.

The empirical section of this study is built on the analysis of 355 smaller manufacturing firms in Sweden. The sampled firms come from various industries and belong to different size groups. Given that Sweden has been consistently ranked among the top three nations in terms of e-readiness (Economist Intelligence Unit, 2005), the influence of macro-factors, such as overall computer literacy and availability of the IT infrastructure, can be factored out.

The remainder of the chapter is structured as follows. The next section introduces the concept of Digitally Enabled Marketing (DEM) and provides an overview of innovation adoption, technology acceptance and product market-strategy approaches. Then the key factors related to DEM adoption are identified and specific research hypotheses are formulated. A discussion of the survey and sampling procedures, measurement and estimation of proposed models follow. The chapter concludes with a discussion of the findings, their implications, the study limitations and suggestions for future research.

BACKGROUND

To begin with, it is necessary to narrowly define digitization of marketing and selling activities. This is not a trivial task, as various authors assign different meanings to the terms. The terms e-business, e-commerce, and Internet commerce are frequently used interchangeably. The term e-business can have a very general scope, and refers to how businesses utilize information technology to achieve competitive advantage. Overall, the existing literature offers a continuum of definitions, ranging from restrictive to general. The first one equates e-business with e-commerce, that is, sales of products to customers over the Internet. The second approach takes a broader view, and includes all Internet-enabled business solutions and applications. To avoid the definitional quagmire, the operational definition of Digitally Enabled Marketing is introduced.

Digitally Enabled Marketing (DEM) is defined for the purpose of this study as the organization's capability to (1) have customers perform buying activities in a self-directed manner using a website and (2) collect information about customers using a website. The first part of this definition is identical to the operationalization of digital selling activity developed by Johnson and Bharadwaj (2005). In practical terms, DEM implies that a firm has the means to receive orders via its website and to process them without direct involvement of a human. It also implies that a firm has the capability to receive feedback from customers via its website, and that a firm actively collects information on how customers use the website (for example, click-per-view or purchase-per-click). DEM is a unitary construct; if a firm intends to adopt DEM, it is likely to adopt all of its features almost simultaneously.

DEM is also conceptually distinct from the use of the Internet for basic purposes[1] (Bengtsson et al., 2007). For example, creating a simple descriptive website or communicating with consumers via e-mail yields immediate benefits without any tangible financial or organizational costs. Adoption of DEM, on the other hand, is costly and can result in a major shift in a firm's business processes. Figure 14.1 sketches the framework that would guide further discussion and analysis, and presents the three major approaches that underlie the decision to adopt DEM. The decision to adopt DEM is likely to be contingent upon management's attitudes towards change and evaluation of market conditions (hence the innovation section), depend on the overall fit of DEM with a firm's market strategy (hence controllable marketing tool), and involve the assessment of its usefulness and ease of use (hence information system). Finally, firm size can be used as a proxy for a firm's financial and human resources. The remainder of this section will review these three major areas of research that can contribute to the understanding of DEM adoption, followed by a range of hypotheses.

Innovation: Willingness to Cannibalize, Market Pressure and Management Support

For a firm, adopting DEM can equal adopting innovation. Entering the electronic marketplace may lead to changes in production, management systems and human resources. Moreover, DEM has features of radical innovation, as opposed to an incremental one, in that it may result in

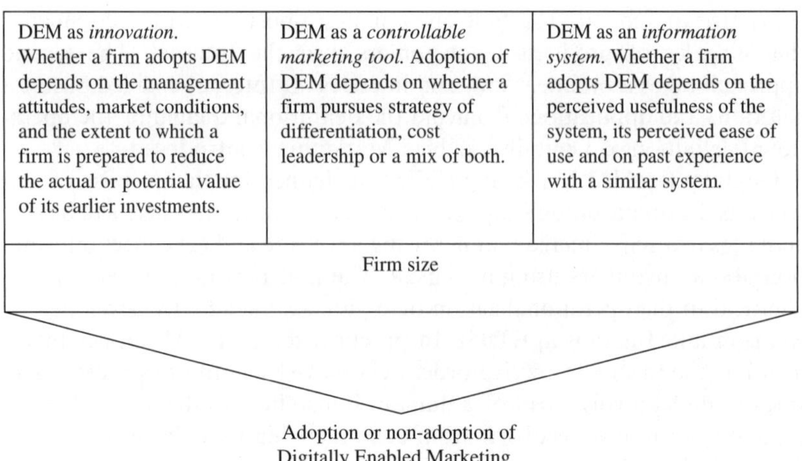

Figure 14.1 DEM adoption from three different perspectives

'fundamental changes in the activities of organization and industry with respect to current practices' (Camison-Zornoza et al., 2004, p. 336) and in rapid depreciation of earlier investments (Chandy and Tellis, 1998). Insofar that adoption of DEM is a subset of a more general innovation adoption, models common to innovation research can be applied. The following three antecedents to innovation adoption are discussed: willingness to cannibalize, market pressure and management support. In general, management support and external pressure are the best predictors of IT adoption by organizations (Jeyaraj et al., 2006).[2] Willingness to cannibalize is particularly relevant given that '[it is] assumed that Internet is cannibalistic . . . will replace the conventional ways of doing business' (Porter, 2001, p. 73).

An important caveat is due at this point. DEM or e-business in general might not necessarily correspond to radical innovation as formulated by, for example, Tushman and Anderson (1986). Nevertheless, the innovation approach has been used in the literature before (Srinivasan et al., 2002; Bengtsson et al., 2007), and these studies have established the link between innovation-related factors and various forms of e-business adoption. It is important to distinguish between suggesting that the Internet is radical innovation itself, which is a matter of opinion, and suggesting that adopting the Internet for marketing and sales can equal adopting a radical innovation. Furthermore, it is precisely this unclear relationship between e-business and innovation that partly motivated this study, which aims to draw on other factors to uncover what actually underlies the decision to invest in an on-line marketing channel.

Willingness to Cannibalize (WILTC)

The concept of WILTC can be traced back to Schumpeter's (1942) notion of 'creative destruction'. It was introduced by Chandy and Tellis (1998) in order to develop a unifying concept of how organizational factors affect radical product innovation. WILTC is an attitudinal variable and refers to the 'extent to which a firm is prepared to reduce the actual or potential value of its past investments' (p. 475). The original study concluded that, other things being equal, firms that exhibit higher willingness to cannibalize are more likely to introduce radical product innovations.

Application of the WILTC to the adoption of DEM is motivated by the fact that DEM may reduce the value of a firm's earlier financial and relational investments. First, introducing a new channel may cannibalize sales through existing channels and result in resellers' alienation (Ghosh, 1998; Porter, 2001; Deleersnyder et al., 2002; Eyuboglu and Kabadayi, 2005). The existing evidence suggests that e-business initiatives of even large and well-established business can be hampered by the resellers located downstream in the value chain. To mitigate the potentially negative effects of introducing a new distribution channel, manufacturing firms may have to implement various measures directed at reducing the potential of channel conflict. For example, Avon pays fees to its distributors for the Internet sales in their area, even if distributor had no role in the sale (Eyuboglu and Kabadayi, 2005). Levi Strauss had to withdraw its Internet channel after one year because of fear of cannibalization losses (Dugan, 1999, cited in Deleersnyder et al., 2002). Second, DEM may affect the existing organizational routines and supporting technologies, such as sales force and call centres (for example, Johnson and Bharadwaj, 2005).[3]

Management Support and Strategy Coherence (MGMTSTRTGY)

As the discussion above implies, adopting DEM is likely to bring change to a firm. It has been shown that management attitude towards change influences the process of adoption and implementation of innovation: 'a greater support of top managers in the innovation process is necessary to initiate and sustain radical departures from the past for that organization' (Ettlie et al., 1984, p. 682). Management is also likely to support initiatives and actions which are aligned with a firm's strategy (for example, Damanpour, 1991; Wu et al., 2003).

Market Pressure (PRESSURE)

Competitive and consumer pressure represent two major external forces that can affect the decision to adopt DEM. A market-oriented business is likely to anticipate customers' preferences (for example, Jaworski and Kohli, 1993). If a firm anticipates that its customers would prefer to shop online, it will respond by adopting DEM. On the other hand, institutional and competitive bandwagon pressures may force a firm to adopt innovation, even if a firm expects that this adoption will yield negative returns (Abrahamson and Rosenkompf, 1993).

Hypothesis 1: WILTC will have a positive effect on the adoption of DEM.
Hypothesis 2: MGMTSTRTGY will have a positive effect on the adoption of DEM.
Hypothesis 3: PRESSURE will have a positive effect on the adoption of DEM.

Product-market strategy (PRODMRKT)

DEM can be viewed as a tool, just one of many available to a marketing manager. Assuming that DEM is a specific form of sales organization, and applying Chandler's (1962) classical argument that 'structure follows strategy', it follows that a firm will adopt DEM if such action is in line with a firm's competitive strategy. From a classical standpoint of product-market strategy, a firm can pursue either a strategy of differentiation (DIFF) or cost leadership (CL) (Porter, 1980),[4] which are roughly paralleled by innovation and efficiency orientations (Porter, 1996). The first orientation emphasizes product and process innovation, differentiation through brand, offering overall superior value and charging price premium. The cost leadership strategy, on the other hand, implies a strong focus on efficiency and lowering costs.

A firm pursuing a DIFF strategy can benefit from DEM by targeting early adopters, and receiving quick feedback and up-to-date market information. For firms pursuing a CL strategy DEM may allow competitive bidding and ease of price discrimination (Brynjolfsson and Smith, 2000). Thus DEM has the capacity to benefit firms pursuing both strategies. Contrary to such reasoning, BarNir et al. (2003) found that 'digitization of advertising, marketing, sales, and customer support is negatively associated with both innovation and efficiency orientations . . . firms that extensively use online processes for marketing, sales, or customer support tend to do so *in lieu of* developing a focused strategy . . . Clearly, this is one of the surprising findings that warrant further study' (pp. 791, 808, 811, emphasis added). Overall, lack of empirical studies (Jeyaraj et al., 2006) and strong conceptual arguments in support of the association between DEM and both strategies allows the formulation of the following hypotheses:

Hypothesis 4a: DIFF will have a positive effect on the adoption of DEM.
Hypothesis 4b: CL will have a positive effect on the adoption of DEM.

Technology Acceptance Model (TAM): Relevance, Ease of Use, Previous Experience

Hardware and software that constitute TAM are a subset of Information Systems (IS), and, therefore, the general tools developed for examining and predicting IS acceptance can be applied. The most prominent model in this field is the Technology Acceptance Model and its extension and variations. The original paper by Davis (1989) introducing TAM has been cited over 870 times in the SSCI database.[5] According to TAM, any IS application is evaluated by the users on two dimensions: 'usefulness' and 'ease of use'. Perceived usefulness and perceived ease of use combined translate into an intention, which, in turn, translates into actual behaviour. Despite its eye-catching simplicity, TAM does explain a significant proportion of variation in the adoption and actual use of IS (Taylor and Todd, 1995). Partly, the explanatory power of TAM is due to its foundations in the behavioural theory of reasoned action (Fishbein and Ajzen, 1975) that accounts for a significant proportion of the variation in actual behaviour (see Sheppard et al., 1988 for a meta-analysis).

The extensions of the original TAM have proceeded in two directions. The first examined the antecedents to perceived usefulness and perceived ease of use (Venkatesh and Davis, 2000; McFarland and Hamilton, 2006); the second established a strong connection between past experience or use of an application and the present intention to use or actual use of the similar or related application (Kim and Malhotra, 2005). Nevertheless, the core of the extended models, as well as of the original one, is the cost-benefit paradigm (Davis, 1989), that is, evaluation of benefits gained – usefulness, and associated costs – ease of use.

Innovation-inspired studies, discussed in the previous section, often do not consider the rational component in the adoption decision, and focus on the general antecedents, such as management support or market pressure. While such an approach is undoubtedly useful and can illuminate a number of relationships between innovation drivers and DEM or IS adoption, the rational component of the decision to adopt cannot be disregarded. The most innovative firm will not invest in an Internet channel if such a decision is entirely irrelevant to its products, and the most rigid firm will do so if the discounted profit associated with such a decision is sufficient and the associated risks are low. It is, therefore, necessary to include a measure of a firm's self-assessment of Internet relevance and ease of use. Given the narrow focus of this study on DEM adoption, the following adjustments to generic measures of usefulness and ease of use are proposed: relevance, ease of use and previous use of the Internet.

Relevance (RELEVANCE)

In the original study by Davis (1989, p. 320) perceived usefulness was defined as 'the degree to which a person believes that using a particular system would enhance his or her job performance'. Perceived usefulness is a highly reliable predictor of adoption by individuals. After reviewing 99 empirical studies published between 1992–2003, Jeyaraj et al. (2006) report that it had been used 29 times and found relevant 26 times. In the organizational context, however, it has been used once, and found significant.

In the context of DEM adoption, perceived relevance is a close analogue for perceived usefulness. That is to say, a firm would adopt DEM if it is relevant to its products and customers. A firm that sells highly customized, complex products that require presentation or lengthy negotiations would be less likely to invest in DEM because of its low relevance. On the other hand, simpler, less customized products may be more likely to be sold via the Internet.

Ease of Use (EASEOFUSE)

The original definition of the perceived ease of use is 'the degree to which a person believes that using a particular system would be free of effort' (Davis, 1989, p. 320). At the organizational level and in the context of DEM adoption, the effort is represented by the complexity of the system and costs associated with establishing DEM. In other words, a firm is less likely to adopt if it believes that DEM operations would be complicated and costly. The opposite is also true.

Previous Use of the Internet (INTUSE)

Kim and Malhotra (2005) have identified strong links between past use of IS and the intention to use it in the future. They also report that past use positively influences future use. The implication is that a firm that used simpler Internet tools in the past is more likely to evaluate a more complicated DEM favourably. Even though this relationship is derived from the research on TAM, other research areas reveal the same association. For example, a pre-existing knowledge base was found to affect the new technology adoption (Cohen and Levinthal, 1990; Srinivasan et al., 2002).

Hypothesis 5: RELEVANCE will have a positive effect on the adoption of DEM.

Hypothesis 6: EASEOFUSE will a have positive effect on the adoption of DEM.

Hypothesis 7: INTUSE will have a positive effect on the adoption of DEM.

Size

For the purpose of this study, firm size is singled out as a separate parameter that is not fully linked to any of the aforementioned approaches. Firm size is an important factor to consider when examining the innovative behaviour of firms, particularly when the unit of the study is small and medium-sized firms. The question to consider here is which firms are more likely to exhibit innovative behaviour, large or small firms? Given that size is a proxy to a range of factors which are difficult to account for, it is hard to provide a definite answer. In the general context of innovation, both positive (Damanpour, 1992) and negative (Wade, 1996) associations between size and innovation have been identified. The same holds true for the specific context of Internet-enabled marketing, both negative (Höst et al., 2001) and positive (BarNir et al., 2003; Bengtsson et al., 2007) relationships have been reported. Overall, a weak positive relationship between innovation and size is present (Camison-Zornoza et al., 2004). In the context of the other frameworks, particularly technology acceptance, size would influence the balance of organizational- and individual-level antecedents. Finally, the size of the firm may affect the applicability of the differentiation/cost-leadership distinction.

Per se, size would be positively associated with adoption. To the extent that adopting DEM is radical innovation, one can expect that the effect of size can be eliminated if other antecedents to innovation, such as willingness to cannibalize or market pressure, are considered (Chandy and Tellis, 1998).

Hypothesis 8: Size will have a positive effect on the adoption of DEM.

METHOD AND RESULTS

Survey Description

Data for this study were collected through the sampling of Swedish manufacturing firms located in four different regions. These different types of industrial contexts represent one metropolitan area and three provincial regions in the south, north and middle parts of Sweden. A random sample of 100 firms in one of the four size groups – fewer than 20 employees, 20–49, 50–199 and more than 200 employees – was drawn. When the number of firms of a particular size group was less than 100, the questionnaire was mailed to all firms in this group. The questionnaire, together with the cover letter,[6] was mailed to a total of 1037 companies.

Table 14.1 Profile of firms in the sample

	No. of respondents	% of sample	% of adopters within each category[a]
Industry Group			
Food, beverages and tobacco	29	8.2	44
Textiles and textile products	6	1.7	60
Wood and products of wood	27	7.6	37
Pulp and paper	9	2.5	89
Publishing, printing and reproduction of recorded media	45	12.7	77
Petroleum and chemical products	46	13.0	48
Non-metallic mineral products	8	2.3	63
Basic metals and fabricated metal products	47	13.2	31
Machinery and equipment	54	15.2	44
Electrical appliances	51	14.4	62
Transportation vehicles	33	9.3	39
Total	355	100	50
Number of Employees			
< 20	86	24.2	35
20–49	115	32.4	50
50–199	111	31.3	53
> 200	43	12.1	76
Total	355	100	50

Note: [a] % of firms adopting the Internet-enabled marketing according to the procedure described in the measurement section of this chapter.

The number of questionnaires returned, after two reminders, amounted to 479 of which 355 contained no missing values or 34.5 per cent response rate. Table 14.1 summarizes the descriptive statistics of the sample. No significant differences in size group or industry affiliation were identified between responding firms and the sampling frame.

Measurement

This section first presents how the dependent variable adoption of DEM was developed, and then the independent variables and coding schemes. The scales, estimates of Cronbah's alpha, its 95 per cent confidence interval and coding schemes are summarized in Table 14.2.

Dependent variable

Four elements of DEM were identified: ordering via a firm's website, collecting feedback from customers, integrating a firm's website with the rest of their systems and collecting information about customers' on-line behaviour. Items for measuring the basic use of the Internet BASINT were: using website for firm's presentation, displaying information about products and communicating via e-mail with customers. Respondents were asked to indicate whether and to what degree they had implemented these elements. The available response categories were: 'not considered', 'considered', 'planned', 'under implementation', 'implemented', 'successfully implemented'.

At the first stage the substantive meaning of the scale categories was ignored and confirmatory factor analysis (CFA) applied to assess the convergent and discriminant validity of the DEM construct.[7] The fit of the measurement model is as follows:[8] GFI = 0.952, AGFI = 0.893, CFI = 0.941, SRMR = 0.057. The model fits the data well. To assess the discriminant validity of DEM, the 95 per cent confidence interval of the correlation between DEM and BASINT was computed. It was significantly below 1 ($r = 0.52$, $p = 0.00$), indicating that DEM and BASINT are empirically distinct from each other. For both constructs, factor loadings were large and significant ($p = 0.00$), indicating acceptable convergent validity. Both the point estimates and the lower bounds of 95 per cent confidence interval of Cronbah's alpha[9] exceeded 0.7, a value that is generally considered acceptable (Srinivasan et al., 2002; Nunnally, 1978).

The CFA results allow us to conclude that DEM is distinct from basic use of the Internet, and that all four features of DEM are likely to be at a similar stage of implementation. However, the substantive interpretation of the scale precludes us from treating it as continuous or ordinal, as different mechanisms generate these responses. A transition from 'considered' to 'planned' indicates that a firm's cost-benefit evaluation favoured DEM; a transition from 'under implementation' to 'implemented' to a large degree is a matter of time; and transition from 'implemented' to 'successfully implemented' is linked, for example, to the quality of contractors' work.

For further analysis, DEM was recoded into binary variable adopter/non-adopter. High consistency in responses indicates that all four elements of DEM are manifestations of some unobservable variable 'utility'. Once this utility exceeds some threshold value, a firm decides to adopt. Below that unobservable threshold a firm chooses to stay out. Such a line of reasoning is a context-adjusted argument for a latent variable model (for example, Long, 1997, p. 40). Therefore a firm has either not implemented DEM (non-adopter), or plans or has done so (adopter). Firms that scored less than 8 on the composite scale ADVINT were coded as non-adopters;

Table 14.2 Variables used in analysis

Measure	Items
Willingness to Cannibalize[a] (WILTC) ($\alpha = 0.77 \pm 0.035$)	1. We are ready to support Internet projects even if it will jeopardize our sales through existing channels 2. We are willing to sacrifice sales through our existing channels to implement Internet-based sales 3. We are willing to bet on new technology even if our past investments will lose value 4. We can easily change the organizational scheme to fit the needs of the Internet-based sales 5. We can easily replace one set of abilities with a different set of abilities to adopt the Internet-based sales 6. We can easily change the manner in which we carry out tasks to fit the needs of Internet-based sales.
Market Pressure[a] (PRESSURE) ($\alpha = 0.71 \pm 0.04$)	1. Our customers want to buy our products through the Internet 2. Our market is ready for e-business 3. Our closest competitor has started to use the Internet for marketing and sales 4. We are forced to use the Internet as our competitors already do so.
Management Support and Strategy Coherence[a] (MGMTSTRTGY) ($\alpha = 0.82 \pm 0.029$)	1. Management pays close attention to the Internet 2. Management supports use of the Internet 3. Use of the Internet is connected with the rest of the firm's strategy 1. We do not want to compete on price 2. Our products have high brand value[b].
Product-Market Strategy (PRODMRKT)	Recoded: answers to both questions ≤ 2 – cost leadership (CL); answers to both questions ≥ 4 – differentiation (DIFF); mixed strategy otherwise (MIXED).
Ease of Use (EASEOFUSE) ($\alpha = 0.73 \pm 0.049$)	1. T costs of establishing the Internet-based marketing are too high (R) 2. Internet-based trade is to complex (R).

Table 14.2 (continued)

Measure	Items
Relevance[a] (RELEVANCE) ($\alpha = 0.76 \pm 0.029$)	1. Our products are too complex to be sold via the Internet (R)[c] 2. Clients often want to have a presentation before purchase (R) 3. Our products are customized to individual needs of clients (R) 4. We discuss our products before purchase (R).
Basic Use of the Internet (BASINT) ($\alpha = 0.80 \pm 0.033$)	Our company uses or plans to use the Internet for the following activities ('not considered', 'considered, 'planned', 'under implementation', 'implemented', 'successfully implemented'): 1. Presentation of our company 2. Providing information about company's offerings 3. Communication with customers via e-mail.
Adoption of Advanced Internet[a] (ADVINT) ($\alpha = 0.79 \pm 0.033$)	Our company uses or plans to use the Internet for the following activities ('not considered', 'considered, 'planned', 'under implementation', 'implemented', 'successfully implemented'): 1. Receiving orders via the website 2. Getting feedback from customers 3. Our website is integrated with other systems (orders processing, logistics and so on.) 4. Collect information on how our customers use our website. Recoded: Non-Adopter: ADVINT $\leq$ 8; Adopter: ADVINT $>$ 8
Firm Size (SIZE) (micro, small, medium, large)	1. Fewer than 20 employees (MICRO) 2. Between 20 and 49 employees (SMALL) 3. Between 50 and 199 employees (MEDIUM) 4. Over 200 employees (LARGE).
Previous Use of the Internet (INTUSE)	1. Years: $<$ 1 year, 1–2, 2–3, 3–4, 4–5, $>$ 5 years.

Notes:

[a] Scales are additive with equal weights;

[b] the Swedish word 'märkesvaror' used in the survey can be translated as 'having high brand value', 'differentiated through brand';

[c] (R) item is reverse-coded.

these firms did not use the Internet for advanced purposes, and did not plan to do so in the immediate future. Firms that scored above 8 were coded as adopters. These firms had either implemented advanced Internet-based operations or were taking active steps to do so in the immediate future.

Independent variables

The innovation-based constructs WILTC, PRESSURE and MGMT-STRTGY, and technology acceptance constructs EASE of USE and RELEVANCE were measured using multiple-item Likert scale 1 – 'strongly disagree' to 5 – 'strongly agree'. The scale for WILTC was adapted from Chandy and Tellis (1998) and adjusted for the DEM adoption context; the scale for MGMSTRTGY is loosely based on Noble and Mokwa (1999). Other scales are new. Again, CFA was used to evaluate the discriminant and convergent validities of the measures. The fit of the model turned out acceptable: GFI = 0.912, AGFI = 0.879, CFI = 0.913, SRMR = 0.0625. The 95 per cent confidence interval for pairwise correlation between constructs was well below 1 ($p = 0.00$), and all factor loadings were high and significant ($p = 0.00$). Therefore conditions for convergent and discriminant validity were met. The alphas and confidence intervals for the multiple item-constructs are reported in Table 14.2. For the multiple-item measures equally weighed additive scales were developed. The independent variable INTUSE was measured by a single question, 'For how long has your organization been using the Internet?' Table 14.3 reports the range, means, standard deviations and bivariate correlations of continuous variables.

The PRODMRKT was captured by dummies. The respondents were asked to evaluate two statements on a Likert scale from 1 – strongly disagree to 5 – strongly agree: 'we do not want to compete on price' and 'our products have high brand value'. Firms that scored ≤ 2 on both questions were coded as CL, cost leadership, and firms that scored ≥ 4 were coded as DIFF, differentiation.

Finally, SIZE was captured by dummies,[10] with large firms ($\geq$ 200 employees) coded as a row of zeros.

Models and Research Hypotheses

Hypotheses presented in the theoretical framework were tested by logistic regression.[11] Table 14.4 reports estimates of coefficients (β), their significance and several measures of model fit. To simplify the interpretation, the estimated probability that a firm of a given size, average on all other characteristics and following a mixed strategy will adopt is presented at the bottom of the table. The odds ratios e^{β} are not reported because they do

Table 14.3 Correlation matrix of variables in the adoption models

	Range	Mean	S.D.	1	2	3	4	5
1. Willingness to Cannibalize (WILTC)	6–30	16.6	4.96	*0.77*				
2. Market Pressure (PRESSURE)	4–20	10.0	3.35	0.48**	*0.71*			
3. Management Support and Strategy Coherence (MGMTSTRTGY)	3–15	11.1	2.72	0.43**	0.34**	*0.82*		
4. Ease of Use (EASEOFUSE)	2–10	6.4	1.86	0.23**	0.09	0.16**	*0.73*	
5. Relevance (RELEVANCE)	4–20	14.5	3.88	0.18**	0.29**	0.12*	0.09	*0.76*
6. Previous Use of the Internet (INTUSE)	1–6	3.8	1.44	0.13*	0.07	31**	−0.08	−0.06

Note: ** – significant at $p<0.01$; * – significant at $p<0.05$; reliabilities of the measures are on the diagonal in italics.

not have any meaningful interpretation given the additive nature of the scales. Overall, five models were tested. To further corroborate the results and to avoid the problem of over-fitting, the split-sample validation was used. The estimation was repeated ten times with 20 per cent random hold-out sample (Lattin et al., 2003). The average value for the correct classification of the hold-out cases is reported in Table 14.4.

The data contained several outliers and high leverage points. To check for the robustness of the results, all the models were re-estimated with outliers removed. The signs and relative magnitudes of the coefficients did not change much, while measures of fit noticeably improved. However, no inaccuracies in data coding were found, so there was no justifiable reason for discarding these observations. The results are reported for models with outliers included.

Model 1 (M1)

M1 tests the model with pure innovation antecedents. As hypothesized, WILTC, PRESSURE and MGMTSTRTGY positively influence adoption. MGMTSTRTGY is the most influential factor. The innovation antecedents do not eliminate the effect of size, confirming the results obtained by Jeyaraj et al. (2006). With innovation-related variables

Table 14.4 Models of factors influencing adoption

Model parameters	Model 1	Model 2	Model 3	Proposed Model	Optimal Model
Constant	−4.18***[a]	0.85**	2.08***	−2.30**	−2.99***
SIZE[b]					
MICRO	−2.03***	−1.71***	−1.45***	−1.71***	−0.98***
SMALL	−1.10**	−0.90**	−0.65(*)	−0.78(*)	–
MEDIUM	−0.89**	−0.85**	−0.76(*)	−0.81(*)	–
WILTC	0.07**	–	–	0.05*	0.06*
PRESSURE	0.11***	–	–	0.10**	0.09**
MGMTSTRTGY	0.27***	–	–	0.20***	0.19***
PRODMRKT[c]					
DIFF	–	0.47**	–	0.30(*)	0.44*
CL	–	−0.47(*)	–	−0.62(*)	–
EASE OF USE	–	–	0.20***	0.15**	0.16**
RELEVANCE	–	–	0.11***	0.90**	0.09***
INTUSE	–	–	0.44***	0.34***	0.35***
−2 Log Likelihood	401.50	469.33	406.48	359.84	389.37
Accuracy. %[d]	70.6	60.8	69.5	75.1	72.5
Pseudo-R^2	0.33	0.11	0.26	0.38	0.35
Pr(Adopt|SIZE)[e]					
Micro	0.27	0.29	0.34	0.29	0.25
Small	0.49	0.48	0.53	0.51	0.51
Medium	0.54	0.49	0.50	0.51	0.51
Large	0.74	0.70	0.68	0.70	0.51

Notes:
a *** significant at $p<0.01$; ** $p<0.05$; * $p<0.1$; (*) $p>0.1$;
b large firms are coded as a row of zeros – reference group;
c mixed strategy is coded as row of zeros – reference group;
d average value of classification accuracy for a 20 per cent hold-out sample over ten iterations; maximum chance criterion $C_{max} = 50.5\%$;
e probability that a firm average on all characteristics (variables fixed at means) and mixed product-market strategy will adopt DEM.

entered, the fit of the model improves considerably to 70.6 per cent hit ratio.

Model 2 (M2)

M2 is the application of product-market strategy and size, similar to a study by BarNir et al. (2003). Size of the firm still matters, however, an indication of the non-linearity is present: small firms are more likely to adopt than micro and medium firms. CL is insignificant, while pursuing a DIFF strategy exerts a positive influence on the probability to adopt. The fit of the model is worse than that of M1.

Model 3 (M3)
M3 is an application of TAM variables – RELEVANCE, EASEOFUSE and INTUSE. All variables are significant and are positively related to adoption. The fit is comparable to M1. However with these variables entered the effect of size shrinks to insignificance for all firms except the smallest ones with less than 20 employees. Furthermore, the gap in probability of adoption between big and micro firms is much smaller than in M1 and M2.

Proposed Model (PM)
PM includes all the variables considered. Contrary to expectations, SIZE effect does not disappear completely. Small and medium firms are not different from large firms, but micro firms still have lower chances of adopting. Product-market strategy also turns out insignificant. All other coefficients confirm the hypothesized relationships.

Optimal Model (OM)
OM is an optimal based on log-likelihood statistics. It is identical to PM, with insignificant variables excluded. As in previous models, SIZE does not have an effect except for micro firms with less than 20 employees; all other variables confirm the hypothesized relationships. To assess the relative contribution of each variable to DEM adoption, the probabilities of adoption at minimum and maximum value of each variable are presented in Table 14.5.[12] The most influential predictor of DEM adoption is management support. With no support from the top management (at minimum) the estimated probability of DEM adoption is 0.17; with full support (at maximum), the probability goes up to 0.70. Thus, for an average firm in the sample, increasing top management support from the lowest to the highest values can translates to 0.53 increase in the likelihood of adoption (range of estimated probability). The second and third most influential factors are previous experience with the Internet and perceived relevance.

DISCUSSION AND CONCLUSIONS

It was suggested at the beginning of this chapter that DEM can be approached from three different perspectives: innovation adoption, technology acceptance and strategic choice. Depending on the perspective, a

Table 14.5 Probabilities of DEM adoption over the range of each independent variable for the optimal model

Variable	At Maximum	At Minimum	Range of Estimated Probability
MICRO	0.28	0.51	0.23
DIFF	0.62	0.51	0.11
INTUSE	0.69	0.28	0.41
WILTC	0.70	0.35	0.35
MGMTSTRTGY	0.70	0.17	0.53
PRESSURE	0.72	0.37	0.35
EASE OF USE	0.68	0.37	0.31
RELEVANCE	0.74	0.38	0.36

separate set of antecedents to DEM adoption was identified and tested. Then, the integrative model (OM) was suggested. The first notable finding that falls out of the models is that DEM indeed has the features of innovation, general IS and a controllable marketing tool. Intermediate models one to three that enter the predictors from each area separately, produce a statistically significant increase in predictive accuracy.

Innovation-derived antecedents in M1 – management support, market pressure, willingness to cannibalize and firm size – produced results similar to what was reported in the extant literature. Management support and market pressure came out as top predictors, in line with results of meta-analytic study of determinants of IT adoption by organizations (Jeyaraj et al., 2006). The innovation-based model also shows a strong association between size and the likelihood of DEM adoption; bigger firms have a significantly higher probability to become adopters compared to smaller firms. Such results are in line with the results of the meta-analytic study by Camison-Zornoza et al. (2004), who identified a weak positive association between the size of the firm and innovation. However, the fact that management support, market pressure and willingness to cannibalize do not fully moderate the effect of size deserves further elaboration. For example, the original study by Chandy and Tellis (1998) showed that the attitudinal variable, willingness to cannibalize, fully moderates the effect of size in the context of radical product innovation; that is, this variable by itself is sufficient to explain the observed differences among firms in introducing radically new products. Even though our study focused on innovation adoption rather than generation, and on smaller manufacturing firms rather than strategic business units (SBUs) of larger corporations, such divergence in results suggests that adoption of DEM cannot be fully accounted for by the identified innovation antecedents alone.

Treating DEM as a marketing tool that should be aligned with either a strategy of differentiation or cost leadership also produced several notable results. The results suggest that firms pursuing the strategy of differentiation – selling differentiated products and charging price premium – are more likely to become adopters of DEM compared to firms that pursue mixed or cost leadership strategies. These results are contrary to the findings of BarNir et al. (2003), who have found that digitization of marketing and sales was negatively related to both efficiency and innovation orientations. This divergence of results may stem from the industry – magazine publishing in BarNir et al. (2003) as opposed to our multi-industry sample of manufacturing firms.

A separate application of constructs derived from the Technology Acceptance Model – perceived relevance, perceived ease of use and previous use of the Internet – showed that all these factors are positively associated with the adoption of DEM; moreover, with the exception of the smallest firms, these factors moderate the effect of firm size. Thus adoption of DEM by firms with more than 20 employees is fully captured by the three TAM variables. If a firm perceives DEM is irrelevant to its products, considers DEM costly and complicated, and has limited previous experience with the Internet, it is less likely to adopt it; the opposite is also true. These results shed some light on the relationship between the age of the firm and IT adoption. BarNir et al. (2003) concluded that established firms digitize business activities to a greater extent than newer firms. The present findings suggest it is not the age per se that is important, but rather the length of previous experience with simpler or related Internet tools. The results of the TAM application provide strong support to the proposition that the decision to adopt DEM has a strong cost-benefit component.

The Optimal Model of DEM adoption includes predictors from all the three approaches. Top management support, previous use of the Internet and perceived relevance are the three top predictors that differentiate adopters from non-adopters of DEM. The measurement model suggests that all the factors considered in this study are empirically distinct. Thus there might be situations where DEM is perceived as relevant and easy to use, and yet the top management does not support the use of the Internet for marketing and sales; the opposite is also true.

One of the objectives of this chapter was to examine the effect of size on DEM adoption. Overall, size has a non-negative, that is, positive or zero, effect on adoption. Per se, size is a significant predictor of adoption, and the direction of the relationship is one way: the bigger, the more likely to adopt. When other control variables enter the equation, the effect of size reduces to no effect except for the smallest firms. Also, when TAM-based predictors are considered, firm size can no longer be viewed as one of top three organizational-level predictors, a result that is contrary to what was reported by Jeyaraj et al. (2006).

The results of this study suggest that individual level adoption models might be better suited for describing DEM adoption in the smallest firms than organization level ones. Such a suggestion fits well with the findings from the entrepreneurship and small-business management literature on the high importance of individual decision-makers. An alternative explanation is that financial capabilities of small firms do not allow them to incur high initial and customer acquisition costs pertinent to DEM (Sharma and Tzokas, 2002).

A general methodological implication emerged from the work on this study. In the studies of IT implementation and digitization it is common to use multiple-item five to ten-point Likert scales to assess the intensity of use of a particular application or tool. Provided that these measures exhibit sufficient convergent or discriminant validity, it is also common to create an additive scale and to treat it as a continuous variable. However, high values of scale reliability may simply indicate that features of the measured construct are at the same stage of implementation, but transition between these stages can be affected by different factors or correspond to significant shifts in underlying processes. To counter this potentially adverse effect, it may be helpful to split the scale in two or more artificial groups, such as adopter/non-adopter, low intensity/high intensity and the like. If the scale is indeed continuous, doing so should not affect the signs and relative significance of the coefficients. The validity of the findings may be further increased by assigning specific interpretation to each point on the scale (similar to the approach used here).

Limitations and Suggestions for Further Research

This study has a number of limitations that need to be addressed. A somewhat simplistic adopter/non-adopter split may obscure many of the subtle distinctions in how various firms implement and use e-business tools. Furthermore, firm size is only an imperfect proxy for a firm's organizational and financial parameters. Additional factors, such as innovativeness, type of products, industry affiliation, centralization, available resources and position in the supply chain should be included in the forthcoming studies model. Operationalization of the product-market strategy employed here omits the focused strategy option, which can be particularly relevant to small firms. Future studies should include more sophisticated measures of the scope of a product-market strategy.

Even though there is no reason to suspect that the country effect may have biased the results, it still may affect the findings. The results presented here are cross-sectional in nature and all the limitations of cross-sectional studies apply. More research effort should be put into conducting longitudinal studies which would allow for the examination of causality, post-adoption phenomena and performance outcomes. Finally, while not within scope of this study, there is no doubt that in-depth interviews and case studies would assist in gaining deeper understanding of the adoption and continued use of the Internet for marketing and sales.

Conclusions

This study aimed to individually assess and integrate several approaches that can explain the adoption of digitally enabled marketing by smaller manufacturing firms: adoption of innovation, technology acceptance and product-market strategy. The construct of DEM was defined, and shown to be conceptually and empirically distinct from basic Internet use. The results of the study suggest that the decision to adopt DEM cannot be fully accounted for by any single approach, and the integration of factors from the three approaches improves the predictive accuracy of the explanatory model. Top management support, previous use of the Internet and perceived relevance are the three top predictors that differentiate adopters from non-adopters of DEM. The effect of firm size is insignificant in the proposed model, except for firms with less than 20 employees.

ACKNOWLEDGEMENTS

The author would like to thank Professors Maria Bengtsson and Håkan Boter for their help in developing this chapter, and an anonymous reviewer for the excellent suggestions on how to improve the manuscript.

NOTES

1. To the best of the author's knowledge, there are no studies that directly assess the empirical distinctiveness of the construct. Many of the earlier studies used mixed measures (for example, Walczuch et al., 2000; Höst et al., 2001). Given the rapid progress in digitization, however, the validity of these measurements can be limited.
2. According to Jeyaraj et al. (2006), size is the third best predictor of IT adoption by organizations. Because of the general complexity of the size factor, it is discussed separately at the end of this section.
3. The role of resellers in the adoption process in further examined in Vanyushyn (2008).

4. Detailed discussion of the relative merits of structure-conduct-performance, resource-based and contingency paradigms is beyond the scope of this chapter.
5. As of August 2007.
6. The cover letter emphasized that a respondent should be closely involved with the marketing activities of the firm. If the firm did not employ a marketing manager, the questionnaire was to be filled in by the top manager or manager/owner of the firm.
7. Reflexive specification explicitly underlies this line of reasoning, as opposed to formative; therefore assessments of reliability and validity are applicable (for example, Steenkamp and van Trijp, 1991). Such specification also has intuitive appeal: to sell its products on-line, a firm is likely to implement a full range of tools necessary to achieve that objective; moreover, one can expect all tools to be at approximately the same level of implementation.
8. While there are no strict cut-off values for the CFA fit statistics, the following values are considered acceptable: Goodness-of-fit index, $GFI \geq 0.90$, GFI adjusted for degrees of freedom, $AGFI \geq 0.80$, comparative fit index $CFI \geq 0.90$ and standardized root mean square residual $SRMR \leq 0.08$ (Hu and Bentler, 1999; Lattin et al., 2003). χ^2 results are not reported because of the sensitivity to sample size.
9. The 95 per cent confidence interval equals $\hat{\alpha} \pm (1.96)(\sqrt{Q/n})$, where $\hat{\alpha}$ is ML estimate of α, n is sample size and Q is variance of $\sqrt{n}(\alpha - \hat{\alpha})$ as $n \to \infty$, given by van Zyl et al. (2000). See Duhachek et al. (2005) for further details. The author is grateful to Professor Duhachek for making the programming code available.
10. Firm size was measured in brackets in the survey instrument. While doing so results in a certain loss of information, using dummies acknowledges the multi-dimensional nature of the size factor that cannot be fully captured by a single continuous variable, for example, number of employees (Bengtsson et al., 2007). Furthermore, it has been shown that the results may be affected by whether the size is measured as number of employees vs log number of employees (Camison-Zornoza et al., 2004).
11. The models were tested with 8 industry dummies, as out of 12 groups, 3 contained too few observations. The dummies were not significant except for the industry 'publishing, printing and reproduction of recorded media'. Because of their low explanatory power, relatively small sample size and collinearity problems these dummies were omitted from the final analysis. Table 14.1 reports the percentage of adopters, as defined in the methods section, in each industry group.
12. Other variable fixed at sample means (see Table 14.3), DIFF = 0, MICRO = 0.

REFERENCES

Abrahamson, E. and L. Rosenkompf (1993), 'Institutional and competitive bandwagons: using mathematical modeling as a tool to explore innovation diffusion', *Academy of Management Review*, **18**(3), 487–517.

BarNir, A., J.M. Gallaugher and P. Auger (2003), 'Business process digitization, strategy, and the impact of firm age and size: the case of the management publishing industry', *Journal of Business Venturing*, **18**(6), 789–814.

Bengtsson, M., H. Boter and V. Vanyushyn (2007), 'Integrating the internet into marketing operations: a study of antecedents in firms of different size', *International Small Business Journal*, **25**(1), 27–48.

Brynjolfsson, E. and M.D. Smith (2000), 'Frictionless commerce? A comparison of internet and conventional retailers', *Management Science*, **46**(4), 563–85.

Camison-Zornoza, C., R. Lapiedra-Alcami, M. Segarra-Cipres and M. Boronat-Navarro (2004), 'A meta-analysis of innovation and organizational size', *Organization Studies*, **25**(3), 331–61.

Chandler, A.D. (1962), *Strategy and Structure: Chapters in the History of Industrial Enterprise*, Cambridge, MA: MIT Press.

Chandy, R.K. and G.J. Tellis (1998), 'Organizing for radical product innovation: the overlooked role of willingness to cannibalize', *Journal of Marketing Research*, **35**(4), 474–87.

Cohen, W.D. and D.A. Levinthal (1990), 'Absorptive capacity: a new perspective on learning and innovation', *Administrative Science Quarterly*, **35**(1), 128–52.

Damanpour, F. (1991), 'Organizational innovation: a meta-analysis of effects of determinants and moderators', *Academy of Management Journal*, **34**(3), 555–90.

Damanpour, F. (1992), 'Organizational size and innovation', *Organization Studies*, **13**(3), 375–402.

Davis, F.D. (1989), 'Perceived usefulness, perceived ease of use, and user acceptance of information technology', *MIS Quarterly*, **13**(3), 319–41.

Deleersnyder, B., I. Geyskens, K. Gielens and M.G. Dekimpe (2002), 'How cannibalistic is the internet channel?: A study of the newspaper industry in the United Kingdom and the Netherlands', *International Journal of Research in Marketing*, **19**(4), 337–48.

Duhachek, A., A.T. Coughlan and D. Iacobucci (2005), 'Results of the standard error of the coefficient alpha index of reliability', *Marketing Science*, **24**(2), 294–301.

Economist Intelligence Unit (2005), 'The 2005 e-readiness rankings', available at http://graphics.eiu.com/files/ad_pdfs/2005Ereadiness_Ranking_WP.pdf (accessed 18 March 2008).

Ettlie, J.E., W.P. Bridges and R.D. O'Keefe (1984), 'Organization strategy and structural differences for radical versus incremental innovation', *Management Science*, **30**(6), 682–95.

Eyuboglu, N. and S. Kabadayi (2005), 'Dealer-manufacturer alienation in multiple channel system: the moderating effect of structural variables', *Journal of Marketing Channels*, **12**(3), 5–27.

Fillis, I. and B. Wagner (2005), 'E-business development: an exploratory investigation of the small firm', *International Small Business Journal*, **23**(6), 604–34.

Fishbein, M. and I. Ajzen (1975), *Belief, Attitude, Intention and Behavior: An Introduction to Theory and Research*, Reading, MA: Addison-Wesley.

Ghosh, S. (1998), 'Making business sense of the internet', *Harvard Business Review*, **76** (March/April), 126–35.

Haynes, P.J., R.C. Becherer and M.M. Helms (1998), 'Small and mid-sized businesses and internet use: unrealized potential?', *Internet Research: Electronic Networking Applications and Policy*, **8**(3), 229–35.

Höst, V., N.P. Mols and J.F. Nielsen (2001), 'The adoption of internet-based marketing channels', *Homo Oeconomicus*, **17**(4), 463–88.

Houghton, K.A. and H. Winklhofer (2004), 'The effect of website and e-commerce adoption on the relationship between SMEs and their export intermediaries', *International Small Business Journal*, **22**(4), 369–88.

Hu, L. and M. Bentler (1999), 'Cutoff criteria for fit indexes in covariance structure analysis: conventional criteria versus new alternatives', *Structural Equation Modelling*, **6**(1), 1–55.

Jaworski, B.J. and A.K. Kohli (1993), 'Market orientation: antecedents and consequences', *Journal of Marketing*, **57**(3), 53–71.

Jeyaraj, A., J.W. Rottman and M.C. Lacity (2006), 'A review of the predictors, linkages, and biases in IT innovation adoption research', *Journal of Information Technology*, **21**(1), 1–23.

Johnson, D.S. and S. Bharadwaj (2005), 'Digitization of selling activity and sales force performance: an empirical investigation', *Journal of the Academy of Marketing Science*, **33**(1), 3–18.
Kim, S.S. and N.K. Malhotra (2005), 'A longitudinal model of IS use: an integrative view of four mechanisms underlying postadoption phenomena', *Management Science*, **51**(5), 741–55.
Kotler, P. (2000), *Marketing Management* (10th edn), London: Prentice-Hall.
Lattin, J., D.J. Carrol and P.E. Green (2003), *Analyzing Multivariate Data*, Pacific Grove, CA: Brooks/Cole-Thomson Learning.
Long, S.J. (1997), Regression Models for Categorical and Limited Dependent Variables, Advanced quantitative techniques series, no. 7, Thousand Oaks, CA: Sage.
McFarland, D.J. and D. Hamilton (2006), 'Adding contextual specificity to the technology acceptance model', *Computers in Human Behavior*, **22**(3), 427–47.
Noble, C.H. and M.P. Mokwa (1999), 'Implementing marketing strategies: developing and testing a managerial theory', *Journal of Marketing*, **63**(4), 57–73.
Nunnally, J.C. (1978), *Psychometric Theory* (2nd edn), New York: McGraw-Hill.
Poon, S. and C. Jevons (1997), 'Internet-enabled international marketing: a small business network perspective', *Journal of Marketing Management*, **13**(1–3), 29–41.
Porter, M. (1980), *Competitive Strategy*, New York: Free Press.
Porter, M. (1996), 'What is strategy?', *Harvard Business Review*, **74** (Nov/Dec), 61–78.
Porter, M. (2001), 'Strategy and the internet', *Harvard Business Review*, **79** (May/June), 62–79.
Schumpeter, J.A. (1942), *Capitalism, Socialism and Democracy*, New York: Harper & Brothers.
Sharma, A. and N. Tzokas (2002), 'Personal selling and sales management in the internet environment: lessons learned', *Journal of Marketing Management*, **18**(3/4), 249–58.
Sheppard, B.H., J. Hartwick and P.R. Warshaw (1988), 'The theory of reasoned action: a meta-analysis of past research with recommendations for modifications and future research', *Journal of Consumer Research*, **15**(3), 325–43.
Srinivasan, R., G.L. Lilien and A. Rangaswamy (2002), 'Technological opportunism and radical technology adoption: an application to e-business', *Journal of Marketing*, **66**(3), 47–60.
Steenkamp, J. and H. van Trijp (1991), 'The use of LISREL in validating marketing constructs', *International Journal of Research in Marketing*, **8**, 283–99.
Sultan, F. and A. Rohm (2004), 'The evolving role of the internet in marketing strategy: an exploratory study', *Journal of Interactive Marketing*, **18**(2), 6–19.
Taylor, S. and P.A. Todd (1995), 'Understanding information technology usage: a test of competing models', *Information Systems Research*, **6**(2), 144–76.
Tushman, M.L. and P. Anderson (1986), 'Technological discontinuities and organizational environments', *Administrative Science Quarterly*, **31**(3), 439–66.
van Zyl, J.J., N. Martin, D. Heinz and G. Nel (2000), 'On the distribution of the maximum likelihood estimator of Cronbach's alpha', *Psychometrika*, **65**(3), 271–80.
Vanyushyn, V. (2008), 'The dual effect of resellers on electronic business adoption by SMEs', *The International Journal of Entrepreneurship and Innovation*, **9**(1), 43–9.
Venkatesh, V. and F.D. Davis (2000), 'A theoretical extension of the technology acceptance model: four longitudinal studies', *Management Science*, **46**(2), 186–204.

Wade, J. (1996), 'A communication-level analysis of sources and rates of technological variation in the microprocessors market', *Academy of Management Journal*, **39**(5), 1218–44.

Walczuch, R., G. Van Braven and H. Lundgren (2000), 'Internet adoption barriers for small firms in the Netherlands', *European Management Journal*, **18**(5), 561–72.

Wu, F., V. Mahajan and S. Balasubramanian (2003), 'An analysis of e-business adoption and its impact on business performance', *Journal of the Academy of Marketing Science*, **31**(4), 425–47.

15. Employment growth of new firms

Erik Stam, Petra Gibcus, Jennifer Telussa and Elizabeth Garnsey

INTRODUCTION

A key outcome of the entrepreneurial process is new business creation. Most new businesses employ only one or very few persons. The creation of new growing firms – a key element of Schumpeter's (1934) theory of economic development – is a relatively rare event. The few new firms that grow substantially face completely different issues during their life course than the many start-ups that remain small. These growing new firms are under pressure to act strategically, especially with respect to the expansion and renewal of their resource base (for example, via organizational learning), innovation, alliances and possibly internationalization). Strategic entrepreneurship (Hitt et al., 2001) is said to be a core issue here, especially the use of dynamic capabilities (Eisenhardt and Martin, 2000). Most studies on dynamic capabilities have focused on large, established firms, despite the flexible, dynamic nature of many small, new firms (cf. Piore and Sabel, 1984; Yu, 2001). Thus far there have been no studies tracing how dynamic capabilities relate to the growth of new firms. This chapter will analyse the association between dynamic capabilities and new firm growth, controlling for measures of firm resources, characteristics of the entrepreneur and aspects of the environment. The central research question is: How strong is the relationship between dynamic capabilities and the growth of new firms?

The chapter opens with a review of empirical studies on employment growth in new firms and then moves on to a discussion on the role of dynamic capabilities in the explanation of new firm growth. After a description of the data and variables we discuss the results and implications of this study.

REVIEW OF EMPIRICAL STUDIES ON EMPLOYMENT GROWTH OF NEW FIRMS

So far there have been no studies tracing the relationship between dynamic capabilities and the growth of new firms.[1] There have been several empirical studies that analyse the factors associated with employment growth in new firms. These studies are summarized in Table 15.1. This table does not give an exhaustive overview of all the factors that have been used in these studies, but all factors that have been examined in at least two studies are represented. An overview of the characteristics of the samples on which these studies are based is provided in the appendix. We have categorized the factors associated with growth in employee numbers in new firms into three sets. Personal level factors include human capital, social capital and ambitions of the entrepreneur; firm level factors include organizational capital and financial capital; variables related to the business environment of the firm are industry or geographical location. Table 15.1 shows that the outcomes of these studies are very scattered: hardly any study takes a similar set of factors into account, and when the same factors are taken into account sometimes contrasting outcomes are presented.

Consensus is to be found to the greatest extent regarding personal level factors. The human capital variables educational level, start-up experience, industry experience and technical experience have generally been found to have a positive relationship with growth.[2] Being a female founder or belonging to an immigrant group has a negative association with firm growth. Social capital, especially in the form of starting a firm with business partners, has a consistent positive relationship with subsequent firm growth. A positive start-up motivation to realize an idea or innovation also has a positive association. Regarding the firm level factors, two have a consistent positive association: the level of start-up capital and being incorporated. Among business environment factors, starting in retail/personal services has a negative association, while starting in manufacturing/construction has a positive relationship with new firm growth.

There is controversy on the relationship between work experience and of the initial (employment) size of the firm. As regards causal factors, work experience might provide opportunities for on the job learning, leading to valuable knowledge for managing a growing business. However, this depends on the type of activity and the type of organization in which experience has been gained. Entrepreneurs with lengthy work experience could become more cautious and conservative than entrepreneurs with shorter work experience.

Contrasting evidence has been found on the relationship between the initial employment size on subsequent firm growth. In the industrial

Table 15.1 Empirical studies on employment growth of new firms

	Factors associated with new firm growth	Cooper et al., 1994	Dahlqvist et al., 2000	Schutjens and Wever, 2000	Bosma et al., 2004	Vivarelli and Audretsch, 1998	Colombo and Grilli, 2005	Almus and Nerlinger, 1999	Brüder and Preisendörfer, 1998	Chrisman et al., 2005
Human capital	Education level	+		0	0		+		0	0
	Immigrant	–	–						0	
	Self-employed parents	0				0				
	Management experience	0		0		+	0		0	
	Unemployment		0			0				
	Self-employment/ start-up experience		+		0		+		0	+
	(Long) work experience			–	+				–	
	Industry experience			0	+		+		0	
	Technical experience						+	+		
	Male founder	+	+		+				+	
	Age entrepreneur			0	0		+			0
Social capital	Entrepreneurial networks				+				0	
	Emotional support from spouse				0				0	
	Business partners	+		+			+	0	0	
Ambitions	Start-up motivation: market need/niche		0			0				

	Start-up motivation: realize idea/ innovation		0			+	+			
	Goal: sales growth			0						
	Goal: employment growth				+					
	Start-up motive: higher income/profit				0	+				
Financial capital	Start-up capital	+		0			+		+	
Organizational capital	Incorporation		+	0				+	+	
	Start-up size: sales			+						
	Start-up size: employees			+				−	0	
	Start-up size: number of hours worked				+					
	Start-up of take over								−	
Environment	Industry: retail or personal services	−	−	0					0	0
	Industry: manufacturing/ construction			+		+			0	+/0
	Industry: high-tech manufacturing							+		
	Industry: business services			+	0	0			0	0
	Metropolitan/urban location		0/+	0				0		

economic literature it is a stylized fact that young and small firms grow relatively fast, because they have to achieve the minimum efficient size (MES) in their industry (Mansfield, 1962; Audretsch et al., 2004). Initial size has been found to have a negative association with firm growth in these studies (Audretsch et al., 1999; Lotti et al., 2001). Smaller start-ups have a higher need to grow (Davidsson, 1991). On the other hand, relatively large start-ups have more resources at hand to realize growth and are more likely to attract financial capital and human resources, which enables them to grow more rapidly than small start-ups (cf. Westhead and Cowling, 1995). These large start-ups may also be more ambitious regarding future growth. This effect can be traced by controlling for growth ambitions.

The review of empirical studies on employment growth of new firms has shown that the relationship between dynamic capabilities and the growth of new firms has not yet been taken into account. Only measures of start-up motivation to realize an innovation might indicate the emergence of a dynamic capability, and two of the three studies that took this variable into account found a positive relationship with new firm growth. In the next section we will discuss the relevance of dynamic capabilities for new firm growth.

DYNAMIC CAPABILITIES AND NEW FIRM GROWTH

Entrepreneurship results in the creation of new firms. Growing a firm to a substantial size involves strategic activities that have been termed strategic entrepreneurship (Hitt et al., 2001). It is necessary for entrepreneurs to create and adapt the resource base of the new firm. New firms often face resource base weaknesses (Garnsey, 1998; West and DeCastro, 2001) and are confronted with subsequent performance shortfalls if these weaknesses are not dealt with. As such, new firms must demonstrate dynamic capabilities to reconfigure the resource base as needed (Teece et al., 1997; Eisenhardt and Martin, 2000). Dynamic capabilities are the organizational and strategic routines by which firms achieve new resource combinations (Eisenhardt and Martin, 2000). They include specific and identifiable processes, such as R&D, inter-firm alliancing, new product development and exporting. With knowledge creation routines (also known as R&D) new knowledge is built within the firm of particular strategic relevance in high-tech industries. Alliancing routines bring new resources into the firm from external sources, also often essential in high-tech industries (Powell et al., 1996; Baum et al., 2001; Tapon et al., 2001). With new product development routines the varied skills and backgrounds of firm members are combined to create revenue producing goods and services. Strategic decision making, for example, regarding the entrance into new (international) markets is also a dynamic capability in which firm members pool their various business, functional and personal expertise to make the choices that shape the major strategic moves of the firm.

Thus entrepreneurs can create and adapt the resource base of the new firm with R&D activities, developing new products, introducing products to foreign markets and alliancing with other firms (Eisenhardt and Martin, 2000). These dynamic capabilities are central elements of strategic entrepreneurship. If an entrepreneur is able to build these dynamic capabilities early on in the life course of the firm, this will increase the likelihood of sustained growth of the new firm. Only few new firms are likely to build dynamic capabilities and these capabilities are not valuable in every context. There may be certain preconditions for the proper functioning or need for dynamic capabilities. On the personal level, the knowledge base of the entrepreneur might enable the effective use of dynamic capabilities. On the organizational level, a munificent resource base would provide the means to create and use dynamic capabilities effectively. The presence of multiple firm members may be a prerequisite for the existence of (dynamic) capabilities (Felin and Foss, 2006). As regards business context, theorists have argued that dynamic capabilities are especially valuable in (technologically) dynamic environments (Teece et al., 1997; Eisenhardt and Martin, 2000). In stable environments the build up of dynamic capabilities might have too high opportunity costs: investing in efficiency improvements might be much more valuable.

We hypothesize that new firms with dynamic capabilities are more likely to grow but that human capital, firm resources and environmental dynamism enhance/moderate the relationship between dynamic capabilities and firm growth. In line with the above explanation of new firm growth in terms of dynamic capabilities, the first hypotheses can be stated as:

Hypothesis 1: New firms with dynamic capabilities are more likely to grow.

Hypothesis 2: The level of human capital of the entrepreneur will moderate the relationship between dynamic capabilities and growth.

Hypothesis 3: The level of firm resources will moderate the relationship between dynamic capabilities and the likelihood of growth.

Hypothesis 4: The relationship between dynamic capabilities and the likelihood of growth is contingent on environmental dynamism.

The hypothesized effects and the relationships identified in the review of empirical studies are summarized in Figure 15.1.

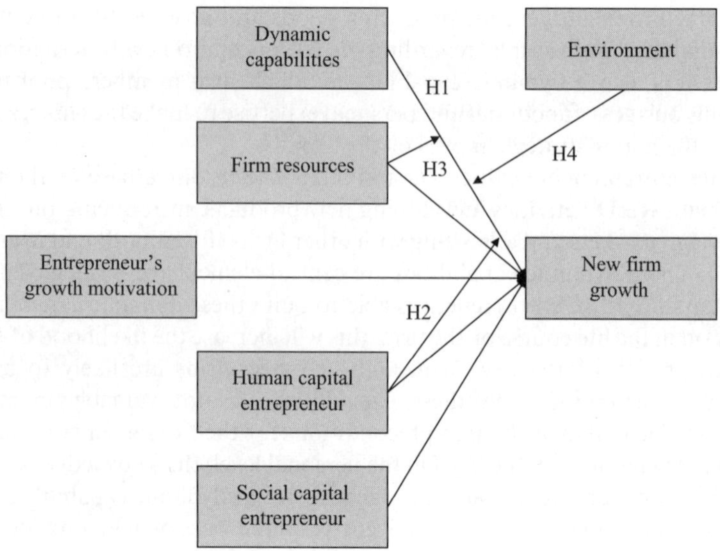

Figure 15.1 Determinants of employment growth of new firms

This dynamic capabilities perspective gives us more insight into the role of 'innovation' in new firm growth. Although it is often assumed that innovation is a necessary or even sufficient condition for new firm growth, the empirical evidence is mixed (cf. Brusoni et al., 2006; Winters and Stam, 2007). Innovation has many different faces (that is, indicators in empirical research[3]), and is not always successful, which explains the lack of empirical support for the effect of innovation on new firm growth.

Although those who conduct enquiries of the kind summarized in Table 15.1 are aware that statistical associations do not prove causal relationships, there is common use of the statistical terms 'determinants and effects' with reference to factors associated with firm growth, which can be confusing for policy makers less familiar with the conventions of regression analysis. We believe that new firms are complex adaptive systems in which complex feedback effects and path dependence are at work (Fuller and Moran, 2001; Garnsey et al., 2006). Causal factors are interactive and involve feedback which is difficult to capture through associations between discrete variables. However the extent of variance in growth performance remaining unexplained in statistical correlation studies is commonly attributed to stochastic factors (Davidsson, 2004; Geroski, 2005) and to methodological weaknesses (Woo et al., 1994). It is therefore illuminating to identify the strength of statistical relationships in a study that addresses methodological weaknesses. Our study does so by using a systematic cohort analysis covering the same business cycle for firms in diverse industries but in the same national economy. This allows for the influence of the business cycle and the national system of innovation on new firm growth. Any relationships revealed in a systematic cohort study between factors associated with new firm growth and actual growth performance outcomes can be assumed to be robust and to provide a guide to further enquiry.

DATA

The data used for this study are based on the 'start-up panel: cohort 1994'. This panel has been set up by EIM Business and Policy Research (EIM). The start-up panel and the sample characteristics are described in what follows.

Start-up Panel

The population in this panel consists of firms in the Netherlands that started their business in 1994. These firms were registered as independent start-ups in 1994. Approximately 12 000 firms have been approached of which almost 2000 start-ups agreed to participate in the panel in 1994. These firms have been followed since 1994. From 1994–99 the participants received a questionnaire by mail, while in the period of 2000–04 the participants were approached through computer assisted telephone interviewing (CATI). In 2000 previous participants were traced and approached. The number of participants therefore increases from 1999 to 2000. Throughout the years only 23 per cent of the initial participants remained in the panel. Some participants refused to participate in the panel in later years, ceased economic activities, went bankrupt or moved and could not be traced. In the end, 435 firms remained in the study from start-up over the decade. Just like in other studies (Baron et al., 1996; Certo et al., 2001), we have taken the age of ten years as a boundary for new firms.

The firms in the start-up panel were interviewed on such subjects as the characteristics of the firm and entrepreneur, finance, bottlenecks, strategy and goals, market and environment, and realizations versus expectations. The main themes have largely remained the same over the years. Therefore the dataset not only contains information about the initial founding conditions, but also information over the life course of the firm.

It must be noted that our study may suffer from survival bias: only the firms that survived during the ten years (over the 1994–2004 period) were included in our research sample.

Sample Characteristics

Of the 435 respondents that were still in the panel in 2004, 354 firms for which the complete growth paths could be identified are analysed here. The entrepreneurs in the sample are most often male (72 per cent) and are often highly educated (71 per cent has a bachelor or master degree). The age of the entrepreneurs in the start-up panel ranges from 19 to 61 years in 1994. The average age in 1994 was 38 years.

The distribution of the firms across industries is as follows: manufacturing (10 per cent), construction (10 per cent), retail and repairs (19 per cent), wholesale (14 per cent), catering (4 per cent), transport and communication (4 per cent), business services (26 per cent) and other services (13 per cent) (Bangma, 2007). The industrial distribution of start-ups in the Netherlands in 1994 in the sectors construction, transport and communication is similar to that in the panel. Furthermore, the industrial distribution shows that the sectors manufacturing (NL: 6 per cent), and retail and repairs (NL: 16 per cent) are slightly overrepresented in the panel. The sectors catering (NL: 6 per cent), business services (NL: 28 per cent) and wholesale (NL: 19 per cent) are slightly underrepresented in the panel.

On average, the firms in the panel employed 3.8 persons in 2004. The average employment creation of a start-up in 1994 was 1.7 persons (Bangma, 2007). The Dutch definition of SMEs includes all firms with less than 100 employees. None of the firms in the panel has grown so rapidly since 1994 that it has become a large firm. In fact 63 per cent of the firms in the panel did not have any employees next to the business owner at all in 2004.

VARIABLES

The independent variables of this study were measured in the first survey in 1994, which covered the first year of the new firms' existence. The dependent – employment growth – variables were measured over the period 1994 to 2004. This time lag between independent and dependent variables enables us to make inferences about the (temporal) causality of the mechanisms tested.

Dependent Variables

Growth

Growth of firms can be measured in terms of inputs (for example, employees), value (for example, assets) or outputs (for example, profits). Here growth is measured in terms of the number of employees, the indicator most comparable with that used in other empirical studies on new firm growth, and provides an indicator of firm assets since human resources are among the most important assets of a new firm. Changes in employee size are a conservative measure for investigating the instability of growth, in comparison to more rapidly changing figures such as sales or capital valuation. Not all firms follow a similar growth path when they grow. Four types of growth paths are explored; continuous growth, growth setbacks (a decline in firm size), early growth and/or plateau and delayed growth (cf. Garnsey et al., 2006).

The growth paths of the 354 firms that survived the first ten years of existence are shown in the pictograms in Figure 15.2.[4] Only one firm has grown continuously over the ten year period. By far the largest group of firms (68.6 per cent) has never grown during the period studied. A substantial group of firms (16.7 per cent) has faced a setback during their life

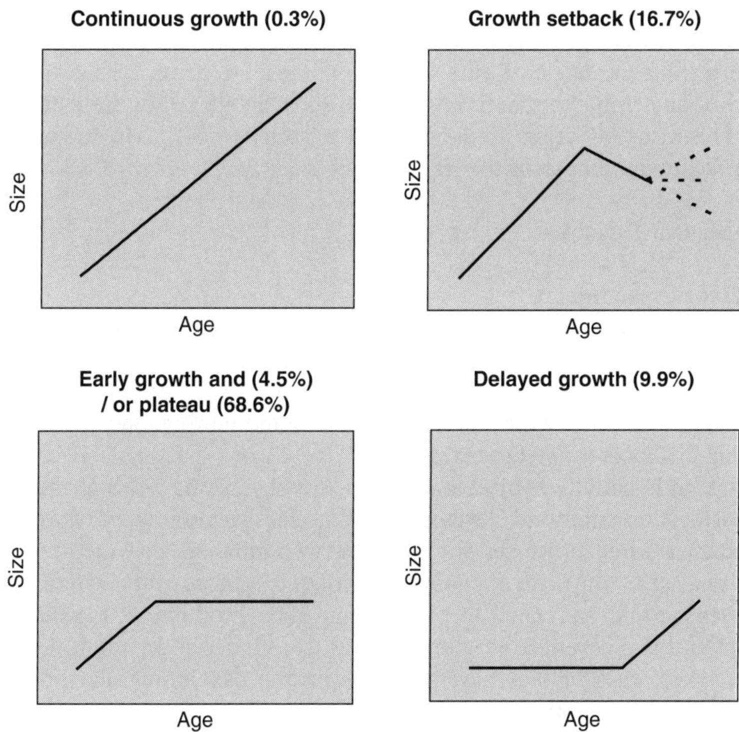

Figure 15.2 Growth paths of new firms

course, while 4.5 per cent of the firms have seen their growth stagnating. Almost 10 per cent of the firms only started to grow some years after start-up.[5]

In order to execute reliable regression analyses a distinction is made between the new firms that grew at least one time period (31.4 per cent) and the majority (68.6 per cent) that did not grow at all during the first ten years of existence. A dichotomous variable was created with a value of one if the firm has grown one or more time periods and value of zero if there was no growth within the first ten years of existence.

A threshold of ten employees is taken to show that a multi-person firm has been created. By our measure of growth this level had to be reached at least once within the first ten years of existence. This measure is somewhat more strict than the first measure of growth (only 12 per cent of the firms reached this threshold once during their early life course), giving a better indication of the creation of a substantial firm. A similar threshold of ten employees has been used in other studies, such as Baron et al. (1996). Most firms never cross this threshold; more than 93 per cent of the firms in the European business population have less than ten employees (Aldrich, 1999). In our sample only 41 firms had reached the ten employee threshold once during the ten post-entry years. Of these 41 firms, 23 had started without any employees, and only six had started with ten or more employees. This measure is thus an indicator of growth in most cases, and not just an indicator of a large initial size.

Independent Variables

Dynamic capabilities

To measure dynamic capabilities, four variables were used to capture the types of processes that have been labelled as dynamic capabilities in the literature (see Eisenhardt and Martin, 2000). These four variables are: R&D activities, alliancing with other firms, developing new products and introducing products to foreign markets.

The R&D activities variable was measured by asking whether the firms performed research and development activities in order to develop new products and/or processes for their firm. Alliancing was measured by asking whether the firms collaborated with one or more other firms in some way (this could be related to purchasing, sales, production, logistics and R&D; but is different from 'pure' market transactions). In addition, firms were asked whether they have been involved in developing new products and in exporting in the prior year.

Different firm resources can be distinguished: financial capital and organizational capital.

1. Financial capital. Financial capital is measured by the amount of start-up capital.
2. Organizational capital. Two indicators of organizational capital have been used: whether the firm has been established through takeover and the start-up size of the firm in 1994 in terms of the number of employees.

Two types of capital on the person level are distinguished: social capital and human capital.

1. Social capital. Social capital is measured by the following variables: entrepreneurial family/friends, entrepreneurs that have contact with other entrepreneurs in their social network (entrepreneurial networks) and the number of business partners (entrepreneurial team).
2. Human capital. Knowledge and experience of the entrepreneur is measured by general and more specific human capital indicators. The general human capital indicator that has been used is the educational level of the entrepreneur. The more specific human capital indicator experience has been taken up in analyses on different fields: experience as a business-owner (prior to the current firm), leadership experience, human resource management experience, experience with financial management, technical experience (in current profession) and industry experience.

Environmental dynamism

Four indicators of environmental dynamism have been taken into account: dynamic industry, rapid technological change, technology-based firm and urban environment. The variable dynamic industry has been composed by adding up the annual number of entries and exits per industry in 1994. The variable rapid technological change refers to the situation in the industry of the entrepreneur whereby they must be on the lookout for technological changes to anticipate. In addition, a variable reflecting the technology base of the firm is taken into account, indicating whether the firm's activities are based on new basic technologies (new materials, biotechnology, medical technology, information technology, energy/environmental technology). The fourth variable is urban environment. This variable distinguishes firms that are located in one of the three largest cities in the Netherlands – Amsterdam, Rotterdam and The Hague and its agglomerations – from those in the countryside.

Controls

Different control variables have been included in the analyses: the (employment) growth ambitions of the entrepreneur, and the age and gender of the entrepreneur. These variables have sometimes been classified – somewhat superficiously – as human capital variables. But, since we do not have a clear theoretical rationale to interpret them as human capital, we have only introduced them as control variables (in order to make the outcomes comparable with other new firm growth studies).

Whether growth firms were overrepresented in certain industries was checked. Growth firms were overrepresented in the retail, catering, transport and communication industries, and underrepresented in financial and business services, and personal services. The ten employee threshold was more often achieved in the catering industry, and less often achieved in personal services. This shows that new firm growth is not restricted, or even concentrated, in high-tech sectors (see also Birch, 1987).

Correlation Analysis

Correlation analyses may be performed to identify the factors which, by our measures, are associated with growth and to check whether the independent variables are highly correlated with each other. Pearson correlation coefficients have been used here as an indicator. The significance levels of Pearson are similar to the chi-square test of independency (linear-by-linear association). High correlation among independent variables may disturb assessment of the relationship through regression analysis. The correlations between the independent and dependent variables have been checked and no high (> 0.7) correlations were found. Several moderately strong (0.4–0.7) correlations could be found within the group of human capital variables: experience with financial management, leadership experience and human resource management experience were moderately correlated. Two other – rather obvious – moderate correlations could be found between employment growth and reaching the ten employee threshold, and between technology-based firms and rapid technological change. Finally, employment growth ambitions and employment growth (not the ten employee threshold!) were also moderately correlated. None of the dynamic capability variables were moderately correlated, providing an indication that these are not interrelated in the firm's first year of existence. This does not mean that firms only use one type of dynamic capability at the time: 38 per cent of the firms use a bundle of dynamic capabilities.

Survivor Bias

A fundamental problem in the analysis of firm growth is survivor bias.[6] If the investigation is only based on surviving firms, it is likely that the selection of the sample is significantly correlated to the same variables that may potentially affect firm growth. In 1994 the panel consisted of 1938 start-ups. For our analysis only 354 cases were used. It is very important to know why an exit from the panel occurred, because of possible biases in our results. We have only used data about the start-ups that survived and were willing to participate, not about the start-ups that left the panel. For example: if a certain start-up left the panel because they had no time or was not interested in participation, it does not necessarily mean that their venture was doing badly. Maybe it was going so well that they needed more time to invest in the venture to keep up the success. It is a totally different case when the non-participation is caused by the bankruptcy of the firm, which also leads to exit from the panel. Unfortunately, there is very little reliable information about the nature of the non-participation of the firms in our panel. An additional 'exit-survey' was held, which did contain some more information about why a firm left the panel (see Stam et al., 2006). However, this additional survey was only performed among a minority of all the exits.

We traced the differences between the firms in our sample, and all the other 1584 firms that started in the same year, but were not among those included in our (ten year survivor) sample. If these two groups do not significantly differ in their initial conditions, our findings are unlikely to be obscured by a survivor bias. The differences between these two groups were checked for all 24 independent variables. We found that, indeed, the majority (19) of the variables had the same value in both samples. Only the values of five variables differed significantly between the two groups ($\chi < 0.05$). Older entrepreneurs[7] and entrepreneurs with high levels of technical experience were more likely to be included in our sample. New firms with low start-up capital were less likely to be included in our sample, while technology-based firms and firms located in urban areas were more likely to be included in our sample. This may indicate that we understate the positive effect of the age of the entrepreneur and of the technical experience on new firm growth (given their negative effect on the chance of 100 per cent negative growth, that is, firm exit). The most important proviso at the level of the firm may be an understatement of the positive effect of start-up capital, of technology-based activities and of an urban location on new firm growth.

RESULTS

Logistic Regression

The hypotheses were tested using logistic regression analysis, a method used to model dichotomous outcomes (here, the probability that the firm grows/probability the firm does not grow (beyond the ten employee threshold)) by modelling the log odds of an outcome in terms of the values of covariates in the model. Multinomial regression analysis could not be performed with the growth paths due to a too small number of observations for each growth path. To test for multicollinearity we used the variance inflation factor (VIF). In none of the models used did multicollinearity appear to be present (VIF < 2.5).

The results are displayed in Table 15.2. There are three consistent effects in both the growth and the ten employee threshold models: employment growth ambitions (positive), age of the entrepreneur (negative) and interfirm alliancing (positive). Firm resources matter, but differently so for both types of growth: a positive relation of start-up employment size with growth in general, and a positive relation of start-up capital with reaching the ten employee threshold. R&D activities in the start-up year is also strongly related with reaching the ten employee threshold. No significant relationships with the human and social capital variables were identified in the multivariate analyses, even though significant correlations were found in the bivariate analyses. The only exception is the negative relationship with having entrepreneurs among the circle of friends and family and reaching the ten employee threshold.

These first analyses give some evidence for the positive association between dynamic capabilities and new firm growth. We can thus confirm our first hypothesis to a limited extent. According to our second and third hypotheses the relationship between dynamic capabilities and new firm growth will vary with the knowledge base of the entrepreneur and/or on the level of firm resources.

On the personal level, the knowledge base of the entrepreneur was expected to enable the effective use of dynamic capabilities. The knowledge base has been measured by the following variables that are significantly correlated with dynamic capabilities: educational level, technical experience and industry experience. No positive interaction effects of these variables with dynamic capabilities could be traced.

On the organizational level, a munificent resource base was hypothesized to provide the means to create and use dynamic capabilities effectively. However the models tracing the interaction effects of human resources and financial resources with indicators of dynamic capabilities did not produce a measurable relationship with firm growth.

The models tracing the interaction effects of personal knowledge and firm resources (start-up size) showed that these hardly changed the relation between dynamic capabilities and growth.[8] Thus the second and third hypotheses are not supported; no moderating effect on dynamic capabilities and growth could be seen to be exerted by the level of human capital and/or firm resources.

Table 15.2 Results of regression analysis for growth and ten employee threshold

Factors associated with new firm growth	Employment growth	Ten employee threshold
Constant	−2.985***	−4.730***
Dynamic capabilities		
New product development	0.022	0.084
R&D activities	−0.542	1.415**
Inter-firm alliancing	0.815**	0.935*
Export	0.517	0.819
Financial capital		
Start-up capital (× 1000)	0.157	0.497***
Social capital		
Entrepreneurial family/friends	0.091	−1.061*
Entrepreneurial networks	0.427*	0.366
Entrepreneurial team	0.608	0.641
Organizational capital		
Takeover	0.001	−0.290
Start-up size: employees	0.737***	X[a]
Human capital		
Educational level	0.092	−0.427
Business-owner experience	0.350	−0.701
Leadership experience	0.278	−0.093
Human resource management experience	0.111	0.399
Experience with financial management	−0.068	−0.090
Technical experience (in current profession)	0.137	0.390
Industry experience	−0.106	0.248
Environmental dynamism		
Dynamic industry	−0.051	−0.124**
Rapid technological change	−0.196	0.400
Technology-based firm	−0.324	0.100
Urban environment	−1.497*	0.400
Controls		
Gender entrepreneur	0.232	−0.777
Age entrepreneur in 1994	−0.778***	−0.832**
(Employment) growth ambitions	0.518***	0.400*
Nagelkerke R Square	0.451	0.387

Notes:
*** Significant at 99% level of confidence; ** significant at 95% level of confidence;
* significant at 90% level of confidence.
[a] Initial (employment) size is omitted due to possible endogeneity problems: firms with nine employees can much more easily reach the ten employee threshold than the majority of one person businesses; the six firms with ten or more employees at the start automatically reach the threshold).

Environments with rapid technological change are often assumed to provide relatively numerous entrepreneurial opportunities, and to be likely to stimulate firm growth (Bhidé, 2000). We found no positive associations of any kind between firm growth and dynamic environments (Table 15.2). Dynamic industries[9] and urban location actually had a significant negative association with the ability to reach the threshold of ten employees, and growth in general, respectively.

Dynamic capabilities are said to be most valuable in dynamic environments, such as environments with rapid technological change. Thus it may be expected that dynamic capabilities have a (stronger) relationship with growth in environments of rapid technological change. The relationship between dynamic capabilities and firm growth/ten employee threshold is analysed in a sub-sample of firms that operate in an environment of rapid technological change. However, for firms operating in an environment subject to rapid technological change, the relationship between inter-firm alliancing and both growth and the ten employee threshold vanishes.[10] The same applies for firms in turbulent industries. Another indicator of the importance of technological change is whether or not the firm's activities are based on a new basic technology. Therefore we explored whether dynamic capabilities were more useful for technology-based firms than the population of firms in general. Among technology-based firms, inter-firm alliancing was found to be the dynamic capability having a positive association with 'growth' and with reaching the ten employee threshold, as for the general population of firms.

The analyses provide only very limited support for the fourth hypothesis which states that environmental dynamism impacts the relationship between dynamic capabilities and growth. The positive relationship with inter-firm alliancing even vanishes in turbulent industries and for firms that operate in environments experiencing rapid technological change. Only a relatively weak positive relationship with new product development on reaching the ten employee threshold in environments of rapid technological change could be found.

The outcomes of the analyses are summarized in Figure 15.3 (growth in general) and Figure 15.4 (ten employee threshold).

DISCUSSION

As regards the relationship between dynamic capabilities and growth, inter-firm alliancing is revealed to have a rather consistent positive association with firm growth and with achieving the ten employee threshold, while R&D only has a positive relation with achieving the ten employee threshold. Exporting showed no association at all with growth. Only in dynamic

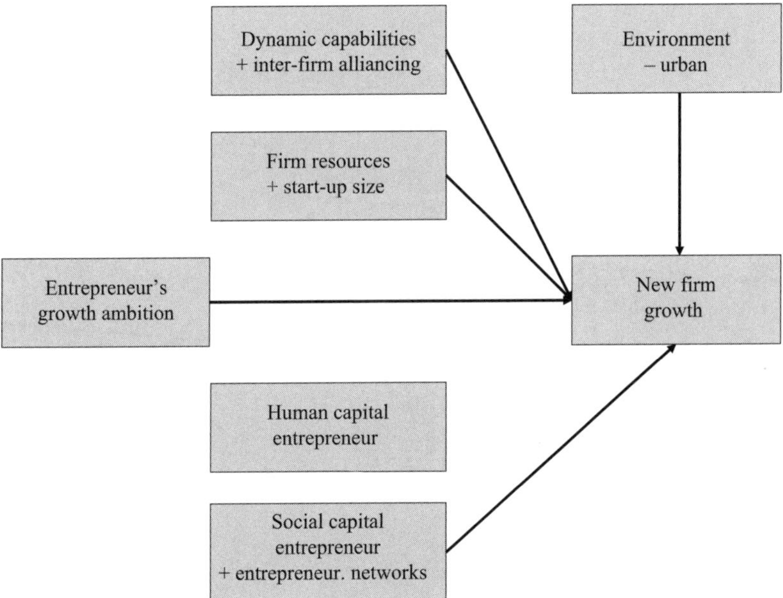

Figure 15.3 Factors associated with employment growth of new firms in general

technological environments did new product development turn out to have a (weak) positive relationship with achieving the ten employee threshold. New product development was not revealed to have any association with firm growth in all other environments.

Assumed opportunity rich environments – environments with rapid technological change, turbulent industries and urban environments – turned out to have no significant relationship with growth or even had a negative relationship in some of the analyses.

Moving from associations to causes, the proposed moderating influence of personal knowledge and firm resources on the effect of dynamic capabilities on firm growth have not been found in this study.

In comparison to the prior empirical studies on employment growth of new firms, many variables (entrepreneurial team, educational level, business-ownership experience, technical experience, industry experience, gender and new product development, that is, innovation ambitions) did not have the presumed relationship. The level of start-up capital only partly had the expected positive association. Employment growth ambitions had a strong positive association with firm growth in general, and a somewhat less strong relation with reaching the ten employee threshold. A large initial

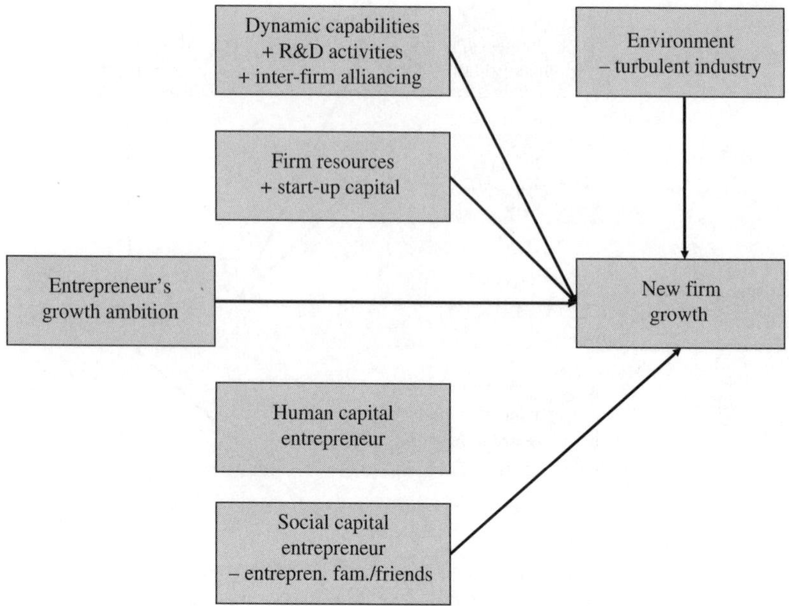

Figure 15.4 Factors associated with reaching the ten employee threshold

size seems to be much more important here than growth ambitions per se. For example, starting with nine employees makes it easier to reach the ten employee threshold then starting with one employee. Another surprising outcome was the negative relationship with having entrepreneurial family/friends and reaching the ten employee threshold. Perhaps it is true that 'ties that bind can easily turn into ties that blind' (Grabher, 1993) in the case of firm growth. Another contrasting outcome was the negative association between the entrepreneur's age and firm growth. The latter outcome may however also be related to the long time span we took into account (ten years in contrast to the 3–6 years of most other studies), perhaps providing fewer incentives for entrepreneurs older than 50 years at start-up to grow their business over this period.

Limitations

Approaches like organizational ecology (Hannan and Freeman, 1984) and evolutionary economics (Klepper, 2002) argue that initial conditions at founding are of decisive importance for explaining the long-term performance of organizations. Several empirical studies have claimed to show the long-term influence of initial conditions on the performance of new firms

(Geroski et al., 2006; Hannan et al., 2006). This does not imply that changing post-entry conditions do not matter. Even though the explained variance of our models are relatively high (ranging from 0.451 to 0.387),[11] we should not expect that initial conditions provide the best explanation of the growth of new firms over a ten year period. A large part of the variance in the relationship between start-up attributes and growth remains unexplained. Factors of this kind defy integration into linear style explanatory models.[12] The responses of firms to the conditions they encounter may be critical and are not readily modelled by conventional statistical approaches. Changing conditions both internal and external to the firm are likely to affect firm growth over the early life course of firms. This is in line with the argument that dynamic capabilities must be built through experience (Teece et al., 1997). Relevant experience can, of course, be built up prior to the creation of the firm, but if it is to be a distinctive asset of the firm (that is, firm-specific) it is more likely to be built up through team work over the years in the early life course of the firm (Penrose, 1959). Accordingly, strategic options pursued and changes in strategy are mentioned in the literature as a mediating factor between capabilities and growth (Wiklund, 1998; Edelman et al., 2005). We have also only used relatively restricted dichotomous dependent variables, which do not differentiate between firms that grow fast and those that grow slowly. Further work will investigate these issues.

Future Research and Implications

Our study provided support for earlier work showing that initial conditions have a major influence on the long-term growth of new firms. There is additional insight to be gained in the growth process by investigating the post-entry dynamics of the firm. Prior longitudinal studies have shown that firm growth is not a linear process, and may take off or be constrained in later phases of the life course. These dynamics in the growth paths may be explained by (random) external shocks (Geroski, 2005). However, the response of firms to circumstances may be a critical factor (Hugo and Garnsey, 2003). There is a need for a systematic analysis of firms' ability to resist external shocks: 'If there is a high probability of any negative event occurring and the hardship it imposes are generic, then one can incorporate the effect of random events through the venture's capacity for withstanding a common set of probable difficulties' (Woo et al., 1994, p. 520). Such an analysis would, for example, imply a focus on keeping open multiple options and on pre-emptive and remedial measures to deal with uncertainty and on the various buffers which enable young firms to reduce or cope with the impact of random jolts (cf. Venkataraman and Van de Ven, 1998). Growth path dynamics should be viewed in terms of the inherent problems of firm growth and the changing ability of firms to solve these problems and accumulate firm-specific competences (Penrose, 1995; Garnsey, 1998) and dynamic capabilities (Arthurs and Busenitz, 2006).[13]

Next to these problem-driven mechanisms, more opportunity-driven mechanisms (innovation) may be important. The EIM start-up panel offers the unique opportunity to trace the emergence of problems and opportunities during the growth paths of new firms (cf. Stam and Schutjens, 2006), and also to take into account the subsequent solution of these problems and the associated learning efforts and investments by these firms over time. Problem solving and learning may be important for the development of organizational capabilities later on in the life course of these new firms (cf. Zahra et al., 2006). Until now such analysis on the growth and problem solving of new firms has mainly been done with case studies (see, for example, Hugo and Garnsey, 2005; Stam and Garnsey, 2006). Future large-scale quantitative research analysing the changing conditions (both firm-internal as firm-external) will deliver insights into whether the dynamic capabilities are developed during the life course of the firm and whether they are effective in changing the resource base of the firm in order to sustain competitive advantage in a dynamic environment. This research should focus on providing improved explanations of new firm growth by analysing process events (problems, innovation) and learning (entrepreneurial, organizational; inter-organizational) during the life course.

ACKNOWLEDGEMENTS

The work by Erik Stam and Elizabeth Garnsey was carried out as part of the Innovation and Productivity Grand Challenge, with financial support from the Engineering and Physical Sciences Research Council and the Economic and Social Research Council through the AIM initiative. This chapter has been presented at the 20th Rent Conference in Brussels. We would like to thank David Smallbone and André van Stel for comments on an earlier version of this chapter.

NOTES

1. There have been some studies on how certain aspects of dynamic capabilities are related to other indicators of new firm growth like sales growth (Lee et al., 2001) or on the probability of IPO (initial public offering).
2. Chandler and Jansen (1992) found similar positive relationships between the entrepreneurial, managerial and technical skills of the entrepreneur on sales growth in new firms. The positive association between industry experience and sales growth of new firms was

also found in Siegel et al. (1993), while Stuart and Abetti (1990) found that only entrepreneurial experience (previous new venture involvements) and not managerial and technical experience were important factors in a composite indicator of new firm growth (based on sales, employment, profit and productivity growth).

3. Kirchhoff (1994) empirically defines innovation on an industry basis: high innovation firms are those firms belonging to industries where business activity is characterized by: (1) above average employment of scientists, engineers and technical professionals; and (2) above average expenditures in research and development. This definition does not take the heterogeneity of firms (other than industry affiliation) into account, and focuses on inputs in the innovation process, not outputs (more relevant for firm growth). Definitions like this one mix up high-tech industries with innovation. Kirchhoff found that during their first six years of existence 'high innovation' new firms are more likely to grow, but do not have higher probabilities to survive than 'low innovation' new firms.
4. These growth paths highlight growth inflections and are based on 5 per cent employment change thresholds; we also used 10 per cent employment change thresholds in another analysis. This however hardly changed the distribution of growth paths over the sample (only the number of firms in the setback category was significantly less in the 10 per cent analysis).
5. These numbers are different from the Garnsey et al. (2006) study, because they analyzed a cohort of firms in the 1990–2000 period (thus before the early 2000s recession) and their sample only included incorporated firms (and thus excluded sole proprietors, which make up the majority of our sample). These differences might be responsible for the relatively small percentage of continuously growing firms, and the relatively high percentage of plateau firms. An analysis of all the firms started in 1977 and 1978 in the USA showed that more than half of all firms that survived for six years did not show any growth in employment (Kirchhoff, 1994).
6. Wiklund and Shepherd (2005) found that firm survival (of all incorporated firms registered in Sweden between 1994–98) is positively correlated with absolute and relative employment growth.
7. This is in contrast with our expectation that older entrepreneurs are more likely to have closed their business (voluntarily) (see Harhoff et al., 1998). On the other hand, young entrepreneurs are more likely to be mobile on the labour and housing markets, which causes a higher non-response rate among them because they are harder to trace year after year (see, for example, Stam et al., 2006).
8. Regression models with the interaction effects are available from the authors.
9. Klepper and Graddy (1990) argued that especially in new, turbulent industries firm growth is rather limited because of the high levels of uncertainty about their costs and product qualities relative to those of competitors.
10. For the ten employee threshold model we found a weak (only at a 10 per cent significance level) positive effect of new product development in environments of rapid technological change.
11. For example, Harhoff et al. (1998) could only explain about 8 per cent of the variance in their models on employment growth of West German firms over a five year period.
12. According to Davidsson (2004, p. 45) we should even be suspicious about research that explains more than half of the variance, because '[t]here is just too much idiosyncratic variation and unavoidable measurement error'.
13. This is not to say that there are invariant stages of growth (Greiner, 1972).

REFERENCES

Aldrich, H. (1999), *Organizations Evolving*, London: Sage.

Almus, M. and E.A. Nerlinger (1999), 'Growth of new technology-based firms: which factors matter?', *Small Business Economics*, **13**, 141–54.

Arthurs, J.D. and L.W. Busenitz (2006), 'Dynamic capabilities and venture performance: the effects of venture capitalists', *Journal of Business Venturing*, **21**(2), 195–215.

Audretsch, D.B., E. Santarelli and M. Vivarelli (1999), 'Start-up size and industrial dynamics: some evidence from Italian manufacturing', *International Journal of Industrial Organization*, **17**(7), 965–83.

Audretsch, D.B., L. Klomp, E. Santarelli and A.R. Thurik (2004), 'Gibrat's law: are the services different?', *Review of Industrial Organization*, **24**(3), 301–24.

Bangma, K.L. (2007), *Bedrijvendynamiek en Werkgelegenheid: Periode 1987–2006* (*Firm Dynamics and Employment: Period 1987–2006*), Zoetermeer: EIM.

Baron, J.N., M.D. Burton and M.T. Hannan (1996), 'The road taken: the origins and evolution of employment systems in emerging high-technology companies', *Industrial and Corporate Change*, **5**, 239–76.

Baum, J.R., E.A. Locke and K.G. Smith (2001), 'A multidimensional model of venture growth', *Academy of Management Journal*, **44**(2), 292–303.

Bhide, A. (2000), *The Origin and Evolution of New Businesses*, New York: Oxford University Press.

Birch, D. (1987), *Job Creation in the America*, New York: Free Press.

Bosma, N.S., C.M. van Praag, A.R. Thurik and G. de Wit (2004), 'The value of human and social capital investments for the business performance of startups', *Small Business Economics*, **23**(3), 227–36.

Brusoni, S., E. Cefis and L. Orsenigo (2006), 'Innovate or die? A critical review of the literature on innovation and performance', no. 179, CESPRI Working Papers, Bocconi, Milano.

Brüderl, J. and P. Preisendörfer (2000), 'Fast growing businesses: empirical evidence from a German study', *International Journal of Sociology*, **30**, 45–70.

Certo, S.T., J.G. Covin, C.M. Daily and D.R. Dalton (2001), 'Wealth and the effects of founder management among ipo-stage new ventures', *Strategic Management Journal*, **22**(6/7), 641–58.

Chandler, G.N. and E. Jansen (1992), 'The founder's self-assessed competence and venture performance', *Journal of Business Venturing*, **7**, 223–36.

Chrisman, J.J., E. McMullan and J. Hall (2005), 'The influence of guided preparation on the long-term performance of new ventures', *Journal of Business Venturing*, **20**, 769–91.

Colombo, M.G. and L. Grilli (2005), 'Founders' human capital and the growth of new technology-based firms: a competence-based view', *Research Policy*, **34**(6), 795–816.

Cooper, A.C., F.J. Gimeno-Gascon and C.Y. Woo (1994), 'Initial human and financial capital as predictors of new venture performance', *Journal of Business Venturing*, **9**(5), 371–95.

Dahlqvist, J., P. Davidsson and J. Wiklund (2000), 'Initial conditions as predictors of new venture performance: a replication and extension of the Cooper et al. study', *Enterprise and Innovation Management Studies*, **1**(1), 1–17.

Davidsson, P. (1991), 'Continued entrepreneurship: ability, need and opportunity as determinants for small firm growth', *Journal of Business Venturing*, **6**, 405–29.

Davidsson, P. (2004), *Researching Entrepreneurship*, New York: Springer.

Edelman, L.F., C.G. Brush and T. Manolova (2005), 'Co-alignment in the resource-performance relationship: strategy as mediator', *Journal of Business Venturing*, **20**(3), 359–83.

Eisenhardt, K.M. and J.A. Martin (2000), 'Dynamic capabilities: what are they?', *Strategic Management Journal*, **21**, 1105–21.

Felin, T. and N.J. Foss (2006), 'Individuals and organizations: thoughts on a micro-foundations project for strategic management and organizational analysis', DRUID working paper 06–01, Copenhagen.

Fuller, T. and P. Moran (2001), 'Small enterprises as complex adaptive systems: a methodological question?', *Entrepreneurship and Regional Development*, **13**(1), 47–63.

Garnsey, E. (1998), 'A theory of the early growth of the firm', *Industrial and Corporate Change*, **7**, 523–56.

Garnsey, E., E. Stam and P. Hefferman (2006), 'New firm growth: exploring processes and paths', *Industry and Innovation*, **13**(1), 1–24.

Geroski, P.A. (2005), 'Understanding the implications of empirical work on corporate growth rates', *Managerial and Decision Economics*, **26**(2), 129–38.

Geroski, P.A., J. Mata and P. Portugal (2006), 'Founding conditions and the survival of new firms', paper presented at the Max Planck Institute of Economics Workshop on Firm Exit and Serial Entrepreneurship, Jena, Germany, January.

Grabher, G. (1993), *The Embedded Firm: On the Socioeconomics of Industrial Networks*, London: Routledge.

Greiner, L.E. (1972), 'Evolution and revolution as organizations grow', *Harvard Business Review*, **July–August**, 37–46.

Hitt, M.A., D. Ireland, M. Camp and D.L. Sexton (2001), 'Guest editors introduction to the special issue strategic entrepreneurship: entrepreneurial strategies for wealth creation', *Strategic Management Journal*, **22**, 479–91.

Hannan, M.T. and J. Freeman (1984), 'Structural inertia and organizational change', *American Sociological Review*, **49**, 149–64.

Hannan, M.T., J.N. Baron, G. Hsu and Ö. Koçak (2006), 'Organizational identities and the hazard of change', *Industrial and Corporate Change*, **15**, 755–84.

Harhoff, D., K. Stahl and M. Woywode (1998), 'Legal form, growth and exit of West-German firms – empirical results for manufacturing, construction, trade and service industries', *Journal of Industrial Economics*, **46**(4), 453–88.

Hugo, O. and E. Garnsey (2005), 'Problem-solving and competence creation in the early development of new firms', *Managerial and Decision Economics*, **26**(2), 139–48.

Kirchhoff, B.A. (1994), *Entrepreneurship and Dynamic Capitalism*, Westport, CT: Praeger.

Klepper, S. (2002), 'The capabilities of new firms and the evolution of the US automobile industry', *Industrial and Corporate Change*, **11**, 645–66.

Klepper, S. and E. Graddy (1990), 'The evolution of new industries and the determinants of market structure', *RAND Journal of Economics*, **21**(1), 27–44 .

Lee, C., K. Lee and J.M. Pennings (2001), 'Internal capabilities, external networks and performance: a study on technology-based ventures', *Strategic Management Journal*, **22**, 615–40.

Lotti, F., E. Santarelli and M. Vivarelli (2001), 'The relationship between size and growth: the case of Italian newborn firms', *Applied Economics Letters*, **8**, 451–54.

Mansfield, E. (1962), 'Entry, Gibrat's law, innovation, and the growth of firms', *American Economic Review*, **52**, 1023–51.

Penrose, E. (1995), *The Theory of Growth of the Firm* (3rd edn), Oxford: Oxford University Press.

Piore, M.J. and C.F. Sabel (1984), *The Second Industrial Divide: Possibilities for Prosperity*, New York: Basic Books.

Powell, W.W., K. Koput and L. Smith-Doerr (1996), 'Interorganizational collaboration and the locus of innovation: networks of learning in biotechnology', *Administrative Science Quarterly*, **41**(1), 116–45.

Schumpeter, J.A. (1934), *The Theory of Economic Development*, New York: Oxford University Press.

Schutjens, V.A.J.M. and E. Wever (2000), 'Determinants of new firm success', *Papers in Regional Science*, **79**(2), 135–59.

Schutjens, V.A.J.M. and E. Stam (2006), 'Starting anew: entrepreneurial intentions and realizations subsequent to business closure', Discussion Papers on Entrepreneurship, Growth and Public Policy 2006–10, Max Planck Institute of Economics, Group for Entrepreneurship, Growth and Public Policy, Jena, Germany.

Siegel, R., E. Siegel and I.C. Macmillan (1993), 'Characteristics distinguishing high growth ventures', *Journal of Business Venturing*, **8**, 169–80.

Stam, E., D. Audretsch and J. Meijaard (2006), 'Renascent entrepreneurship', Working paper, Max Planck Institute of Economics, Jena, Germany.

Stuart, R.W. and P.A. Abetti (1990), 'Impact of entrepreneurial and management experience on early performance', *Journal of Business Venturing*, **5**, 151–62.

Tapon, F., M. Thong and M. Bartell (2001), 'Drug discovery and development in four Canadian biotech companies', *R & D Management*, **31**(1), 77–90.

Teece, D.J., G. Pisano and A. Shuen (1997), 'Dynamic capabilities and strategic fit', *Strategic Management Journal*, **18**, 510–33.

Venkataraman, S. and A. van de Ven (1998), 'Hostile environmental jolts, transaction sets, and new business development', *Journal of Business Venturing*, **13**(3), 231–55.

Vivarelli, M. and D. Audretsch (1998), 'The link between the entry decision and post-entry performance: evidence from Italy', *Industrial and Corporate Change*, **7**, 485–500.

West III, P.G. and J. DeCastro (2001), 'The Achilles heel of firm strategy: resource weaknesses and distinctive inadequacies', *Journal of Management Studies*, **38**(3), 417–42.

Westhead, P. and M. Cowling (1995), 'Employment change in independent owner-managed high technology firms in Great Britain', *Small Business Economics*, **7**, 111–40.

Wiklund, J. (1998), 'Small firm growth and performance: entrepreneurship and beyond', PhD Thesis, Jonkoping International Business School, Jonkoping.

Wiklund, J. and D. Shepherd (2005), 'Knowledge accumulation in growth studies: the consequences of methodological choices', paper presented at ERIM workshop 'Perspectives on the longitudinal analysis of new firm growth', Erasmus University Rotterdam, the Netherlands, 18–19 May.

Winters, R. and E. Stam (2007), 'Beyond the firm: innovation and networks of high technology SMEs', in J.M. Arauzo and M. Manjón (eds), *Entrepreneurship, Industrial Location and Economic Growth*, Cheltenham, UK and Northampton, MA, USA: Edward Elgar, pp. 235–52.

Woo, C., U. Daellenbach and C. Nicholls-Nixon (1994), 'Theory building in the presence of randomness: the case of venture creation and performance', *Journal of Management Studies*, **31**(4), 507–24.

Yu, T.F.L. (2001), 'Toward a capabilities perspective of the small firm', *International Journal of Management Reviews*, **3**(3), 185–97.

Zahra, S., H.J. Sapienza and P. Davidsson (2006), 'Entrepreneurship and dynamic capabilities: a review, model and research agenda', *Journal of Management Studies*, **43**(4), 917–55.

APPENDIX

Table 15A.1 Data used in studies on employment growth of new firms

Authors	Time period	Industries	Number of firms	Region
Cooper et al., 1994	1985–87 (3 years)	Representative for new firm population	1.053	USA
Dahlqvist et al., 2000	1994–97 (3 years)	All except agriculture, forestry, hunting, fishery and real estate	6.377	Sweden
Schutjens and Wever, 2000	1994–97 (3 years)	All except agriculture and mining	563	Netherlands
Bosma et al., 2004	1994–97 (3 years)	All except agriculture and mining	758	Netherlands
Vivarelli and Audretsch, 1998	1985–93 (< 9 years; mean age 3 years)	All	100	Emilia (Italy)
Colombo and Grilli, 2005	1980 (or later)–2004 (max. 13 years)	High-tech sectors (computers, electronic components, telecommunication equipment, optical,medical and electronic instruments, biotechnology, pharmaceuticals, advanced materials, robotics and process automation equipment, multimedia content, software, internet services and telecommunication services)	506	Italy
Almus and Nerlinger, 1999	1992/ 1996–98	Manufacturing industries (both 'high-tech industries' (R&D intensity above 3.5%) and 'non-high-tech industries' (R&D intensity below 3.5%)	8.739	Germany

Table 15A.1 (continued)

Authors	Time period	Industries	Number of firms	Region
Brüderl and Preisendörfer, 1998	1985/ 1986–90 (4 years)	All except crafts, agriculture, physicians, architects and lawyers	1.710	Munich and Upper Bavaria (Germany)
Chrisman et al., 2005	1992/1997–2001 (3–8 years)	All (received outsider assistance at start)	159	Pennsylvania (USA)

Index

Abetti, P.A. 200, 345
Abrahamson, E. 304
academic entrepreneurs 275; *see also* university spin-offs, academic staff typology; university spin-offs, role of academic staff
academic entrepreneurship, *see* university spin-offs
academic spin-offs, *see* university spin-offs
Achtenhagen, L. 94, 96, 97
Acs, Z.J. 15, 194
adhocracy 256–7
affordable growth, *see* sustainable growth
agency theory 118
Ahl, H.J. 20
Ahlstrom, D. 183
Ajzen, I. 305
Albers, S. 179
Albert, P. 276
Aldrich, H.E. 5, 334
Allinson, C.W. 30, 33, 34, 44, 45, 47
Aloulou, W. 35
Alsos, G.A. 16, 199, 201
Álvarez, L.I. 221
Alvesson, M. 97
Amason, A.C. 163
ambiguity, *see* Flemish entrepreneur profile study, tolerance for ambiguity
Anderson, P. 302
Anderson, R.C. 118, 135
Antoncic, B. 16, 22
Ardichvili, A. 172
Arrow, K.J. 166
Arthurs, J.D. 344
Astrachan, J.H. 117, 144
Atuahene-Gima, K. 141, 218, 220
Audretsch, D.B. 15, 328
Auger, P. 35
Autio, E. 215, 216
autonomy
  of companies 95
  in family firms 110–12
Axelsson, R. 250–51

Badger, B. 33, 45
Bailey, D.E. 166, 168, 175, 176
Baines, S. 22
Baker, T. 5, 262
Banbury, C. 142
Bandura, A. 32, 54
Bangma, K.L. 332
Barney, J. 216, 219
BarNir, A. 299, 304, 307, 314, 317
Baron, J.N. 331, 334
Baron, R.A. 29, 32, 33, 44
Baron, R.M. 147
Bartholomeusz, S. 108
Barton, S.L. 79, 82
Bateman, T.S. 32, 39
Bates, T. 195
Baum, J.R. 18, 328
Baumol, W.J. 16
BCERC (Babson) conference 21
Beamish, W. 22
Becattini, G. 16
Becchetti, L. 122
Becherer, R.C. 32, 44
Becker, G.S. 172, 195
Begley, T.M. 42, 47
Belgium, *see* Flemish entrepreneur profile study
Bellon, B. 142, 143
Bengtsson, M. 299, 301, 302, 307, 320
Bentler, M. 320
Berger, A.N. 122
Berggren, B. 122
Berr, S.A. 45
BFS (case study pseud.)
  Formality/Informality duality 105–6
  Historical/New Path duality 101

Independence/Dependence duality 103
main characteristics 98
primacy of the proactiveness and innovativeness 109–10
Bharadwaj, S. 301, 303
Bhave, M.P. 16
Bhidé, A.V. 78, 79, 173, 340
Bhuian, S.N. 216, 220, 221
Bierly, P.E. 218
Bigné, J.E. 219
Birch, D. 336
Birley, S. 16, 164, 165, 168, 199, 200, 270, 271, 272, 273, 276
Bjerke, B. 243
Blackburn, R.A. 37, 46
Blau, G.J. 32
Blesa, A. 219, 220
Boden, R.J. 196
Bollen, K.A. 181
Bolton, R. 246
Boone, C. 32, 36
Bortz, J. 178
Bosma, N. 195, 196, 198, 199, 200
Bouckenooghe, D. 30, 34
Boyd, N.G. 32, 46
Braks, B.F.M. 260
Braunerhjelm, P. 16
Braunstein, D.N. 39
Breton-Miller, I. Le, *see* Le Breton-Miller, I.
Brett, J.M. 147
Bridge, S. 31
Brower, R.S. 257
Brown, A. 151, 154
Brown, F.H. 95, 97
Bruce, N. 121
Brüderl, J. 166, 168, 173, 195, 196, 205
Brundin, E. 18, 20
Bruno, A.V. 163, 166
Brusoni, S. 330
Bruton, G.D. 183
Brynjolfsson, E. 304
Bullvåg, E. 199, 200
Burgelman, R.A. 96
Busenitz, L.W. 219, 344
Buttner, E.H. 34, 45
Bygrave, W.D. 200
Cadogan, J.W. 221
Calantone, R.J. 218
Camelo-Ordaz, C. 163
Camison-Zornoza, C. 302, 307, 316, 320
Campbell-Hunt, C. 215
Capon, N. 141
Carayannis, E.G. 270, 271, 272
Carbonell, P. 218
Carlock, R.S. 124, 144, 152
Carlsson, C.G. 249–50
Carpenter, M.A. 165
Carree, M. 22
Carsky, M. 119, 142
Castanias, R.P. 197
Cavusgil, T. 216, 218
Certo, S.T. 331
Chalmers Innovation 82
Chandler, A.D. 304
Chandler, G.N. 163, 183, 194, 195, 205, 344
Chandy, R.K. 302, 303, 307, 312, 316
Chatman, J.A. 171
Chell, E. 22
Chen, C.C. 32, 33, 44
Chen, G. 39
Chetty, S. 215
Chia, R. 245, 262
Chiesa, V. 268, 269
Child, J. 153
Childs, M. 263
Chin, W.W. 181
Chittenden, F. 122
Cho, H. 218
Chowdhury, S. 165, 170, 172
Christoplos, I. 261
Clapp, R.G. 45
Clark, K. 142, 143
Clarysse, B. 274
Cliff, J.E. 18
cognitive approach, Flemish entrepreneur profile study 33–4, 43
Cohen, S.G. 166, 168, 175, 176
Cohen, W.D. 306
Cohen, W.M. 221
Coleman, S. 119, 142
Collins, C.J. 15, 33, 44
competitive aggressiveness of companies 95

relative seclusion in family firms 108–9
Congcong, Z. 215
Cools, E. 34, 39
Cooper, A.C. 55, 163, 166, 172, 195, 197, 198, 201, 202, 205, 206, 211
Cooper, R.G. 141, 151
Corbin, J. 97, 98
corridor principle 199
CoSI (Cognitive Style Indicator) 34, 39
Covin, J.G.30, 35, 39, 94, 95, 121, 217, 219
Cowling, M.142, 146, 152, 328
Crant, J.M.32, 36, 39, 46
crisis management 255
  literature 257
Cromie, S. 29, 31, 33, 44, 120, 124, 135, 136, 142, 144
Culture dimension (F-PEC scale) 144
Curran, J. 37, 46
Cyert, R.M. 153
Czarniawska, B. 247

Daft, R.L. 142
Dahlstrand, Å.L. 270, 271, 276
Daily, C.M. 142, 151, 152, 153
Damanpour, F. 142, 303, 307
Daniel, E. 22
Davenport, D. 257, 260
Davidsson, P. 15, 16, 17, 22, 144, 328, 330, 345
Davis, F.D. 305, 306
Davis, P. 119, 153
Day, G.S. 215, 218, 221
Dekkers, E.J.M. 141, 146, 151, 152
Deleersnyder, B. 303
Delmar, F. 16, 22, 31, 178
Demirgüç-Kunt, A. 117, 123, 128
demographic heterogeneity, in NVT 186
Dependence/Independence duality 102–4
Dess, G.G. 30, 35, 93, 94, 95, 97, 109, 110, 112, 217, 219
Dhanaraj, C. 22
Dickson, K. 272, 275, 291, 294
differentiation 143
Digitally Enabled Marketing (DEM)
  adoption study
    background 300–307
    discussion 315–18
    limitations 318–19
    measurement 308–12
    models 312–15
    survey description 307–8
  definitions 300–301
  as innovation 301–2
  overview 299–300
Dimitratos, P. 217
Dimov, D.P. 19
Dollinger, M.J. 142, 151, 152, 153
Donckels, R. 124, 141, 144, 151, 152, 154
Dosi, G. 142
Douglas, K.S. 164
Doz, Y. 97, 113
Drennan, J. 173
Drucker, P.F. 32
du Gay, P. 243
dualities 96–7; *see also* Formality/Informality duality
Duchesneau, D.A. 197, 200, 201, 202
Dugan, S.M. 303
Duhachek, A. 320
Dunn, B. 120, 135
DuRietz, A. 22
Dutch SMEs, *see* family orientation, and innovation study
Dyer, G.W., Jr 93
Dyke, L.S. 212
dynamic capabilities
  and employment growth of new firms
    definitions 328–31
    discussion 340–42
    dynamic capabilities 334–5
    environmental dynamism 335
    growth 332–4
    implications 343–4
    limitations 342–3
    results 337–40
    survivor bias 336–7
    variables 332–7

e-business 300; *see also* Digitally Enabled Marketing
Ebert, R. 143
Eckhardt, J. 217
Eddleston, K. 121

education/predisposition interaction study
  future research 74
  hypotheses 58–61
  implications 73
  measures 63–4
  method 61–5
  overview 54–6
  theory development 56–8
  see also human capital attributes of business founders, business performance study, education level
Efron, B. 181
Eisenhardt, K.M. 98, 168, 171, 172, 219, 248, 324, 328, 329, 334
Elfring, T. 171
emergency entrepreneurship
  case study stories
    civic associations taking charge 248–9
    incapacitated corporate structures 251–2
    intermediators in broken structures 252–3
    moment of truth for the municipality 249–50
    small businesses disconnected from their customers 250–51
  definitions 260–62
  organizing under pressure 255–60
  overview 243–4
  study analysis 253–60
  study method 246–8
employment growth
  and dynamic capabilities study
    data 331–2
    definitions 328–31
    discussion 340–42
    dynamic capabilities 334–5
    environmental dynamism 335
    growth 332–4
    implications 343–4
    limitations 342–3
    results 337–40
    survivor bias 336–7
    variables 332–7
  literature 325–8
  overview 324
enactive entrepreneurship 245–6, 254–5
Ensley, M.D. 163, 165, 170, 175
entrepreneurial orientation, *see* EO
entrepreneurial professors 293; *see also* university spin-offs, case studies, professor entrepreneur
entrepreneurial scientists 275; *see also* scientific entrepreneurs
entrepreneurs
  definitions 5–6
  personality traits 15–16
    see also Flemish entrepreneur profile study
entrepreneurship
  alternative images of 246
  as career issue 14
Entrepreneurship and Regional Development 21
Entrepreneurship Theory and Practice 21
entrepreneurship/small business research
  challenges for 17–20
  in Europe 3–5
  Europe vs North America 20–23
Entrialgo, M. 46, 153
EO (entrepreneurial orientation)
  applied to family firms
    Formality/Informality duality 104–7
    Historical/New Path duality 100–102
    implications 113–14
    Independence/Dependence duality 102–4
    interpretive analysis 107–12
    methodology 97–100
    overview 93–4, 112–13
  definitions 217
  dimensions 94–5
  Flemish entrepreneur profile study 30, 35–6, 39
  and international competitiveness 217–19
  and market orientation 219–20
  market orientation/EO/international performance study
    limitations 233–4
    measurement 224–7

methodology 222–7
overview 215–16, 230–33
results 227–32
measurement 224–5
E.ON (Swedish power company) 248–9, 251–2
ephemeral organizations 247, 254, 257
Erdogan, B. 30, 35, 36, 44
Ettlie, J.E. 303
Evan, W. 142
Evans, M.G. 19
Evans, P. 97, 113
Evans, R.E. 119
Eyuboglu, N. 303

family firms
definitions 6
entrepreneurial orientation study
Formality/Informality duality 104–7
Historical/New Path duality 100–102
implications 113–14
Independence/Dependence duality 102–4
interpretive analysis 107–12
methodology 97–100
overview 93–4, 112–13
financing/growth linkage 121–3
generational differences study
data and methodology 125–8
financing behavior 118–20, 128–31
financing/growth linkage 121–5, 133–4
growth behavior 120–21, 131–3
overview 117–18, 134–6
results 128–34
sectoral representation 142
family orientation
definitions 8
and innovation study
comparison with previous research 151–3
data analysis 147–8
effects of family orientation on innovation 146, 148, 151
effects of strategy on innovation 145–6, 148
key concepts 142–4
overview 141–2, 154
research limitations 153–4
research model 145–6
sample 146–7
intergenerational differences 120–21, 124
literature review 96
Fayolle, A. 35
Felin, T. 329
Fernández, Z. 120
Fernhaber, S.A. 215
Fillis, I. 299
financial bootstrapping
definitions 77–8
literature review 78–80
motivations survey
conclusions 88–90
data analysis 83
data collection 82
description of the sample 83–4
design 80–82
results 84–8
Fishbein, M. 305
Flemish entrepreneur profile study
cognitive approach 33–4, 43
cognitive style differences and EO 36
data measures 38–40
data sample 37–8
entrepreneurial orientation 30, 35–6, 39
locus of control 32–3, 39
need for achievement 33, 39
overview 29–30, 47–8
proactive personality 32, 39
research limitations 46–7
self-efficacy 32, 38–9
tolerance for ambiguity 31–2, 38
trait approach 31, 43
traits and EO 35–6
see also family firms, generational differences study; family orientation, and innovation study
Fletcher, D. 218
Flören, R.H. 141, 144, 151, 152, 153, 154
Florin, J. 44
Flynn, F. 171
Folkesson, M. 252–3
Fontes, M. 269, 272, 273
Ford, C.M. 178

formal organizations 247
Formality/Informality duality 104–7
Fors, J. 252–3
Foss, N.J. 329
Francis, D.H. 163
Frank, H. 178
Freear, J. 77, 78
Freel, M.S. 22
Freeman, J. 342
Fritsch, M. 15
Fröhlich, E. 124, 141, 151, 152, 154
Frontiers of Entrepreneurship Research 21
Fuller, T. 330
Furnham, A. 31, 38

Gaglio, C.M. 171
Gallén, T. 36
Garnsey, E. 328, 330, 333, 343, 344, 345
Gartner, W.B. 16, 197, 200, 201, 202, 243, 245, 253
Garud, R. 218
Garvis, D.M. 217
Gascon, F. 198, 206
Gemünden, H.G. 163, 165, 166, 168, 169, 171, 178
general human capital 195
General Self-Efficacy scale 38–9
George, G. 215, 217, 221
Gephart, R.P.261
Geroski, P.A.330, 343
Gersick, K.E.95, 105, 118
Ghosh, S. 303
Giddens, A.166
Gimeno, J. 195, 201, 202, 205, 211
Gioia, D.A. 178
Glaser, B.G. 97, 98
glocal matrix organizational structure 252, 259, 262
Göbbels, M.W. 144
Goel, S. 126
Goldsmith, R.E. 34, 45
Gomez-Mejia, L.R. 152
Gordon, I. 221
Grabher, G. 258, 342
Graddy, E. 345
Granovetter, M. 171
Grant, R.M. 216, 222
Gratzer, K. 23
Gregory, B.T. 122
Greiner, L.E. 165, 345
Grenier, S. 38
Grieshuber, E. 163, 173
Griffin, R. 143
Grimm, C.M. 172
growth, *see* employment growth; sustainable growth
growth behavior, family firms 120–21, 131–3
growth orientation 144, 152
growth/financing linkage, family firms 121–3
Gryskiewicz, N. 34, 45
Gudmundson, D. 141, 151, 154
Gudrun (hurricane) 243–4; *see also* emergency entrepreneurship, case study stories
Gumpert, D. 217
Gundry, L.K. 32, 46
Gurdon, M.A. 276
Gustafsson, V. 16, 20

Habbershon, T.G. 93, 94, 95, 96, 97, 113
habitual entrepreneurs 173, 199
Hall, A. 96
Halman, J.I.M. 260
Hambrick, D.C. 165
Hamel, G. 218
Hamilton, D. 305
Hamilton, S. 119, 124, 136
Hanks, S.H. 195
Hannan, M.T. 342, 343
Hansemark, O.C. 31, 47
Harhoff, D. 345
Harker, M. 221
Harman, H.H. 39
Harris, D. 152
Harrison, R.T. 77
Harveston, P. 119
Harvey, M. 119
Hauschildt, J. 172
Hayes, J. 30, 33, 34
Haynes, P.J. 299
Helfat, C.E. 197
Heller, T. 256
Helsloot, I. 257, 258, 259
Henderson, R. 142
Henrekson, M. 16, 22

Higgins, R.C. 117, 122
Hildebrandt, L. 179
Hill, D.D. 271
Hillmann, K.-H. 174
Hine, D. 286
Hirschman, A.O. 258
Hisrich, R.D. 29
Hitt, M.A. 218, 324, 328
Hjorth, D. 243, 245, 255, 259
Hoang, H. 16, 22
Hodgetts, R.M. 153
Hodgkinson, G.P. 34
Honig, B. 16, 22
Höst, V. 307, 319
Hough, J.R. 36
Hough, M. 257
Houghton, K.A. 299
Hoy, F. 95
Hu, L. 320
Huang, X. 151, 154
Huber, G. 221
Hughes, M. 217, 218
Hughes, W.P 257
Hugo, O. 343, 344
Hulshoff, H. 144
Hulsink, W. 171
Hult, G.T. 218
human capital attributes of business founders
  business performance study
    business ownership experience 199–201
    early business performance measure 204
    education level 198
    general human capital variables 196–8, 204–5
    managerial experience 197
    method 203–6
    overview 194–6, 210–12
    parental self-employment/business ownership 201–2
    previous businesses similarity 202–3
    results 206–10
    specific human capital variables 198–203, 205
    work experience 196–7
human capital framework 195
Hurlbert, J.S. 261
Hurt, H.T. 38
hybrid spinouts 272
Hymer, S. 215

incremental innovations 142
industrial entrepreneurs 294
innovation 142–3
  definitions 217
innovation 'funnel' 143
innovation performance 142–3
innovativeness
  of companies 95
  primacy of, in family firms 109–10
intention
  interaction with self-efficacy 56–8
  see also education/predisposition interaction study
Internal-External (I-E) scale 39
internally financed growth rate 122–3
International Award for Entrepreneurship and Small Business Research 21
International Small Business Journal 21
Internet, *see* Digitally Enabled Marketing
Ireland, R.D. 173

Jackson, W.A. 94, 96
James, H.S. 93, 108
James, L.R. 147
Jansen, E. 205, 344
Janssens, M. 97
Janszen, F. 152
Jantunen, A. 217, 218
Jarillo, J.C. 217
Jaworski, B.J. 219, 303
Jensen, M.C. 119
Jevons, C. 299
Jeyaraj, A. 299, 302, 304, 306, 313, 316, 318, 319
Johannisson, B. 16, 243, 245, 246, 255, 259, 260
Johannisson, J. 254, 263
Johnson, B.R. 31, 33
Johnson, D.S. 301, 303
Johnstone, H. 243
Jolly, V.K. 268
Jones-Evans, D. 272, 274
Journal of Business Venturing 21

Judge, T.A. 40, 46
Jungbauer-Gans, M. 163

Kabadayi, S. 303
Kahn, R.L. 261
Kangasharju, A. 198
Kapeleris, J. 286
Karau, S.J. 169
Kasvi, J. 259
Katz, D. 261
Katzenbach, J.R. 164
Kaye, K. 119, 124, 136
Keegan, A. 256
Kellermanns, F.W. 121
Kennedy, J. 44, 173
Kenny, D.A. 147
Kenny, J. 142
Kerr, J.R. 34, 45
Kessler, E.H. 218
Ketchen, D.J. 218
Khavul, S. 215
Kickul, J. 32, 34, 40, 46
Kim, S.S. 299, 305, 306
Kirchhoff, B.A. 345
Kirton, M.J. 40
Klein, S. 142, 144
Kleinschmidt, E.J. 141, 151
Klepper, S. 342, 345
Klofsten, M. 276
Knight, G.A. 216, 218, 221
Ko, A. 220
Koh, H.C. 32, 44
Kohli, A.K. 219, 303
Kolvereid, L. 16, 199, 200, 201
Kotler, P. 299
Krafft, M. 180, 181
Krauss, S.I. 30, 35
Kreiser, P.M. 35
Kreitner, R. 39
Krueger, N. 34, 40
Kruglanski, A.W. 38
Kuratko, D.F. 153
Küster, I. 221
Kyd, C.W. 117, 122

Lambin, J.J. 221
Lambrecht, J. 243
Landström, H. 4, 29, 47, 48, 77, 79, 171
Langley, A. 98
Lank, A.G. 153
Lanzara, G.F. 247, 254, 256, 257, 258, 259, 261
Larson, A. 255
lateral information flow 259
Lattin, J. 313, 320
Laukkanen, M. 269, 276
Le Breton-Miller, I. 109, 119, 121, 128, 135
Lechler, T. 163, 165, 166, 168, 169, 171, 178
Lee, C. 344
Leonard, D. 45
Leonard, N.H. 30, 36
Lévi-Strauss, C. 262
Levinthal, D.A. 221, 306
Li, H. 141
Liesch, P.W. 216, 221
Lionais, D. 243
Liu, S.S. 221
Locke, E.A. 18
locus of control, Flemish entrepreneur profile study 32–3, 39
Long, S.J. 309
Loosemore, M. 257
Lotti, F. 328
Low, M. 15, 20
Lumpkin, G.T. 30, 35, 36, 44, 93, 94, 95, 96, 97, 109, 110, 111, 112, 121, 217, 219
Lundvall, B.Å. 269
Lussier, R.N. 126
Lyon, D.W. 93, 95, 97, 108, 109, 112, 194

MacMillan, I.C. 199, 244
Macneil, I.R. 87
Mahoney, J.T. 218
Maillat, D. 16
Maksimovic, V. 117, 123, 128
Malhotra, N.K. 299, 305, 306
Malmqvist, A. 248–9
Malone, D.E. 271, 272
management support 302
Manimala, M.J. 36
Mansfield, E. 328
March, J.G. 153, 259
market orientation
  and international competitiveness, literature 220–22
  measurement 225–6

market pressure 302–4
Markman, G.D. 32
Martín, E. 221
Martin, J.A. 324, 328, 329, 334
Martin, J.J.S. 144, 152
Martin, W.L. 96, 109, 111, 112, 121
Martins, L.L. 170
Mason, C.M. 77
Mason, P. 165
Matthews, C.M. 79, 82
Maurer, J.G. 32, 44
Mazaira, A. 221
McClelland, D.C. 33
McConaughy, D.L. 121, 126
McDougall, P.P. 215, 216, 217, 220
McEntire, D.A. 257
McFarland, D.J. 305
McMahon, R. 122
McMullen, J.S. 32
Meckling, W. 119
Melin, L. 94, 96, 97
Mellewigt, T. 163
Meyerson, D. 262
Mikl-Horke, G. 171
Miller, D. 39, 94, 109, 111, 112, 121, 153, 217
Miller, L. 119, 121, 135
Milliken, F.J. 170
Mintzberg, H. 141, 173, 243, 257
misalignment costs 121
Mitchell, R.K. 16, 30, 33
Mitchell, W. 142
Moe, T.L. 257, 259, 260
Mokwa, M.P. 312
Moran, P. 330
Moray, N. 274
Morgan, G. 97
Morgan, N.A. 222
Morgan, R.E. 217, 218
Mueller, P. 15
Murphy, G.B. 206
Myers, A. 257
Myers, I.B. 40
Myers, S. 119

Nachtigall, C. 179
Naldi, L. 94, 96, 108
Narver, J.C. 219, 220, 221
Nayyar, P. 218
Ndonzuau, F.N. 269, 270
Neck, C.P. 32
need for achievement, Flemish entrepreneur profile study 33, 39
Need for Cognitive Closure scale 38
Neeley, L. 77, 78, 79, 84
Nelson, R. 262
Neubauer, F. 153
New Venture Teams, *see* NVT
Nicolaou, N. 270
Nieto, M.J. 120
Nilsson, A. 243
Noble, C.H. 312
Nordqvist, M. 109
Norton, E. 79
Norway, *see* human capital attributes of business founders, business performance study
Nucci, A.R. 196
Nunnally, J.C. 309
Nutt, P.C. 36
NVT (New Venture Teams)
  communications within 169–70, 172, 174, 175–6, 186
  definitions 164
  fluctuation 176–7, 178, 183, 187
  heterogeneity 170–72, 178, 185–6
  previous experience within 172–4, 186
  reflective measurement model 180–81
  size 165, 168–70, 178, 183, 185
  structural model 181–2, 184
  team characteristics/processes study
    discussion 182–7
    measurement 178
    method 178–9
    overview 163–4, 187–9
    results 180–82
    sample 177–8
    theoretical background 165–8
  theoretical model 167
  upper echelon perspective 165, 187–8
  work norms 174–5, 185

Ogilvie, D.T. 36
Ok Choi, S. 257
Olaison, L. 254, 263
Olsen, J.P. 259
operative adhocracy 256

opportunity-driven entrepreneurship 244–5, 254
Organ, D.W. 39
organized anarchy 259
organizing under pressure 255–60
orthodox spin-offs 271–2, 275
Ottum, B. 143
Oviatt, B.M. 215, 216, 217, 220
Ozkan, A. 128, 130
Ozkan, N. 128, 130

Pandian, J.R. 218
Pardasani, M. 257
Pathranarakul, P. 257, 259, 260
Pearce, C.L. 163
Pearson, A.W. 165
pecking order theory 118
Pekkala, S. 198
Pena, I. 197, 198
Penrose, E. 343, 344
Perricone, P.J. 144
personality heterogeneity, in NVT 186
Peteraf, M. 222
Peterman, N.E. 44
Peterson, R.A. 256
Pettigrew, A. 98
phenomenon-driven research 18–19
Phillips, G.M. 121
Piccaluga, A. 268, 269
Picot, A. 163
Piore, M.J. 324
Pirnay, F. 243, 271
Pistrui, J. 93, 94, 95, 113
Podsakoff, P.M. 39
Poole, M.S. 97, 113
Poon, J.M.L. 30, 35, 36, 39, 40, 43, 44, 46
Poon, S. 299
Porter, M.E. 143, 302, 303, 304
positional advantage 215, 218, 227
Powell, W.W. 328
Power dimension (F-PEC scale) 144
Prahalad, C.K. 218
Preisendörfer, P. 166
pressure, organizing under 255–60
price discounting 143
proactive personality, Flemish entrepreneur profile study 32, 39
Proactive Personality scale 39
proactiveness
  of companies 94
  primacy of, in family firms 109–10
production managers 295
professors, *see* entrepreneurial professors; university spin-offs, case studies, professor entrepreneur
project organizing 255–7
Project Venture Creation course 61–2
prosaic entrepreneurship 246, 254
Pucik, V. 218

radical innovations 142–3
Radosevitch, R. 272, 274, 292
Raffa, M. 23
Rajan, R.G. 128
Randøy, T. 126
Rasmussen, E. 276
Rauch, A. 33, 95
Rayner, S. 34
Reid, R. 120, 124, 135, 136
RENT (Research in Entrepreneurship and Small Business) Conferences
  Conference XX, keynote address 13–23
  early conferences 14–15
  lessons learned 15–17
research oriented entrepreneurs 294
Reuber, A.R. 211
Reynolds, P.D. 16, 194
Rialp, A. 215
Ribchester, T. 31, 38
Riding, R.J. 34
Rigotti, L. 46
Ringle, C.M. 179
Ripollés, M. 220
risk orientation 144, 152
risk-taking
  of companies 95
  relative seclusion in family firms 108–9
Roberts, E.B. 271, 272
Rodríguez, A.I. 218
Rohm, A. 299
Romano, C.A. 119
Ronstadt, R. 199
Rosenkompf, L. 304
Rotefoss, B. 201
Rotter, J.B. 32, 39

Ruef, M. 16
Ruitenberg, A. 257, 258, 259
Runyan, R.C. 257
Ruther, S. 251–2

Sabel, C.F. 324
Sadler-Smith, E. 22, 29, 30, 33, 34, 36, 44, 45
Samson, K.J. 276
Samuelsson, M. 15, 16, 20
Sandberg, W.R. 163
Sanner, L. 261
Sapienza, H.J. 172
Sarasvathy, S. 16
Sauri, D. 260, 261
Schmidt, A.G. 178
Schoonhoven, C.B. 168, 171
Schulze, W.S. 108, 124, 136
Schumpeter, J.A. 217, 244, 303, 324
Schutjens, V.A.J.M. 344
Schwarz, E.J. 163, 171, 173
Schwass, J. 119
scientific entrepreneurs 275, 291; *see also* entrepreneurial scientists
Scott, M.G. 201
self-efficacy
  Flemish entrepreneur profile study 32, 38–9
  interaction with intention 56–8
  see also education/predisposition interaction study
Services, Farmers' 252
Shane, S. 15, 16, 19, 29, 31, 55, 217, 218, 243, 245, 267, 270, 271
Sharma, A. 299, 318
Sharma, P. 95, 117, 136
Shenhar, A. 256
Shepherd, D.A. 32, 216, 345
Sheppard, B.H. 305
Sherer, M. 38
Shih, C. 221
Shook, C.L. 29
Siegel, R. 345
Simon, H.A. 153
Sirmon, D.G. 218
situational altruism 258
Sköldberg, K. 97
Skutle, A. 259
Slater, S.F. 219, 220, 221
Slevin, D.P. 35, 39, 94, 121, 217, 219
small business/entrepreneurship research
  challenges for 17–20
  in Europe 3–5
  Europe vs North America 20–23
Smircich, L. 97
Smith, K.G. 163, 165, 169, 176
Smith, M.D. 304
social contracting 244–5
social loafing 169
Sogorb-Mira, F. 122
Sonfield, M.C. 126
Späth, J.F. 163
specific human capital 195
Spector, P.E. 37
Spieker, M. 165
Spillan, J. 257
Spilling, O.R. 268, 276
Spinosa, C. 245, 260
Srinivasan, R. 302, 306, 309
Stam, E. 330, 337, 344, 345
Stankiewicz, R. 276
Starr, J.A. 200, 255
Starr, J.R. 244
Steenkamp, J. 320
Steers, R.M. 39
Steffensen, M. 270
Stevenson, H. 217
Stewart, A 243
Stewart, W.H. 34, 40
Steyaert, C. 29, 30, 97, 243, 245, 246
Stinchcombe, A.L. 202, 215
Stine, R.A. 181
Stockley, S. 164, 165, 168
Storey, D.J. 15, 194
Storper, M. 257
Stoy Hayward 144
strategic entrepreneurship 328
strategic process 143
Straus, S. 45
Strauss, A.L. 97, 98
strong ties 200
Stryjan, Y. 260
Stuart, R.W. 200, 345
Stuart, T. 55
Suarez, K.C. 144, 152
success syndrome 200
Suddaby, R. 98
Sultan, F. 299

supportable growth, *see* sustainable growth
surrogate entrepreneurs 292–3
sustainable growth 122–3
swift trust 262

tacit market knowledge 215–16
Tanewski, G.A. 108
Tapon, F. 328
Taub, R.P. 171
Taylor, S. 305
Teach, R.D. 163
team foundation 163
technology spinouts 272, 275
technology use, *see* Digitally Enabled Marketing
Teece, D.J. 216, 328, 329, 343
Tellis, G.J. 302, 303, 307, 312, 316
Tibishirani, R. 181
Todd, P.A. 305
tolerance for ambiguity, Flemish entrepreneur profile study 31–2, 38
Toulouse, J.M. 39
trait approach, Flemish entrepreneur profile study 31, 43
Trijp, H. 320
Trovato, G. 122
Tsai, M. 221
Tsang, E.W.K. 117, 136
Turner, J.R. 256
Tushman, M.L. 302
Twomey, D.F. 201
Tzokas, N. 299, 318

Ucbasaran, D. 22, 166, 170, 174, 176, 194, 195, 197, 199
Udell, G.F. 122
Uhlaner, L.M. 144
university spin-offs
  academic staff typology 293–5
  case studies
    industrial entrepreneurs 281–2, 292
    laboratory manager 280–81
    professor entrepreneur 278–80
    research based entrepreneurs 280
  commercialization 268–70, 282–6
  institutional and systemic context 276–7, 290–91
  literature 270–74
  overview 267–8, 295–6
  processes characteristics 286–90
  role of academic staff 275–6, 291–5
  study method/data 277–8
upper echelon theory 165
Usher, J.M. 19
Utsch, A. 33

Van Auken,H.E. 77, 78, 79
Van de Ven, A.H. 16, 97, 113, 270, 286, 343
Van den Broeck, H. 34, 39, 128
van Zyl, J.J. 320
Vanyushyn, V. 319
Vázquez, R. 221
Vecchio, R.P. 31, 44
Venkataraman, S. 15, 29, 217, 343
Venkatesh, V. 305
Verheul, I. 144
Verser, T.G. 95
Vila, N. 221
Virtanen, M. 269, 276
Vorhies, D.W. 221
Vozikis, G.S. 32, 46
Vyakarnam, S. 163

Wade, J. 307
Wagner, B. 299
Wahren, H.-K.E. 169
Walczuch, R. 319
Waldman, M. 121
Ward, J.L. 119, 120, 124, 135, 144, 152
Waters, J. 141
Watson, W. 196, 197, 198
Watson, W.E. 163
wealth effects 152
Webster, D.M. 38
Weick, K.E. 245, 253, 259
Wensley, R. 215, 218
Wernerfelt, B. 222
Westerveld, E. 259
Westhead, P. 16, 126, 142, 144, 146, 152, 195, 199, 200, 215, 255, 328
Westlund, H. 246
Wheelright, S. 143
Whetten, D. 32, 44
Whiteside, M.F. 95, 97
Whittington, G. 142, 143

Wickham, P.A. 29, 30
Wigren, C. 20
Wijers, E.J. 141, 151, 152, 153, 154
Wiklund, J. 20, 22, 30, 35, 216, 217, 343, 345
Williams, K.D. 169
Williams, M.L. 96
WILTC (Willingness to Cannibalize) 302–3
Winborg, J. 77, 78, 79, 80, 81, 82, 83, 84, 85, 88, 89, 171
Winklhofer, H. 299
Winters, R. 330
Woo, C. 330, 343
Wright, M. 16, 173, 199, 200, 255
Wu, F. 299, 303

Yin, R.K. 98, 100
Yu, T.F.L. 324

Zahra, S.A. 30, 35, 93, 94, 96, 97, 108, 112, 113, 120, 215, 216, 217, 218, 221, 344
Zhao, H. 32
Zimmermann, P. 174
Zingales, L. 128